Big Blue Sky

'. . . something much greater than a political memoir. It is a true autobiography, which deserves to escape the gravitational pull of the author's fame and be considered among the best examples of the craft. Garrett evokes the past as another, familiar country as easily and vividly as some of the greats of the Australian literary canon . . . It should be read for the pure enjoyment of such well-crafted prose, but it should endure within the national archive as a document of much greater significance than most political memoirs.'

JOHN BIRMINGHAM, *SYDNEY MORNING HERALD* AND *THE AGE*

'Among the 400 sprawling pages there's a lot of great passages, and the inside story of a man who set the agenda for many . . . buy it as much for insights into recent policy formation as for the hits and memories. The passion, then the power.'

GUY RUNDLE, *CRIKEY*

PETER GARRETT

Big Blue Sky

a memoir

ALLEN&UNWIN
SYDNEY·MELBOURNE·AUCKLAND·LONDON

All attempts have been made to locate the owners of copyright material. If you have any information in that regard please contact the publisher at the address below.

This edition published in 2017
First published in 2015

Allen & Unwin
83 Alexander Street
Crows Nest NSW 2065
Australia
Phone: (61 2) 8425 0100
Email: info@allenandunwin.com,
Web: www.allenandunwin.com

Cataloguing-in-Publication details are available
from the National Library of Australia, www.trove.nla.gov.au

ISBN 978 1 76063 274 8

Internal design by Lisa White
Design of illustration inserts by Bookhouse, Sydney
Index by Puddingburn Publishing Services
Set in Garamond by Midland Typesetters, Australia
Printed and bound in Australia by SOS Print + Media Group

10 9 8 7

I dedicate this book to Doris,
the love of my life,
and our three beautiful girls, Emily, May and Grace.

CONTENTS

SUITE M1 52, PARLIAMENT HOUSE, CANBERRA, FRIDAY, 28 JUNE 2013, 5 P.M.

IT'S GONE ALL ghostly quiet and frozen still.

Everything is in silent outline, like the mountains of the moon when it rises close, fat and yellow over Weereewa, the mystery lake up the road.

Other than the background hum of machines on standby, and the tick of the clock bouncing off the walls in my office, there's no sound. The phones have stopped ringing—in this giant cubbyhole of politics and power a sure sign that an endpoint has been reached. Double-strength fixed windows and solid doors muffle loud noise but there is none right now.

The vast tiled courtyard below, where the prime minister's press conferences take place, is at last empty. I can still see the faint outlines of body shapes, the spectral residue of human heat from the crowd here earlier: before the doors closed, before the changing of the guard, before the rats and angels went scurrying for the outside world.

I've never suffered the affliction of loneliness; just lucky I suppose. I like people, but I like the measured beat of my own company as well. Still, there have been times when I've felt alone.

Sitting in the gutter, sober, listening to the distant whoops and whistles of a New Year's Eve party.

Squatting on the edge of a dry salt lake in the Western Desert with no sign of another person.

Standing in front of the microphone late into the night when everyone else has gone, the headphones replaying an orchestra of sounds as I try to find the words and melodies to match.

At those times and others I've been a castaway on my own island, but they were nothing to what I'm feeling now. The previous afternoon I'd phoned Doris, my sweetheart of nearly thirty years, to tell her this adventure was finished. She was about to head overseas for a month to attend to distant family business. Bad timing, but at least we'd be seeing more of each other in the months and years ahead.

I take a deep breath, and then another, and slowly look around the room.

A massive wooden desk still groaning with paper and, behind it, racks of books and piles of reports, some small family photos.

Hanging on the walls are my sustenance: photographs and art and memorabilia. There's a big Freddie Timms painting that I look at every day. For me it's got more power than a dozen Monets. He's sung it into life and even if I don't understand all its meanings—and I don't—it's ever strong. An elder from the Kimberley, Freddie was renowned for challenging the claims of certain historians who, discounting the oral evidence of local Aboriginal people, denied that some of his family had been killed by white troopers in a massacre barely a hundred years before. The great man surprised me by turning up at the office one day, with a group of community leaders from the east Kimberley in tow, to seek support for education programs for their young. They sat directly under Freddie's work but no one mentioned it; the talk was all business. On the way out, though, Freddie paused, glanced over his shoulder and said, 'Not a bad painter that one.' I know I won't remember the scores of meetings, the endless sea of faces, the fine detail of every policy, but I will remember that old man's wry humour.

Like a newsreel in reverse, images are racing through my mind: a small blond-haired boy who is sure he knows the answer, thrusting his hand up again and again and again in grade six at Gordon West Public School; twenty years later balanced on the edge of a stage, looking out at a heaving mass of bodies swaying and singing in unison as 'Lucky Country' rings out across a huge field; on the street, megaphone in hand, calling for us to become a more independent nation and start caring for the fabric of our ancient land; crammed into the boardroom of the Randwick Labor Club, shoulder to shoulder with supporters and family, as the votes come in and I'm chosen as a new member of parliament.

My staff are now gone, the younger ones dispatched early, before emotions spilled over. My ever-loyal deputy and my chief of staff are the last to leave, but leave they must: to go to homes in other cities; to catch their breath with loved ones; to gather their thoughts and try to make some sense of what has just happened; to grieve and rage against the injustice, the bloody ordinariness, of the past few days.

I poke my head into the long corridor, all heritage colours and solid furniture. To the left are the public areas of Parliament House and the labyrinth of meeting rooms and backbenchers' suites. To the right lie the ministerial wing and the offices of my colleagues. There is no one; no people, no movement, just an eerie silence.

I feel like I'm on a giant abandoned raft drifting across a familiar stretch of water. For the last time, I walk the wide corridors, slowing to take in the paintings that hang on the walls. Some of Australia's best art is here, morsels that feed your spirit in the crazy times, although I know most people rushing by take little notice.

I head down the stairs and past the cabinet room and the prime minister's suite.

Solemn guards look up and nod. 'Good afternoon, Minister—sorry, er, Mr Garrett.'

I walk past the offices of the ministers for Defence, Employment, Environment, Resources and Energy, and up the stairs past Trade, Health, before finally returning to School Education, Early Childhood and Youth.

It's time to finish packing my bags. The leader of the nation has gone, and soon her conqueror will occupy the office below with his minions and their plans. For now I am in the gap between, the calm before another storm, with giant plastic bags full of shredded paper dumped in the corridors the only sign of the revolution just passed—other than the parade of talking heads offering post-mortems of victory and loss on the television screens in every room. Thankfully, the volume is turned down.

Although only twenty-four hours have passed, already the howling cesspit that is the House of Representatives feels like a lifetime ago. It's darkening outside when I leave the vacant office, stepping over cardboard boxes and abandoned files, flicking the lights off as I go. A pause to reflect and give thanks—no regrets.

The door is heavy. I pull it closed and it thuds behind me.

After a mourning day that's gone on forever, it's the loudest sound I've heard.

1
HOMEBODY

The kangaroo tail glints in the sun
As the freckle boys paddle out at Curly
Mascot smells sweeter than eucalypt gum
I'm coming home to blue hills in the morning

It's a journey that's lasted as long as my youth
I never was one to quit early
But the miles of white lines are a sign of the times
I'm coming home to blue hills in the morning

I wish all my friends could see with my eyes
What I can't re-create just by telling
Acres of red roofs in early sunlight
Out of the gullies massed wings taking flight

I've seen wars and dark places glass castles of kings
Jewels and junkyards, the craziest things
The satellite salesman's glittering nose ring
I'm coming home to blue hills in the morning

Yes, I yearned to see sandstone cliffs washed by the dawn
Longed for the white cradle that guards the lagoon
To the arms of my sweet love I'm coming home soon
Coming home to blue hills in the morning

B LUE WAS THE colour of my earliest years.
        The clearest big blue skies that soared whichever way you looked.

The blue dresses my mum wore, fifties-style, fresh from the copper tub, drying crisp on the clothesline that stood, arms out like a solitary soldier, in the middle of the backyard.

I'm the first of three boys, and boys wear blue. No wonder I like Miles Davis, and Brett Whiteley, and being outside.

I grew up in Australia, the lucky land for most, born in a quiet suburb on the edge of a city picking up speed and starting its spread. Sydney, the prettiest, take-your-breath-away town in Australia, bordered by the Pacific Ocean on its eastern side and to the west by the Blue Mountains we could just see from our home.

Such good fortune: big patches of bush splashing in the valleys and across the spiny sandstone ridges, the most brilliant harbour in the world—surely—with beautiful beaches stretching north and south, only half an hour away.

And there, a succession of arcs of white sand between rocky headlands, tranquil lagoons, rolling surf—a child's perfect playground. Splash in the clean blue water, swoon in the soft warm sand, with the gentle swishing sound of waves washing in and out. Clear light cascading in from all sides.

'When I'm dreaming, I dream in blue.'

I strain to drag back early memories: low murmuring voices—my mum and dad's—in the kitchen; a toy Sydney Harbour Bridge, made of steel like the real thing; the smell of freshly washed linen; and, later, the radio.

Radio has been my lifelong companion. I was surrounded by its crackling hum from an early age, particularly the live broadcasts of the Test cricket matches between Australia and England. If it wasn't on in the kitchen, it was blasting out of someone's garage or echoing over the back fence. The pop of ball on bat, the sudden eruption of the crowd if a wicket fell, and always the pitter-patter, ambling commentary. Even today, when I care less about who is winning or losing, I have it on. It's a comforting noise. I must have heard the broadcasts of countless games, the vibrations and timbres of a day on the green, while still in the womb.

Years later Mum maintained she'd become so tired of keeping an eye on me once I started crawling that she put me in a large peg bag and hung me out on the line with the washing. We couldn't quite believe it, but maybe it explains why I don't have a fear of heights.

We always listened to the world's longest-running radio serial, a soapie about life in rural Australia. It came on before lunch every weekday, introduced by a melancholy classical theme, strings with French horns, repeated and supplemented with oboes, and then the sombre English accent voiceover: 'The ABC presents *Blue Hills* by Gwen Meredith.' I remember those words more clearly than the lyrics to some Midnight Oil songs. When you're very young, you take it all in, especially sound—and whatever your mum is doing. And it sticks; it makes you who you are.

...

I have my birth certificate in front of me.

> When and where born: 16 April 1953, Sydney Sanitarium and
>   Hospital, Wahroonga.
> Father: Peter Maxwell Garrett, Departmental Manager, born Rabaul,
>   New Britain.
> Mother: Betty Collin, born Murwillumbah, New South Wales.

I hardly knew my dad's parents. His father, Tom Vernon Garrett, was a returned serviceman who had been granted land outside the town of Rabaul at the end of World War I. Rabaul was on the island of New Britain, which later became part of Papua New Guinea. He owned a copra and cocoa plantation there called Varzin. He was lost at sea in World War II, along with nearly a thousand other Australian civilians and Allied prisoners of war, on board the Japanese merchant ship SS *Montevideo Maru*. Following the Japanese attack on Pearl Harbor in December 1941, fighting had raged across the Pacific. Rabaul fell in early 1942, followed by a mass evacuation of what was left of the army and locals. En route to China, the *Montevideo Maru* was mistakenly torpedoed off the coast of the Philippines by an American submarine, the USS *Sturgeon*. It went down in minutes. It was Australia's greatest maritime tragedy, and is still little known. I wrote about it in the song 'In the Valley'.

Tom Vernon's father, my great-grandfather, was the Test cricketer Thomas William (Tom) Garrett, famous as the youngest to play in the first game against an English team in 1878 (the first game, that is, if you don't include the Aboriginal cricket team that toured England in 1868). A medium-pace bowler, he was a stayer, and captained New South Wales till he was fifty. After a long career in the public service, notably as the first public trustee of New South Wales, he went on to work as a solicitor until he was in his eighties. His father, also named Tom Garrett, was a newspaper publisher who, in an interesting career segue, later became a conservative politician; at one point he was the New South Wales Minister for Lands.

My father's mum, Nora, was sickly, and regularly came down from New Guinea to Sydney to convalesce in hospitals and boarding houses. I only saw her once during one of these visits. She had long, elegant hands like my dad.

My father had grown up on the family plantation in New Guinea, but with the outbreak of war he and his twin brother, Tom, were sent to Mosman High School in Sydney. Dad, who—like his mother—suffered poor health, was hospitalised on and off for most of the war years. After the war, there arose the question of which brother would stay in New Guinea to run Varzin, there being room for only one boss. The matter was settled by the toss of a coin—my dad lost. I later discovered that the brother who missed out on the property would be entitled to a share of the profits, but only a dribble made its way to the unlucky twin. Dad then found work as an office boy in a chemicals company called Henry H. York & Sons. After spending years as a salesman he rose to the position of general manager of the Sydney branch of the same company, BASF, which was established after Henry York was split into three following the war.

Dad was a man of natural charm; tall, with thinning hair and a generous moustache, he stood out in the crowd, especially when wearing one of his trademark cravats. Despite his various ailments—including a bung leg and relentless bronchial troubles—he was keen on and good at sport, hard to match in backyard cricket. He coached my under-eights soccer team, though he'd never played. To the end of his days he loved golf and, like the raven-haired beauty he married, was extremely social.

My mother had grown up in the Southern Highlands town of Bowral, one of the few bits of cool-climate country within cooee of Sydney. She was a warm, high-spirited person, and belonged to one of the earliest generations of women to graduate from Sydney University, in 1949. She worked all over Sydney as a social worker for many years.

Her parents, Len and Emily Collin, were permanent fixtures in our lives, especially after they moved from Bowral to Sydney to be closer to our family. Before their relocation, we spent mid-year holidays and occasional weekends visiting them in their home in Aitken Road, next to Bowral High School.

The drive took forever. The back seat of the FH Holden was a big mobile playroom we could roam around on, as there were no seatbelts. I would range between my brothers—Matthew, still a baby tucked up in a bassinet, and Andrew—as we wound out through the suburbs towards Liverpool and then over the Great Dividing Range. Eventually, my favourite landmark would come into view. This was a huge Port Jackson fig in the Razorback Range near Picton. Erected next to the tree, in full view of the passing traffic, was a sign bearing the slogan of Sydney department store Anthony Hordern's: 'While I Live

I'll Grow'. As a young boy I found this message, framed by spreading branches, deeply reassuring. The tree itself seemed timeless, and its sighting meant we would soon be careering down the hill, past the villages of Bargo and Mittagong, and into Bowral.

My grandparents' house smelled of pine needles outside and camphor mixed with old people's cooking odours and pipe tobacco inside. Full of dark timbered furniture, each window engulfed in heavy curtains, it felt a world away from home. Adjacent to the house was a big paddock where a single large horse quietly grazed. Of course I wanted to catch it and ride bareback after imaginary baddies like a Texas Ranger (*Tales of the Texas Rangers* being one of my favourite TV programs at the time). Armed with a stepladder, reins and bridle, I'd spend hours working my way into position, with the bridle bit at last wedged into the horse's mouth, only to have my steed move off just as I was about to make the final leap. Undeterred, I'd drag the ladder across the paddock to the horse, still nonchalantly chewing grass, and try again. Finally, one year, a tad older and stronger, I at last managed to get everything in place and clamber onto its back. Triumphant, I was now ready to gallop across the paddock and chase down the marauding gangs still lurking in my imagination. Instead, the horse stood stock-still, and I couldn't get it to move at all. My dreams of successfully pursuing swarthy robbers and cunning thieves were dashed by a horse now pretending to be a statue.

My grandparents had lived through two world wars and the Great Depression—a tougher time by far—and never forgot it. They were frugal and industrious to a degree that intrigued me as a child. So much effort was given over to labelling and storing food, in stark contrast to Mum's regular Friday afternoon supermarket run, in which the boot of the car was crammed with a jumble of shopping bags whose contents were demolished within a week. In my grandparents' home, tins of used rubber bands, bits of string tied up in a ball and an assortment of paperclips, old pens and pencils all jostled for space on shelves neatly stacked with tinned food and preserved fruit. Shopping coupons advertising the latest specials were cut out of newspapers and stuck up on the kitchen wall; clothes in need of repair were sewn up and made good. Everything had a place and everything was marked, nothing was thrown away. The expression 'waste not, want not' rang in my ears for years afterwards. It's such a stark contrast to the way we live today. Now, mountains of waste are a sign of the times, included in the national accounts on the positive side of the ledger. Massive bins sit outside most homes, filled to over-flowing with food scraps and rubbish that end up in landfills, which are overflowing too. Our recycling efforts are outweighed by the tonnes of stuff we chuck out by a factor of ten to one.

My grandfather Len was one of the gentlest men I ever knew. He had seen the Great War up close, stationed in Egypt and the Middle East as the Allies staggered to victory. He came home to convalesce with half a lung, and most of his hearing gone from the noise of battle. The doctors said he wouldn't last long, but he thumbed his nose at this miserable diagnosis, put up with a giant hearing aid inserted in his ear, retrained, and worked for the rest of his life as a dentist.

After a long day in the surgery he'd retire to an enormous double garage full of tools, a lathe and other (to my eyes) mysterious machines. Here, pipe on the go, humming quietly, he'd busy himself weaving fabrics, building model railways—the engines, tracks, rolling stock and furniture—or just plain pottering. When not in the garage, he could be found hammering away on a braille typewriter translating books for the blind. This unsung service to others was incomprehen-sible to me at the time, but I later found it a great inspiration.

My grandmother, Emily Jane Collin, was a no-frills person and incredibly tough. She was tiny, and carried herself like a determined sparrow unwilling to cede the smallest breadcrumb. She'd grown up in the small western Victorian town of Nhill and in her early twenties travelled to Western Australia—in those days an epic journey of over 3000 kilometres lasting up to three months, travelling by horse and dray across the arid Nullarbor Plain—to work as a nurse. There she

joined Daisy Bates, a well-known journalist and amateur anthropol-
ogist, caring for survivors of first contact—Aboriginal people with
leprosy—who were confined to Bernier and Dorre Islands off the
remote Western Australian coast, well away from the public eye.

These were my ancestors, the ones who came before me, whose
genes I carry in my blood.

...

Today, West Pymble, the suburb where I grew up, is picture-perfect,
its tree-lined streets boasting well-maintained houses and gardens.

Yesterday was another story altogether.

In the nearby Lane Cove River valley, home to the Guringai people,
there was plenty of food—oysters, crabs, possum, kangaroo and water-
fowl. Described at the time of settlement as 'friendly', by 1856—only
a hundred years or so before my birth—they had been pummelled by
disease, a fact that was hardly registered by the European settlers then,
or afterwards. Here the bush was full of good timber—stringybark,
turpentine, blue gum and ironbark—and as in many parts of the new
country, logging was the first recorded industry.

The area was subdivided not long after 1900—another great Aussie
tradition: subdivide and development will follow—but it was rugged
and hilly and so slow to be settled. When my parents moved there,
it was still a frontier suburb. (Less than a mile from where I grew
up, a notorious illegal gambling ring operated on weekends into the
mid-1950s.) As tracks were pushed into the bush, two- and three-
bedroom weatherboard cottages started to appear, home to defence
personnel and families like ours, with modest means and ambitions.

Our house was the first built in the Broadway, the last street on the
edge of West Pymble. To the east, behind the back fence, was order
and calm, with tidy streets leading up to a small collection of shops. To
the west, out the front door and across a dirt road, a sandstone ledge
drop-off led to dense bush and a river valley filled with native birds,
whose screeches and lilts—C'mon, sunrise!—woke me most mornings.

West Pymble was fast becoming populated with up-and-coming professional and business types, leavened with a smattering of manual workers who'd bought early, before land and house prices began their inexorable climb. When I was five, we moved up a notch to a three-bedroom, red-brick bungalow at 22 Grayling Road. We were now smack bang in the middle of the suburb and more firmly ensconced in the middle class. Though a mere half a kilometre further east, we were now on a tarred road and closer to schools and the North Shore railway line that ran into the city. In other words, we were closer to civilisation. It was here that I spent my first fifteen years. Also living in the vicinity was Johnny O'Keefe, the famed Oz rocker, but I never saw him and there was no graffiti to announce his whereabouts. So too was Jacki Weaver, who went on to become one of Australia's best-known actors. I was at primary school with her brother and glimpsed her a few times around the traps. That sent the pulse racing even at my tender age.

By the time we reached our new home, another boy had arrived— my brother Andrew—and Matthew followed two years later. We were a tall family in a smallish house. Andrew and Matt, closer in age and several years younger than me, shared the second bedroom while I occupied a small, windowless room at the back. An enclosed rear verandah with steps leading down to a sloping backyard had been turned into guest quarters, and doubled as a playroom when it rained. Timber paling fences on either side, covered in choko and passionfruit vines, separated us from our neighbours, and there was an acre of bush not yet built out at the rear.

Black-and-white television arrived not long after we moved in, and proved a sensational drawcard. This blinking, moving diorama sucked children in like insects to neon. I pitied the affluent trailblazers in the street who'd been the first to acquire this magic box; they didn't get a moment's rest. Despite the magnetic attraction of moving pictures on tap, even when we got our own idiot box I loved being outside, and this was where I spent most of my time, playing with my brothers or the neighbourhood kids.

Along with many of my friends I walked and later rode my bike to Gordon West Public School a kilometre or so away. Other than the skinny eucalypts that now dot the grounds, it hasn't changed that much since then. It was here that I strained to keep up at mathematics but sailed through English and, along with my friend Grant Andrews, who went on to become a notable rugby union player, represented the school and the district in athletics. We must have been one of the last generations to receive free milk, in half-pint bottles with silver caps, inevitably warmed in the morning sun.

After school we'd gather in the street. There were no cement gutters to crack our shins on and mercifully few big front fences. Most importantly, it was a safe arena for play, until increasing traffic made setting up cricket stumps in the middle of the road impossible. We roamed through the bush, played soccer and cricket in the backyard or down at the local oval, rode our billycarts and, later, primitive skateboards down the steepest hills, made cubbyhouses and climbed the tallest trees.

As we got older we ventured further into the nearby Lane Cove River valley. Here, especially in the holidays, I would spend endless hours with my mates, Steve Adams and Bruce Diekman (who later went on to work for the Nature Conservation Council of NSW), whose mums also let them roam freely, exploring, damming small creeks, building makeshift rafts to float down the trickle that was the headwater of the river in summer. Fanging down the bumpy tracks on our bikes was the best feeling, and who knew what lay in store as we entered our hidden hideaway—stands of thick forest—only a hundred metres from the road? We never saw another person and, left to our own devices, invented a gritty fantasy world to play in. This gave rise to a blended feeling of contentment and challenge that happens when you're exploring nature without an adult issuing directions. You just felt so alive.

Sunset was the cut-off. Mum would relent to yet another plea to head out and play with, 'Okay, but just make sure you're back before dark', the words already fading as I tore out of the house. But inevitably I ran late, a habit that stayed with me for years. There was just too much going on: massive games of hide-and-seek involving twenty or more of us with plenty of options for concealment, friends' houses to visit for cordial and biscuits before heading back out to kick a ball around, more tracts of bushland to explore. At a nearby disused quarry, which became a favourite haunt, the paths around the quarry walls were narrow and rough, and even for agile ten-year-olds on the run, escaping from rival Lilliputian gangs who roamed the amphitheatre playing out mock battles, a fall was always on the cards. So extra care had to be taken, and that took more time, didn't it, Mum?

Such open-skies freedom must have given rise to a fear on the part of some parents that sooner or later someone's kid would be seriously hurt. Scrapes and bruises were already common and, as it happened, around this time I was proudly displaying six stitches sewn to close a large gash over my knee, courtesy of a misjudged jump from one rock platform to another. A committee of local parents formed to encourage the establishment of a boys' Cub and Scout troop, to be followed later by a girls' Brownie troop as well. More fun, except now we had uniforms and badges. Our escapades would be legitimised and our thirst for adventure and risk-taking at least partially slaked.

First land needed to be located and a hall built, and so began the community fundraising effort to secure a space in which to contain this wild gaggle of kids. The main source of funds was multiple progressive dinners and bottle drives. The progressive dinner was exactly as it sounds. Individual families hosted one course of dinner as people who'd paid for tickets 'progressed' from house to house until, at the final destination, coffee and tea were served. Bottle drives were an early form of recycling. The neighbours were letterboxed and asked to put any empty bottles or jars out on the nature strip between their house and the street, to be picked up and later sold.

Weekend after weekend—or at least that's how it seemed—we were either sticking notes advertising an upcoming bottle drive into assorted letterboxes, or scouring the streets of West Pymble, emptying various bottles of their dregs before stacking them in cardboard boxes and loading them into the boots of various dads' cars. Like our school milk ration, the smell of stale beer warmed by the sun and dripping into boxes was ever-present, and even today if I catch a whiff when passing by a pub, it instantly takes me back to this time.

That these frantic rounds of raising much-needed cash quickly bore fruit was evidence of the truth of another of my Gran's favourite sayings, namely that 'many hands make light work'. In no time we had our new hall and a more controlled environment in which to let off steam, learn some new bush skills—like tying knots and reading a map—and, most importantly, make plans for numerous thrill-seeking escapades, which were now officially sanctioned by the New South Wales scouting movement. While this new knowledge proved useful over the years, no more so than when I went seriously bush in the 1980s, the most salient lesson I took from my time in the Cubs was how the wealthy got that way, and how they behaved towards others.

At that time, the annual fundraising activity for Cubs and Scouts was Bob a Job Week. Over the course of a week you would knock on a neighbour's front door and ask if there was any small job you could do for a 'bob'—the nickname for a shilling—which roughly equates to $1.40 today. Competition to raise the most money was fierce and as a Cub leader I was determined to show the way. I spent most afternoons trudging the streets, cajoling the parents of friends and close neighbours to give me jobs. One year I hit a dry patch near home as lots of families were away, so I decided to head up the hill towards the railway line and into the well-heeled suburb of Pymble. Here, estates with driveways longer than three cricket pitches laid end to end abounded, with spacious gardens and substantially bigger houses than the modest fibro and brick dwellings of West Pymble. And so I reasoned the fruits of my labour would be greater as well.

As it turned out, I fared poorly. In some cases, despite my Cub uniform and obvious willingness to work, I was turned away. If the lady of the house was home alone, there was a chance I might get a simple gardening chore or a car to wash—this I was used to. If, on the other hand, a man answered the door, then sometimes I wasn't sent off, the temptation to abuse my offer proving too great. I'd be ordered to rake a lawn the size of the Sydney Cricket Ground with specific instructions on how to do the job properly, or to sweep and clean a garage the size of the house I lived in. The stern male who'd issued the instructions would then disappear inside and I'd battle on, spending at least twice the usual time taken on these chores. Once the job was finally completed, and duly inspected at length, one single bob would be pressed into my, by now, blistered hands.

The first time it happened I put it down to unusual circumstances. I'd struck a real-life Scrooge, I marvelled—in Pymble of all places! But the pattern never wavered and after two days of hard labour I headed back down the hill. There I was greeted, as was the norm, with a cheerful, 'Sure, love. Work for half an hour, will you, and then just chuck the rubbish/lawn clippings/bucket over there.' Two bob or more would then be pressed into my hand. It was an encounter with the polar opposites of generosity and greed that I never forgot.

...

The only shadow on the wall in those carefree days was my health. My parents, like many in their time, were lifelong smokers and I was born with asthma. Dad was already prone to the same condition, which worsened over time. I was allergic to numerous things: different foods and various pollens and grasses. I'd put in time in an oxygen tent when very young and, despite the ceaseless outdoor activity and generally being pretty fit, I was still vulnerable if any of these triggers crossed my path.

On these occasions I'd have no choice but to hunker down and wait it out. The lack of windows in my bedroom can't have helped, but it was my struggle and I wanted to meet it, front on, in my domain. And so Mum would sit with me, and if it got bad we'd pace through the house together in the midnight hour as I strained to get enough oxygen, waiting for whatever medicine had been optimistically prescribed that year to kick in.

These attacks continued through to my mid-teens, stymieing my efforts at sport and causing some anxiety if I was spending a night with a friend or relative whose house might be full of animal hair or dust, both guaranteed to cause wheezing. After one particularly nasty attack, while staying with family friends at Pacific Palms, a remote village on the Mid North Coast, a long way from doctors or a hospital, I feared I might cark it and got a massive attack of the panics as well.

From that point on I chucked out all the drugs and threw myself into a tougher fitness regime with lots of surfing and breathing exercises. Thankfully these efforts saw it off, or possibly I simply grew out of the ailment, or one complemented the other. Whatever the case, it no longer flared up to flatten me and I never looked back.

Ten years later, when I was spending a lot of time touring, trapped in hotels and hire cars, I took up tai chi to help keep my lungs open. I learned it from a ponytailed rock singer called Erle Montaigue, who'd been to Taiwan to study with exiled grandmasters and held classes in a warehouse near Central Station. I bypassed the esoteric philosophy but it really helped to keep me healthy and on an even keel, and I practise to this day.

···

I always loved music. The cadences and melodies of nursery rhymes and Christmas carols locked into my head early and singing felt like the most natural thing to do.

My dad could often be heard whistling or humming a tune. He was a bit of a showman, courtesy of his days as a member of the Killara Liberal Party younger set who put on fundraising concerts for the blue bloods of the North Shore.

Occasionally he'd launch into one of my favourite songs of the time, Perry Como's 'Catch a Falling Star'. The lyric was ever so simple, hinting at mysteries that were a long way out of my reach.

Catch a falling star an' put it in your pocket
Never let it fade away
Catch a falling star an' put it in your pocket
Save it for a rainy day
For love may come an' tap you on the shoulder
Some starless nights
Just in case you feel you want to hold her,
You'll have a pocketful of starlight.

An unforgettable melody, imprinted forever on my brain.

I sang at school and at Sunday school, but to this day I have no idea how I ended up as the youngest member of the choir of St John's Anglican Church in Gordon, a suburb up the hill, next to Pymble. This was high church—all ritual and mysterious incantations—where religion was taken very seriously. It was dark inside, candlelight flickered on the crossbeams and trusses that held the giant roof in place, faint light fell from stained-glass windows with medieval illustrations and the smell of incense hovered in the air. We wore cassocks and sang the liturgy in Latin. And this was the early 1960s!

Despite its brooding solemnity, and the air of pomp with a dash of boredom that hung like a low cloud over the congregation, I loved the singing. Once underway, the soaring organ was as loud as anything I'd heard and I came to love the music too. The notes oh so naturally falling in the right place and the content was stirring. With the great hymns and carols of the English tradition, courtesy of composers like Wesley and Britten, booming and echoing through this elaborate theatre, it was my first encounter with the transformative power of music. I hope to sing in a choir again one day.

···

There couldn't have been a greater contrast between the solemn rituals and reverence that characterised St John's and the constant toing and froing that happened at home.

Grayling Road had a dual personality. During the day, ours was just one in a row of indistinguishable brick houses in a leafy, suburban street. Here, family rules dictated that beds were made every morning before school and teeth were cleaned every night, while chores and, later, homework had to be finished before we could jump into any other activities.

Come nightfall it was a drop-in house; the door was always open to impromptu visits from neighbours and friends on the way home from work in the city.

On the weekends, and occasionally during the week, it could expand like a giant piano accordion with music and laughter, and the mingling smells—perfume, cigarette smoke, alcohol, potato chips— of a party. If a big one was planned, the grog would be stashed in laundry tubs filled with ice on Saturday afternoon. As evening fell, modestly made-up wives would gather in one corner, chatting and gesticulating, while their red-faced husbands, sleeves rolled up and with a glass of beer in hand, would congregate in the kitchen telling jokes and catching up on news. The gramophone would be fired up and Gershwin's *Rhapsody in Blue*, Gilbert & Sullivan, Sinatra, Rodgers & Hammerstein, especially Richard Rodger's *Slaughter on Tenth Avenue*, Elvis and early Beatles would all get a run. Later, there would be dancing to Chuck Berry. At only eight or nine years old, I was the sober one—as I've since been most of my life—watching and helping. It looked exciting but at the same time exhausting, and I couldn't understand how my parents still managed to get up early and do household tasks or, harder still, head off to work the morning after.

The frequent mid-week socialising wasn't without consequence. Phone calls would come in from angry wives demanding to know where their husbands were and vice versa. Sometimes uninvited guests who'd overstayed their welcome would be gently nudged, swaying, out the door, only to reappear a few weeks later with a sheepish smile and a bottle of brandy in hand to say sorry.

I learned a lot about people at this time. With a few drinks under their belts they started to relax and it didn't take too long for their personalities to emerge: the flirt, the joker, the tense and nervous, the kind, the distant. I came to see that my parents' friends were just older versions of young people like me. I became quite close to a number of them, the Saxton and the Vasey families in particular. Both Pam Vasey and Trish Saxton were pert, engaging women with a ready-for-a-party air about them. Russ Vasey worked at Qantas and, surprisingly to me, loved classical music. When Mum dropped over to visit the Vaseys I'd tag along, and he and I would listen to Mozart—the Horn Concerto No. 3 in E flat major with the Australian soloist Barry Tuckwell was a favourite—sitting on a vinyl couch in their living room and following the score with a pencil.

Not surprisingly, there seemed to be lots of minor car accidents at this time, and sometimes I'd lie awake with one ear listening to the adult conversations filtering through my bedroom wall, the other ear cocked for the screech of brakes and, occasionally, the sound of metal hitting metal, a brief moment of foreboding. Luckily, no one suffered much serious injury.

One evening my father appeared at the front door, red-faced, to explain he'd run into a parked car—a black Rolls-Royce, what's more—fifty metres from our house. It was obvious to me, and I assume to Mum, that he'd been drinking, but he was insistent that he'd done nothing wrong. The car was jet black, for starters, and the careless driver hadn't left the parking lights on and so, unusually for Dad, he subsequently refused to pay the owner for the necessary repairs. The fact that he'd made contact with the same make of car the Queen was driven around in was a matter of some pride, and so the accident quickly entered into family folklore without too much speculation as to how he had managed to hit such a large object in his own street.

...

Above all I loved being in the water, and on weekends and in the holidays we'd head down to beaches close by—Harbord, Bilgola or Palm Beach—or go north to the Central Coast in the summer break.

We often rented a house at Norah Head, overlooking a long strip of open beach. Hidden away at the southern end, between a giant bluff and a massive rock that was fully exposed at low tide, was a small cove. The biggest thrill of all was running across the sandhills and down to this spot when we first arrived. Surges of water and seaweed would wash up and back into the narrow gap of the cove, carrying us along for the ride. My brothers and I would spend day after day swimming, exploring the rocky headland and catching waves.

Very few families came to this wilder spot and here, with Mum and Dad perched on their beach chairs, reading and chatting, I was happiest. Other than playing golf, these were among the few occasions my dad truly relaxed. At night a board game would keep us going for hours until at last we'd fall into bed exhausted. With sand in the sheets and the muffled crash of surf interrupted by snatches of laughter from the kitchen, all was right in my small world.

For any trip to the beach you needed to be well prepared: beach umbrella stuffed under one arm, clinging on to a big bag overflowing with towels, flippers, a bottle of Johnson's Baby Oil to ensure everyone went copper brown, books, magazines and some fruit which quickly went soggy as the day wore on. Laden families would lurch out of the car park and down onto the sand, little ones trailing behind, older kids hanging on to surfboards, chafing to get into the water as soon as possible.

For a young Australian the stages of the surfing experience are a mini marine version of the Stations of the Cross. You begin with making sandcastles and paddling at the edge of the water under someone's watchful eye—sheer bliss.

When you're a little older and able to swim, you're ready to go further out and learn how to dive under waves and get back to shore in one piece—great for confidence building.

Then you graduate to flippers, or a boogie board or surfboard, and catch as many waves as you can until your arms ache so much it feels like they're going to drop off and salt has seeped into every pore—excitement, total satisfaction and a challenge overcome.

I saved up and with a bit of help from my parents got my first surfboard in my last year of primary school. It was a Barry Bennett nine-footer, so long and heavy I needed help to carry it down to the beach, me holding the nose of the board and Mum or Dad or a helpful stranger clutching the other end. You had to paddle like an iron man to get beyond the waves, but once out the back, the board floated like a fibreglass boardroom table. You could eat your lunch on this monster, it was that big and stable.

Paddling onto the rising wall of water that was the incoming swell and jumping to your feet, a new world opened up. Time was suspended, the water and the translucent reflections around you breathed sparks, as some hidden hand thrust the wave, the board and you—half crouching, half standing—towards the shore. It took hours for the exhilaration to subside.

If these recollections make my early years seem idyllic, that's because in many ways they were. In the early 1960s we weren't constantly bombarded by the woes of the world, nor its enticements. I was living in a cocoon of family and neighbourhood, with each day's adventure unfolding at its own pace, and sleeping happily night after night.

2
QUIET AT THE BACK

WHEN I FINISHED primary school at the end of 1964, I had no strong feelings about which high school I should go to. Friends were scattering up and down the North Shore, some to local high schools, some to private schools that mimicked English public (but actually private) schools like Eton and Harrow. The main carryover from these nurseries of the English class system was the embedding of a clear pecking order between older and younger boys, and between prefects—appointed to exercise authority—and the rest of us. This, and the arcane school uniforms that owed a lot to *Tom Brown's School Days* and took no account of Sydney's warm climate.

My father's choice of school for me was Barker College, at the upper end of the North Shore. I knew he wanted his sons to enjoy the best possible sports facilities, superior to the ones at his public high school. I suppose, too, he wanted us to have the advantages that a private-school education would confer in a class-conscious society. It is inevitable that he would have seen how effective the old boy network could be. I didn't know enough or care enough to protest. If going to Barker meant pleasing my dad, then I was happy to go.

Overnight, my life was transformed beyond recognition.

Barker was then an all-boys Anglican school, located on the Pacific Highway at the end of the North Shore train line in Hornsby. It consisted of a series of low, brown-brick, thirties-style buildings—sober in scale and demeanour—including classrooms and boarding residences, a large chapel and a library. Behind the older buildings sat a modern assembly hall and a series of science labs and newer classrooms, plus numerous playing fields and, further down on the far side of the school grounds, a junior school. Above all, and especially to my young eyes, Barker was big.

Out had gone the scruffy school shoes, shorts and loose shirts, to be replaced by long trousers, shiny black shoes, crisply ironed long-sleeved shirts, a blazer with the school emblem embroidered on the pocket and, in a final ridiculous touch, a straight-brimmed straw hat called a boater.

My fifteen-minute bike ride to Gordon West Primary School with my friends had turned into an hour's slog each way as I trudged from home to bus stop to train station, to be joined on the crowded platform by hordes of other boys and girls in similar attire going to similar schools, our bags weighed down with books and sports gear. If you were unlucky enough to have a prefect living in the same suburb, then you would have to run the gauntlet of his watchful eye, always on the lookout for minor dress infractions and the opportunity to punish the miscreant.

The overwhelming regimentation came as a shock, and not only to me, judging by the comments from kids in my class. It included North Korean-style mass rallies, at which the assembled student body would be exhorted to rise to superhuman heights for the weekend sporting competition against other private schools, and to turn out in force for the First XV rugby contest in winter, where Barker's reputation was on the line. 'But it's only a game', a tiny voice inside my head reminded me. The hardest part was that I now hardly saw my West Pymble playmates. My free-range afternoons had been replaced by regular homework and practice for team sports, and my donkey walk home from the bus stop often happened in the dark. It was the end of an era I'd loved and I felt miserable for the first year.

To be fair, despite its overwhelming air of privilege, Barker attracted a range of students. Some boys were there automatically as their families had always gone to schools like these; the sons of doctors, lawyers, graziers and businessmen predominated. But there were others like me, from the 'wrong' side of the railway line. A few had earned scholarships, others had parents or grandparents who scrimped and saved to cover the fees. Everyone assumed his or her children would be happier and get a better education at a school like Barker, where tradition and discipline were taken seriously.

I can't help but feel that my father's decision to send my brothers and me to a private school contributed to his declining health without a corresponding increase in opportunity for his sons. None of us ever reached the giddy heights of the top sporting teams, although my brother Andrew, a tenacious rugby player, nosed in and out. Matt was a more rebellious spirit and ended up being expelled, escaping to an alternative school in Balmain, lucky boy. None of us excelled academically. With the exception of the music and theatre programs, which I alone took advantage of, we would have been just as content and likely just as successful—however this is defined—had we gone to a government school nearby. The school fees had to be paid each term and once three boys were enrolled it was a hefty sum. Add to this the increased mortgage when we later moved to a two-storey home in Lindfield closer to the city, and Dad's office-manager salary was stretched to breaking point. Even with Mum working nearly full time, the budget wasn't easily balanced and we tipped further into debt. Dad fretted, smoked and drank too much for his own good. His already precarious health deteriorated bit by bit as the years rolled on and pressure from work mounted.

Meanwhile, I gradually adjusted to my new existence. I became familiar with the private-school routine and eventually made some new friends as the carefree days of West Pymble receded into memory. I joined the chapel choir and my familiarity with the

English music canon—the parallels between the music at church and at Barker were eerie but entirely predictable, as both were Anglican institutions—meant that, in this environment at least, I was more confident, standing on solid rock. Still I spent most of my years at Barker in the B class. It was lots of rote learning—chalk and talk—with the teacher standing in front of the class, writing lessons on a blackboard, which we dutifully copied into exercise books and regurgitated at exam time. I enjoyed English and geography, especially when a teacher with a bit of get up and go managed to turn our lights on. The science lab remained a place of bewilderment, though, as did the constant emphasis on beating other schools at sport.

There was a plethora of dos and don'ts that seemed to exist for the sole purpose of curbing the effervescent spirits of boys like me. I was gregarious and was frequently punished for chattering in class. ('Garrett! Quiet at the back!') Barker still practised corporal punishment and if you pushed things too far, as I occasionally did, you'd be frogmarched to the feared deputy principal's office for six of the best, applied to your bum with a bamboo cane.

This was both scary and potentially very painful. Yet all students knew the trick to minimising the hurt was to stuff a couple of exercise books down your pants. We all did it, and while it must have been glaringly obvious to the chief enforcer, he never asked me to pull the packing out.

...

By 1966 I'd graduated from Cubs to Scouts and had been designated troop leader. We were a brand-new troop and I was the youngest to take this role in the district. But as the stack of school duties and obligations swallowed more time, it became clear I'd have to quit. A great adventure was planned for my swan song and a gaggle of twelve- and thirteen-year-olds, without any adults or senior scouts, caught the train north, taking some rudimentary camping gear and a collection of ropes and twines; we were going to sea. In my mind's eye we were following in the wake of explorer Matthew Flinders in his tiny *Tom Thumb*, usurping the latter-day adventurer Thor Heyerdahl, who'd led the famous *Kon-Tiki* raft expedition from South America to Polynesia. Who knew where we'd end up and what excitement lay ahead?

We camped near a secluded beach and scoured the area for materials to build a raft. Having gathered two ten-gallon drums and assorted bits of wood and iron—Aussie settlers discard everything—we lashed them together using every knot we knew.

The next morning dawned fine and seemingly calm. The raft, now trussed up like a chook with a life sentence, was duly launched and then, with some difficulty, dragged out through a moderate swell.

Once past the shore break we clambered on board and aimed for the open sea, rowing furiously with our makeshift paddles, which were in no way equal to the task of propelling our rickety vessel at sufficient speed to make good progress through the breakers.

A much larger set of waves loomed up ahead of us, and when the first giant broke the raft fell apart as a wall of white foam knocked us to smithereens.

Unhurt, we swam to shore, pieces of our brave vessel floating past on the swirling current. The glorious excursion had lasted no more than five minutes.

...

My scouting career had ended but the thirst for adventure remained, even as the options were narrowing. I loved reading adventure yarns but wanted to get out and explore the world even more. For the time being, however, I had to endure the weekly, monthly then yearly routine of commuting, classes, sport, homework, choir practice and end-of-year exams. There was some welcome respite from the tedium, though.

On Fridays I would take the train into town and walk up past The Rocks—the collection of old cottages and warehouses that clustered around the western side of Circular Quay—and through the Argyle

Cut, a roadway that had been tunnelled through sandstone by hand with convict labour. I was on my way to Millers Point Community Centre, where Mum had been appointed the first community social worker, to the Friday-afternoon singalong.

Here I'd reef off the boater, loosen my tie and entertain the retired merchant seamen and wharfies and their wives, salt of the earth in every pore, as we roared our way through old classics: 'The Road to Gundagai', 'Pack Up Your Troubles in Your Old Kit Bag', 'Daisy, Daisy'. It was amazing to me how many of the denizens of Millers Point could play the battered piano that was pressed into service for these singalongs. Otherwise the only interruptions to the long march of schooling were the holidays and the chance to spend some time at the ever-enticing beach.

One year, following my fifteenth birthday, I got lucky when this monotonous calendar of activities was spectacularly interrupted and I was allowed to travel by myself to visit the family plantation, Varzin, in Papua New Guinea, with a detour on the way back to stay with a schoolmate whose family had settled in the Eastern Highlands town of Goroka. Now this was a real adventure.

I flew to Port Moresby, the capital of Papua New Guinea, and then changed to a smaller plane to fly to Rabaul. This was my first taste of long-distance air travel, and despite decades of flying since, including ten years on the Canberra–Sydney shuttle as a member of parliament, I've never tired of it.

I exited at the ramshackle collection of huts masquerading as the Port Moresby airport to be hit full in the face by oven-force heat; I was dripping wet in an instant. Then came the overwhelming smells, the strange vegetation and the different-looking people. I could feel my stomach tighten and nerves tingle as my eyes opened to a world beyond the northern suburbs of Sydney, drinking in the wildness of the place into which, as if by magic, I'd been catapulted.

On the second leg, to Rabaul, we ducked in and around the afternoon storms that are common in the tropics, flying over the empty beaches and reefs that fringe the island of New Britain, and then over great stretches of jungle, with occasional flashes of lightning sparking on the near horizon. I could clearly see the huts of villages scattered across the island, mainly on the lower slopes and along the coast.

And then the ancient DC-3 descended into Rabaul, after dipping like a lumbering pelican into a ragged caldera dominated at either end by prominent volcanoes. To the east, easily visible, was the low, flat shape of New Ireland. The names—Britain, Ireland—might have been familiar, but it was impossible to imagine a starker contrast between them and their Melanesian counterparts. Here it was hot and brimming with wild growth; the earth could quickly turn malevolent and I was awestruck. If travel is a drug, from that time on I had the taste.

My uncle picked me up and we drove for half an hour south-east along a winding coast road towards the small town of Kokopo. Occasional villages dotted the route, with small groups of people sitting outside their huts. They wore bright sarongs and gave a nod or a wave as we drove past. There were very few other cars. It was so different to anything I'd ever seen I was jumping out of my skin at the sight of it all: the intense cobalt sky, azure colours wherever you looked, with deep green vegetation hugging the sides of the road, and the Coral Sea, a soapy, aqua pond to our left. By the time we'd turned off onto a smaller dirt road that led up into the low hills where Varzin was situated, Australia had temporarily disappeared off my map.

My aunt and uncle lived in a spacious bungalow, with views down to the sea and across to New Ireland. With its cane furniture, ceiling fans whirring overhead, extensive verandahs and a guest wing that I had to myself, it was light years away from our brick bungalow in West Pymble. There were no other signs of human settlement, just rows of cocoa and copra trees, and rainforest spilling across the road and surrounding the house on three sides. I was amazed at the strangeness of the place I found myself in, but no one had prepared me for a further inversion of my teenage worldview—the fact that my relatives also had servants who worked on the plantation and in the family home. They were Tolai people from a nearby village. Unbeknown to me, I'd landed at the epicentre of claims by these people for their land. It was now the final years of the colonial occupation of Papua New Guinea by European nations.

The Gazelle peninsula, where Varzin was located, is among the most fertile parts of New Britain and the Garrett family holdings were the jewel in the crown. The peninsula had been colonised by Germany in the 1880s, becoming a part of German New Guinea. It was captured by Australian armed forces at the beginning of World War I in 1914, and in 1921 Australia was granted a mandate by the League of Nations to administer the region. Following World War II, the newly established United Nations determined that the territory should be administered as a trusteeship by Australia. The Tolai made numerous claims for return of their land, with the first, and initially successful, being a claim for 'native customary rights' over Varzin. This decision was successfully appealed to the High Court by the plantation owners, including my uncle. But their victory was short lived, as around the world colonised states fought for recognition and standing. Within four years of my visit, the Whitlam government had initiated discussions with local leaders with a view to granting independence, which subsequently took place in 1975.

The hangout of expatriate Australians was the sports club at Kokopo, a ten-minute drive down to the coast from the Varzin plantation. They'd gather around five each evening for drinks—and earlier on the weekends, after completing a few rounds of golf or bowls—to gossip and sip gin and tonics. It was very Somerset Maugham; the planters were not outwardly racist but cocooned from the outside world and blindly resistant to the pressures building around them. Papua New Guineans performed all the manual labour, and most Europeans had a cook and housekeeper whom they paid a pittance. It had been this way as long as anyone cared to remember. One evening after dinner I tentatively raised the topic of why this unequal state of affairs should be allowed to continue. But my uncle cheerily brushed my questions aside as the impertinence of youth. Nor did he make any mention of the land claims for Varzin. I left Papua New Guinea thinking it couldn't and shouldn't last, and sure enough, in very quick time the colonial era came to a sudden halt. I subsequently studied the region and highlighted the Varzin court case for my Higher School Certificate (HSC) geography exam.

Through the whole trip I was in a state of wide-eyed amazement, and, not surprisingly, vivid memories of the trip stayed with me. There was the earthquake that rumbled across the road just as my aunt and I were changing a flat tyre, tossing the car off the jack; an emergency landing in the jungle on an old World War II airstrip when a wild storm closed in across the ranges; walking into a highlands village with my schoolfriend Nigel Cluer (a future breaststroke champion), the two of us alone among tribal people from Goroka, with pigs and dogs scampering by as I stared, transfixed, at the nose rings and wild hair of the men who greeted us.

...

Back home, the world was moving ahead in other ways, and pop music was tugging at my sleeve, stoking my interest. A distant relative visiting from the UK brought a bunch of records fresh from London. They included Every Mother's Son's 'Come on Down to My Boat', plus early Monkees' singles. We constantly played 'Pleasant Valley Sunday', written by 1960s pop rock icons Gerry Goffin and Carole King, with its tart commentary on suburbia as 'status symbol land'. Good melodies and sharp observations, an unbeatable combination. Later on, when we had a bit of spare pocket money, Andrew and I signed up to the Australian Record Club, which dispatched at least one album every three months by mail. This was the only correspondence I ever received and what riches—Eric Clapton playing searing guitar as a member of John Mayall's Bluesbreakers, Creedence Clearwater Revival's seminal *Cosmo's*

Factory—we pored over the album covers while repeatedly playing the black vinyl discs on a His Master's Voice record player, the size of a large shoe box, which had pride of place in the lounge room.

I'd started going to a church youth group on Sunday evenings where older guys with an acoustic guitar would occasionally show up and sing folk songs, some with a religious bent. For someone with a yearning to know more about why humans acted the way they did and how they interacted with their God—and who was entranced by live music—these gatherings were a new awakening. I'd often join in with the singing on the lookout for opportunities to perform—somewhere, anywhere; I just didn't know how to make it happen.

Then halfway through high school, when I was in year nine, Dad announced he'd have to work overseas for six months. Mum started working nights as a waitress to raise the airfare to visit her sister in Canada, my brothers were sent to stay with friends who had a farm in the far west of the state and I subsequently put in a term as a boarder at Barker.

It wasn't the easiest of times. I was tall and skinny and maturing slowly, surrounded by burly farm boys, many of whom were already starting to shave. I was an occasional target for bullies, but managed to keep most of the ape behaviour at bay. If I couldn't bluff my way out of trouble, I could usually talk my way out, as most of my fellow boarders weren't that bright.

Because of my recurrent asthma, I'd had a nose operation to improve my breathing. It was sore for months afterwards and, on the one occasion I volunteered to fight a younger but tougher boy whose bullying I'd objected to, I finished the worse for wear. One direct punch to my still-tender nose forced me to a teary and humiliating surrender. Even so, I resolved that, if I could help it, this would be the last time I'd come off second-best. I came to deplore violence of any kind, and still do, but I vowed to better prepare myself for a world that had little in common with Sunday-night youth group. This was a harder place where you had to be able to take care of yourself and others, if need be.

We slept in a large dormitory and once 'lights out' was called I pulled up the blankets and, with a pillow over my head, stuck my ear directly on the speaker of my tiny transistor radio. I was mesmerised by the frenetic sounds of the British music revolution, with a smattering of Aussie bands in the mix: the Kinks, the Stones, the Beatles, the Who, the Easybeats and Masters Apprentices blasting out their early best.

This music, and humming hymns and old remembered melodies, helped sustain me, for boarding was a solitary experience. Most boys already had well-established friendships and those I was close to went home on Friday afternoons. At least I had my one good friend, Nigel, with whom I'd jaunted through the jungles of New Guinea. But if he wasn't around, I spent the weekends after school sport and chapel walking by myself through the school grounds, just mulling over tunes and thinking. My trip to Papua New Guinea had stirred up all kinds of thoughts: about politics and society, how the world worked, and what part I might have in the future.

My boarding experience soon came to an end and I couldn't wait to get back home, away from the predictable food and conversations that I'd endured for months, relieved only by the occasional postcard or letter from overseas cataloguing my parents' travels. By now ensconced in a bigger house in Eton Road, Lindfield, we were still on the western side of the railway line but had more room to accommodate three big teenage boys. It was here that adolescence—in my case late and relatively uneventful—unfolded.

As in West Pymble, visitors were frequent, and I enjoyed listening to and then joining in the often heated discussions about the topics of the day. Later on, the war in Vietnam featured extensively. These debates would continue around the dinner table at night and we were given a fair hearing. My parents held opposing political views. My father, while not gung-ho, was a Liberal Party supporter. Mum, on the other hand, had grown up in Bowral, and experienced the blanket conformism that went with conservative communities. As it happened, Gough Whitlam was friendly with her elder brother and had visited the family home in his student days. Whitlam was now leader of the Labor Opposition and, like a number of her friends, she was drawn to the modern vision he embodied.

Even at Barker it was impossible to ignore the scent of big changes and I became more interested in politics through 1969, my second-last year at school. I'd been to a big anti-Vietnam War demonstration in the city with a few like-minded classmates. Conspicuous in our uniforms, awkwardly holding our straw boaters behind our backs, we were heckled mercilessly by the crowd when we arrived. But then a few voices rose up to argue that these pimply youths shouldn't be held responsible for their parents' decisions and that everyone's support was needed—even that of these young refugees from the conservative classes—if the war was to be quit in time. We carried on listening to the speeches in uncomfortable silence.

It was also a federal election year and our home became an unofficial campaign base for the Labor Party. While Dad went off to play golf on the day of the election, Mum and I got up early and marched up and down the leafy streets of Lindfield and Roseville, in one of the nation's safest Liberal seats, pushing how-to-vote cards into letterboxes. I was convinced a change of government was necessary, although most people we ran across didn't seem to share my conviction.

Meanwhile, in an effort to get serious about my studies, with the final exams only twelve months away, I'd taken to sitting up the front at school. In the economics class the following Monday, the teacher—somewhat surprisingly—asked the students, 'If you could have voted in Saturday's election, who would have voted Labor?'

Without hesitation, I thrust up my hand, only to hear an outbreak of titters and laughs behind me. I swung around to find I was alone. One out of thirty; enough said.

When the headmaster decided on an experiment in democracy by instituting the first student representative body in Barker's history, my political instincts gelled. I stood for office for the first time, and as there were very few (if any) nominees, was elected president of the senior student council.

I took the role seriously. A common room had been provided for final-year students where we could meet and engage in intellectual discussion and debate. Instead, we mainly played table tennis and hung around. Despite the general level of apathy among my peers, and a lot more realpolitik as it turned out, I drafted a manifesto proposing regular meetings of the student council so we could make suggestions to the headmaster on how the school could be run better. I then sent our proposals up the food chain, but I never heard back. Democracy, to paraphrase Sir Elton, lay bleeding in my hands.

...

My final two years at school passed in a blur of study and some tentative socialising. The North Shore girls I liked—alabaster beauties with sweet dispositions—already had steady boyfriends, or were pretty choosy. Dancing classes were held at Turramurra on Friday nights and a huddle of boys would congregate in one corner, trying to summon the courage to ask a girl they really liked to dance. This was no big deal for me as I enjoyed the company of the opposite sex, but at the same time I couldn't get on the girlfriend/boyfriend wavelength— I was only just out of short pants. When a friend's sister I was drawn to actually kissed me one night, it put me into meltdown. Although nothing came of it, I lived off the memory until I left school.

There was one girl I'd met at a youth fellowship folk night whom I liked a lot. Rayna, a beautiful, gentle girl, was special. But she lived many suburbs away on a different train line altogether and it took five hours on public transport to get to her place, spend half an hour in polite conversation with her mum, head out on a movie date or go into the city, escort her home and then get myself back to Lindfield. The logistics of getting together saw the relationship falter and then stop; in short, the rail system defeated us.

With everyone around me making plans and scoping out possible careers, I had decided to try to get into law. My parents had floated it as a possible profession and it seemed like one of the few things I might have had an aptitude for—namely, arguing. But as is the case today, you needed good marks to get in so I stepped up my efforts.

In fact, I'd already applied to the Australian National University, which was trialling a new entrance scheme for students who showed real promise, offering early entrance without requiring a top-level mark. It sounded like an attractive initiative, especially for someone in the B class. As it turned out, my application wasn't accepted, but it did put the germ of an idea in my head. Here was a way of getting off a well-trodden path that everyone seemed to take for granted.

I'd made some good friends at Barker and no enemies that I was aware of. I'd enjoyed my time in the choir and various music productions. I'd taken my Sunday school beliefs with me and led the Crusaders Christian group for a time, and I'd learned a bit along the way: about the heart and soul through English literature, and the land and the way it's used through geography. But the narrow habits and material aspirations of the North Shore were looking increasingly monochrome to me, the landscape predictable and flat. I wasn't angry or sad, and I certainly didn't resent my parents for sending me to a school like that nor the privilege that surrounded me. I just couldn't wait to leave.

It was nearly forty years before I returned to my old school to give an address to students studying music. By now I was Minister for the Environment, Heritage and the Arts in a federal Labor government and we'd been in power for less than a year. I was greeted with muted restraint—I didn't expect anything more.

3

THE PLACE TO BE

THE ROUTINE WAS tougher than I was used to. Out of bed early, summer's on the run, the dry air still warming to its mid-afternoon peak.

Help kick off the morning fry-up, breakfast for the few guests— mainly commercial travellers who'd stayed overnight.

Get the pub ready for the day. Rolling kegs with TOOHEYS and RESCHS stamped on their metal girdles up from the cellar on a wooden ramp—and, God, they were heavy—and into the bars: the public bar at the front, and the ladies' lounge at the rear. The familiar smell of stale beer was in everything, wafting through the rooms and across the verandahs like cheap perfume at a hens' night.

Then hunker down and work in the front bar till late. Ease out the drunks, empty the till, clean up, and start all over again.

It was the beginning of 1971 and I'd come down to work at the Great Eastern Hotel in Young, in southern New South Wales, before commencing study in Canberra.

With better exam results than expected, I'd qualified for Arts/Law. The Australian National University, where I'd had a go at early entry, far away from the cloistered vibes of the North Shore, was my first choice.

The Great Eastern was owned and run by the Kerrs, a husband-and-wife team whose daughter-in-law, Penny, was a good friend of the family. Located past the northern end of the Monaro, this was sheep and, where farmers had access to water, cherry country. To the west, treeless hills, scarred and devoid of life, dotted the landscape. In between, the plains were grey and droughty, with dry creeks snaking through paddocks, and miles of fencing laid out every which way.

Young was a rural hub and the hotel, which was in the main street, was patronised by a mix of locals from the town, farm hands, stock and station agents, fruit pickers and other itinerant strays who wandered in at all times of the day and night.

Between the time I'd agreed to work as a roustabout and my arrival, Old Man Kerr had a heart attack. He survived, thankfully, but was out of action. That left his wife, Margaret, a refined woman in her late fifties, and me, fresh out of school, to run the pub until a permanent replacement could be found. Getting thrown in at the deep end was the best learning experience for the novice that I surely was—only just starting to shave and with long blond hair and well-rounded vowels from a city private school. In other words, I came from a planet far removed from a town like Young.

During the day the drinkers didn't so much converse as grunt in shorthand, and it took me a while to decipher what they were saying. It was a kind of mumbled song cycle: weather, weather, sport, gossip, local news, weather. Once you'd picked up the rhythm of the words, and which stage the cycle was at, you could safely chime in.

But what really mattered, apart from whether the town would experience the blessed relief of rain, was how a glass of beer was poured. I quickly learned that a millimetre too much froth—head, as it is known—in the glass or, alternatively, a millimetre under, was tantamount to treason for the beer drinker. 'What are you, mate? Some kind of mug?' Such ineptitude could spell disaster for the publican, as there were several other hotels in the main street and holding on to your regulars was crucial for business. I stayed up late at the end of the first day practising pulling beers from the dregs at the bottom of a keg. As I got the hang of it, Mrs Kerr breathed a bit easier.

There were some Aboriginal workers among the customers, and this was the first time I'd encountered Aboriginal people. Ironic given that I'd already had contact with Papua New Guineans.

The tempo during the week was like a shambling funeral march and I counted down the days until the weekend. Friday and Saturday nights were much livelier, especially when thirsty men came in from outlying areas. One recurring problem during my stay was that the weekend crowds were often reluctant to leave once 'last drinks' had been called.

The 1960s counterculture revolution had rolled across the Pacific from San Francisco and into suburban lounge rooms, and was now pushing into the hinterland. In January 1971 I was one of the few visible embodiments of this radical new era in town. Not everybody took kindly to being ushered out at closing time by someone they didn't know, who looked like a hippie or a surfie or some such sub-species of the modern generation. If a fight broke out at closing time, which wasn't unusual, I'd try to manoeuvre the brawlers outside, ducking punches and hoping the rest of the bar would follow to watch, then quickly dart back inside and lock the doors.

The end of my first week came. The law required hotels to be closed on Sundays, so I was looking forward to a day off. Instead, Mrs K asked me to bring a keg around to the rear yard and set it up for Sunday morning.

At ten o'clock sharp, out of nowhere, a smattering of regulars appeared, with the local police sergeant joining in for a few schooners and a late breakfast of fried sausages and onions. It was a pretty smart arrangement for the publican's wife and the cop. She kept her serious drinkers happy, and the sergeant had the errant characters herded into one place, where he could keep an eye on them, and do a little socialising at the same time. The town ran pretty well, from what I could judge, and I couldn't help thinking this arrangement was one of the reasons.

I slept in a small room on the second floor with a window that looked out over the town to bare brown slopes in the west. In those rare times when I wasn't working I read like a demon—Hemingway, Keneally, Tolstoy, Dostoevsky ('I have seen the truth . . . in one day, in one hour everything could be arranged at once! The chief thing is to love . . .' stayed with me)—and rested my aching limbs. Apart from the hum of trucks doing the night-time run, it was a lot quieter than I was used to. The real noise was the buzzing in my head. I was wound up like a spring, permanently excited. Out of uniform, out of school, out of Sydney and raring to go, getting a little more life experience under my belt.

. . .

Summer wound down and my stint at the Great Eastern finished. I drove to Canberra with Mum to enrol at university and then headed over to Burgmann College, which would be my home for the next three years.

Some Barker friends had raised an eyebrow over my choice of university. Why quit the pulsing, emerald city, with its great beaches and cosmopolitan pubs, at such a promising time? The question wasn't so much asked as implied. As my big burst of swotting over the previous year had paid off, I could have gone to Sydney University and rubbed shoulders with the serious lawyers in Phillip Street. Yet here I was, leaving the bright lights to go to a planned metropolis seen as dull and artificial, full of politicians and bureaucrats, dry and hot in summer, very cold in winter. As comedian Barry Humphries once screeched, 'Canberra, darling, I couldn't live there. It's just a bunch of suburbs searching for a city.'

But I found the nation's capital ideal. Sure, it had a sterile air. The city centre was a haphazard collection of shops and modest office blocks that people couldn't get away from fast enough. The houses were little boxes in uniform, scattered across the Canberra plain and spreading out to the hills. No sharp edges or wild colours, no messy experiments in design, everything cantilevered and constructed to the same standard.

None of this mattered to me. I loved the natural character of the city, with generous areas of parkland and open space surrounded by wooded hills and ranges.

I loved the placement of the lake (named after American architect Walter Burley Griffin, who, along with his wife Marion, had designed Canberra) smack in the middle of town, bisected by the two main avenues that linked the northern and southern sides of the city.

I was infected by the low-key sense of national purpose that seemed to radiate from the creamy white, low-slung Parliament House, the serious air around the big modernist National Library and other stern-looking government buildings on the southern side of the lake.

Most importantly, I was now free to spread my wings without causing my parents too much grief, yet still close enough to charge back to Sydney, only three hours with the foot flat to the floor on the deadly Hume.

In my earlier enquiries about ANU I'd discovered that it drew students from across the nation, as well as from overseas. The Colombo Plan scholarships scheme supported by Australia meant the keenest from Africa, South-East Asia, PNG and the Pacific came there to study. This was the clincher. Living with students from varied backgrounds sounded interesting, a stark contrast to the samey middle-class tribe I'd been a member of all my life.

I'd applied for Burgmann College for the same reason, plus it was brand-new and had the added bonus of being a co-ed college. Like most people, I didn't know a soul before I arrived, and so friendships were quickly made—including with another Sydney private-school refugee, Mark Dodshon, instantly nicknamed Doddo by his new friends—and have lasted to this day.

The college was located on the southern perimeter of the university, close to the lake, and was still under construction when the first intake of students arrived. L-shaped with elongated two-storey wings and surrounded by trees, it was hip 1970s in style, with lots of glass and open areas leading to the grounds outside. I lived in Barassi, which became the partying wing. Named after legendary Australian Rules player and coach Ron Barassi, it had views across the lake and westwards to the Brindabella Mountains. The panorama through my college room window became my inspiration. Sometimes it seemed to change each hour, a reminder of the pulsing flux of weather bearing on water and land, with the mountains constantly changing colour throughout the day.

The university and its colleges were experiencing big social changes. Students, unlike the drinkers in Young, were fully embracing the freedoms that the 1960s had ushered in. There was something in the air that reached its zenith with the mass movements against the Vietnam War, the campaign for racial equality in the US, the quest for women's liberation and a host of other social causes. Many students rejected what they saw as the suffocating mores of their parents, reinforced by seventeen years of conservative rule in which authority wasn't widely questioned and social stirring was frowned on.

This high-water mark of change was backed by a dazzling soundtrack of protest music across genres: folk, pop, rock and the avant-garde. It was a time for new relationships and new experiences. Society was definitely in transition and there was a feeling that anything was possible. I jumped right in.

The only curb on my lust for life (apart from a nod to self-preservation) was my need to work. I was determined to pay my own way given the straitened circumstances at home, and so during my time at ANU I held down a variety of part-time jobs, including as the inaugural Burgmann College barman. The college had decided to have its own bar in order to foster college spirit. After my stint at the Great Eastern, I was the logical choice as no one else had much experience, and so most evenings during the week saw me mixing drinks and playing confidant to my fellow students.

Where I could fit it in, I took on other occasional work. I'd managed to get a truck driver's licence just after leaving school, hoping to get work in a Sydney factory, and this useful document helped a lot. I trundled second-hand furniture around for St Vincent de Paul, sold Sharpe Brothers soft drinks door to door, worked in a carpet warehouse and on the weekends did time as a labourer at a woodchip factory, of all things, on the outskirts of the city.

This last gig required an early start and Sundays were hard going. Once the factory floor was swept and the boss had disappeared, I'd sneak off and grab a quick nap in the massive pile of woodchips that were dumped next to the factory building. The stack made for warm and surprisingly soft bedding. I wasn't the only casual who'd discovered this hideaway and it wasn't uncommon to bump into other students half buried in the pile, happily snoring off the night before. One morning I collapsed on top of someone who would become a close friend and colleague many years later in government: Warren Snowdon, the Member for Lingiari in Central Australia.

...

Burgmann College's motto was 'The Place to Be', and it wasn't far off the mark. As the newest college on campus it attracted its share of lively people. Nominally Anglican, it had been established by a collection of Canberra churches, and was lucky to have as its first master Dr David Griffin, who was open-minded enough to preside over a unique social experiment. Unlike similar colleges of its ilk, there was no student hierarchy or senior common room. The facilities were not segregated between men and women. There were no rules other than to be socially responsible; it was a modern version of the great second commandment, 'Love thy neighbour as thyself'. As a result, Burgmann wasn't cliquey, and it was relatively free of the cant and pompous chiacking, inherited from English university colleges, that often passed for culture at these institutions. We were the first intake, tradition-free, with a blank canvas on which to paint, and so we made it up as we went. As in nature so in life, diversity produces healthy communities; and the colour of beige—in my eyes, where I'd come from—was thankfully absent from this lively college next to the lake.

Burgmann later became well known as the breeding ground of a prime minister (Kevin Rudd) and cabinet ministers of different stripes (yours truly and Nick Minchin, Minister for Finance in the Howard government), along with senior diplomats—John Dauth, who served as ambassador to the United Nations; Judy Pead, ambassador to Sweden; and Hugh Borrowman, ambassador to Vietnam—and lawyers and public servants, many of whom spent their formative years there.

In 1971 it was buzzing. A kaleidoscope of youth had gathered from home and abroad: kids from the bush, overseas students, the reckless and the studious, the drinkers and the pot smokers, the well-off and the poorer students on scholarships.

Like many colleges we produced our own annual revue. It was light-hearted stuff, all about lampooning the social and political foibles of the day: playing Beethoven's Fifth on wine bottles, pretending to be members of the Russian Ballet dancing to a bushranger ditty. There was plenty of talent on offer: pianists, guitarists, thespians and comedians poured out of the woodwork.

One typical performance by a raconteur of great skill, John Terry, who later went on to work for legal aid in NSW, saw him simply read out the names of suburbs and their postcodes from the Canberra phone book in an exaggerated ABC newsreader's accent, which made everyone collapse in hysterics. (Well, it seemed funny at the time.)

On another occasion a group of students dashed off to a Canberra hotel to kidnap the famous English comedy duo, Peter Cook and Dudley Moore, who agreed to the heist and came back to have dinner at the college, tossing off a truncated but hilarious routine on departure.

I don't have many regrets from this period, but not putting in more effort while at university is one. An occasional student at best, I struggled to concentrate. The law seemed stodgy and dense, and there was so much going on that I missed most of my classes, leading to a predictable end-of-year ritual: borrowing notes from studious mates and cramming like a speed freak in the final weeks. Sometimes on the morning of exams I'd wait for ten minutes after everyone else had gone in and were already furiously scribbling their answers, just to generate some adrenalin. Not the best way to pass, but the only method of motivation—blind panic—that worked for me.

Politics classes were more interesting, especially the lectures by Professor L.F. Crisp, who was an authority on Labor prime minister Ben Chifley. I occasionally joined the honours students who congregated in his study after class to hear him reminisce. He actually *knew* a prime minister. We sat on the fraying carpet in his office, mouths agape. Some of those students were already playing politics, and the student union meetings echoed loud with red-hot rhetoric on the rights and wrongs of the world, who was to blame and what needed to be done about it.

We were basking in the afterglow of the 'summer of love', and the slogans and lyrics rolled off the tongue easily: 'Make love not war', 'If you can't be with the one you love, love the one you're with'. And I fell in love quickly, and on more than one occasion. This earth-shaking part of growing up had mostly eluded me until then, but was suddenly centre stage. It was heady mind and body contact, a supercharging of the senses. Some relationships didn't last that long, but emotions were always on the boil and break-ups, and making up, commonplace. In fact, the freedoms we were experiencing were a kind of mirage, because most people were really looking for the perfect mate. Eventually the ship of young fools righted itself, and the search for an authentic relationship began in earnest, as it has since the first of never.

Still the campus pulsed with an energy that, when directed, was potent. One of the big issues of the day, Australia's involvement in the Vietnam War, was dividing the nation. The conflict was long-running, having started in 1965. Young men were chosen by lottery to do 'national service' and serve in the army. But as the war grew increasingly unpopular, some young men who were picked simply refused to cooperate. I was due to be considered in the next selection process and, if my birth date was drawn, I would have to decide then if I'd chance my luck or go on the run. The second issue attracting attention was the system of apartheid that had divided South Africa into a two-tier society, with black South Africans on the bottom. The student leaders and much of the student body were of one mind. Both issues had to be remedied immediately, whatever it took.

In the case of the campaign against apartheid, ANU students were well placed to make an impact. The national parliament was just across the lake, as were various embassies and consulates that had a presence in Canberra. The South African embassy became a target for student activists who planned a succession of actions, including a permanent posse standing outside the embassy with signs reading: TOOT AGAINST APARTHEID. This meant the sound of car horns blasted across the parliamentary precinct all day and, courtesy of those students who had cars, all night as well.

The tour of Australia by the South African Springbok rugby team was an opportunity to intensify the campaign. Games were interrupted by spectators who took to the field, smoke bombs were set off, the police presence was significant and civil disobedience was legion. We marched in large numbers from the university into the centre of town to protest the arrival of the Springboks in July 1971. Looking back down University Avenue at a crowd that took up all the available space, ten people wide and stretching for half a kilometre or more, brought home the latent power that people have when they gather en masse for a cause, if they are willing to use it. In the ensuing tussles with police a number of students were arrested (and later released) as the game staggered on. In the stands surrounding the pitch chaos reigned. Even though it was another ten years before the South Africans were banned from playing international rugby so long as apartheid was in place, the seeds of change were well planted during this time.

Burgmann College became an occasional refuge for those students on the front line. One evening a short, stocky student rushed into the college, soaking wet. Dave Bradbury, later to forge a career as a documentary filmmaker, was a student radical who had narrowly escaped the clutches of the police—leaving his wristwatch behind. The arresting officers were determined to track Bradbury down under the guise of returning his watch.

Spotted by the federal police walking over a bridge that crossed Sullivans Creek, which separated the colleges and the university, Bradbury chose the superhero option, leaping off the bridge and into the creek. He then scrambled up the bank with the police in hot pursuit and, dripping wet and covered in muddy reeds, scampered into Burgmann. David Griffin refused the police entry and the college provided a safe hiding place for the fugitive until things quietened down.

The university colleges also provided a bolthole for those students avoiding conscription. These were the brave ones, hanging in the shadows and moving on each night to avoid arrest.

...

In search of something outside the norm I enrolled in a new subject called Man (women weren't part of it in those days) and the Environment, a brave attempt at cross-disciplinary studies, combining sociology and ecology. The subject's intellectual enquiry stirred up my dormant interest in the way the world worked. It focused on the intersection between the planet's physical processes, such as weather, geography and climate, and the way people acted in relation to nature informed by their values.

It is usually assumed that economic drivers help to explain the impact that human society has had on the environment. It makes sense that people act rationally by always seeking to maximise the use of resources, even if the end point is to deplete the resource stock, like a fish species, to the point of extinction. But this is not the full picture and fails to account for other factors—social, spiritual, political—that might influence behaviour. Some thinkers believed then that modern man and woman were suffering alienation, a sense of separation from the outside world. If this was the case, what did that mean for their relationship with nature? And, importantly, what did it mean for the emerging awareness that there was now palpable damage happening to the environment in many corners of the earth—and what were we to do about it? The subject was discontinued after a year but the questions it raised lingered in the back of my mind, only to resurface years later.

Apart from occasional flashes of interest provided by diversions like this, student life outside lectures was my main focus. There were multiple enjoyable distractions, and I was easily distracted.

If I didn't have a casual job going we'd while away the daytime hours playing volleyball and table tennis, ride our pushbikes across the campus to catch up with friends or just hang out in each other's rooms. I'd bought a cheap motorbike to get further afield, and would skip classes and set out with my mate Doddo for boys' own adventures. We'd head around the lake to the open space that surrounded Government House at Yarralumla and weave through the trees, chasing each other like kids playing hide-and-seek in a big garden. Yet no one in uniform materialised to quiz us about why we were fanging around in broad daylight on noisy motorbikes just over the fence from the nation's nominal head of state.

One of the popular books doing the rounds was called *Be Here Now* by the Buddhist author Ram Dass. It was a basic primer on non-attachment and valuing compassion, and a ready partner to the general 'do what you want to do, be what you want to be' ethos that was considered the way of the moment. I wasn't so influenced by the bracing unorthodoxy that I dropped out and headed for the hills like some friends, but I carried a bit of hippie sentiment with me. It was a kind of Christianity with a small 'c', plus marijuana. While the hippie culture was derailed by hard drugs and furry thinking later on, in the beginning there was a peaceful, take-it-easy feeling I liked that was in stark contrast to the competitive, blokey atmosphere that characterised many colleges and social settings.

The regular rites of binge-drinking prevalent in nearby colleges were, to my mind, an unfathomable part of Australian culture and of university life. Perhaps I'd already spent too much time in close quarters with alcohol, serving drinks to all and sundry—from my parents' parties to the pub in Young and now the bar at college—but these boorish vomit-ridden escapades with their deadly hangovers and ritual humiliations looked like a macabre joke to me.

This antipathy probably explains why a handful of longhairs trying herbal alternatives—dope, mushrooms, tea leaves even—would still be skipping about in the early hours while our fellow students slept off an evening's hard drinking. In the dead of night we'd jump on our motorbikes, kick over the engines and ride to the top of nearby Mount Ainslie, which overlooked the Australian War Memorial and the avenues leading to Parliament House. There we'd take a deep breath, and then tear down the hill as fast as the bikes, engines squealing, would go, screaming at the top of our lungs.

We didn't see the sun come up through bloodshot eyes; instead, we hungered to explore the world taking shape in our heads as the night wound down and we'd sit till dawn, talking, listening to music, hanging out with our girlfriends of the time. On quiet nights I'd lie on the floor of my tiny room on my back with a speaker next to each ear—luckily my closest neighbours, including Doddo on one side, shared my taste—and listen to whatever the album of the week happened to be, over and over again. I could probably play the drums and sing every track on Neil Young's *Harvest* today, if called on.

Sport entered the scene too, as Burgmann had to field sporting teams for the existing college competitions, even though we mainly comprised first-year students, and so I ended up playing everything for a while. We were easily beaten in rugby league, although we fared better in table tennis due to my years of playing in primitive conditions at home and at Barker. The presence of students from Victoria meant that Australian Rules was highly popular. I was tall and could catch and kick a ball and so was drafted to play, despite knowing little about the game. I loved it, although after years of rugby I could never work out how to get in the right position to make an impact. A visit with friends to see a game in Melbourne turned me into a lifelong fan. Unlike the Sydney rugby crowds, which mainly consisted of men from roughly the same background, this crowd was surprisingly diverse, ranging from little kids to grannies, and all sorts in between, from all walks of life. The spectacle was great to see but the atmosphere was even better; I was hooked.

...

Music was the other great distraction from studies and sport, and there was plenty around. Towards the end of the week crowds would congregate in the student union bar where the resident band, Wally and the Wombats, were starting their career. We'd hang out, drink cheap cider and, in my case, listen hard. The more I listened, the more I wanted to be a part of the alchemy that was happening between long-haired guys wielding guitars and massaging drums, making a wondrous noise together on a small stage only metres away—but how?

Whenever somebody was playing, I jumped at the opportunity to go and listen. An early highlight was a visit from blues legend Muddy Waters and his band. They played in a circus tent out in the burbs. Western Australian band Chain, who knew their way around a twelve-bar and were at the peak of their form, supported. It was a stand-out night.

For starters there was the smell of sawdust, a galaxy of childhood memories to mull over. The tent resembled a big, brightly lit cave and was sound heaven. The canvas walls softened the pings and echoes that erupt when amplified music hits hard surfaces like concrete or glass. It was muted and warm, perfect for bluesy rock. Muddy came onto the stage grinning from ear to ear. We'd worked our way to the front, and were so close to the stage we could see the wild patterns on his socks and the sweat breaking out on his forehead. Within minutes he was cooking with a red-hot band. When he shouted 'I got my mojo working!', you believed.

Maybe the promoter was holding on to their return tickets. I'm guessing they were as far away from Chicago as they'd ever been. Maybe this was what they did every night. One thing was for sure: they played like their lives depended on it—the only way to play. The drummer anchored a beat, which the bass player reinforced and then stretched, like a lace stocking sliding up the long leg of a beautiful girl, when it suited. The guitars were human voices: murmuring, pleading, screaming. The mouth harp punched out phrases like a cheeky gatecrasher, pushing the sound up into the roof where the circus trapezes were tethered. It was like listening to a fit, well-oiled, highly tuned part-animal, part-machine mow down everything in its path.

I'm getting the shudders just writing about it. The only performance that ever came close in my experience was one by the Sufi mystic singer Nusrat Fateh Ali Khan, whom I saw at a WOMAD (World of Music, Arts and Dance) concert in Adelaide twenty years later. Both performers were able to keep building the song so that it continually lifted to a higher level, washing over you in waves of supercharged intensity, and both were over forty years of age.

The song 'Eagle Rock' was on its way to becoming a household anthem when Melbourne band Daddy Cool showed up and played the Aquarius Festival, one of the first outdoor music festivals Canberra had seen. Held on the lawns in front of the student union building, it was chockers, the space not big enough to accommodate a crowd that had gone hippie overnight. A pall of dope smoke hung in the air and most of the crowd, including me, were wearing regulation San Francisco garb—tie-dyed T-shirts, jeans, sandals and shoulder bags—and giving off a general feeling of bliss and laidback calm.

I stood at the back but could hardly hear. After Muddy Waters and the intimate, in-your-face experience of the circus tent, it seemed tame and lite. Not because the band couldn't cut it—far from it—but because the amplification wasn't up to the task. I made a mental note then about the importance of sound. Music is best enjoyed loud, and this was too wimpy by far.

Bands were constantly turning up at the uni, and when Split Enz and, a week later, Renee Geyer came through, they both left a big impression.

Split Enz, fresh from New Zealand, were light years away from anything I'd so far seen or heard. Dressed like harlequins, they produced a choreographed performance of broody, jerking melodic rock. With singer Tim Finn conducting the moves, it was eye-popping, the music an unpredictable excursion—M.C. Escher wired up to amps and drums.

Renee Geyer's band featured the cream of local jazz-rock players who seemed freakishly comfortable with their instruments. The music was more soul than jazz. Unlike a lot of jazz players, they didn't waste many notes, and Renee's timing was impeccable. It didn't cater to my taste, but she was, and still is, a great soul singer. Again I was mesmerised—more alchemy.

The surprise gig of the year, though, was the appearance of one of my first discoveries as a fifteen-year-old, John Mayall & the Blues-breakers. I'd pored over their records for years, brought the albums with me to Burgmann and driven my neighbours mad playing them endlessly—and here they were, in person, in Canberra. Who would have believed it?

They played the Albert Hall—Canberra's version—and things took a turn for the better when Mayall announced during the show that he and the band would be doing a music workshop the next day at the same venue. They must have had a day off, but it was still unheard of for an international band to hang around and share their tricks with the local proles. Clearly one glance out the window of their motel would have told them there wasn't much going on in downtown Canberra and some wise member of the outfit had decided they might as well stay occupied.

There would have been no more than thirty people when I arrived at the hall the next morning eager to learn; a smattering of stickybeak fans and local musicians listened intently as the band, which included some of the best-credentialled black players around, showed us the ropes. As with Muddy Waters before him and countless others, Mayall was working in a time-honoured musical tradition that stemmed from America's slave past. This was music based on Negro spirituals and gospel hymns. It was the music of people working for scraps in the fields, living in shanties, identified and condemned by the colour of their skin. Early black troubadours then worked this music up into popular songs of the time. The crying out of a people in chains became the blues: the humming tunes of prisoners marching to be free.

Modern rock music fed off and stole the music of these same blues pioneers: Robert Johnson, Lead Belly, Howlin' Wolf, Bessie Smith, Champion Jack Dupree, Mississippi John Hurt . . . the rollcall of greats is a long one. When Muddy sang 'The blues had a baby and they named it rock and roll', he was calling it, naming the state of the game. The Stones and Beatles supped at the table, Led Zeppelin too, and got rich beyond imagining along the way, but they weren't the only ones—just listen to the Black Keys. This isn't necessarily a crime; all art is imitation and borrowing. The artist is like a bower-bird picking at baubles left lying on the ground after the party's moved on. It depends on what they do with the jewels they uncover or, in the case of the blues, rediscover. Here was Mayall, a white English guy, playing the blues and it sounded right. But he had an ace band made up of great musicians steeped in the tradition, and they were the ones making it work, holding it down.

The main thing I took from this memorable day was that it wasn't the number of notes or chords played. In the blues it's usually only a three-chord progression with variations. Dead simple. It was *how* it was played that counted. You needed to feel it, not think it. It happened in your gut, not in your head. It was a groove you furrowed, and you needed to play with soul.

I left the hall with my head spinning. It sounded straightforward enough, but though I could think it out, I couldn't always feel it. I spent years trying to reach that still point where the notes and the rhythms exit your brain and lodge in your gizzards.

...

As well as checking out as many bands as possible, I'd signed up with my gentle, I'm-up-for-it mate Doddo to train as an announcer for Radio ANU, a new university radio station, which later became 2XX—more sounds, more songs.

The decision to go on air came so quickly that within a few days of learning the basics of operating a small radio console we were broadcasting across the campus. The infant station had few resources so volunteer student announcers brought along records they owned or had borrowed for their shows. People played whatever they wanted, and we drew heavily on friends who'd amassed collections by mail order, picking albums that featured in *Rolling Stone* or the English music mag *New Musical Express*.

The era was post-Beatles and early Stones but pre-punk. Songs were getting longer, the listeners were more likely to be stoned; albums were meant to be listened to over and over, not just three-minute pop songs. The field was full of talent: Bob Dylan; Neil Young; Joni Mitchell; Taj Mahal; B.B. King; Crosby, Stills & Nash; the Band; the Mamas & the Papas; the Byrds; Jefferson Airplane. And from the other side of the Atlantic there were Van Morrison, Pink Floyd, mid-period Who and the Kinks, Family, Fairport Convention, Traffic. Australian free-wheelers Tamam Shud and Spectrum—and their alter ego Indelible Murtceps—and country rock band, The Dingoes, also got a run.

At times it tended towards dozy, but the best songs made the hair on the back of your neck stand up. There were pungent attacks on the military mood of the time, ear-twisting excursions into sound-scapes, gritty blues, soaring pop and lots more in between. We were drenching ourselves in music, as young people do, and it washed us up on a distant shore.

My friend Andy Richardson was a year older and part of the motorbike crew at Burgmann. They rode big, grunting bikes quite unlike the little chaff cutter I was pushing around town. Andy was out of the Melbourne establishment, had been to the right schools and his father was one of Sir Robert Menzies' best friends. A stellar career in business or law would have been expected of him.

Early one morning he disappeared into town, re-emerging a couple of hours later clutching a peculiar-looking silver metal stick which, on closer inspection, turned out to be a flute. It was hardly the stuff of rock'n'roll. He had no idea how to hold, let alone play, the delicate instrument. Forty years later, with thousands of performances and scores of albums under his belt as Howlin' Wind, he still approaches his instrument with the same fierce fervour.

...

I was relishing student life, so primed were my senses on all fronts, when a year after I'd left for Canberra, my father had one of his recurring asthma attacks at home. I'd come back to Lindfield to visit, not knowing anything was amiss. Mum and I, along with a relative who was staying over, had rushed into my old bedroom where Dad had holed up, when he called out shortly before 11 p.m. He was in trouble, and we grew more worried as his breaths became shorter and shorter, until each one was a drawn-out, horrendous struggle.

By the time the ambulance reached the emergency department at Royal North Shore Hospital, a twenty-five-minute drive away, he was dead.

I was devastated but at the same time not shocked. In the last few years we weren't so close that I felt I'd lost a friend. He had travelled a lot, and when he was at home he was often unwell. I'd got used to his downhill slide to the point where it almost seemed normal, and from a young age had taken up more responsibilities as the eldest, helping out when I was around. The thing I missed most was the smiling, dignified presence of the old dad I'd grown up with.

There wasn't much in the way of savings and no gold watch in the mail from the company he'd given his all to, an effort that had impacted on his health. It was a sacrifice he'd made so his family could enjoy the kind of life he had missed out on. Dad had been a popular boss, and the women who worked in the office and came to his funeral were inconsolable, the senior management cool and reserved.

I wasn't sure how my mum would manage but expected she'd pull through. She was strong, with a decent job and, most importantly, a good circle of friends. I'd bought an old Peugeot 403, nicknamed Bess, and having a car meant I could get up to town to see her a bit more.

My father's death was a reminder of the fragility of life. For a while I was content to enjoy the unfettered existence of the young student, as I zoomed around the campus with like-minded comrades. One moment at an experimental film festival starting at midnight in the city, the next, skipping lectures to picnic down by the lake. The colours were bright, the air a sweet vapour, and on the surface it probably appeared that I didn't have a care in the world. Yet deep down I had an inkling that something had to give. It wasn't a fully formed feeling and I doubt I could have given voice to the sensation if someone had asked. There was plenty going on, lots of hanging around, watching, laughter and listening. But actually doing something, something real and new? That was yet to come.

4

SCHOOL OF ROCK

I T WAS EIGHTEEN months after Dad's funeral when I heard a whisper that a band had formed in a college up the road. They had equipment, they could play—allegedly—and they were on the lookout for a singer.

I didn't tell a soul I was interested. I just walked across the lawns to listen in and see what they were up to.

It couldn't be that hard, I said to myself. I'd sung plenty of times before, even if it was only to captive audiences at school and church. I had chimed in at a few folk nights before leaving home and I was *always* joining in with whatever was spinning on the turntable.

A couple of months earlier I'd gone up to Sydney to see Rod Stewart and his band, the Faces, play a big open-air concert at Randwick Racecourse. Success had clearly gone to Rod's head as they arrived by helicopter an hour late, strutted onto the stage, fell over a few times, played a stop-start set, and then disappeared into the night. The audience didn't seem to notice, or, if they did, they didn't seem to care. But I knew then that, given a chance, I could do better than this shambolic outfit. At the very least I'd try harder. All I needed was a band.

There wasn't much going on when I fronted up to hear the students play. Bits of musical gear were strewn around a small room, and a few young blokes sat chatting and toying with their guitars—it seemed pretty haphazard and a bit aimless. Someone would play a few bars, stop, and then someone else would start another song, only for it grind to a halt midstream when no one could remember how it finished.

This was Devil's Breakfast. On bass, Damian Street, a trainee accountant with a big black moustache, bell-bottomed jeans and a cheeky grin. The guitarist, Trevor Thomas, was like most guitarists I've ever known: fixated on his equipment and making the six-string beast sound off as loud as possible. Nigel, the drummer, sat melancholy and out of scale behind an enormous drum kit, with cymbal stands that looked like transplanted traffic signs.

It turned out the only song everyone knew from start to finish was Deep Purple's heavy-metal chestnut 'Smoke on the Water'. On the strength of getting through it a couple of times we were ready to go.

We played our first show, a selection of cover songs, in a small hall in Burgmann. A handful of friends showed up and endured a barrage of guitar and wailed indistinguishable vocals echoing around the empty room.

A few months later Nigel moved on, to be replaced on the kit by another Barker College escapee, Richard Geeves, a curly-haired honours history student and lover of Brit pop.

Devil's Breakfast quickly turned into Rock Island, a name taken from a Lead Belly song, 'Rock Island Line', that UK skiffle artist Lonnie Donegan had had a hit with in the mid-1950s. Armed with a more credible moniker—painted on the bass drum skin for maximum effect, naturally, just like the bands on TV—the new group was primed to sail forth and take Canberra by storm.

We needed to rehearse, get a lot more songs under our belt, and then get work. But synchronising these tasks was tricky, and by the end of the year we'd only played a handful of times to the ever-tolerant students on campus, and we weren't getting any better.

We also needed our own PA, a set of large speakers that would amplify the voice and drums. It signified that you were a real band, and meant you didn't have to rely on borrowing or renting a rig, which took time and blew the budget.

I went home over the Christmas break and mentioned to Mum that without a PA we were stuck and my new career stalled before it started. Out of the blue a few days later she offered to lend me some money to buy a decent sound system.

I returned to Canberra the proud owner of two big white speaker boxes we christened 'the fridges', along with a tangle of leads, a set of amplifiers and a couple of microphones. Later on I added a gizmo called an Echoplex that put various echoes and reverbs on the voice and was frantically operated by foot—a precursor, maybe, to my stomping movements. Damian sold his motorbike and bought an old post office van to cart the gear around. We were now a viable touring outfit.

The time and energy I'd expended on Rock Island inevitably had a detrimental effect on my education in the study of the law, and 1974 was shaping up as a year of reckoning in more ways than one. As the door was opening on the music front, so was it in danger of closing shut on my studies. Up to now, I'd rarely attended lectures, instead relying on friends' notes to scrape by, submitting assignments the minute before midnight, just squeezing over the pass mark in exams. Then came the inevitable first fail, in administrative law, along with a sterner than usual talking-to from my lecturer, an eminent legal scholar. I'd been warned.

A choice now had to be made. I was flat broke again. Rock Island was on the cusp of great things—of that we were certain. We now had more than twenty songs under our belt that we could get through without stuffing up. My studies would have to wait. So law was deferred for a year as I resolved to push the band as far as possible and at the same time pay off my debts, including the latest and largest owed to my dear mum.

I took a series of driving jobs. The first and best was delivering Arnott's biscuits around Canberra in a bright red truck with a giant illustration of a rosella on the side. Arnott's was quintessentially Australian then, their products a part of my life for as long as I could remember—and, encouragingly, they were still going strong, if the hectic delivery schedule was anything to go by.

I slept on Damian's floor in college and lived on surplus shredded wheatmeal biscuits until I had enough money to share a rented house—I've never been able to face that variety of biscuit since. Once solvent, I then moved into a plain brick house close to the university in the suburb of Ainslie with our drummer Richard and another law student and computer buff, Karl May.

We stored the band's gear in the lounge room and began to rehearse in earnest. Armed with a grab bag of top-forty faves and rock classics, equipment that worked and reliable transport—the basic necessities of a working band—we took whatever gigs were thrown our way. We went all over Canberra and to outlying country towns, even as far as Young! Loading and unloading the gear, wiring up the PA, writing the song list, hacking through thirty or so songs a night, hustling for a feed and then heading home, turning the engine off to save fuel as we coasted silently downhill, four of us crammed into the front of the van with a heater that didn't work.

It's a scenario as old as the hills. It was our school of rock. Whenever we were due to play the day would drag like the last school period on a Friday. I could visualise a great night coming up, anticipating the moment when the lights went down and we took the stage. Even if we played to a handful of bystanders in a freezing hall, as happened on more than one occasion, I never felt the cold, just the thrill of fitting the pieces of music and tentative movement together. A flesh-and-blood rockin' band is in town, and no, we don't do requests.

Most times we were incidental music, the live backing tape for people to hang out to. It was only towards the end of the night, when the audience had a few drinks under their belt and started to loosen up a little, that we then rolled out the tried and true standards, like 'Johnny B. Goode' or 'Roadhouse Blues', turning it up a notch so the dancing could start in earnest.

In terms of pecking order, Rock Island sat on the lowest rung, yet we were getting plenty of work. Having a band play at your event had become the in thing to do. So apart from the usual round of pubs, we found ourselves at all kinds of strange locations: school fetes, college balls, and even in windblown paddocks, playing for farmers and their wives as they celebrated the end of the shearing season.

One Saturday evening, we were booked to play at the local speedway to entertain the crowd between races. We set up on the back of a truck (not the last time I'd find myself playing on one of these) in the middle of the racetrack, cranked it up, and were midway through the third song only to be drowned out by the roar of engines as the starter's flag came down and the gaggle of cars, with massive fibreglass quiff-shaped ailerons over their chassis, emblazoned with decals and sponsor names, roared off in a blaze of noise and smoke. Our tough rock routine morphed into limp pantomime as the song petered out and the stampede of hot rods continued to tear around us, while the crowd cheered and the icy evening turned mauve, then deep purple and finally black.

We were working hard but our sound was bog standard, and unlikely to create a sensation. Even when our housemate Karl joined the band with the stage name of Dr Technical and we raised our sights by meshing standard twelve-bar rock and blues with weird sound effects courtesy of his primitive synthesisers, no one took much notice.

There were a few exceptions to this general disinterest, however. Towards the end of the year we were booked to play a mid-week show at the Croatia Deakin Soccer Club, one of Canberra's leading venues, supporting what was billed as 'Australia's Craziest, Zaniest, Bizarre Group (Neat casual dress—No jeans, no cords)'.

Skyhooks were already making waves. I'd only just heard their first album, and it had hit me like a gale blown straight up from the Antarctic it was so fresh. This was the kind of music I wanted to make. The songs were snappy and inventive, all about their hometown Melbourne, with lots of pithy reflections from a young person's perspective; they sounded real. And in a long overdue departure, there were none of the faux American accents or maudlin rock clichés about being an outlaw or finding true love (again) that served as the staple formula for many Australian bands at the time.

They went on before us, a smart thing to do at that time of the year in Canberra; at least the audience was still awake. And their set list was a killer. They played their debut album, *Living in the 70's*, back to back. And they looked the part too: dressed in bizarre costumes, wearing make-up, but with smart, cheeky chitchat from lead singer Shirley Strachan, whose voice soared like an eagle. The guitarists were ever in sync, the rhythm section locked in tandem. I was transfixed.

Even more surprising was that after they finished their set they stayed on to watch the local crew do their best.

More surprising still was guitarist Red Symons walking through the crowd and up onto the stage carrying a replacement amplifier after Damian's bass amp died mid-song. We'd recently supported teen idols Sherbet at a picture theatre in a town outside Canberra and their road crew had refused to allow us onto the stage at all. Instead we had to balance the drum kit and amps on the steps leading up to the stage. It was a clumsy performance, literally, and there was no court of appeal.

The final Hooks gesture set a new template. As we were packing up they came backstage and showed some interest in the novel marriage of mainstream rock and blues with strange signals from homemade sound generators we were trying to pull off.

'Keep at it, there's something good happening up there,' said Greg Macainsh, the bass player and main songwriter.

These few words of encouragement were all the fuel I needed to stoke up the fire in the belly.

...

The year settled into something approaching a predictable pattern when I got a permanent full-time job delivering heating oil for Linfox Transport to the ever-spreading suburbs of Canberra.

Other than the early starts—when if you didn't have gloves, your hand would freeze and stick to the metal nozzle as you pumped oil— I enjoyed shunting my truck around Canberra with no one looking over my shoulder. Most of my workmates had left school early and were no-nonsense types, who worked to live and lived to play. The atmosphere was down to earth, with lots of poking fun and talk about the horses and the greyhounds. I felt at home except I couldn't get anyone interested in the rollercoaster ride of the Whitlam government, which I was avidly following.

As my mechanical skills were limited, I took to buying a slab of beer—two dozen cans—and propping it up on the bonnet of my truck on Friday mornings when we were due to do a basic service of our vehicles. Other drivers would wander across to see what was going on and lend a hand. The job was done and the beer gone in super-quick time. I never did work out how to replace a fanbelt on one of those behemoths.

Besides a much-needed income, my new job had another practical benefit. Our share house in Limestone Avenue—a squat three-bedroom white-brick structure—was always Canberra-cold in winter and autumn. We played out our own version of the tragedy of the commons by using the paling fence as fuel for the fireplace in the living room during an early frosty spell not long after I moved in. Other than that, there was no heating. Then we bought an old oil heater and I was able to keep it filled for the rest of the year.

It was a congenial place to live. We would squeeze into the tiny kitchen and sit around jive talking. Often there'd be a cacophony of different sounds filtering through the bedroom doors and down the hall as each of us fired up our record players and tape machines: Hawkwind and Roxy Music from Karl's room, the Kinks from Richard's, and Crosby, Stills, Nash & Young and Johnny Winter from mine.

The black-and-white television was rarely watched, with the exception of two ABC music programs that were reshaping the local music scene. One, *Get to Know* (*GTK*), was a five-minute filler featuring a range of folk, jazz and alternative groups that showed up and played live just before the country soapy *Bellbird* during the week. The other was *Countdown* on Sunday evening, and it came out of the blocks with a bang. As the music–youth culture mix was heating up, and with more bands emerging, *Countdown*—hosted by the perennially positive Molly Meldrum, with an hour-long time slot every Sunday night at six—became mandatory viewing. It proved a huge boon to the music industry, with Meldrum spruiking upcoming concert tours, profiling new singles, spreading gossip, introducing new bands. *Countdown* featured a never-ending procession of personalities, from Iggy Pop to Abba and the ubiquitous Elton John. Even Prince Charles showed up one night.

Sure, it was a pure pop program, but never before had so many local acts had access to such a large audience. AC/DC, the Ted Mulry Gang, John Paul Young, Dragon, Hush, the Divinyls, Icehouse and INXS all became household names—along with whomever the powerful Melbourne music mafia, led by Michael Gudinski of Mushroom Records, could persuade Molly was the next big thing.

A *Countdown* appearance guaranteed mass exposure as it was watched by just about everyone, but showing up regularly carried a long-term risk: being seen performing to an audience predominantly made up of teenage girls could turn off the older, more serious music fan. Then, in time, the young screamers would swivel their eyes towards the next up-and-comer thrust in front of them, the caravan would move on and the big-name act featured so heavily in the past lost both their credibility and their audience. This phenomenon contributed to the demise of my semi-idols, Skyhooks, who became frustrated playing Beatles-style to auditoriums full of prepubescent girls, while the finer points of the band's music and between-song repartee was lost in a welter of hysteria.

Of course, Rock Island was a universe away from the flashing *Countdown* logo and hyperventilating host and audience. We numbered among the legion of armchair critics dissecting bands and artists every week, and watching closely to see how they fared. Even then it was obvious that appearing on the program was no guarantee that you'd make it.

But still we were determined. If we weren't playing on the weekends, we'd set the gear up in the living room and practise for a couple of hours, but mostly we toured the local circuit. Everyone was dreaming of making it, getting into the glow of Sydney or Melbourne's bright lights. But Canberra was hard to break out of, even with a bit of audience interest and positive chat on your side.

The students' favourites, Wally and the Wombats, styled up like a US West Coast guitar band with long hair and denims, could play Steely Dan and Eagles covers all night and not lose the current. But with the 1970s now well underway and the public always hungry for new looks and sounds, they morphed into a super group—the Ritz— got dolled up in snazzy clothes and headed up the Hume Highway with their first album fresh under their belt.

They stiffed. Sydney was too far away, moving at its own accelerating pace, and anyway, the nearest comparable act was New Zealand band Dragon, whose songs were better.

The same thing happened to the next big thing: Baby Grande, featuring Steve Kilbey, who went on to serious music-making in The Church. Even armed with substantial financial backing and reams of attitude, new equipment and sharp haircuts, it didn't work.

Rock Island just kept trundling out to play. Our hair was long, our denim fading and our limitations increasingly apparent, as the stars in our eyes dimmed. Just four, occasionally five, young blokes on stage, making noise you could sway and jump around to. At least we were earning more than we would pulling beers and it was fun.

We'd mastered the four half-hour sets, with a selection of crowd pleasers to see the night out on a high. We'd contemplated a big band format with female backing singers and Electric Light Orchestra-type arrangements but couldn't fit the pieces together. We'd even mucked about with a few originals, including one song brought in by Trevor, the guitarist, called 'Made in Australia'—but again there was no magic moment of uplift. We were starting to plod, and with exams pressing in on those still studying, Rock Island wound down as the year drew to a close.

I headed up to Sydney to visit Mum and my brothers and to catch a few waves, hoping to get some holiday work before resuming my studies.

Unbeknown to me at this time, a bunch of younger North Shore students who'd played together while at school were planning to take their band Farm out on tour. They'd decided to play the surf clubs and halls along the coast south of Sydney, which would be crammed with holidaymakers over the Christmas period. It was an ambitious undertaking. They were completely unknown, and there was one major flaw: they didn't have a lead singer.

I saw their ad in *The Sydney Morning Herald* of all places. It stood out in a sea of 'Situations vacant' ads for cleaners, labourers, car detailers and so on.

I rang the number and spoke briefly to an up-tempo voice—'I'm Rob the drummer'—and headed off to the audition, which took place in the hall of Sydney Grammar School. Here I was, back at the very kind of school I'd only just escaped four years earlier.

This 'What am I doing here again?' sense of deja vu, was a fore-taste of an experience that is common to the touring musician whose working life goes around in ever-increasing and then ever-decreasing circles. Inevitably you find yourself back in a town or venue you never dreamed you would return to and, in some instances, after shaking the dust off your shoes, had vowed never to visit again.

To my grown-up eyes (I was all of twenty-one), the group I encountered—Jim Moginie, Andrew James and Rob Hirst—appeared to be mere kids, although they had just started at university. But there was no question they could play.

Jim, the guitarist, stood stock still and fixed his eyes on some imaginary point in the distance. The bass player, Andy, was likewise singularly focused on his instrument. The songs thundered, a water-fall after heavy rain, as the boys' fingers flew up and down their respective fretboards. Rob, grinning under a shock of black, spiky hair, smashed at his drums in a flurry of staccato movements as the sound cannoned off the walls of the genteel school's hall.

There were no other obvious candidates for vocalist. After all, what self-respecting Sydney musician would be reading the daily newspaper looking for a gig? To top things off I had a PA, so the arrangement was sealed and Farm's tour of places bands rarely played was confirmed.

I drove by myself in Bess, surfing all day and jumping up on stage at night, as we headed down the coast, sleeping in caravan parks, under our cars and, once we were further away from the bigger towns, on the beach.

It was do-everything-yourself touring. This meant booking the halls, putting the posters up on telegraph poles and in the windows of shops, loading the gear in and out, manning the ticket office, administering first aid. This was a new school of rock for me, with more subjects to master.

Then there was the climax of this frenetic running around: doing the show each night to mixed crowds of locals, holidaymakers, hoons and music fans of all ages.

There were plenty of magic moments of take-off, even if Farm was jamming on a twelve-bar. With zinc cream still smeared on my face from a day out the back, the power of the unit exploding behind me was a wonder. Other than Rob, no one seemed much interested in interaction with the crowd. Friends who could play sax and mouth harp and were helping on the tour jumped up during the set as we blistered through a diverse range of cover songs—Cream's 'Cross-roads', Jethro Tull's 'Locomotive Breath', the Doors' 'Roadhouse Blues' (which by now I was very familiar with)—and a smattering of originals the boys had been notching up.

It was more intense than Rock Island and I admired the chutzpah of my temporary band mates and their team of fresh-faced helpers, schoolfriends Rob had recruited for the jaunt, rewarded with free beer and the promise of good times. That this was a temporary arrangement was understood by all. I was due to return to ANU to finish my law subjects while they continued their studies in Sydney. Farm would keep looking for that elusive permanent vocalist. Accordingly, once the tour was over, we shook hands and went our separate ways.

Back in Canberra, Rock Island soldiered on for another six months. I'd now been on stage with a band that could play just about anything, with a ton of push. The experience had opened my ears a whole lot more, and I couldn't see us going any further. In any case, we were part-timers, and I needed to make up ground with my law studies or I'd never graduate, something I'd promised myself I would do. I didn't want to throw away four years of study—and who knew how handy a law degree might be in the future? Very handy, as it happened.

Damian got married young and Richard Geeves was concentrating on finishing his master's degree. My first band was fading to black.

. . .

Throughout Rock Island's brief career, a storm had been building in the real world. After twenty-three years of conservative rule, the penny had finally dropped. It was time for change.

A new ship of state was ploughing through the political waters of the country, with a giant captain at the helm, and I was one of many willing passengers on full alert for the journey. Less *Queen Elizabeth II* and more turbo-charged tug, the great new Labor vessel was pushing and prodding us into relevance with a long overdue priority list that had been locked away by the forces of caution and retreat for many years.

For the patricians who'd ruled for over a decade it was an affront to the natural order.

For those patriots who longed for change, for contemporary ideas to emerge from hibernation, it was a gale of fresh air.

The first couple of years of the Whitlam government had, by any measure, been fireworks spectacular. Captain Gough had been plotting out this voyage for most of his working life, and even though his crew lacked experience, he knew only one way: crash or crash through. No matter how large a wave was looming, nor how sound the counsel to slow the vessel a little and make for safer ground, he neither slowed nor changed direction.

To the passenger watching from below deck, it was both thrilling and unsettling: there was always a sense of imminent disaster. Sure enough, the tumultuous voyage quickly came to an end—and by devious means at that—and the ship foundered and sank. But Australia would never be the same again, and the lessons learned—the need for probity, discipline, policy rigour and economic responsibility—were of great value to the Labor governments that followed.

Whitlam's ascension to the leadership in 1967 had finally made Labor competitive. For the generations born in the 1940s and 50s, the opportunity to reset the agenda had to be grasped. Labor's breathtaking start, after victory in 1972, is now political legend. Establishing diplomatic relations with China, ending conscription and seeing off the war in Vietnam—which included releasing seven conscientious objectors still in prison—putting in place measures to protect the Great Barrier Reef, introducing Medibank, establishing the Australia Council for the Arts, abolishing university tuition fees, instituting an Australian honours system, passing the *Racial Discrimination Act*, instigating SBS TV and ABC youth radio station Double J . . . on and on the 'must-do' boxes were ticked.

This was a government unlike any before it, drawing in anyone with a serious interest in politics, even more so if you lived and worked in Canberra, where you could smell the action up close. It was a government quick to make decisions and usher in big reforms, but was brought undone just as quickly by Whitlam's overconfidence and the ineptitude of some ministers. Labor enthusiasts watched in horror as a succession of political crises unfolded when the government's attempts to borrow money off line from Middle East sources unravelled. There were months of high drama as ministers resigned or were sacked, the economy was fragile, the air filled with claims of incompetence.

Soon the Opposition leader, Malcolm Fraser, smelled power and the press smelled blood as he determined to force the government out. The Coalition, with the numbers evenly balanced in the Senate, settled on the tactic of refusing to pass the budget through the upper house—the first time this had ever happened. The nation was brought to the verge of a standstill as the government faced the very real prospect of having insufficient funds to pay the wages of public servants or the defence forces.

In Ainslie, stepping up the study necessary to make up for a year away, I was closely monitoring the unfolding drama, unsure of what the circuit-breaker might be. After weeks of building pressure, at home with my housemates on the afternoon of 11 November 1975, we listened in disbelief to radio reports that Whitlam had just been sacked by Governor-General John Kerr, a man Whitlam himself had appointed. Surely not, just ten minutes down the road, in our easygoing democracy?

We jumped into someone's old car (I don't remember whose) and tore down the main thoroughfare, Commonwealth Avenue, over the lake and shuddered to a halt across the road from Parliament House.

Breathless, we joined the crowd of people pouring in from surrounding office blocks and off the street to hear the reedy tones of the governor-general's official secretary, David Smith, echoing from the steps across the forecourt, announcing the dismissal of an elected prime minister to the bewildered throng.

Then came Whitlam's now-famous riposte: 'Well may they say God save the Queen (pause) for nothing will save the governor-general.'

Cheers and jeers swelled around us as the significance of what they had just witnessed dawned on the heaving crowd. Malcolm Fraser and the conservative forces had abandoned accepted practices that held the Westminster system in place, so desperate were they to get their hands on the levers of power. The man who'd previously said 'I'm not one of those who believes that any means are justified by the ends' had changed his tune.

It is to Whitlam's credit that, while exhorting supporters to 'maintain the rage', he made clear that this was to be by peaceful demonstration, and then through the ballot box.

I maintained the rage at this breach of our democracy, as did many others. There were plenty of us at the mass rallies to protest Kerr's and Fraser's actions. I called around to my friends to ask: 'You going?' No one needed to ask where. We all knew and we were out in force. But overall the public mood had soured; the stuffing had been taken out of Labor. The brief golden age was over, and in the bruising election that followed, Labor was thrown out of office.

And I returned to Sydney. I'd been back a few times since the previous summer to play with the Farm crew, who'd been trying without success to find another singer; apparently no one could crack it.

Maybe we could do something together, I mused—but I'd have to go back to the city of my birth to give it a try.

5
A WEIRD MOB

RETURNING TO LIVE in Sydney in 1976 was part pleasure and part shock.

The pleasure lay in anticipating the possibilities ahead, with a band that just might amount to something.

The shock was the increased pace, back in the hurly-burly, surrounded by screeching and clanging, getting familiar with the big sprawl after the quiet of the small bush capital.

Along with a friend who, like me, had decided to transfer to the University of New South Wales to finish his law degree, I headed out to Kensington in the city's east to enrol.

The law school was located in an ugly ten-storey building at the top end of the campus. Wherever you looked there were cement paving and plain buildings; unlike the picturesque ANU, there was very little grass and few trees.

As we queued for the lifts to go up to the faculty office to finalise our applications, my friend suddenly said, 'This is too much. I'm going back to Canberra.' And just like that he walked off.

I headed in alone to begin my last eighteen months of stuttering study.

This time, I was determined to be disciplined. Whatever else was happening—be it a big surf running or casual work at the local squash court—I had to go out to the campus for lectures, put the time in at the library and finish my degree. That it was a sterile and

crowded environment compared to ANU helped, for there was little
to do on campus other than to stick your head into a textbook.

...

Back in Sydney, I moved into Eton Road, Lindfield. Mum had chosen to
stay on there after Dad died and my brothers were constantly in and out.

It was a brick and timber two-storey house, built, so the rumour
went, by a retired sea captain who still haunted the upstairs and could
be heard rattling around at night. I loved this home perched on a
ridge at the end of a street looking over the treetops of the Lindfield
valley. There was a large liquidambar in the backyard, and we'd sit in
its shade on summer evenings and on the weekends when the barbie
would be fired up. This was where my sunny-natured mum was in
her element, with a few friends around to gossip and debate the night
away, a drink in hand, ready to welcome all comers.

The rooms were laid out according to a formula only the captain
could have known. My bedroom was downstairs, at the front of the
house, along with a tiny kitchen equipped with a small bench and op
art Jetsons-shaped stools we'd squirrel onto for breakfast, a tiny front
study, and a lounge and dining room that faced the rear yard.

Upstairs was my parents' bedroom, and those of my two younger
brothers; Andrew's was three times the size of the others, under a sharply
pitched roof with the beams not quite square. It was all a bit mad.

However, facing north meant the transit of the sun was perfectly
in sync with the habits of the household: starting from the bedrooms
in the early morning, then warming the linoleum under our feet in
the kitchen, by late afternoon the sun's gentle, amber light would
stream into the living room. To this day, I can't believe how dumb it
is to design houses any other way, especially on greenfield sites where
planning can start from a blank page.

I would drive across the fabled coat hanger after the morning's
peak-hour rush had subsided. Craning to glimpse the sails of the
Opera House, glimmering in the sunlight, I was seeing Sydney with

fresh eyes. I'd put in the requisite hours on campus, then head back home in the evening, content to spend time with Mum as friends—hers and increasingly mine—dropped by. The rest of my days were taken up with odd jobs and, having reunited with my band mates from the previous summer, rehearsals with whoever made up Farm at the time.

By now, the basic subjects that all students need to pass, like contracts and commercial law, had given way to electives, and there were some interesting options to choose from. The law school was a relatively new addition to the university and its founders, led by the first dean, Hal Wootten, wanted the law to play a constructive role in society, with an emphasis on areas such as social justice and Aboriginal rights. It felt like an institution with a beating heart.

One of my choices was penology—the study of prisons—as I was thinking of becoming a barrister and practising criminal law, spiced with some international subjects like air and space law, anything out of the box and interesting. We visited jails in the Sydney area, including the Long Bay Remand Centre, still the biggest prison complex in the state. (In later years I would return in quite different circumstances, when I was a member of federal parliament. I tried to get there when I could for National Aboriginal and Islander week—the week of celebrations organised by the National Aborigines and Islanders Day Observance Committee [NAIDOC]—as there were lots of Pacific Islander and Aboriginal inmates in this jail and visitors and senior figures supporting their culture might help turn prisoners' heads around a bit.)

But it was the visit to Parramatta Gaol, half an hour west of the city, that had the greatest impact on me.

While I understood the need for imprisonment in some circumstances, seeing a small, barely furnished prison cell for the first time brought me up with a start. Inspecting the notorious Circle at the colonial-era Parramatta Gaol was like touring the set of *The Silence of the Lambs*. The Circle took the deprivation of liberty to the extreme.

It was an internal cage, with spokes leading to various corridors that high-security prisoners could access in order to exercise for a limited period before returning to their cells. Constructed of steel and wire and concrete, its design left inmates with no possible means of seeing others—unless they too were in the Circle—or the outside world, even if only as a flash of sky above the stone walls of the prison. The inmates were being treated like animals. There was no other way to describe it. Who could fail to be surprised if, in the absence of any meaningful attempts at rehabilitation, they reoffended once they were out of this state-sanctioned hellhole?

During the late 1970s, in the flow-on from the anti-war movement and the surge of women's liberation, prison reform had become a more prominent issue.

In time the Circle went, as Parramatta Gaol and several other prisons were either closed altogether or modernised, and steps were taken to make prison administrators more accountable and rehabilitation and treatment efforts more comprehensive.

Unfortunately, the momentum for reform stalled in the 1980s as simplistic calls for law and order and sensationalist coverage of isolated notorious cases became the norm. The political and media warriors of the 'lock 'em up and throw away the key' school were banging the drum ever louder, happy to ignore the fact that countries like the US, with one of the highest imprisonment rates in the developed world, had one of the highest homicide rates as well. Or, closer to home, the fact that Aboriginal and Torres Strait Islander men were many times more likely to be in jail than any other group.

The Christian gospel is unambiguous about keeping a weather eye out for prisoners and widows, but these sentiments were conveniently ignored by the noisy punishers, who held themselves up as defenders of the Judaeo-Christian ethic to which they barely paid lip service.

It is too easy to blame the powerless, and those who have fallen, no more so than from the great bully pulpit of a radio station microphone. I used to drive past the Long Bay jail often and think how simple (and heartless) it is to talk about locking people up and throwing away the key. Some people need to be in jail to protect members of society and to do the time for their crime, but for many jail is no solution. The harder task is to try to assist individuals to recover their potential before they are released. So too in areas like mental illness and education, society needs to allocate the time and resources to maximise every person's chance of leading a fulfilling life, reducing the likelihood they will end up in jail.

...

Between law lectures and casual jobs, I started to spend more time in a garage at the rear of a house in Chatswood, owned by Rob Hirst's father, where Rob and various students lived. The garage was the new line-up's rehearsal and writing space (although we also took over the lounge room on occasion). The walls were covered with carpet underlay and egg cartons; there were no windows or ventilation, just four suburban boys, dreaming of a life of music, crammed up against speakers, amps, drums and assorted paraphernalia. It was usually stinking hot, always loud and close, with a stale, sweaty odour thickening the air—a good training ground for what lay ahead.

We worked on a backlog of songs including 'Blue December', 'Getting Gone' and 'Your Funeral', but at the end of the day none made the final cut. This was the region of poppy musicality versus feel that would remerge on and off as contested ground in the future. The challenge of playing complex pieces of music appealed to the players in the band, but as the new frontman I felt we needed a tougher, pushing sound, with punchy songs that would stir people, and in time they came.

At this stage, though, the first task was to settle the line-up, which until now had been floating, and sort out the issue of who would play keyboards. A wild, Cream-style three-piece was an option—we'd toured the previous summer in that format, and it gave the band plenty of space to wig out—but the music that was emerging needed extra texture. While Jim could play anything from a tin whistle to a Moog synthesiser, guitar was his first instrument, and the off-the-wall emotes from his gold Les Paul were already a signature sound, so there was an ongoing search for the right keyboardist. People would look the part but not be able to play, or could play Chopin and boogie-woogie blindfolded but look like a fish out of water. We wanted to bring a bit of yin into the dominant yang make-up, so we tried to find a female keyboardist, but we had no luck.

For a while we were hitting a sweet spot with multi-instrumentalist Murray Cook, who could also play bass if Andrew 'Bear' James was unwell. Murray went on to serve in various outfits, including Mental As Anything, and was a keen surfer—which appealed to me, as no one else in the band had much interest in waves of any size. He made a welcome reappearance in my life at a NAIDOC concert and barbecue in July 2011 at Long Bay jail. By this time Murray had become a marine scientist and taught music to the prisoners in his spare time. He was one of the many gods of small things making a difference for people in a tangible way: a spark of hope in a some-times gloomy landscape.

But the band's sound wasn't surging the way we felt it should, especially with Rob's drumming propelling the tempo. The solution was ultimately found by recruiting Martin Rotsey to play guitar. Martin was another product of the schoolboy band scene the boys had inhabited, and had also filled in on bass a couple of times when Bear couldn't make it. With a similar slim build to Jim, he too was quiet until he picked up his instrument and then watch out. Martin could partner Jim on guitar, but if Jim went across to keyboards, Martin could step in and play solo till the sun came up. Theirs was a partnership based on mutual respect for each other's playing, with an instrument both loved dearly, and it has lasted to this day. It didn't hurt that Martin always looked the part, initially with flowing locks and bell-bottomed jeans, and later with a cigarette clenched between his lips, tight jeans and a black shirt. He was the personification of a mean guitar slinger and we were a tougher-looking and tougher-sounding unit with him on board.

We sought out places to perform, all the while sweating it out in the garage, note by note and line by line. Once Martin had settled in, the songs tightened up and it started to sound right. We were set to go—now all we needed was an audience. But where to find it? Other than a few inner-city nightspots and the club circuit, there were hardly any places to play. Cover bands performed the hits of the day and yesterday's heroes the hits of the past, but there was little space for bands fermenting sounds for tomorrow unless you were lucky and scored a university gig.

There was an established career route: signed by the record company for peanuts, pushed to commercial radio, thrust onto TV via *Countdown*, then, with a few well-attended national tours under your belt, shoot off to England or the States to make it—overnight, of course. In the majority of cases, bands would be defeated by the experience, strangers in semi-strange lands, easy prey for the Aussie-bashing English press or simply minnows in the much bigger pond that was the US. Inevitably there was the silent return with their tail between their legs. All through this rollercoaster ride their fans and the public, blissfully unaware of the actual progress of the Aussie hopefuls, were fed endless hype about how successful they had been.

The agents who booked the local venues ruled with an iron fist. The shop was closed to new bands unless you signed with an agent who, in turn, had a direct relationship with the venues. In some cases the record company and the booking agency were in cahoots as well, as was the case with Mushroom Records and Premier Artists. In the search for new talent, the record companies were constantly looking over their shoulder for fresh faces who could replicate the sound that had just succeeded. It was a set-up that favoured mediocrity and copycats; no originals need apply.

As the 'unemployed, hyperactive truck driver'—according to Bear's diary notes of a year with the band, which he circulated on his departure—my role, as I saw it then, was to get better at what I was doing and to help think our way out of the stuffy rehearsal room and permanently onto stage.

Some of the early songs had been written in difficult keys, so I decided to take some singing lessons to get on top of the material. I rang John Forrest, one of Sydney's leading singing teachers at the time, to make an appointment, found out the cost—high, more part-time work needed—and months later booked a lesson in which the secrets of vocal mastery would be revealed.

On the appointed day, Forrest ushered me into his studio and, after ascertaining that I was a 'rock singer', started by playing sets of scales on the piano and inviting me to follow.

It was an inglorious journey. So much so that after five minutes of clear single piano notes followed by my howling responses he politely, but firmly, suggested that I might like to think of an alternative occupation. It was clear, to him at least, that I couldn't sing.

He wasn't alone in this assessment. A set of early demos was hawked around to record companies to be met with, 'Why don't you get another singer?', or, 'Maybe if he wears a Silver Surfers suit . . .?'

I wasn't deterred. The only jury I cared about was in the street, and one thing churning it out in Canberra had taught me was that people responded to effort, to the sweat of a real performance. Still, this view of me as unconventional, and the combination of members as an odd fit, was common enough among some of those close to us and parts of the music industry for years after. We were a weird mob, with a visible fault line between the energetic performers—the gangly, dancing singer and the effervescent showman drummer—and the rest of the band (with Martin in the middle somewhere), who appeared introverted, interested solely in their instruments and the sounds they were making. This lack of a unified look and a united approach to performing meant people were ambivalent about the band. They could hear something happening, but when they opened their eyes it looked out of whack—the visual clues were confusing because they appeared contradictory.

In fact, what was happening on stage was just a reflection of the personalities who made up the young band. And there wasn't any Kiss make-up to mask the difference. It was enough to raise the question in people's minds—how far could this outfit go? According to some, the answer was not very far at all.

This kind of scepticism quickly morphs into knocking, in the form of 'What makes you think you're so good?', that is lodged deep in the Australian psyche. At the lighter end of the spectrum, it's about not taking yourself too seriously, where ribbing mates helps grease the social wheels, and it accounts for Australians' lack of pretension. At the darker end it shows up as a relentless antipathy towards anyone's desire for success, as well as success itself. It's a national trait that anyone who aspires to be the best, be they sportsperson, entrepreneur, creative artist or local builder, must confront. It helps to have a tough hide, and ego cannot be a dirty word if you're going to defy the detractors and survive.

'Just don't give up your day job, mate,' was a common refrain, better in some ways than the boozy indifference of the pubs we encountered in the early years, because it was clear that the heckler hadn't thought it through. We didn't have a day job at that stage and we never expected to have one—that was the point! In fact, all the negative chatter did was strengthen our determination to break through or bust—there was no middle ground. And the more emphatic the rejection, the stronger our resolve, and the more certain I was that we would succeed in striking out on our own path. Not for fame or fortune, whatever that might actually mean, but simply to wrestle an amorphous bunch of different individuals into a blazing aural experience, a band with something to say that couldn't be ignored.

Meanwhile punk was in the wings and Australian groups were at the forefront—another kind of 'golden' age was dawning. Here was the great irony of the flowering of the Australian music scene: when it came to the punk/new-wave revolution, we got there first. The defining date when staid and pretty gave way to bold and brutal is usually identified as the release of *Never Mind the Bollocks, Here's the*

Sex Pistols in London in October 1977. In reality, punk as a term, and the music that embodied the attitude—nihilistic, anti-establishment, no frills and extreme—had been bubbling along in the US for some time. Think Iggy Pop and the Stooges, MC5, the Ramones, James Dean even.

In the UK, the impact of the Sex Pistols was so great that overnight the music world changed. It helped that the Pistols' manager, Malcolm McLaren, was a master manipulator whose partner, fashion designer Vivienne Westwood, created the clothes worn by the pioneers of the new movement. In one fell swoop a trifecta of cultural change—novel fashion, raw attitude and even rawer sounds—was happening in your face and on the street, and it arrived with a bang. The media were mesmerised by the pretend anarchy and the old guard was pushed aside, if not altogether, certainly out to the bleachers for a while.

Yet Brisbane band the Saints recorded their first single, the very punkish '(I'm) Stranded', in June of that year. In Sydney, Radio Birdman had been performing their meld of Stooges-like Detroit rock and surf music to increasingly manic crowds at the Oxford Funhouse at Taylor Square since mid-1976. I went in early to see them play: the sound was laser-bright and ferocious, and frontman Rob Younger was riveting, stalking the tiny stage with a leonine fury. The audience wrestled with each other and went berserk as the songs sped ever faster. Somehow the coolest of the crowd managed to keep their sunglasses on—chic and white-noise mayhem, another neat combination.

In Adelaide, two outfits—one the chugging, charging Angels, the other the bluesy swing band Cold Chisel—had already started out. The attitude, especially Chisel's, was punkish, even if their musical roots were in the blues.

In Melbourne, Lobby Loyde and the Coloured Balls had been playing since the early 1970s, loud and fast and hard, with a skinhead audience and utter disdain for success. Lobby's bass player, Ian Rilen, then came up to Sydney and, with Steve Lucas on vocals, formed X, red-blood raw with the menace of heroin lurking in every distorted note they played.

Later on, Rose Tattoo, with pint-sized, ink-covered Angry Anderson up front, ate new-wave posers for breakfast. And what was Billy Thorpe—the pop singer turned rock god playing at blistering volume at the Sunbury Festival in 1973, with his cry of 'Suck more piss'—if not an archetypal Australian punk?

And there were plenty of others.

Call it the butterfly effect—sure, songs and hair were getting shorter, but it wasn't just that: a changing mindset that would shake up the music industry was beginning to take hold.

Farm started to crawl out of its cocoon and into this energy, settling the line-up, turning into the iron butterfly that was Midnight Oil. We can thank a temporary keyboard player, Peter Watson, for the name, which was drawn out of a hat in Chatswood one afternoon. Everyone put in a couple of suggestions; mine included Television and Southern Cross, Rob offered Sparta and Schwampy Moose. But Peter put in Midnight Oil. It came out first and it stuck.

I shaved my head, in part so I could take surf photos from the water—a hobby I shared with my brother Andrew—without strands of hair getting stuck on the lens, but it was also a signal to all and sundry that we were serious. As Abba-style white slacks and hippie gear gave way to black jeans and runners, we got louder and faster. As music surplus to requirements was jettisoned, a lean and hungry beast emerged.

Towards the end of 1976 and through early 1977 we'd started playing occasional gigs at a wine bar on Oxford Street, Darlinghurst, called French's, and on weekends at a northern beaches pub called the Royal Antler, in Narrabeen. It was increasingly slash and burn, playing all the songs we had, taking them as far as we could, as the sweat of the audience condensed on the roof and returned to the stage as smelly rain.

We were hot-wired by the instinctive attitude of punk. It wasn't the sneering cliché of being anti-everything (although Johnny Rotten's sneering at the Queen was endearing), but, instead, the do-it-yourself ethic that rang true. With a pair of scissors, a spray can and a couple of safety pins you had a ready-made wardrobe. Why wait for the record company to see the light when you could start your own label? Just load the gear into a cheap studio and lay down whatever you wanted.

A wild-eyed local surfer-cum-real-estate salesman called Gary Morris had presented himself as manager in waiting. He'd even turned up at intermission when I'd headed out to the movies mid-week to outline his plans for success. I was taken by his single-minded determination and we accepted his hand in a marriage that would last, on and off, for the life of the band.

Together we were the antithesis of most emerging groups chasing success, and shaping their look and sound to get there. In time, years of thinking about the music scene and hundreds of hours of playing live saw us develop a hybrid model that included democratic decision-making, fair treatment of fans, management as part of the band, taking as much control of the process of touring as possible and not giving way on our music or views. It was about crafting songs that had the musical bones to get us moving, the riffs and chorus rushes to take us over the top, welded by performances that could work anywhere.

These were the elements that would mark out Midnight Oil's career as we strapped in for a wild ride that lasted a quarter of a century. The only constant was perpetual motion. We were always on the move, driven by a desire to keep it as pure as possible, and so on top of the road work, we scheduled endless meetings in which we thrashed out the finer details and turned our precocious vision into reality.

It was at the Antler that we first sought to control our environment, advocating for reasonable ticket prices. When the promoter reneged, we went out on strike—unheard of before or since—but the lines of punters waiting to get in just grew and grew.

It was at the Antler that Rob and I got into the habit of pushing our bodies as far as we could. I learned to keep at it even when dark spots appeared at the edges of my vision and things went a bit erky, as all the fresh air was sucked out of the room. Legend has it that one night it got so hot all the windows and glass doors in the hotel misted over. This torrent of condensation dripped onto the floor, already awash with spilled beer and sweat pouring off the crowd. As people down the front passed out, I leapt from the stage and tore across the road to grab a night-time surf. It's true, and the Pacific Ocean held me in her cool embrace until I could see again. Head clearer and body cooled, I ran back to the pub and up onto the stage to finish the night.

Once the crowds got too big we put on entertainment—clowns and buskers—in the hotel car park for those who were queuing up or who got turned away.

It was at the Antler that Gary Morris saw a band called the Farriss Brothers taking the stage with long hair and blue jeans. He ordered new clothes, renamed them and put them out on the road with the Oils so they could hone their craft with a fresh look. It was obvious even then that Michael Hutchence could reach right into the audience and take them along for the ride.

Gary showed up one morning at the share house I was living in, as he was wont to do. By this time the habit of applying nicknames to all and sundry was in full swing, and mine, given I was always willing us to play faster and harder on stage, was—predictably—Rock, and later Uncle Rock.

'Rock.'

'Yes, Gary, what is it?'

'I know what the Farriss Brothers should be called.'

Me: 'Oh yeah, and what's that, mate?'

Gary: 'INXS.'

Me, incredulous: 'INXS?'

'I was at the supermarket with all the cans of IXL fruit and jam,' he said, 'and I saw that slogan, "I excel in everything I do", and then I knew—INXS. Get it?'

Me: 'What about X, X-Ray Spex, XL Capris? Have another think, Gary; there are way too many bands with X in their name already. It'll never work.'

Later, it was at the Antler that we introduced the Warumpi Band to an unsuspecting crowd of blond surfers and their girlfriends. As the lights came up to reveal the band on stage I can still hear singer George Rrurrambu delivering his opening words to a wide-eyed audience that had fallen quiet. Most of them would never have seen an Aboriginal man in person before, let alone in tight black jeans and a Prince-style jacket. 'Don't be shy just because I'm black,' he said. Funny man, George. Here he was channelling James Brown, the Godfather of Soul, whose 'Say it Loud—I'm Black and I'm Proud' had topped the American R&B charts and become an anthem for black America a decade earlier.

All along we kept plugging away, fronting up to any dive that would put on a band and treating each gig like it was the last night on earth. Fixated on our music and figuring out the Oils way of doing things, we were getting ready to take on the world.

We weren't alone among new combinations busting out. With punk's fierce have-a-go attitude, everyone was in a band now, everyone fancied themselves a chance. The ever-present challenge for this crate full of innocents was how to make ends meet. One or two gigs a week hardly covered expenses, let alone gave band members enough to live on, and many bands went on the dole just to survive. Our solution was to forgo the inner-city scene and the pretensions to cool that went with it, and head further out to the suburbs where most people actually lived.

There was a palpable sense of excitement as the boys finished their studies at the end of 1976 and a few months later, I finished mine. Now we could go anywhere any time; now things could really take off.

No one could have expected what happened next: the death of my beloved mum in the early hours of the morning in April 1977, when our family home in Lindfield burned down—and everything in my world suddenly came to a shuddering halt.

6

LOSSES AND GAINS

DURING THE COURSE of writing this memoir I came up against a giant stumbling block—the death of my mother. I knew I'd need to address it; after all, she was a central figure in my life, and the circumstances of her death were already publicly known. But even though I thought I'd come to terms with losing her, the thought of revisiting that night and trying to understand her death in the broader narrative of a rollercoaster life, with all the inevitable ups and downs, filled me with dread. I wanted to retell this part of my story honestly, but at the same time I was fearful of rendering it in too extreme a way. My feelings and those of my brothers ran deep; we loved her so much. How to find the words to sum up this cauldron of emotions without seeming trite?

Some commentators later singled out this traumatic event as an explanation for my extreme stage performances and a take-no-prisoners approach to life in general. They may have been right, though it's not a theory I've ever been particularly interested in addressing. I'm a fairly private person and I've always hated the idea of parading misery to gain sympathy or publicity. All I can say is that the grieving process took time, it was so searing and personal, but it was my pain and I felt I best honoured her memory by bearing it alone. Furthermore, I am hardly the only person to have experienced a family tragedy. They are a constant of life, and I'm only too aware that others had gone through a lot worse.

Now I can see that Mum lives on in me and my brothers, and in our children. In the end, I have let her voice guide me. She was someone who fully embraced life, greeting friend and visitor alike with open arms. 'Make the most of life,' she'd exhort us, and that is what I've tried to do. Because no matter what befalls you along the way, in the end it *is* all you have.

...

When the house in Eton Road burned down I was the only other person at home. Woken by the popgun sound of windows shattering, I tried to reach Mum's bedroom upstairs, which was already engulfed in flames, but was driven back by the heat and thick smoke.

I ended up sitting, howling, in the gutter, covered in only a blanket offered by kind neighbours, as the house turned into a blazing inferno in minutes. By the time the fire engines arrived it was way too late. The sound of her screams still haven't completely faded away.

I was in so much pain, numb with shock. My brothers and I closed ranks and battled the cloud of grief that enveloped us as we tried to make sense of what had happened. The coroner's report was brief: 'But as to the cause of such fire, the evidence adduced does not enable me to say.'

When the tragedy struck we lost everything. It turned out the house wasn't insured; neither Mum nor Dad believed in it. And, like Dad when he died, Mum didn't have much in the way of savings, and with a bank overdraft there was a mortgage to repay.

An uncle lent us a one-bedroom flat in North Sydney as we pulled ourselves together, sleeping on three single mattresses on the floor. We were consoled by close friends and sympathetic strangers, including the Chatswood police who investigated the incident—no easy job.

We took whatever jobs we could find, including cleaning taxis in the early hours of the morning as they returned to base, the drivers bleary-eyed and punch-drunk after a twelve-hour shift. As the city slumbered, Andrew and I would wash out the 3 a.m. leftovers, and whatever else had happened on the back seat.

The night after the fire, the Oils were booked to perform at French's in Oxford Street in the city. Its minuscule, dingy basement was the in place to play and we were building a loyal following. Mum had come to see one of our first shows there, and of course ended up in animated conversation with a bunch of strangers, who were bemused that someone over fifty was actually in the room.

Even though I could still smell the singed hair on the back of my arms, we played the show. I was determined not to fold up and crawl into a hole, even though for more years than I care to remember, I would wake during the early hours and be taken back to that moment.

In the weeks that followed the fire, I went back to assess the damage. Like an automaton, taking one heavy step at a time, I slowly picked through the rubble and the waterlogged timbers to see if anything could be salvaged. There wasn't much left: a few blackened tins of letters and papers, seared and peeling from the heat, and that was it. It was painful, tedious work and often I'd find myself squatting, teary, staring at the debris, weighed down by a mass of sorrow pulling me towards the ground.

It took us a few months to clean up, sell the block of land and pay off the bank. Then I packed what was left of my belongings into a blue sailor's bag. I had no more than a couple of pairs of T-shirts and black jeans, a handful of books, a mono cassette player for writing songs and flippers for body surfing.

Along with Andrew's girlfriend, Lyndall, my brothers and I moved into the top floor of a house in Neutral Bay. Matt, six years younger than me, went back and redid his HSC while working part time in an old people's home. Andrew was in his first year of uni, studying to be a surveyor. He picked up whatever odd jobs were going, including as a roadie for the occasional Oils gig.

We lay low, licking our wounds, watching telly, listening to music and, if the band didn't have a gig, sharing cheap wine on the weekends. Eventually the dark lifted a bit and I started inching back into the bright light of day again.

···

The strategy from then on was simple. Play to the people where they lived, as often as was needed to get the music lodged inside their head. Never rip the audience off. Forget about pleasing the critics or pandering to the in crowd, who would sooner or later consign you to the outhouse. Find those who shared the vision: road crew, staff and music-industry people who were fans, and play, play, play, hoping like hell that you wouldn't crash and burn.

After Gary's arrival, other pieces of the puzzle started to fall into place. As the crowds kept building on the strength of word of mouth and some publicity from ABC radio station Double J, record companies came back for a second look.

After the obligatory 'You guys are great!', they wanted to talk money, singles and marketing. Like many young musicians, we simply wanted to talk music and impose our take on things—it had to be our way or not at all. The normal criteria of success weren't the measuring stick, least of all for me, given what I'd just been through. We had our noses in the air, sniffing the wind, trying to figure out the best way to avoid diluting our precious work and insisting on having the final say. We had chosen to climb a very different-looking mountain compared to other bands that were courted by major record companies, and the dialogue was frustrating everyone. At the same time, the do-it-yourself ethic was energy-sapping and there were only so many 2 a.m. poster runs to let people know about the next gig, and only so many visits to the same suburban pub we could make. If we wanted to break out to a wider audience, we needed a machine that could enable the music to fly a little bit further.

Among the suitors was Channel 7, the television station that happened to own a pressing plant and had established a label to flog cheap compilations and cover records on TV. The manager of the plant, Ken Harding, was an old-school, down-to-earth business-man who, for some reason, liked what he saw and, importantly, was willing to chance his arm on the rogue outfit that had swung into his quiet village.

We were unlikely but ideal partners, as Ken's knowledge of the music scene was scant at best. Channel 7 would give us our own label, subsequently named Powderworks, and promised no interfer-ence. We could record whatever we pleased, with the added incentive of television advertising if things went well.

We also found a fledgling agency called Nucleus, run by a gruff, grassroots operator, Chris Plimmer, who was prepared to place the band on its own terms and break the stranglehold of the mainstream agents. He was also willing to put up with Gary Morris and me badg-ering him at all hours of the day and night about some aspect of our touring schedule.

By now the Angels and Cold Chisel had built large followings and had set up their own booking agency, Dirty Pool. All of a sudden a raft of new venues opened up, as hotels and clubs across the country became the new stomping ground for the 1980s local music explosion.

Success on the charts was still likely to be elusive with a singer the industry hadn't warmed to and with songs that didn't fit radio formats, but the work plan was clear enough: play hundreds of gigs a year, following in the footsteps of troubadours and journeymen and -women since time immemorial.

In Australia there had always been those who'd put in the miles: artists like Slim Dusty, whose biggest hit, 'A Pub With No Beer', we would subsequently record for a Slim tribute album. Slim Dusty, the King of Country, had played places Midnight Oil couldn't get anywhere near, including a few remote Aboriginal communities in the far outback. I later got to know Slim and his wife, Joy McKean, an accomplished songwriter in her own right. It turned out the Oils and Slim had a bit in common: marching to the beat of our own drum, not afraid to talk politics and write music about the here and now. We were cultural patriots; singing nasal and local—touching base, not channelling a distant headline or, in Slim's case, a Nashville by-line. The country crew never stopped touring and recording, and Slim, by dint of regularly showing up in just about every town on the map for as long as anyone could remember, ensured his relationship with the audience got deeper and deeper as he gigged into legend.

When Slim died in 2003 it was an honour to be asked by the family to speak at his funeral. I spent hours trying to craft a speech that did justice to his contribution. Slim had been on the road for nigh on fifty years and had over a hundred albums under his belt; he was the biggest Australian artist ever—there was a lot of ground to cover.

Ours was a full-frontal, revved up version of the practice pioneered by Slim, playing and returning in quick succession. The concentric circle spread out from Sydney and the inner city to the coastal suburbs. Next up were mid-week excursions to Newcastle and the Ambassador Night Club. Located in the main drag, Hunter Street, it was a scungy, forlorn dive that eventually came alive after repeated visits. Then to another steel city and Wollongong Workers' Club the next night, then to far-flung suburbs we hadn't known existed.

Necessity dictated that we continue to seek out new horizons. So off we went to Melbourne for our first southern tour, excited at the thought of being in funky town and pouring it out to fourteen people in a club in Carlton, most of whom we came to know well, in a circle that included Deb Conway, about to form Do-Ré-Mi, and Paul Hester, a great mate, who ended up drumming in Crowded House. And so it went, on to other capitals, Adelaide and the Arkaba Hotel, then Brisbane and, eventually, the west. In Perth the pattern repeated itself, except bands played on Sunday afternoons at 'Sunday sessions' after which everyone, but especially the bands, were definitely at a loose end. The solution? Regroup at one of the few pubs still open on a Sunday night, work the juke box over, ducking and weaving the wild-eyed looking for company before the town shut down. These pubs were our equivalent of the Kaiserkeller nightclub in Hamburg, where the Beatles honed their craft and learned to play all night, fuelled by beer and speed and fast food. As in Sydney, we kept coming back until the rooms were full and punters were turned away.

...

Unlike the rest of the band, who were in steady relationships, I was so focused on the task we'd set ourselves, still nursing my grief, that I had room for little else. Girls drifted in and out of my life, but I couldn't hold things down for long enough and the sparks were intermittent. Friendships, for the most part, were suspended.

I lived around the Lower North Shore, occasionally sharing a house with Andrew and Matt, sometimes with other friends, including Richard Geeves from Rock Island days.

If there were earth-shattering events happening I didn't much notice them. Wherever I happened to be sleeping, a routine of sorts emerged. I'd rise after twelve, slowly get the body back to a semblance of normal, then head down to Curl Curl Beach for a quick surf and a run. Then it was off to the gig, where I'd spill my guts for ninety minutes, drink gallons of water and Staminade, wind down with a beer or two, deconstruct the night, iron out the bugs in lighting and sound with the crew. And then do it again the next night, and month, and year. Winding down after the show was always the hardest part. It's the time when lots of people in the entertainment industry come unstuck. In the very early days, I'd drive back into town when the others—quieter at this time—had headed for home. Martin would often come with me and we'd grab a pizza and play some pool or, mid-week, we'd hang out at Kings Cross, occasionally bumping into other bands having a late-night drink and telling war stories. Other nights we'd finish with a cup of tea at Martin's flat overlooking Wedding Cake Island at Coogee as dawn broke. One early morning I was lamenting the dearth of surf songs in the set. A few weeks later he walked in with a guitar theme that would resonate for years. 'Wedding Cake Island' was our first big song; the fact that it was purely instrumental might have helped.

Later on, I'd often stay at the venue for hours decompressing, just hanging round, deconstructing the show with the crew, letting the after-burn of the night fade until the dreams of ordinary men took over again.

Our musical spirits now unleashed, we'd happily play on after the show with whatever instruments were at hand. At the Ritz in Manly, previously a picture theatre, a small crowd would gather around the piano still sitting in the mezzanine and hit us with requests as we sang the night away, Jim massaging the ivories through old radio classics, the Doors, Elvis Costello, anything that was singable into the early hours.

If we finished early it was important to find something to do or the night would spoil with our body clocks set to peak after midnight. After playing to a bewildered first-time crowd at a pub in the South Coast town of Tathra, we were done by ten and so retired to the roof of the motel in the main street. It was flat and made of concrete, an ideal place to pull out the guitars and sing and drink and smoke until dawn.

The after-show jams were by no means routine, and over the years they happened less and less, and then usually in a hotel room—the second home of the touring musician—but they were pure outings and I fed off these moments; they were solid preparations for the marathon haul we'd embarked on.

At this time there wasn't anything like the travelling one-day rock extravaganza of Aussie pub rock anywhere else in the world. Bands would bring all their musical equipment, as well as sound and lights, into an empty room comprising four walls, beer-sodden carpet and a couple of power points behind a basic stage. A desolate drinking trough would be turned into a 'you've got to be there' rock cauldron in the space of six hours, as road crew lugged in box after box of gear: mixing desk, lighting rig, speaker boxes and drapes, completely transforming the empty space.

Along with our new-guard peers, the Angels and Cold Chisel, we pioneered the door deal, a basic form of capitalism that meant you got paid on the basis of how many people showed up. It was an honest model but needed proactive management who were skilled in promotion to make sure fans knew you were playing at a particular venue on a particular date. It also required someone with the instincts of a bloodhound to be simultaneously checking off the numbers as the audience came in the front door and making sure no one was sneaking in through the back.

On a good night, a thousand people or more would pour into the pub, share the songs, then pour out again, leaving the same handful of crew to pull it all down. This involved packing up in super-quick time then carrying tons of equipment outside to be loaded into waiting trucks that would set off into the night, sometimes across the city, sometimes interstate.

And on it went, night after night. It was grinding, exacting work—an extreme version of the musician's life on the road, when most time is spent travelling or waiting, with the high point that is the performance over in a flash. The crews were as determined as any technician in any opera house to honour the entertainment industry's first commandment—the show must go on—but under far more difficult conditions. It was a small miracle that more road crew weren't seriously injured by the inevitable mishaps that happen in a pressure-cooker environment. There was no shortage of electrocutions, rollovers, clashes with authority figures and wilful fans, scrapes and near misses.

The early Midnight Oil road crew was fiercely proud, with a staggering work ethic but few communication skills. Most interaction with others was short and brutal, along the lines of, 'Fuck off and get out of my way, I've got a job to do.'

At rougher venues there was some risk in this approach, as we discovered when playing the Comb and Cutter Hotel in Blacktown—where, surprisingly, the publican took offence at this phrase being uttered within earshot of his wife at the end of the night. He came up onto the stage—hallowed ground for road crew—to complain, only to be met with the automatic response.

In the ensuing discussion he was flattened by a sudden right-hand jab from the roadie in question and a nasty brawl followed. We struggled to separate the warring parties and, in the face of increasing numbers on the publican's side, grabbed our bags and retreated to the hotel car park. Attempts to negotiate a ceasefire with the hotel security staff were abandoned. The finer details of who said what to whom no longer mattered and they were clearly in no mood for making up. At last it was agreed that if the roadie in question—known to all and sundry as the Pig—was kept out of sight (by now I fervently wished to see the last of him as well), they would allow us to finish loading out the equipment.

More reinforcements—theirs, not ours—had arrived, and several vehicles, one with four large occupants, circled the hotel, going past us every few minutes. After the third circuit a window was wound down and the end of a shotgun appeared. Its owner, who looked awfully like an off-duty cop, sneered, 'This is for you and your fucking smartarse mate.'

Surely we weren't going to get shot now, when we were just getting the hang of touring and recording, and in suburban Blacktown of all places?

Time froze as we awaited the next development—which failed to materialise. But the threat had the desired effect: we were scared witless.

The crew hurried the pack-up, and at last we were able to quit the battleground, relieved to get everyone home in one piece.

...

We had blasted through recording our first album, simply titled *Midnight Oil*, in six days in the winter of 1978 with Double J's live broadcast engineer Keith Walker. We pretty much put all the songs down live at the Alberts Studios, then located in the middle of Sydney's business district. It was the closest thing Australia had to the famed Brill Building on Broadway in New York City, where songwriters like Burt Bacharach and Hal David, and husband-and-wife team Gerry Goffin and Carole King, wrote hit after hit through the 1960s and 70s. Here Harry Vanda and George Young, formerly of the Easybeats, worked as in-house writer/producers for AC/DC, John Paul Young, the Angels and others, composing and recording a raft of hits. Was that the bass line to 'Love Is in the Air' wafting through the wall? We were in the company of champions.

Our first single, 'Run by Night', didn't travel quite the distance that 'Love Is in the Air' managed, and the album closed out with an eight-minute track full of solo guitar called 'Nothing Lost—Nothing Gained'. Not very punk. Still, at long last we had some recorded material available for our growing fan base—and we were well and truly out of the garage.

There is nothing like having your first album under your belt, maybe even hearing one of your songs played on the radio. I'd listened for so many years to other bands, and to friends who'd finally got a run, but now the joy of discovery was magnified—it was us! Thus proudly equipped with a round piece of vinyl with our name on it, we continued to play far and wide.

Head Injuries, a tighter and tougher album, was recorded nearly as quickly less than a year later at Trafalgar Studios in Annandale. It was produced by Lez Karski, who'd toured Australia with English funk band Supercharge. His only complaint was that the songs contained too many ideas, but by now most of the tunes had been well honed in the pubs. During recording we often came in after a show to lay tracks until nine or ten the next morning.

The injection of politics on songs like 'Stand in Line' and Rob's 'No Reaction' gave the record bite. My take on the archetypal Australian surfing odyssey emerged as 'Koala Sprint', and one of Jim's wild pieces (with some additional lyrics), called 'Is It Now?', ended the album in a flurry of noise, just as the shows did. *Head Injuries* was everyone pulling in the same harness, paring down the songs to reflect the intensity of the live performances that, in the absence of healthy record sales, were keeping the wolf from our door.

...

My grandmother Emily, by now in her mid-nineties, was still living at her home in West Pymble. Her husband and closest daughter gone, she'd set her jaw and pressed on.

If I was in town I'd go up on Sundays to mow her lawn and we'd go on her favourite outing, a drive down to Newport Beach for lunch, Gran with a blanket on her knees and a box of Kentucky Fried Chicken, me with a burger and my flippers in the boot in case there was a decent swell running.

When we played a free outdoor afternoon concert put on by radio station Double J at St Leonards Park—reasonably close to home—in April 1978, it was time for Gran to see what her grandson had actually been up to for the last few years.

Doddo brought her down for the show and she sat in a wheelchair up the back behind a monstrous crowd that had materialised out of nowhere. There was plenty of noise as the bands pushed the PA to the limit, and people danced and swayed, stepping around groups who'd set up camp for the day with blankets and eskies, amid growing piles of cans and food wrappers that carpeted the park.

Afterwards, when I asked Gran what it was like, she said firmly, 'It was very enjoyable, dear.'

After the manic pace, and all the losses and gains of the past couple of years, what more could I ask for?

7
OUT AND ABOUT

BEING ON THE road lifts the scales from the musician's eyes to a wider world. In the era before Walkman players and iPods, once the local radio had been exhausted, you spent a lot of time gazing out the car or van window as the landscape rushed past.

You could see the physical shapes, the different outlines of locations, but also the way people lived, and you got a sense of their habits as well. Coming into any town for a break I'd look out for the markers: street names, the descriptions in 'For Sale' signs, notices in the local supermarket window, headlines in the local rag, Tidy Town awards, the noticeboards outside empty churches, garage sales, graffiti—all these visual clues to be read like a detective searching for the ideal settlement. It was interesting, too, to see what people had stashed in their backyards. Old caravans, multiple car bodies, maybe a vintage model covered by long grass and dandelions, abandoned play equipment, scabby concrete statues, well-tended vegie gardens, fire pits, dilapidated sheds, trail-bike tracks, granny flats. There was no end to the variety, or to the endless, unfinished projects that littered these quarter-acre paradises.

I was sucking in parts of the country I hadn't seen before and still enjoying the novelty of being in a different town most nights. Constant touring meant the opportunity to explore and the thrill of possible new discoveries. One day you're checking out amusement parks and beer gardens, overgrown cemeteries and sports grounds;

the next, you're exploring shell middens and marvelling at drawings on the wall of a cave, the outline of the sail of a prau from the Celebes that last cruised the northern coast hundreds of years ago.

I could see more clearly that Australia isn't uniform. Each state is different, each city and town a product of its past, with different geography, histories, stories. There was plenty going on above and below the surface. We found that touring Queensland in the late 1970s and early 1980s was noticeably different from other interstate locations. Heading north you could taste the tropical flavour as grevillea and palms took over from dry-weather eucalypts. But it was the politics of the state, playing out like a 1930s newsreel, that hit you in the head. These were the final years of the regime headed by Premier Joh Bjelke-Petersen. Corruption in the police force, and in the highest levels of government, was rampant. Furthermore, this right-wing crowd came down hard on those who dared to criticise.

As is often the case, activists and artists were singled out for attention. We'd heard Queensland called a police state but were still incredulous to discover an unmarked police car nestled in a parking bay, right in front of the motel we'd checked into on our first visit. It said something about the reach of the regime, and its stupidity, if some young Sydney rock band with a few political songs in its repertoire—although none yet about Queensland—was judged a threat to the government.

My old friend from Barker College, Nigel Cluer, was now studying dentistry at the University of Queensland and had been swept up by the police and locked up overnight as he tried to make his way past a demonstration. Until then he'd been apolitical, but the shock of finding himself behind bars for no reason quickly turned to anger, and like many other Queenslanders, he became an implacable opponent of the conservative government.

He was living in a state where the government held power by gerrymander (with voters in rural areas effectively getting more say than city dwellers), led by a man who'd benefited from insider knowledge in share dealings, who had actively fostered corruption in the police force, planned to mine the Great Barrier Reef, and then sent a delegation to a United Nations meeting in Paris to oppose the federal government's push to have the reef added to the UN's World Heritage list.

This was a state where the premier was so in league with property developers, the so-called white shoe brigade, that at one stage they backed his push to become prime minister. During his time, no building, however culturally significant or historically important, no wetland or rainforest, no matter how environmentally sensitive, was safe from the bulldozer.

A prime example was the pre-dawn demolition of the popular Cloudland Ballroom in Brisbane. Built in 1940 on a hill overlooking the city, Cloudland was unlike any other venue in Australia: a classic two-storey white building with a gracious entrance featuring an eighteen-metre arch, a specially sprung wooden dance floor, decorative columns running around the internal walls and a spacious upstairs viewing area. The scene of much of Brisbane's social and cultural life in its early days, Cloudland hosted dances and jazz band concerts. Buddy Holly had played his only Australian shows there, and many entertainers of the 1950s and 60s had graced its beautiful stage.

In the 1970s and early 80s, as the local music scene exploded, it again became a popular venue. It was a wonderful place to play, with the made-for-movement floor a brilliant feature. Once a show got going it would start to flex, as crowds up to two thousand strong bounced up and down in unison, under a roof thirty metres high. The audience would then stream outside to cool off in the breezes that blew across from the Brisbane River and Moreton Bay, with the lights of Brisbane twinkling below—pure magic.

Over the strenuous objections of the public and without any warning, this heritage-listed treasure was flattened in the early hours of the morning to make way for blocks of flats in 1982. We eventually recorded the song 'Dreamworld', which referenced the sorry incident, on the *Diesel and Dust* album. A year after Cloudland was demolished, the Liberal/National Coalition was finally swept from power.

...

In the early years, to get from city to city we drove and drove, along the way blowing tyres as if we were bursting balloons at a kid's birthday party. *Bang!* went one on the way from Sydney to Brisbane.

A few days later—*bang!*—another one blew outside Albury as we were driving home from Melbourne. Short on sleep, and pushing as fast as I could, I managed to pull the swaying rental wagon up before we careered into a dusty paddock.

We were all a bit shaken, but at this point Andrew James decided he'd had enough. The Bear had now used up a couple of his nine lives; it was early 1980 and the touring schedule was only just kicking in. Added to which he'd been crook and was homesick, an affliction that everyone would fall prey to at different times in the years ahead. There's nothing natural about being constantly on the move, but it satisfies the nomadic instinct for some. Others are just not built for life on the road, and our first bass player was one of these.

Once Bear announced his early retirement we needed a replacement quickly. We were geared up to keep playing, and finding someone in a hurry meant broadcasting for a new member as widely as possible. Peter Gifford, a carpenter from Canberra who'd moved up to Sydney to find a band, heard on the radio that we were holding auditions for a bass player and came in to try out. Giffo thought like a member of King Crimson but played like he was in AC/DC, with a tradie's voice to match. He was in, and in the deep end at that, as we were back on stage days later.

The pressure, with Gary Morris directing traffic, a phone on each ear and only a few hours' sleep a night, was by now building to an unnatural level. In the space of a year or so we'd gone from playing a couple of nights a week to year-round touring, doubling as record company, promoter and publicity machine in between—but we still struggled to break even.

The workload piled higher as we tried to make every show better than the last, driven by the conviction that we shouldn't repeat ourselves. It was a whirlwind of costly self-improvement: new poster artwork, better sound equipment, trying new instruments, different arrangements and songs, capped ticket prices, organising our own events, doing fundraisers and even more extensive touring schedules.

Endeavouring to cover all the possible bases—ensuring adequate security, liaising with community groups, producing media, and more songs to soar—was stretching the people around us to breaking point, but on it went. We would continue to sweat across the stages of Oz as the audience kept us alive and we, in turn, kept giving back to them. We were honouring an unwritten contract, and despite the wear and tear on everybody involved it kept us in good shape for years to come.

An epiphany at a Billy Graham crusade saw Gary suddenly depart the scene in 1980 for a few years. Initially we did his job ourselves, and I was the bagman, getting in late and stashing the night's takings on top of my wardrobe, but the hours were insane and it couldn't last. Gary had suggested we look up a young Melbourne promoter, Zev Eizik, and eventually he took us on.

Zev was another one not built for the road. He had other business interests to keep an eye on so he delegated tour-managing duties to a young Californian, Connie Adolph, aka the Boogie Queen. Constance came with impeccable showbiz credentials: she'd been an original Walt Disney Mouseketeer. This meant she could muster enthusiasm in any situation, however dire or uninspiring. And with her effervescent personality, the Boogie Queen was the perfect foil for the sometimes dour and determined Oils she was charged with safely getting from gig to gig.

There seemed no reason to alter an approach built on sweat, loud noise and outrage, so we went around the block again, and then headed off on our first overseas jaunt, beginning with New Zealand,

and after that making tentative forays to small clubs in Canada and the US.

The Kiwi trip was like going back in time. New Zealand was mostly sleepy, with lots of sheep and cows, and very green. Outside the two big cities, Auckland and Wellington, everything was closed by ten, except the quaintly named dairies (milk bars), where even the fearsome Maori gang, the Mongrel Mob, could be found.

One night, following a show in the regional town of Hamilton, a couple of us headed out to eat, only to find ourselves crammed into a small dairy with a bevy of tattooed and drunk gang members. It was the kind of situation that could end in pain, and when the largest of them wandered over and demanded a bite of our sound engineer Colin's burger, the stage was set for confrontation.

'You want some of my burger?' Colin asked.

'Yes, now,' came the grunted reply. A pause.

'Are you sure?' Colin asked.

'Yes,' came the menacing growl. Another pause, and shuffling from the rugby pack of massive hulks now glaring at us with evil intent.

Suddenly Colin thrust the entire hamburger into the inquisitor's mouth as the bikie froze for a moment, agape at the audacity of the move.

'Run!' Colin, shouted and we took off out the door—pure shock and awe. Col's quick thinking saved the day.

This isolated incident belies the fact that most New Zealanders were hospitable to a fault; you just needed to know where to connect with them. After playing a club show in Queenstown in the south, we repaired to a party held in a restaurant at the top of the cable car that took skiers to the nearby snowfields. In the early hours, when it came time to leave, we jumped into the swinging cable car; the last passenger having pulled the switch to set the cable car in motion, he then leapt in as we careered back down the mountain. No one blinked an eye.

I admired the plucky resolve of the Kiwis in the face of strong international pressure when they took an antinuclear stance in the

80s, and their music scene is endlessly inventive and spreads wide for such a small nation.

What makes something original and different in music will always be a matter of opinion laced with taste. The topic is subject to endless debates, usually conducted at the end of the night when the crowd has drifted away, or, in our case, on the big buses that served as our home away from home once we gained a foothold in America.

Everyone strives to be different, but when different is the norm then nothing much is that, well, different. In trying to stand out, lots of performers end up in uniform, unconsciously parodying themselves; just think most heavy-metal outfits.

The Oils didn't wear our sources on our sleeve because we each had different tastes and no slavish devotion to one band or era of music. After the beginning period, when the band was Rob's project, Gary and I took up greater roles, conducting the operation and speaking by phone to one another constantly, sometimes for hours on end, as we tried to find the ground where the band's composite personality could merge with the business we were in.

Midnight Oil was often a mystery to itself. We'd start with one person's chunk of clay on the potter's wheel—notes, riffs, a sketch, a piece of music in draft form from Jim or Rob usually, but importantly an original idea—then all five sculptors would work away to make it a Midnight Oil song. On one level it was plain rock, played by five white guys, mainly with regular four-beats-to-the-bar time signatures, the songs around four minutes long, most with traditional verse, chorus, verse, chorus, middle, chorus, outro structures. But it sounded different and we weren't easily pigeonholed. When a journalist asked me who my musical heroes were, I replied, 'The band.' Because we didn't sound like anyone else, the energy we threw out made me want to move and the music matched the semi-ordered chaos of my brain and the deeper currents of Australia.

There are literally millions of pop songs. Some are instantly forgettable, some are competent and palatable, and some take you a lot further. Then there are songs transcendent, which stand the test of time: the Drifters' 'On the Roof', Burt Bacharach's 'Anyone Who Had a Heart', countless Dylan classics, the Triffids' 'Wide Open Road', to mention a tiny number on my list. What counts is whether the truth of the song rings through, how it speaks to the listener, how the chords, the rhythms and the melody bring the words alive. So it doesn't sound like anyone else, it just is.

While punk and new wave favoured a minimalist mindset, with people who'd never played an instrument before forming bands—an approach that delivered plenty of hallelujah moments—we were a reverse-engineered version of this prototype. This meant plenty of 'let's go for it' attitude, tempered with some inkling of the pitfalls that lay ahead, but being players and writers at heart, the band had to search out a route that was both musically satisfying, and short and sharp enough to hold everyone's, but especially my, interest.

It was a strange, unusual tension, but it served us well for a long while. If a song like 'Don't Wanna Be the One' worked on stage, we could be pretty confident it would work in the studio. Once budgets increased and songs entered the studio in finished form, it got harder, but that's another story.

Still, endless road slog will eventually take its toll and strip some shine off the duco, so not long after we finished *Head Injuries*, the time came for a real break, and the chance to search out some fresh terrain. Being at home reminded me of how much I missed my mum, so early in 1980 I took off on a cheap round-the-world standby ticket, travelling west in a stop-start fashion, pulling up for a few unplanned nights in cheap hotels on the outskirts of Seoul and Tokyo while waiting for a seat to become available so I could continue my journey.

I couldn't have a schedule, and had no plans other than to satisfy a long-standing desire to surf in Hawaii, the home of big waves, and to drink in the atmosphere of different lands now there was a welcome pause in the endless season of touring.

I eventually landed in London and stayed with my college mate

Andy Richardson, who'd moved to the UK to further his flute studies. He was putting food on the table by busking to commuters in the London tube. They were as tough an audience as you could ever find, but with thousands of commuters passing by every hour it could be lucrative, so long as you grabbed a good spot.

I took in the sights and sounds of the empire fading, taking care to skirt around suburbs like Earl's Court, where many young Australians would gather in a predictable rite of passage that seemed to involve lots of beer and not much else.

I was also keeping watch on upcoming tours and noticed that a new Irish band making waves was due to play their first gig at the legendary Marquee Club. Andy and I headed down to join a smattering of punters as U2 went through their paces. They were cranking out a pretty good sound for a three-piece, especially when Edge's trippy guitar and Bono's voice met in the upper register. I stayed back to say hello, figuring the Irish and Australians have a bit in common—our attitude to the English for one—and that proved to be the case.

Apart from the abundance of culture, especially the non-stop procession of music performances, there was little to hold me. The institutions and ways of the English were familiar enough, which was why lots of Aussies ended up there, but the odious class system was still in full swing. This meant heaping reams of condescension on colonials, who were considered to be even lower down the rung than the working classes, a mentality that was irritating and out of date. Added to which the Poms were a morose lot, given to constant complaining about everything under the ever-sodden skies. They seemed perpetually unhappy, not my disposition at all.

A visit to a new exhibition on the Great War at London's Tate Gallery cemented these feelings. I was intrigued to see how the war would be portrayed, particularly given that Australia and New Zealand had played a loyal supporting role across Western Europe and the Middle East, one that was magnified in our history by the experience at Gallipoli.

I knew the military encounter had been a tragic fiasco. This was due in no small part to the decision taken by the First Lord of the Admiralty, Winston Churchill, to attack the Turkish forces at a location that was too easily defended. The ANZAC soldiers trying to advance up the steep slopes from the beach could have reasonably been expected to suffer serious casualties, and they did.

I also knew that the Gallipoli campaign was the first time Australia as a young nation joined others to fight as part of the British Empire. The exchange ended in retreat but the bravery and camaraderie of the Aussie and Kiwi soldiers became the stuff of legend. The diggers were predominantly young men. A visit to any country town's cemetery shows how innocent in years and life experience many were. They displayed a refreshing resistance to authority, including refusing to salute their superior officers, especially the British.

How would the exhibition present these events? What paintings would the curators choose to show what happened when the Australians and New Zealanders came ashore and attempted the near-impossible task of taking higher ground and defeating an enemy that quickly marshalled far greater numbers?

To my surprise there was nothing on the walls—no paintings or sketches, no written descriptions—referring to 25 April 1915, our Anzac Day. Not one skerrick.

Whether the ANZAC tradition as it has evolved deserves the attention it receives today, sometimes at the expense of equally deserving chapters of our military past, including the first resistance of Aboriginal people, is an open question. But my grandfather had been injured in the deserts of Arabia. I knew every note of the Last Post, the bugle call that had rung out once a year for as long as I could remember. The example and sacrifice of the young diggers in that place is rightly honoured. This is an event seared into the consciousness of Australians and Turks. It defines, to some extent, the nationhood of both countries. Yet it had been left out of the exhibition completely.

I doubted the omission was deliberate, rather Australia just wasn't in their viewfinder. It was consistent with the tone of conversations I'd already overheard. Many English looked down their nose at or made fun of Australians, typecasting them as ex-convicts who were only good at sport and drinking. You couldn't be too precious about this, and we inevitably gave it back in spades, but nevertheless I felt a deep sense of anger welling up.

Even though I'd soon be back with the Oils to play and record *Place Without a Postcard* in the English countryside, and not long after that, *10, 9, 8, 7, 6, 5, 4, 3, 2, 1* in London, we could never dig in there, of that I was reasonably certain. The only way England welcomed bands from Australia was if they moved over and took on some of the English habits, dressed the part and played their game. This was never likely to happen with the proud outfit I was in. No matter what, we would always drink from the well of connection to home. My visit to the Tate underscored this a thousand times over.

Europe was a different kettle of fish: magnificent public buildings, especially churches, a crowded, cosmopolitan cafe culture, inter-twined histories that after centuries of war and peace meant there was a lot to chew on. They were putting things back together again, trying to join as one. The goal of a united Europe, where they no longer resolved conflict on the battlefield, seemed a very long way off but their stoic, rational stance after so much turmoil was impressive; you got the feeling they might just make it.

I feasted on a surfeit of culture and art and craft, expressed over centuries, revealed layer by layer in museums and towns. The usual spots sucked me in and lifted me up. I got stuck with busloads of gawkers for hours in the Van Gogh Museum in Amsterdam, a place I would return to whenever I got the chance, so utterly compelling and accessible were Vincent's paintings, so tragic the backstory.

Continuing west, I dropped in to New York to see a few of my friends from ANU: David Bradbury, now busy making left-oriented documentaries, and Paul Sheehan, veering to the right, who was studying at the Columbia School of Journalism. I was planted some-where in between. But we were joined, as so many of our countrymen and women have been, trying to make it on a wider stage.

The streets of the Big Apple were overflowing as hurrying crowds surged through the city, and muggers and derelicts lurked on the periphery, getting braver as the shadows grew longer. The air was filled with the smell of hot bagels and roasting chestnuts from the street vendors in the day and the strains of jazz from the clubs at night. I stayed at the YMCA, with the heaviest security grilles I'd ever seen across the windows, completely blocking the view, and just walked along the giant avenues of this in-your-face high-rise town.

This was a city I could get to like. I was drawn to its energy and constant hustle, and to New Yorkers: black, Irish, Italian, Jewish, Hispanic, all pushing their way forward. It became our East Coast base in Midnight Oil's latter stages, a place that made touring manageable, with a raucous voice louder than the homesick blues.

Then I was off to LA via El Salvador.

I was on a pilgrimage of sorts to visit the cathedral in the capital San Salvador, where the Catholic Archbishop Óscar Romero had been recently gunned down by a right-wing death squad while conducting mass; he had criticised the military dictatorship who had ruled the country on and off for decades. El Salvador, one of the poorest and smallest nations in the region, was experiencing a civil war, and when I applied for a one-day visa in New York I'd been surprised to be granted one.

As I exited the plane I saw soldiers everywhere, and I fell into a conversation with an American woman who, it turned out, was taking the same trip. Figuring it would be safer to pose as husband and wife, once through customs we took a cab straight to the cathe-dral square and pretended to be dumb tourists. The poverty of El Salvador was plainly in view, but it was the air of fear and dread permeating the city that slapped you in the face. The cathedral was empty, with a handful of young soldiers standing outside in the blazing sun, nervously fiddling with their carbines. We paused briefly to pay our respects and then hightailed it back to the airport, where we went our separate ways.

The Reagan administration ended up providing billions of dollars to the right-wing El Salvador government and the army. The left-wing opposition received some support from Cuba and peasants in the rural areas, not surprising given that 2 per cent of the population held around 90 per cent of the wealth. It wasn't until 1992 that a process sponsored by the United Nations brought the warring sides together in an uneasy truce that staggers along to this day.

My funds were running low as I overnighted in LA on the way out of the States. I could hardly see the Hollywood sign, but when I did glimpse it through a veil of pollution it looked crooked and tawdry. I felt like I'd landed in a Raymond Chandler novel, and I wanted out.

I hung around Los Angeles airport until eventually I got a flight to Hawaii. Camped in a cheap motel in Honolulu, I awaited the arrival of giant waves, glancing occasionally at the weather channel where the announcers, talking in tongues, never stopped smiling. I knew the names of the breaks by heart: Waimea Bay, Makaha, Sunset Beach, Banzai Pipeline. They'd been plastered over my bedroom walls since my early teens. My skills as a board rider were limited, in fact they'd stalled altogether, but I'd long wanted to test myself as a body surfer in this crucible of world surfing.

Each day I made my way from Honolulu, in a cheap rent-a-bomb, out to the North Shore (another one), to scan the horizon for the big lines of swell that chug across thousands of miles of Pacific Ocean, then rear up out of deep water and thunder-dump onto the Hawaiian shoreline.

This part of the island was reminiscent of New Guinea: uncrowded and undeveloped, hilly, with dirt tracks winding around the verges of tropical rainforest, which came down almost to the coastline, on the edge of which many Hawaiians had built small homes.

I was reasonably confident that I could hold my own in the bigger waves. I was super fit and just before leaving home had swum out

to the infamous Queenscliff Bombora, a break about half a kilometre offshore, on a day when huge seas whipped the coast and all
of Sydney's beaches were closed. The rush of adrenalin that coursed
through me as I shot down the face of a growling monster before
ducking down under the crunching lip left me quivering. I wanted
more and Hawaii was the place to get it.

By the end of the week, just as I was running out of money and
running short of patience, the ocean at last began to stir. I drove
north for the final time to find the flat conditions of the past week
had vanished. A solid three- to four-metre swell was pushing in to the
shore. It was bigger than I was used to but not that big.

I chose Pipeline, famous for its extreme waves that pitch up over
shallow reefs, as it was a shorter swim to get out to the break. It was a
left-hander, a difficult wave to get a grip on, with a much thicker lip
and a sudden throw, and a lot more power than the easygoing rollers
of Curl Curl.

More surprising was that out of nowhere scores of board riders had
materialised and were already positioned beyond the break, sitting
patiently like a flock of seagulls, waiting for the next set.

I picked one of the littlest, and hopefully easiest, waves that
suddenly reared up. But in an instant its sheer force flung me from
the face and I speared into white foam, went around the spin cycle
a couple of times, hitting the lava-encrusted bottom with a sudden,
scarifying thump—not good.

I was the only body surfer who'd ventured into the water and there
was an outbreak of cackles from the boardies around me. I took a few
more small ones to salvage a bit of self-respect before retreating to the
shore to watch the locals rip it up.

I'd fulfilled a boyhood dream, having escaped with a few scratches
and a vivid memory of getting dumped at Pipeline. The next morning
I flew home.

8

THE HURDY-GURDY MEN

W E WEREN'T GOING to just f-f-fade away, and we certainly weren't running on empty. Once back from the brief sojourn overseas, albums and tours came round as quick as the morning headlines.

We weren't chasing the charts either. We were chasing something more elusive: the distillation of a moment in which five (six if you include Gary Morris) odd fits—extroverts and introverts, some focused on making music, some intent on making waves—could find common ground.

I always saw the band as family, sharing a mission. We would socialise now and then, still do, but the years of being together for an ideal and for the music meant we were more like brothers—fragmented, perverse, affectionate, loopy and difficult to explain as any family can be. You might not always agree with or even like your brother every step of the way, but the bond that holds partnerships of this kind together is not easily described—let's just call it tight.

And one thing we always agreed on was taking a chance to go further if the opportunity presented itself, as happened when the legendary English producer Glyn Johns, who really did deserve that description, saw us play at Selina's in Sydney at the beginning of 1981. Selina's was a big room at the back of the Coogee Bay Hotel just across from Coogee Beach—extra sweaty and very, very crowded.

He came on a typically humid Saturday night, standing amid a crush of about two thousand punters, mostly young blokes, T-shirts stripped off and tied around their heads, who knew every word. The singing was louder than the monster PA the crew had squeezed into the room. The aircon struggled to keep up.

We played song after song, barely pausing between, as the roiling crowd surged towards us with their arms outstretched, crashing and falling into each other, getting thrown to the floor only to be hauled back onto their feet to resume the crazed stampede.

Buckets of ice were stashed backstage, ready to be tossed into the throng to revive the hard-core fans who were now wilting in the front rows. Before the encore, the crew poured leftover freezing water over our heads to stop us from conking out in the furnace—the show *will* go on.

Outside, couples and families would be ambling up the Coogee shopping strip, clutching melting ice creams. Inside our brick box, the spectacle raged. Racks of lights flashed madly and the groaning rumble of the bass and walls of guitar noise spewed from the bank of amplifiers lined up across the back of the stage like techno centurions preparing for battle. To close the night out, I clambered onto the top of the speaker stacks and leapt back down onto the stage floor (what was I thinking?!). At the same moment, Rob, standing on his drum stool, slashing at his cymbals, kicked his drums off the riser and onto the floor—take that, Pete Townshend! The pale-faced Johns had come straight off the plane, jetlagged and blinking, from a London winter. No wonder we made an impression.

Glyn was unlike the toffy English I'd met in London. He was an East Ender who'd risen from working-class roots to produce the cream of 1970s artists like the Who, the Eagles, Joan Armatrading. He'd even worked with the Stones and knew them as mates. All this naturally piqued our interest, and he was keen.

Like many people, he'd fallen in love with the spectacle of the Oils live, but his lights had dimmed a little when we brought our new songs in, determined to craft a deeper album than the last. Glyn was coming from years of increasingly painstaking sessions with bands that could afford to spend forever in the studio. But for him there was to be no more taking two weeks to get the bass drum sounding right. Glyn wanted fresh, and that meant making the album quickly.

We lived and recorded in England at his home studio out in the Sussex countryside through the European summer of 1981. The best part of the stay was roaming the fields in the long twilight, wandering across the commons and along the ancient walking paths—finding a bustle in a hedgerow at last—with the smell of fresh-cut hay and English blossoms saturating the air. That, and sneaking a listen to old demo tapes and backing tracks of the greats (the Stones, the Who, the Beatles) he'd secreted away in a storeroom. Surprise, surprise, they sounded kind of normal—but no, not ordinary, because of the distinctive, oh-so-familiar voices. Still, there were these legends, sounding like just another bunch of musos stepping through different arrangements, drifting in and out of tune, stopping and starting, trying different keys and debating the best way to finish a song—the perspiration before the alchemy.

We were stretched for cash so couldn't afford to do much more than hang around and write songs and grab the opportunity to get tracks down when Glyn was in the mood. *Place Without a Postcard* was recorded on the run (sometimes literally, as the vocal for 'Lucky Country' was done after tramping through the fields, and then tearing back breathless to the studio), to record something with urgent bite. Other tracks were put down in one or two live takes, as was the case with 'Loves on Sale', 'Quinella Holiday' and 'If Ned Kelly Was King', which were all recorded in a row without pause.

We were proud of our third album, spare and unmistakably Antipodean, but A&M Records, our putative label for the rest of the world at the time, couldn't hear a single and asked us to go back in and record more songs. We refused.

Glyn was also proud of the album. So much so that, dissatisfied with this turn of events, he took it upon himself to fly to the record company headquarters in LA to play it to the label heavies.

'Where's the big song, which track should I listen to first?' one demanded.

'Put it on anywhere,' was Glyn's defiant response.

They passed.

We were back at square one and broke again, having spent all our money travelling to England, and now there was no prospect of an international record deal. Dreaming of the sun, we just wanted to get home. Another stint on the road awaited but at least we had a batch of new tunes under our belt to keep things fresh.

From a music-industry point of view the band had reached a plateau, with a strong cult audience in Australia, and the beginnings of one overseas, but with very little reach for our records, although eventually CBS picked up the album for worldwide release. It didn't bother us greatly. We'd never been in sync with popular taste, and there was no reason that should change now. But at some point we'd need to reassess, if only to square our ambition with the reality we found ourselves facing—big name, small records. So small, in fact, that when the Australian record company requested a greatest hits package— well-known live songs in actuality, as we'd had little airplay—Zev Eizik, in an inspired moment, offered a B side, 'Armistice Day', with a special edition T-shirt as a single. It promptly made the charts.

Once *Postcard* was released locally in November 1981, we took in the whole country, finishing in Cairns, the last big town in Far North Queensland, full of cane farmers coming in for supplies and tourists heading out to visit the reef and the Daintree Rainforest a little further up the coast. I then detoured for a week to drive across to the Northern Territory with my Rock Island mate, Richard Geeves. He was going to teach in a small community called Numbulwar on the east coast of Arnhem Land, a long way from anywhere.

I was looking forward to the escape. The further from the big cities, the more difficult it was to find suitable venues that could accommodate our equipment, for the Oils were always loud and large no matter the size of the gig. We'd been at it for a while now and yet would often end up playing in sleazy pub rooms or makeshift nightclubs, which served as temporary pick-up joints, playing mutant disco, running wet T-shirt competitions, and on quiet nights offering girls free entry to bulk up the crowd. There was a depressing familiarity to this scene, and the Cairns club was oppressively chauvinistic, so escaping to the big spaces as we headed west across Queensland was a welcome relief.

As the flat landscape opened up and I wound the window down to suck the air in, I felt the tingle return: new faces and new places heading our way. We'd pull up stumps to sleep wherever we happened to stop, grab a roadside burger for breakfast, then set off again. On the second night out we got spooked by the Min Min lights, a strange natural phenomenon of flickering low flashes on the horizon that seemed to be tracking us at a distance outside the driver's-side window. With no inkling they were a feature of these parts, we had a few eerie moments imagining that we were being chased by UFOs.

By the time we reached Mataranka a few days later, I was in heaven. This was a part of Australia I felt at home in, even though I'd never visited before. The eyesore of roadside signs flogging cheap land and cheaper furniture was gone. And there were interesting types around: wanderers like us, a lot more Aboriginal people, truck drivers I could yarn with, missionaries looking for easy game and a smattering of pioneer grey nomads. It was remote and sparsely populated, but it felt intimate, real.

And so we motored across Queensland in Richard's ancient Holden, chatting about old times, reprising the Beatles songbook, often going for hours without seeing another vehicle. The country was given over to hard-hooved grazing with the odd mining tenement popping up every now and then. As we crossed the border into the Northern Territory, the landscape slowly turned rocky as we left the big dusty plains and entered escarpment country. Here the jagged landforms gave off an air of permanence and mystery. With *Please Please Me* and *With the Beatles* thoroughly worked over, we turned north on the only road leading to Darwin. We were on the upside of the Tropic of Capricorn and thick, perfumed air as sweet as fairy floss whooshed in the window.

Then came large chunks of Top End frontier flavour as we entered Darwin, the end of the line. The mix of people out and about increased: bankrupts, misfits, get-rich-quick types, adventurers and idealists, all rubbing shoulders at the Roma bar, then the only cafe in town that served a decent coffee. You could always close out the night at the appropriately named Birdcage. This was no-frills drinking with concrete floors and perforated wire walls that finished a metre off the floor to enable patrons to make a quick escape if things got hairy.

We put in a couple of nights at the YMCA and then said goodbye. As we stood on the high cliffs, looking out to sea, there wasn't a boat in sight. Yet a day or two under sail would bring Timor—part of the East Indies on the old maps—into view. I was entranced and decided then and there to return when conditions were right.

...

By now I'd moved into an old rundown four-storey block of flats called the Ritz (another Ritz) in Cremorne, on the north side of Sydney Harbour. It was close to the foreshore and some rooms had spectacular views across the harbour to the city and the Opera House. Most of the tenants were pensioners, as it was dirt cheap and buses ran close by. I could hear my neighbours listening to the races on the weekends as cooking smells seeped under the door and through the walls: tinned spaghetti and baked beans—my staples as well.

Mark Dodshon was back in Sydney working night-shift radio, and if the Oils were playing around town I'd drop in at the Lavender Bay boatshed he'd holed up in to debrief following the show. The melange of distorted guitar feedback and cymbal crashes, and the crowd braying, would bounce around in my head for hours after the final chords sounded out, and it was a good wind-down to sit listening to the water lapping against the harbour walls with cockroaches scuttling to and fro. Across the silky bay Luna Park had long fallen silent. Sometimes we'd step outside to stretch our legs, and if we looked up to Brett Whiteley's house we could see him padding about in a kimono, prodding and gesticulating at imaginary friends and enemies. If Doddo asked how the night had gone, I'd dissect the evening's performance song by song, sometimes bar by bar—the poor man.

After a few hours there, I'd walk a couple of kilometres through the quiet streets that ran along the harbour back to the Ritz, where residents were just starting to stir. In my basement flat—a single room with a bed in one corner and a kitchenette on the far wall—I'd pull the blankets up over my head to keep the dawn at bay as sneezes, shuffles and the whistle of the first kettle of the day merged into a soundscape above me, drifting in and out of reverie until my body finally gave way to sleep.

I got to know Whiteley a bit later on as he was friendly with Mark Knopfler from Dire Straits, who'd found big favour with Australian audiences with their 1985 album, *Brothers in Arms*. Musicians would often stay at the Sebel Townhouse Hotel in the Cross. Away from the main drag, it was a good place to hang out after shows and wind down. I'd bumped into Knopfler there and was struck that he didn't seem the least bit carried away by the mega success Dire Straits was enjoying. At the peak of their fame, he'd agreed to co-sign a statement with us directed to Prime Minister Bob Hawke, calling for the protection of Tasmania's ancient forests.

He liked to talk politics and art and had become friendly with Whiteley, who dropped by to shoot the breeze. Brett was a brilliant painter and his death by overdose a few years later threw me off balance. Whenever I was at the Art Gallery of New South Wales, I'd grab a moment in front of *The Balcony 2*, one of his large Sydney Harbour paintings that was part of the permanent collection. Sails scattered across the iridescent water, the quick arc of a sea bird in flight, dashes of white against luminous blue and green. The painting shouted life in the epicentre of the glistening city of Sydney.

Occasionally we'd hang out with other bands, although most were nightclub habitués, and I've never been in a nightclub I didn't want to get out of asap. More often we would cross paths with the road warriors of the time: Mental As Anything, the Angels, the Sports from Melbourne and Cold Chisel. The Mentals were art-school guys, having fun and making quirky pop. Chisel were already cutting strong records and burning up the stage like we did. We ended up jamming with them at the Music Farm studio near Byron Bay one year. The evening became the stuff of minor rock folklore, but like most encounters of this kind, it was as much talk as it was music.

It was always interesting to see how other people were handling the pressure cooker of rock marriage, where you end up spending more time, in more extreme circumstances, with the members of the band than anyone else. In this petri dish of different and often-colliding personalities, what you loved and wanted more than anything could turn into a slog. And then the question rears up: when the merry-go-round stops, do you still feel the shiver when syncing up on a song, or walking onto the stage with these same people, night after night? If the answer is yes, then most else is forgiven or more likely forgotten until such time as you can afford to do it by yourself. That's when bands tend to go their separate ways.

I loved that Jimmy Barnes sang till his throat bled; we were soul brothers on that score alone, and he was great company. Don Walker's songs were pithy short stories, the melodies abundant, and to cap it off, Ian Moss sang and played guitar like a young Muddy Waters. Chisel in full flight at Cloudland in Brisbane doing 'Wild Thing' is one of my most cherished memories. They left nothing to chance and could swing while going off the dial—that's rare. I always felt they deserved more critical acclaim and could have gone a long way internationally if the stars had aligned, which, sadly, they didn't.

For Midnight Oil, endorsing a direction, and the decisions that followed, even if some members weren't so concerned about offstage matters, was more an emotional reaction than a strictly rational process.

The Oils tended to respond intuitively, trusting the direction 'the band' was taking, while still being aware of what was going on around us. If anyone had doubts we could hold a meeting to thrash things out, and the right to veto was always an option if an individual member wanted to exercise it. Throughout, we were usually unanimous in agreeing to take up an issue.

This was the case from day one, when we put our hands up for our first benefit concert, Save the Whales at Balmain Town Hall on 29 April 1978, to coincide with the date the Greenpeace vessel *Rainbow Warrior* left London for Iceland to contest commercial whaling. As late as the 1970s, whales were being pursued to extinction. Boats armed with high-powered harpoons, launched from ports like Albany in Western Australia and Eden in New South Wales, would hunt them down and drag the bloodied creatures back to shore, where various parts of the carcass would be hacked off and sold to make perfume, candle wax and even soap.

Our first benefit show was a chaotic evening, never mind that it was a noble cause. The anarchists and community activists running the show couldn't tie anything off properly. And we were doing a double, and due to play again later that night at the Bondi Lifesaver in Sydney's eastern suburbs, one of the few venues then dedicated solely to live music.

After a while, knowing people would be showing up for the politics *and* the music, we took to handling the organisation of these events ourselves, with Gary and our office taking the reins. Benefit shows were a way of directly helping activists and community groups who were often engaged in a David-and-Goliath struggle against powerful forces with deep pockets. If anyone deserved a hand it was the planet savers, everyday citizens often armed with little more than good intentions.

These shows were also an antidote to nuts-and-bolts touring, a means of putting some flesh on the bones of our songs and inviting our audience into a new arena that showed our values. The night at

Balmain Town Hall marked the start of us hooking up with the like-minded—young and old—who weren't content to sit on their hands and whinge. They actually wanted to do something about what was going on around them and so did we. Some of the issues we encountered have faded from view, and that's a good thing. Others have stuck around, none more dramatically than whaling, an issue that returned with a vengeance during my time in government three decades later.

...

In the early days we played a few times at the Lifesaver. It was a notorious industry hangout, featuring a long bar at the rear of the room, and a big fish tank that provided cheap entertainment for punters who could no longer see the stage or had overindulged. Everyone went, played or partied there, and it was the place where a lot of acts got a run, including Rose Tattoo, Richard Clapton, Chisel, Dragon and Split Enz—even AC/DC were early regulars.

In the late 1970s, with a stagnating economy, rising youth unemployment and Malcolm Fraser in the Lodge, and propelled by the punk explosion, the stage was set for a resurgence of live music. You could sidestep the doldrums and scope out one of the many new bands emerging overnight—or, better still, you could form one. The Civic Hotel at the southern end of Pitt Street in the city was emblematic of this period, and, unlike the Lifesaver, was willing to take a chance on little-known bands. Up a flight of stairs, with big windows looking down to the street, it was an L-shaped room that held about 300 with a small stage wedged into a far corner. The doors were open seven nights a week to a huge range of acts, some with a career already in hand, others just starting out and hoping this was the beginning of something solid. In a typical week you could catch locals—Chisel, Mentals, Flowers (later to become Icehouse), Oils, Wasted Daze, Lipstick Killers—and the latest interstate up and comers, like the Models and Paul Kelly. Some nights there'd be three bands for three dollars, the equivalent of around ten dollars today—sensational value.

As the crowds grew, drawn to the novel excitement of the burgeoning scene, so more venues sprang up in and around the city to
accommodate them, including the Chevron, the Rex Hotel at the
Cross, the Trade Union Club and the notorious Stagedoor Tavern.
The cream of Sydney's crop was regularly in full view, supported (and
on some nights usurped) by the breadth of talent on offer: Johnny
and the Hitmen, recyclers of the Detroit sound; the XL Capris, architecture students having fun à la Television; the Laughing Clowns,
Saints guitarist Ed Kuepper's startling left-field homage to jazz impro;
Jimmy and the Boys, a revue-style outing with singer Ignatius Jones
and keyboardist Joylene Hairmouth dressed to offend; and the Reels,
quirky keyboard-based pop/rock all the way from Dubbo.

It's easy to idealise the past. The mind seems to have a self-protect
mechanism in that we tend to remember the good times and bury the
bad, but by any measure this was a special period. The sheer number
of bands that were around was remarkable. There was nothing
uniform in the breakout. Everyone was chasing a different sound,
trying to land on something that stood out, channelling their inner
cool, spewing angst and attracting fans who travelled from all points
of the compass, any night of the week, to catch the shows.

Then the multiplier effect took hold, with the cluster of new bands
providing work for a growing cast of technicians: poster artists, road
crew, agents and, later, as careers started to take off, lawyers, design-
ers, film-clip makers—this was a creative cottage industry on the rise.

It has always been the case that Australia's huge distance from the
rest of the world meant local artists had to travel to bigger markets
overseas to test their wares and try to make a go of it. But in the late
1970s to the mid-1980s, there was critical mass right here at home.

Occasionally, when tomorrow was looking too much like yesterday, the Oils would feel the need to break out a little. So we'd put
on our own shows—mini events that were a bit different, like 'Sex
and Drugs and Rock and Roll' at Paddington Town Hall. This night
predictably drew a super-keen mob. They seemed content enough

until the power was mysteriously pulled, plunging the hall into darkness mid-set. Crouched backstage in the gloom as the audience screamed ever louder and threatened to trash the venerable old hall, we wondered if there was too much rock and too little sex and drugs, and now we were being judged guilty of misleading advertising. Finally the power was restored and the event ended on a high, with very loud music and a kaleidoscope of frustrated gig goers raging the night away.

The Stagedoor Tavern was in an unlikely location—a basement below a huge office block opposite Sydney's Central Station—but had a brief yet wild term. Inside it was dark with low ceilings, a huge bar dividing the room and great rock atmospherics with 1500 on the chant. The promoter, Pat Jay, was a big burly redhead of the 'colourful Sydney identity' school, and bands were paid on the spot in contraband, with mountains of cash piled up in his office like freshly washed nappies in a crowded nursery. No one knows where he ended up, but he was last heard of heading for the Philippines. He was a 'bad bugger', to quote Don Walker, so I suspect, if he's still alive, he works in entertainment.

When word came through that the Stagedoor had to close down, local fans saw this as a bureaucratic slap in the face to the swelling music scene that was spicing up the city. We were booked to play the final night and, as a way of livening up proceedings, had produced a set of posters promising, among other things, that Midnight Oil would 'destroy' the Stagedoor. This was pure Colonel Tom Parker—Elvis Presley's legendary manager—on Gary Morris's part, and the oldest trick in the book: teasing punters with over-the-top claims to draw the crowds and make a splash.

The state government panicked and the police took out an injunction to prevent the show from going ahead. By a strange twist of fate, my North Shore background came in handy when, at the eleventh hour, the judge, Michael Helsham, whose wife had been at uni with my mum, dismissed the case on the grounds that he knew my family (true), and he was confident that 'Mr Garrett would do no such thing' (sort of true).

The tabloid press and Sydney radio were all over the story and by evening thousands had gathered in the street and on the steps that led down to the Stagedoor entrance. The authorities didn't take the judge's decision too well and armed up. Paddy wagons materialised from nowhere, and the riot squad took up position in the forecourt while others lurked in side streets. To cap things off, a phalanx of mounted police were watching from the park opposite.

As promoters were wont to do, Jay took the opportunity to maximise his swan song and packed the room to overflowing and beyond. It felt hotter than anything we'd previously experienced, if that was possible, and the mood was wild and dangerous.

Music solid as granite would be needed to assuage the multitude of raging spirits, as well as some cautionary remarks about confronting those outside. After we finished the set, I duly destroyed the wooden stage—cheaply built, prone to the wobbles and the subject of numerous complaints because of its condition—with a steel microphone stand; it was time for some spectacle, I figured, and Pat Jay wasn't likely to take the makeshift infrastructure with him. We then staggered off what was left of the stage, drenched in sweat and completely drained, stumbling over bodies slumped in the narrow passage that led to a grotty dressing room. The air was on fire; it felt like all the available oxygen had been vacuumed out of the room, and I wasn't faring well.

A decision was taken to get out quick via the fire escape, but it had been locked and chained by Jay to stop anyone getting in, and now we couldn't get out. There was no hope of getting through the crowd, densely packed and wound up tight. Slumped on the floor, feeling faint and numb, I pressed my lips to a small crack at the bottom of the door and sucked desperately. I can still taste that cool nectar. Outside was a concrete stairwell littered with building rubble, empty beer cans, cigarette butts and condoms, and reeking of vomit—but nothing since has ever tasted as good as that sweet air.

9
LIFT-OFF

WE HAD ALWAYS been grateful for the growing crowd that kept us alive, but by 1982, six years in—or ten, if you counted Farm's first forays—the rollercoaster ride was becoming a rutted road. It was increasingly obvious a circuit-breaker was needed.

We'd spilled our guts in so many intimate settings that most fans had favourite songs and a definite idea of our style, and they assumed we would stick to it. These expectations were winging into cafes where we'd stop to have breakfast, barking back at us when we pulled up for fuel—and they would be sure to feed into the studio if we chose to record at home. We were three albums in and needed to push down the fence and graze in a bigger paddock. So it was back to England's green and pleasant land: first to a big house in St John's Wood in London for rehearsal time, and then to the Townhouse Studios in Shepherd's Bush for the serious business. Part of the Oils' working method was to react to what had come before, to learn from the experience, and then to throw the dice and head in another direction. I'd liked the natural spirit of *Postcard*, but the recording experience had been unsatisfying as the opportunity to really explore where songs could be taken had been limited. And for the players, itchy to expand their palette, there was a strong sense that we needed to go the other way and find the missing link—technology as a sixth instrument.

So we picked a studio we knew could cook a sound, and went left field, as far from Glyn Johns and our previous old-school producers as we could get. We chose a young engineer/producer, Nick Launay, who had a handful of non-mainstream singles but only one album—by English new wavers the Gang of Four—under his belt. Nick had a refreshing approach to knob twiddling (namely, 'Can't we make this sound more extreme?'), and with Jim working up all kinds of noises to insert throughout the album, he had a willing ally. And there was no rule he didn't want to break. At the same time, he was smart; he'd seen Midnight Oil in full flight. We were co-producers and he wasn't going to let any fits of indulgence get in the way.

The Townhouse turned out to be a choice location. With Van Morrison in one studio, Hall and Oates in another, engineers staying back late to mix a new Clash track and, just outside the studio door, a constant procession of international acts coming through London, you just had to get infected. Plus it had a special configuration that produced a big, whacking drum sound (later made famous by Phil Collins on songs like 'In the Air Tonight'), which would be amply used by Rob once the sessions were underway.

On the street, London was grumpy and jittery. Iron Lady Margaret Thatcher was prime minister and had begun to dismantle the welfare state brick by brick. The Labour Opposition, in full shop-steward mode, were sticking by their cardigans and socialist values, but picking and losing all the wrong fights. They weren't helped by a hysterical English press, chafing at the bit to demonise Labour at the behest of proprietors like Rupert Murdoch.

Meanwhile, the political situation in Northern Ireland was boiling over and the Irish Republican Army had stepped up their guerrilla activities in England's capital, setting off bombs and generally terrorising the populace.

We woke one morning to a large cracking sound, followed by a long period of silence and then sirens. A bomb had been detonated under a bandstand in Regent's Park, not far from where we were staying; at least one soldier had been killed and a number injured.

It seemed unreal, and was a vast remove from the placid suburbs of Sydney, but daily life didn't pause on the high street. Sure, the mood was a bit nervous, but the red double-decker buses kept careering around Trafalgar Square, people still crowded into the tiny corner pubs for a slurp of warm beer; the only noticeable change was the tooled-up soldiers patrolling the streets. On hard days like this, when people were entitled to feel put upon, you had to credit their stoicism.

At the Townhouse, we weren't to be distracted. To save money we'd moved into the first floor of the studio, sharing a couple of tatty rooms still undergoing renovation. The builders' jackhammers started early, so there was no straying from the task. We had to put the time in to make the music add up, pushing against the grain, using the technology in our quest for a sharper, wilder, more atmospheric sound.

It helped that there was a bundle of good songs—Jim and Rob were hitting their stride. The ideas were solid; we just had to doggedly pursue each one to the end point, where justice was done to the lyric and the music. If that meant throwing out some of the tried and true ways of working, then so be it.

We no longer thought of the studio as just a stage where you play your songs and record the moment. It could also serve as a laboratory for experimentation, a way of working that was initially hard for me to grasp. I'd always liked the immediacy of live performance, and trying to capture the sound of the band going off was never easy. In the case of *10–1*, as it became known, the massive Solid State Logic mixing desk with its myriad knobs and buttons, the rows of instruments and effects machines, both high- and low-tech, and a willingness to try anything meant there was a fresh kind of alchemy—and at last it was going to tape. The trick was not to drift too far away from the core of the band. In our case, this meant not losing the energy that made Midnight Oil a pungent rush of sound, and movement, with word play to match.

The preliminary writing and working out of tunes took place in a bog-standard live-rehearsal complex on the outskirts of London. It had the typical grimy vibe of rehearsal rooms worldwide, with a procession of heavy-metal acts tooling in and out to remind you what a circus rock can be. We knew the stakes were high—a fact that caused Rob, with his long-time ambition for the band, no end of grief. He ended up coming close to a nervous breakdown, and then played the best drums of his life on 'Only the Strong'.

Start the album with a bed of low strings and keyboards, followed by ricochet drum punctuations before you hear a word in Jim's 'Outside World' and let the rest follow. For 'US Forces' use a sea of acoustics and dobro guitars and an isolated snare drum to set the song up. In 'Power and the Passion', lay up a drum click track, sing the verses in rap mode—a precursor of things to come—and finish with a steaming brass section outro; pasty-faced London session players with their cheeks puffed bright red and the mixing desk melting down.

Lo and behold it worked—we were now a very long way from pub rock.

The day after recording finished, the band took off for home. I stayed behind with Nick to round some vocals off and mix the tracks—each one distinctive, zinging at last—and then jumped a jumbo for Sydney.

We'd been going all day and most of the night for months, but it didn't matter. A g'day from the Qantas crew perked me up and I must have listened to the finished album at least ten times on the way back.

It sounded good at all hours: looking down at the sharp peaks of the Himalayas shimmering white in the crystal air, and later at the scattered villages of Asia nestled in tiny green fields.

10–1 stayed in the Australian charts for over two years and got a decent run on college radio in the States. The critics fell in love too.

Success was like a drought breaking, and the passage of the album changed our lives in more ways than one.

At last we were out of debt, so we could properly settle into family life, buying new cars or guitars, and our own homes. Our local ANZ bank manager, who, unbeknown to his superiors, had backed us with an overdraft that was never called in, could finally sleep at night. We salute you, Mr Willis.

And we could at last buy some relief from the never-ending touring, which meant freedom to experiment, and time to get deeper into issues and give them a nudge. We didn't always have to worry about the dollars if we wanted to give something a go.

We'd finally proved to ourselves, and a loyal band of supporters, that we could pull it off in the studio. And now the foundation had been laid for a longer career, if we wanted it. While no one could ever mistake where the Oils came from, we'd gone international on parts of *10–1*, the lyrics picking up on such topics as the prospect of a nuclear war, and this would resonate with music fans across the globe.

...

Nuclear proliferation was an issue increasingly on our minds. At the time we were writing and recording the album, the world as we knew it had gone mad; literally, as it turned out, in the case of the military doctrine of mutually assured destruction (MAD).

The world's two super powers, the US and the USSR, were faced off against one another, with thousands of the most destructive weapons on earth—nuclear bombs—aimed directly at population centres in both countries. The MAD doctrine maintained that these weapons would never actually be used, because to do so would invite blanket retaliation, thus guaranteeing the annihilation of both nations, with some nasty spillover to the rest of the world. The logic was perverse; who could possibly know where things might end if even one shot was fired in anger or by mistake?

Since the deliberate use of the first atomic bomb over the Japanese city of Hiroshima in August 1945, quickly followed by a second days later at Nagasaki, the number and destructive force of these weapons had grown inexorably. Notwithstanding a raft of accidents and false alarms, in which nuclear weapons had come perilously close to being used, the main efforts around nukes had been so-called 'improvements' that made them more lethal and accurate. One of the consequences of this continual refinement was the emergence of the military doctrine of first strike. This new strategy advocated shooting first and asking questions later; in other words, the super powers were now prepared to launch a pre-emptive strike. It sounded like the Wild West, but it promised Armageddon.

The placement of nukes in Western Europe—in Germany in particular—was vehemently opposed by people living in those countries, and demonstrations protesting the build-up of weapons had escalated dramatically.

Then there was the issue of their huge cost—an obscenity by any measure. US president Ronald Reagan encouraged a new Strategic Defense Initiative, dubbed 'Star Wars', which involved the technical impossibility of shooting down nuclear weapons from space to counter any launch by the Soviets. It would certainly have sped up Soviet bankruptcy, with estimated costs on the American side of more than $500 billion in 1980 figures (no, that's not a misprint), to be spent on unproven technology—money that could have been put to better use addressing such issues as poverty, the environment and education.

In Australia, we contributed to the nuclearisation of the globe by hosting American communication bases that would relay information and be used by the US in the event of any nuclear conflict. We also welcomed US nuclear submarines into our ports, the practice being that the Americans would neither confirm nor deny they were carrying nuclear missiles. Really?

It wasn't as if we in Australia didn't have our own painful experience of nuclear damage. We'd already suffered the disadvantage of empire when Australian soldiers were used as guinea pigs in early experiments by the United Kingdom, in concert with the Australian government at the time. Primitive atomic devices were tested in the desert at Maralinga in South Australia and on the Montebello Islands off the coast of Western Australia in the 1950s. The authorities had failed to adequately warn Aboriginal people living in the area. Some had been rounded up and moved away from the fallout, but others were exposed; illness and suffering, especially for people in the Pitjantjatjara lands on the border of South Australia and the Northern Territory, and for some servicemen involved in the tests, were a dreadful consequence of this time.

The Oils attacked this history on *10–1* with songs like 'Maralinga'. When we toured the album, a public phone box was installed on the stage and in the middle of the show I'd put in calls to the White House or, closer to home, Parliament House to put the case. Usually there'd be a recorded message or I'd swap a few words with a receptionist, but one evening I was put straight through to Prime Minister Bob Hawke's office and had a tense conversation with a staffer about nuclear policy, broadcast live to an audience 16,000 strong.

We put on benefit concerts to raise money for the cause, including Stop the Drop at the Sidney Myer Music Bowl in Melbourne with INXS, Goanna and folk rockers Redgum. The mood backstage was unanimous; we were outraged that a mushroom cloud was hanging over our future. The younger generation was being held hostage by a system that seemed to have lost its way.

We would need to search out ways to fight the madness. Turning swords into ploughshares wasn't going to happen overnight. Throwing up our hands or throwing things at the television wouldn't do. I could sense the ferment, and I wasn't the only one. It was as if the cosmos was willing something to happen; people were scanning the skies for some real action and my inner voice was getting louder, saying, 'Why don't you get out and do something concrete, now?'

10
BIG MOVES

IN THE MIDST of this craziness I'd fallen for a beautiful German girl, Doris Ricono, whom I'd met out of the blue at a friend's place one night. After spending some time in Australia, she was moving back to Germany to live.

Doris had no real idea who I was and what I was up to, and neither did I have a bearing on her—but I was smitten (I still am), heart pounding like a kettledrum as I struggled, after being solo for so long, to adjust to the arrival of a person with whom I might share my life.

In fact, meeting my soul mate transformed my world. From our first date—fish and chips at Doyles in Watsons Bay—we knew we wanted to be together. But this proved to be harder than expected. First Doris had to spend time in Germany. Then, once she'd returned and moved into the boatshed at Lavender Bay where I'd set up camp (Doddo having moved on), I promptly headed out on tour again.

I owe a great deal to this incredible woman who became my wife. She took the huge step of making Australia her home, so we could be together. And on top of this, she committed herself to a wandering musician and activist, who would be away from home for long periods of time, forever jumping on a white charger and disappearing out the door. We've always had a deep bond, but her willingness to hang in through my many absences was based on an absolute conviction that we were meant to be together. This was the invisible thread that bound us tight and I've been amazed and thankful for it ever since.

...

Before heading back to the studio to record the next album, which would end up as *Red Sails in the Sunset*, I'd started reaching to the outside world in a different way. The extended silent grieving for my mum had run its course, and I was deeply in love. Despite pouring everything I had into the Oils for as long as I could remember, I felt recharged and re-energised, ready to go out and get stuck into issues that were important to me.

Along with a couple of friends, including Richard Morecroft, originally from Adelaide and now reading the news for the ABC in Sydney, and film director John Duigan, Doris and I had formed Nuclear Disarmament Projects to raise the alarm about the nuclear madness we feared was infecting the world.

We enlisted the help of Joanne Langenberg, a Canberra expat, and set up a small office in Kirribilli (right next to Michael Hutchence's mum's beauty salon, as it turned out). Here we put together a series of ads and designed media campaigns to mobilise the public, while catching up on news of INXS's progress overseas. It was small beer but a start, though the rush of ideas we were generating was limited in the end by our dwindling resources.

The enormity of the task we had undertaken was still swirling around in my mind as the Oils headed off to record in Tokyo in the first half of 1984. On *10-1* I'd been asking who was running the world, but more pressing now was the question of what I could actually do about it. My mind wasn't fixed on songs and recording; in fact, I had little to bring to the table and ended up throwing lyrics at some of the tracks once they were done.

Nick Launay would be producing again, and we had picked the Victor Studio in the Tokyo suburb of Aoyama, reasoning that the Japanese were bound to have first-class recording equipment. We were aiming for another left turn that would insert unpredictability into the creative process. It was a pricey exercise for those times but typical Midnight Oil. We had a few dollars to play with now, and the opportunity to go left field, so why not?

After a while we had to let our expensive interpreter go, and so the negotiations with the record company on some finer points around the album took nearly as long as making it. But we became variously proficient in Japanese as a result of living there for months, and the exposure to a totally different culture, where we were complete strangers, was refreshing. I took to fasting at the weekends to clear my head and worked my way through Gideon's Bible and the sayings of Buddha, the only English-language books in the typically tiny Tokyo hotel room that was my home for the duration. In a touch of synchronicity, Rob introduced the song 'Kosciusko' with a phrase from Isaiah 61: 1–4, 'bind up the broken-hearted'.

The band played studio gurus with Nick, as bewildered local sound engineers tried to fathom sessions where constant change and daily experiments were the norm. What possible reason was there to record the drums in the toilet, or to have two studios on different floors going at the same time, or to completely change all the settings on the mixing desk after spending a day getting it right? The answer: because we can, and let's see where the song might end up.

I worked hard on songs like 'Who Can Stand in the Way' and 'Sleep', but my mind was on the big screen. After taking some small steps I was ready to do more, in whatever shape or form that turned out to be.

...

Between albums I'd got steamed up about the kinds of policies I thought the government should adopt to help the local music industry, and I'd travelled to Canberra armed with a paper setting out the arguments: a stronger quota for Australian music on radio, loans for overseas touring support and so on.

I presented the proposals to the arts minister, Barry Cohen. He wasn't in cabinet and didn't seem to know much about the Australian rock scene, so I wasn't confident of a positive response—nor did I receive one. The only sound I heard was the report dropping into the bottom drawer of his filing cabinet and the door slamming shut. (Twenty-three years later, when I was arts minister, I went looking for the submission, knowing that bureaucrats don't throw much away. There was no trace of it.)

Meanwhile, the mood had been building to mount a more determined opposition to Australia's role in an increasingly nuclear environment. People who'd previously opposed the war in Vietnam, peace activists, some church groups and a smattering of artists (including the novelist Patrick White, who had publicly opposed Australia's role in preparations for nuclear war) were coalescing into a broad antinuclear movement.

I'd already had some interaction with the local peace organisations and found them splintered around ideology and mired in personality conflict. Up to that time, they had been campaigning hard to hold the Labor Party to its controversial no-uranium-mining policy. I had a difference of opinion with some groups, a number of whom were offshoots of the Communist Party of Australia, over the question of what the right response to nuclear overkill should be. I wasn't a pacifist and so didn't unreservedly support its policy equivalent, unilateral disarmament. I could not conceive of modern nations with opposing ideologies trying to maximise their sphere of influence while one decided unilaterally to lay down its weapons. Nor that the only country laying down arms would have to be America. Martin Luther King Jr was right to say that true pacifism is not 'unrealistic submission to evil power'. I knew that, if faced with the prospect of submitting to an aggressor or defending my family or my country, I'd stand my ground. Sometimes turning the other cheek was the right thing to do, if it was an act of defiant, deliberate non-violence, but that didn't mean lying down and letting someone walk over you.

Mum and Dad in Martin Place, Sydney, holding hands in the early days.

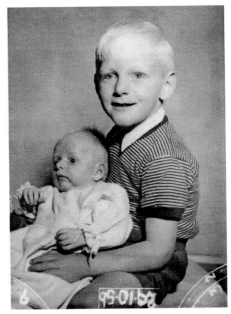

With my brother Andrew, 1956.

Posing on the bonnet of our Holden, around 1957. Top: Mum and Dad with Andrew and me.

With Emily Jane Collin, our gran, in about 1960.

Barker College athletics team, 1965. I'm the one with the blond hair in the back row, third from the right. BARKER COLLEGE

Young, and waiting for a wave.

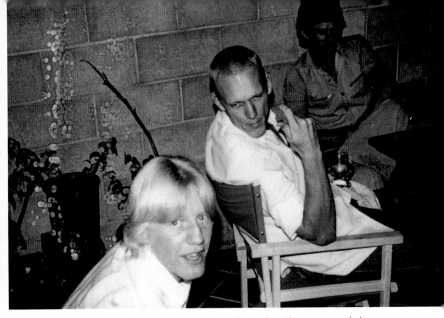

Andrew and I at Lyndall's twenty-first birthday party. Soon after, they were married.

An early Devil's Breakfast gig at Burgmann College, ANU, with bass player
Damian Street, 1974.

Graduating with an arts degree, ANU, 1975.

Fresh-faced band in front of our rehearsal studio, 77 Albert Avenue, Chatswood, 1976.
PHILIP MORRIS

Getting physical, Mawson
Hotel, Newcastle area, 1978.
GEOFFREY MOORE

Early Oils at the Flicks Theatre,
Manly, 1979. JAN PAUL

Going through a few songs, 1979.

The Sun, 31 October 1979.

No 39: PETER GARRETT.

Born: Tennants Creek, sometime in 1954.

Plays: Lead singer in Midnight Oil.

Likes: A good lather up.

Dislikes: Journalists.

Favourite recording artist: Normie Rowe.

Eats: Chicko Rolls.

Drinks: Glucodin and Staminade.

Favourite actor: Telly Savalas.

Good Habits: Walking Old ladies across busy streets.

Single: Cold Cold Change — Used and Abused, from the Head Injuries album on Powderworks Records.

It gets louder
towards the end
of the show.
MIDNIGHT OIL ARCHIVE

Close and hot, Stagedoor Tavern, Sydney, 1979. DAVID KNOWLES

Trying to get a song going, with Jim Moginie in the background, 1980.

Grabbing some takeaway, location unknown, about 1980. PHILIP MORRIS

Taking off at the end of the night, early 1980s. MIDNIGHT OIL ARCHIVE

Above: Shooting our first film clip, 'Run by Night', 1978. PHILIP MORRIS

Below: Sweetwater Festival, 1983. G.R. CARROLL

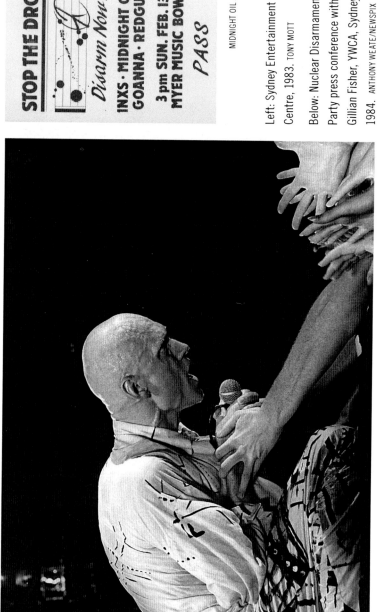

STOP THE DROP

Disarm Now!

INXS · MIDNIGHT OIL
GOANNA · REDGUM

3 pm SUN. FEB. 13
MYER MUSIC BOWL

PASS

Left: Sydney Entertainment
Centre, 1983. TONY MOTT

Below: Nuclear Disarmament
Party press conference with
Gillian Fisher, YWCA, Sydney,
1984. ANTHONY WEATE/NEWSPIX

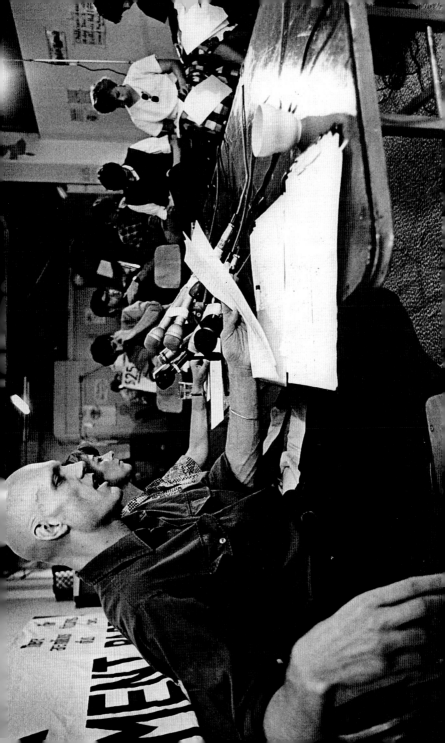

With Wayne 'Rabbit' Bartholomew, Surfers Against Nuclear Destruction (SAND) competition, Alexandra Headland, Queensland, 1985.

'Oils on the Water', Goat Island, Sydney Harbour, Australia Day, 1985. ADRIENNE OVERALL

With thousands of weapons armed and dangerous, we urgently needed measures that reduced the threat of nuclear war. The do-nothing proposition was morally objectionable, and the argument that you had to destroy the world in order to save a part of it (in God knows what shape) was nonsense.

When we finished recording *Red Sails* in June, Doris and I took the bullet train down to Hiroshima for the annual commemoration ceremony marking the use of the first nuclear weapon when 'Little Boy' was dropped on the city on 6 August 1945. What we witnessed there provided the final push for me to do something concrete.

At Hiroshima, everything other than the steel skeletons of some buildings at ground zero had been reduced to ash. Nearly all the doctors and nurses in the city had been killed by the blast, leaving the hideously injured survivors to fend for themselves. When multiplied hundreds of times, in even a limited nuclear exchange, this first horror-filled experience showed there was simply no way the arms race and the strategies that attempted to justify it could be tolerated any longer.

With a federal election in the wind, the single-issue Nuclear Disarmament Party (NDP) had been formed by a Canberra doctor, Michael Denborough, and anti-war groups around the country were standing candidates for the Senate as a way of giving the issue greater prominence. I heard about a meeting of the Sydney groups, and spent some time talking with Victorian candidate Jean Melzer, who'd already been chosen to run, about the possibility of standing as a candidate myself. She was an experienced Labor Party activist and I valued her counsel. She was positive about the idea, as were a number of local contacts, including Sean Flood, a well-known public defender. I touched base with the Oils, who said I should go for it and, finally, talked it through with Doris and got the same response. On the basis that I could head the ticket and so maximise the vote, I decided to throw my hat in the ring.

There was one complicating factor that was to bedevil the campaign and which still exerts undue influence on left politics in

Australia, and that was the presence of members of the Socialist
Workers Party (SWP), or 'Trots' as they were then known. These
were mainly young activists attracted to a virulent form of anti-
capitalism, who'd been specifically trained by older members with a
hard left background, some with ties to communist countries. Many
in number and skilled in organising, they knew how to mount a
public campaign, how to get a street demonstration going, how to
disrupt a meeting and, crucially, they could infiltrate other organisations if it suited them.

It sounds far-fetched, but at that time they were a destabilising fact
of political life. They saw the rise of the antinuclear movement as an
ideal opportunity to further their specific aims, which I, and many
others, did not share. We simply wanted to remove 50,000 weapons
of mass destruction from the face of the earth, however impossible a
task that might appear to be.

I enlisted Doddo's help as campaign manager. I needed someone
I could trust if we were going to take this unexpected step. Michael
Denborough was also intending to stand, but it was hard to see how
that could work as he was based in Canberra and unknown. A call
was made over radio station Double J inviting potential members to
join the party.

The meeting to select a candidate was fractious as a consequence.
Denborough had flown supporters up from Canberra and Patrick
White was miffed at the sudden appearance of new members, but
we prevailed by a narrow majority, and set about establishing an
office underneath the YWCA just off Whitlam Square—the kind of
address I could live with—calling on volunteers and friends from the
music and arts community to lend a hand.

The stopper was out of the bottle and people flocked to the cause.
A small committee was established to coordinate the start-up effort,
including the maverick Liberal MP Ted St John QC and the number-
two candidate, Gillian Fisher. John Ward, a doctor who took a broad
view of the Hippocratic oath, served as chair. The distinguished

historian Russel Ward, the deputy chancellor of the University of New England, joined the ticket and lent an air of authority to the growing swirl of activity that surrounded this new political party.

Peter Carey, just branching out as an author, offered to help. He and his advertising agency partner Bani McSpedden came up with the slogan 'The future is ours', and, not surprisingly, much of the subsequent written material read pretty well. Other early helpers included the opera singer Janet Kenny, writer and psychologist Alex Carey, and Judy Richter, who'd worked on the Franklin Dam campaign in Tasmania with Bob Brown. Split Enz frontman Tim Finn phoned in his support, and film director John Duigan came and went depending on his work schedule. Strangers would just turn up at the campaign office and pitch in, like the softly spoken nurse Diana Lindsay, who walked in one day and without a word started efficiently sorting leaflets and answering phones. She stayed to the end and then came across to work for me and the Oils in our office in Glebe.

My diary entry—one of the few I have for that time—for 7 October 1984 reads: 'No more dope, this is really it.' That really was it, and that's the way it stayed. We'd been playing on the North Coast, and the night before the announcement of my candidacy had shredded the tiny stage at Forster RSL. I drove to Sydney late, still steaming after the show, and early next morning headed in to start work. All of a sudden I was a Senate candidate.

Initially, the NDP was seen as purely a novelty: a rock singer from a single-issue party that had sprung up overnight trying to get into the Senate in an election where bread-and-butter issues were expected to dominate. We almost didn't get off the starting blocks when there was an amateurish attempt to derail the dawn launch of the campaign at Mrs Macquarie's Chair, overlooking Sydney Harbour. Just as we arrived, a woman suddenly lurched out of a taxi swigging from a bottle, lipstick smeared all over her face. Falling out of her blouse and visibly staggering, she made a beeline for me, calling out, 'Pete! Pete!' Luckily Doris sniffed the set-up. There were photographers lurking behind trees ready for the compromising moment but I managed to steer clear as the dishevelled saboteur was hustled away. To this day I've no idea who was behind that piece of nastiness, but I suspect right-wing Labor Party heavies might have had something to do with it. That and a break-in at the NDP offices following the election were the only dirty tricks we experienced.

The NDP was constantly dismissed as a joke by the major parties and written off by most of the media before we'd even produced any policies. This worked to our advantage. By night the Oils were touring big shows in the capital cities, with a specially designed backdrop illustrating the futility of war, featuring songs like 'Read About It' and 'Minutes to Midnight'. By day I campaigned with as much energy as I could muster, trying to get in front of as many voters as possible, reaching out to disillusioned parts of the electorate: the young, those from the left, disenchanted Labor supporters and a growing body of Australians wanting independence of mind in our foreign policy and apprehensive about the massive build-up of nukes.

The Democrats, a small party established by former Liberal minister Don Chipp that sat to the left of the Coalition, went feral as their vote drifted. They received extensive coverage from *The Australian* during the campaign. A typical headline on 20 November 1984 read: CHIPP LAUNCHES BARRAGE AT NDP. There were plenty more in that vein.

When I joined the Labor Party in 2004, some questioned how I could take that step, having campaigned against Labor twenty years earlier. It was Finance Minister Lindsay Tanner who made the observation that back then he'd never once heard me attack the Labor Party as a whole. That was true, but I certainly was highly critical of some of their policies at the time, especially in the area of nuclear issues.

The fact is we'd caught the political establishment napping. One of the assumptions that underpinned our reliance on America's protection in the event of a conflict was that we would acquiesce to the use of nuclear weapons. It was a fatal concession that had to be challenged and, if possible, changed. It's never easy to judge how well a campaign is going when you're in the thick of it, but at one point support for the NDP reached 17 per cent. In Western Australia, stalwart anti-nuke activist Jo Vallentine was running a cheeky, media-savvy campaign, and she eventually won a spot in the Senate.

We knew we were making an impact when, at the last minute, Foreign Minister Bill Hayden finally agreed to a live television debate with me. The Hawke government was now under significant political pressure, with votes leaking to the left. Under the direction of right-faction chief senator Graham Richardson, Labor exchanged preferences with the Liberal Party, and the remaining parties adopted the same tactic, which ensured I received very few flow-through preference votes. My primary vote ended up at 9.7 per cent, short of a full quota but historically high in relation to any single-issue candidate. The party bosses' action meant I just missed out on taking a seat and at least six years of concerted political activity.

That I would have leapt into the job boots and all had I got over the line was never in question, and that was my intention at the time. But once the count was finally concluded there was a tinge of relief from all quarters that things could return to normal, or at least to our definition of normal. Throughout, the Oils had backed me without qualification, and I was grateful for their solidarity. It would soon be time to grab the microphone and guitars and get out to play again. My close encounter with a dose of party politics would surely add to the store of experiences we were accumulating; we'd broken new ground for a rock group—and the band was still intact.

As it turned out the NDP was not so solid, however. The election was held on 1 December but, because of the vagaries of the Senate voting system, the result wouldn't be known until weeks later. At one point Channel 10 mistakenly announced that I'd won the seat, not the last time that the media would get something so basic completely wrong. I was conscious that, whatever the result, following through on the momentum we'd built up would require a lot of effort on everyone's part, so I scheduled a meeting for early January, before the final count was in, to make preparations for the next phase of work. However, on the appointed day very few members showed up. Sure it was the holiday season, and it did happen to be a stunning summer's day, but I was deflated by the low turnout, other than a few close allies and the usual SWP supporters. If we couldn't muster decent numbers so soon after a tumultuous campaign that had succeeded in shaking up the political status quo, and with the possibility that I might still win the seat, then it seemed to me we stood little chance of keeping this ship afloat.

Even though the party could not hold together over the long term, a moral victory belongs to the NDP and its many initial supporters, as that period saw some discernible changes made in Australian politics and policies.

The 1984 election was the first to see a haemorrhaging of two-party support, a trend that has continued to the present day, with the emergence of the Greens party, occasional independents and other minor parties that have altered the composition of the Senate. The major parties could no longer take their traditional base for granted.

It should be noted that during the campaign Bill Hayden tried to distance Australia from American efforts to develop first-strike capability. Displaying commendable independence of mind, he held out the possibility of a reassessment of the relationship between our two countries if the Americans didn't up the ante on arms-control negotiations. Within a week of the election, *The Sydney Morning Herald* was reporting that the US had protested about Australia's policies because of our support in international forums for a nuclear test ban.

Barely two months later, Prime Minister Hawke was forced into a humiliating backdown following the government's decision to assist the US in testing long-range MX missiles in the South Pacific. The public uproar that followed, due in part to the coverage nuclear issues had received courtesy of the NDP campaign, saw the initiative founder only four days after it was announced.

A stronger degree of partnership was initiated in relation to the operation of US communications bases on our soil, with America nominally sharing 'all' information and Australian security agencies more fully informed about US operations. From that point on, according to defence ministers up to the present day, Pine Gap—one of the largest satellite ground stations in the world—'operates with the full knowledge and concurrence of the Australian government'.

But the activities of the bases, especially Pine Gap, have expanded over time, and the chief of the facility is an American officer, with the deputy chief an Australian. While Pine Gap plays an important role in arms-control monitoring, it also scoops up information that is used for intelligence and military purposes by the US, an issue that accompanied my entry into parliament.

I had qualified my earlier view by saying that the bases could play a constructive role in anti-terrorism efforts, and this was Labor's position at the time, but my wording was imprecise and gave the impression that I'd completely reversed my position. I should have simply reiterated my reservations on the question of Australian control at the facilities and their potential role in any nuclear exchange, while noting that since the 1980s the bases could play an important role in anti-terrorism and arms-control verification. In fact, my thinking on the bases had changed since the NDP campaign. The NDP was right to question the extent to which Australian sovereignty was compromised by US bases, and to oppose their existence as key parts of a nuclear war-fighting strategy; the arrangements governing their operation are too opaque, and require greater clarification and a higher level of oversight by parliament. But because of its unique location the base can, and in the future should, play a greater role in current disarmament efforts. We are now reaching the stage where the verification capacity of Pine Gap and its many satellite antennas should be utilised and shared more widely. If the world is finally going to get serious about ridding itself of these weapons, then Pine Gap could service a multinational verification project aimed at speeding nuclear disarmament as the push continues towards a nuclear weapons treaty.

It's worth adding that the supposed advantages that flow from the arrangement to host the bases, other than the security dimension, are mainly illusory. Bob Hawke admitted as much in his 1994 book, *The Hawke Memoirs*. Trade was the single most important issue that Australian prime ministers raised in Washington, but as he 'readily concedes', 'we were never really able to get a satisfactory outcome from the Americans'.

Following the elevation of Paul Keating to prime minister, the government initiated the Canberra Commission to review and make recommendations on advancing nuclear disarmament globally. That work remains important today and the foreign minister of the time, Gareth Evans, has subsequently continued these efforts through his co-chairing of the advisory board of the Centre for Nuclear Non-Proliferation and Disarmament at the Australian National University in Canberra.

Notwithstanding the decommissioning of thousands of warheads by both sides in recent years, the progress towards disarmament has stayed frustratingly slow, despite Barack Obama, in his Prague Speech, committing the US to 'seek the peace and security of a world without nuclear weapons'. Most recently Russia, under Vladimir Putin, canvassed increasing its weapons numbers. To break this logjam a proposal has emerged, with substantial backing from eminent former political and military leaders (including former prime ministers Fraser and Hawke) for an entirely new nuclear weapons convention that would see the possession of nuclear weapons made illegal under international law. These stockpiles are a waste of precious resources, a threat to life on earth, and embody an old way of thinking that is both immoral and devoid of reason. This is a crucially important area where disarmament efforts should be directed in the years ahead.

11

KEEP ON THE SUNNY SIDE

YOU DIDN'T NEED to be a clairvoyant to see what the future would be like for Midnight Oil once *Red Sails* was released in October 1984 and the NDP campaign finished—planes and trains (if we were lucky and in Europe) and buses, touring and more touring.

At the same time we were in a position to settle down a little. Some of us had now married long-time girlfriends. After years of me living out of a suitcase, Doris and I were finally ready to make a home and be a family.

The band could also afford to support more people who we thought were doing the right thing. We did benefit concerts, and funnelled profits into a donation register to provide grants to individuals and organisations working on causes that were important to us: peace, youth homelessness and the environment. In one case we funded the Brotherhood Christian Motorcycle Club to acquire demountable accommodation for street kids around Parramatta, a program that is still going to this day.

This was the time when the fate of native forests, those great swathes of eucalypts which are the lungs of the eastern seaboard, was front of mind for many. The issue blew up in Tasmania, where a campaign to stop a proposed dam on the Franklin River drew nationwide attention. I headed down to a rally in 1983 and afterwards we sent some dollars through. We also put on Reef to Rainforest shows at the Entertainment Centre in Sydney in the same year, and then subsidised the preparation of scientific reports to enable a case to be made for the protection of the Daintree Rainforest in Far North Queensland. Rare in beauty, the rainforest stretches from the ranges inland right down to the coast and inshore reefs, and was home to a dazzling variety of plant life that had evolved over aeons. The Queensland state government, led by Premier Joh Bjelke-Petersen, was intent on opening up the area to development and housing subdivisions, which would have spelled the end of the intact rainforest. Fortunately, he didn't get his way. In 1987 the Daintree became a national park, and not long after it entered the World Heritage list—created to recognise globally important natural and cultural areas—and of course is now, along with the magisterial Great Barrier Reef, one of Australia's most important tourist destinations. There was no shortage of worthwhile campaigns like this to support, but it took time to assess every proposal to make sure the money would make a difference, and time was always in short supply.

To keep our fans up to date with our musical and political activities, we produced mini newspapers called *Oil Rags* to coincide with albums and tours, with the help of our old friend Andrew McMillan, a rock journo who'd written extensively about the rise of independent bands on the street in the early days. They were avowedly anti-corporate and anti-fashion, the polar opposite of most fan mags, providing another media platform on which to profile the issues the band was getting behind.

...

We were now aiming to influence two continents at the same time. If you wanted to build an audience, you had to get in their face, so after a long stretch of doing just that at home, the Northern Hemisphere started to feature more prominently in the itinerary.

Our sights were set on North America. By the early 80s we were blasting in and out of club and college gigs at night and local radio stations by day, grabbing food and sleep on the run. With Gary Morris headquartered in Kangaroo Street, Manly—a handy talking point address for an Australian group trying to break into the US—and us on a bus somewhere between Washington and Florida, attempting to forge a path in the States while trying to keep our hands on every aspect of the career—it was chaotic, intense and constantly verging on breakdown.

We'd kissed big dollars behind in the past while fighting for the right to song choices and album titles, marketing ideas, tours, ticket prices, the colour of T-shirts—anything and everything imaginable that reflected Midnight Oil—and we wanted to maintain this control as much as possible. This meant constantly testing the patience of Gary and our supportive US agent, Mitch Rose, who were charged with rewriting the rulebook.

As we moved higher up the food chain, one vexing issue was the mass of beer and tobacco signage that adorned many of the bigger venues. Unlike in Australia, these sponsorships operated directly between the companies and the venues, and were set in stone. Wherever possible we had the crew slip in under the radar and surreptitiously cover up the offending logos with drapes and whatever else they could lay their hands on just before we took the stage, and no one even noticed.

The political nature of the band was always going to challenge America, but not because they didn't have a tradition of political artists. As with most aspects of western popular music, they did it first and best: just think of Woody Guthrie or Pete Seeger and, later on, Bob Dylan and Joan Baez and Gil Scott-Heron, Bruce Springsteen and Michael Franti, Ani DiFranco, Rage Against the Machine—and legions of similar artists in the wings.

In the Oils' case, our vantage point wasn't shared by the audience, or by the music industry at large. Sure, we sang in English and played with guitar, bass and drums, but as far as many Americans were concerned, we were from another planet (often referred to as Austria). A fair portion of our narrative attack was directed at them, or at least their companies and politicians, especially the Republican president, Ronald Reagan.

Added to this, our willingness to play the game was zero. We'd always done things a certain way and it was hard to find an entry point to the American music-industry juggernaut, whose support (in some form) was essential if we were to get by, let alone succeed. While we'd moved on from having our own label, Powderworks, to inking a contract with CBS Records, in order to free up more time for writing and playing and to increase our reach, it was on the basis—unusual at the time—that we would continue to exercise creative control over every aspect of our recording career. The local company knew what they were signing up for and included people who were either fans, or at least empathised with what we trying to pull off, so we had a good chance of finding a happy marriage between commerce and art. In the Northern Hemisphere, however, interest in our way of doing things ranged from negligible to downright hostile.

We were talking big, but running the race sideways. So in the beginning we aimed low, starting at the small inner-city clubs where the band might be judged on its merits, and then stepping up to the college circuit, where a younger crew would listen without prejudice and our songs could get a run on campus radio. We sensed an audience hungry for more, if we could just manage to keep coming back. But a key part of Midnight Oil's make-up was our Australianness. This was what made us tick and it needed regular refills, otherwise fatigue and longing for home would set in pretty quickly.

Still, putting in the hard yards—and the long miles—we quickly discovered that America was not at all homogenous, definitely not one nation under God. The south was so starkly different from the north (they had, after all, fought one another not that long ago) and California, with its sun-drenched, Hollywood-flavoured atmosphere was a universe away from the stolid Midwest, which, in turn, was light years removed from cosmopolitan, edgy Manhattan. From the redwood forest to the Gulf Stream waters, the US was a study in contrasts. In the space of twenty minutes you could go from glittering high-rises to exclusive gated estates in the suburbs to card-board-box shantytowns under bridges and around bus stations and railway yards. At its best, America was always capable of renewal. Its political system had been designed by a coterie of wise owls who had a pretty good grasp on human nature and the lure of power, but there lurked a deeply conservative strain that could quickly veer into selfish isolationism.

Yet one thing was a constant wherever we fetched up: from top to bottom, the country was drenched with music. We were in the home of the blues and just about everything that followed. For any musician, getting up on stage to play your songs was the endpoint: you . . . had . . . finally . . . arrived. Americans loved music, and if nothing else, you generally received a fair hearing.

Even in the early stages of touring there, when we played only five of the potential twenty-five cities that were on the must-do circuit, we could see a very faint light at the end of a very long tunnel that signalled the point of critical mass.

No matter how dingy the club or filthy the dressing rooms, no matter how far off the map the touring schedule was—once we were booked to perform at the foot of a chairlift in the snowfields outside Salt Lake City at five in the afternoon—one thing was for certain: someone had come this way before. The only question was who or what would break first: the audience, the industry or the band.

For some bands from home who'd had a go earlier, the pitfalls were clear. In Dragon's case, lead singer Marc Hunter's habit of testing the limits of audience tolerance came undone when he called a crowd in Texas 'faggots'. It wasn't a good choice of word in that location and the band was lucky to get out of town alive. Skyhooks fell foul of the notorious ego-driven side of the industry; manager Michael Gudinski's legendary big mouth wasn't quite as effective in Tinseltown, where big talkers were a dime a dozen. Later the Divinyls, with a swag of great radio-friendly songs and a sassy Chrissy Amphlett up front, came undone as Australian and US managers squabbled over money and some of the band fell into a pit of drugs and couldn't crawl out in time.

We had our share of scrapes, mainly around the perception of the band as anti-American. 'US forces give the nod' was pretty clear in meaning, and led to the odd record burning in the south. We could live with that; it gave us a bit of cred and meant a couple of states could be deleted from the touring schedule. Audiences could get touchy when it came to insulting the president, too. I copped the odd shellacking, and on one occasion objects were aimed at the stage when my mouth got away from me, including at one open-air show in Boston, where missiles rained down on us from all over the park—which was surprising, given its reputation as a liberal, progressive town. In the firestorm of stage rhetoric it was all too easy for the audience to misinterpret us. The band's distaste for what the US government was doing didn't mean we disliked America or Americans; far from it. But our message of 'We don't like your commander-in-chief but can we still be friends?' was often lost in the din.

This became crystal clear when, later, I was invited to present at the American Music Awards in Los Angeles, a big deal at the time, where the cream of the music industry gather to schmooze and lay bait. The Oils had always taken the line that TV awards ceremonies have little to do with the intrinsic value of what artists produce—they are more like marketing exercises than celebrations of music—so we'd steered clear of them in the past. In this case, however, the opportunity to get in front of a big crowd, and on national television as well, with a distinctly Midnight Oil message was too tempting to refuse.

After tossing a few ideas around with Gary Morris, I decided to dress like Abraham Lincoln and deliver a stern message to the crème de la crème of the rock and pop world. Instead of reading the cue cards word for word, I'd riff a little on how it was false security for a strong democracy to rely on threatening others, and that the most important thing was to rid the world of nuclear weapons. I'd finish with an emphatic: 'And that means you, America!'

I came on to a smattering of applause only to see a shocked Molly Meldrum, the legendary Australian music personality, sitting ten rows back staring at me, eyes widening as the hubbub subsided; he alone at that point might have guessed something unpredictable was about to unfold. Ignoring the trepidation on his face, I launched into my spiel. By the time I'd finished, the crowd was as cold as frozen fish fingers. Backstage, amid the usual pretend mateyness of air kisses and hugs, I was treated like a leper. The rebellious nature of rock be damned; I'd overstepped the mark—Lincoln of all people!

But for the most part, peace reigned. If you were going to repeatedly insult a head of state, it was safer to do it in the US than in most other countries. Thankfully, they took freedom of speech seriously. And so we ploughed on.

Because music was everywhere, you could fasten on to songs and block out the ugly. It started when you flew in to LA, with a dozen lines floating in your head about that city alone. Jim Morrison howling 'LA Woman', the Red Hot Chilli Peppers' latest—the buzz persisting across the length and breadth of the Union.

Popular music served as escape, as it does all over the world, but it was also a vehicle for the country's conscience.

Music was one of the signposts for the Vietnam years and the rise of the counter-culture, which had seen America experience a shake up which took the country decades to recover from (if indeed it ever has), and all the eras that followed.

And it wasn't just the protest songs or the conveyor belt of the top forty. Black soldiers play Hendrix loud as the bombs rain down on them in *Apocalypse Now*. Brass bands oom-pah-pah up the main street on the 4th of July. Gospel singing soars out of white timber churches in the south on Sunday mornings.

The air hums as big city radio stations with powerful transmitters blast classic rock from Anchorage to New Mexico. If you tire of

wailing guitars and formula vocals you can dial up any era of pop/
rock/country/blues/rap/jazz/classical/world.

I always found it hard to sleep on the tour bus: I was too tall
for the bunk and too fidgety with someone else at the wheel, so the
country stations became a favourite. Swinging down the interstate at
two in the morning, with fields of corn and canola stretching away
either side and the Soggy Bottom Boys harmonising on 'In the Jail-
house Now' with a touch of static as backing. Towns like Chicago,
steeped in the blues, likewise New Orleans for jazz, Nashville for
country, Memphis, San Francisco, Austin, all with music blasting
into the truck stops and bars, anywhere with a set of speakers and a
crowd of more than one.

We played, played and played, as hard as we could. And Americans talked, talked and talked, so word of mouth, as it always will,
travelled up from the street to the attention of the opinion makers.
But still, Australia called. Just as we were being drawn ever closer to
the belly of the beast, we turned inwards to face the mirror, to have
another look at our own country.

12

A CONTINENT IMMENSE
IN THE WORLD

I FINALLY GOT away from Cessnock Workers Club at around 1 a.m. one Sunday, late in January 1985. It had been a business-as-usual night, brutally hot and heavy. A small stage, sound overload, and a room full of miners' and farmers' kids who didn't often see a band of the Oils' size and wouldn't go home—fair enough.

When the show finally ended the Boogie Queen undertook one of her least favourite tasks: picking up the sweat-drenched stage clothes (actually dungarees and workman's shirts) and, holding her nose, squashing them into a giant plastic bag. Meanwhile, aching joints were straightened out, the recovery soothed with a few beers while we caught our breath—sometimes literally. Towards the end of the set I'd had to take a quick visit to the oxygen bottle. After early brushes with mortality in the furnaces of the Stagedoor Tavern and the Royal Antler Hotel, it was a permanent fixture on tour, with its own road case stacked next to the guitar racks in the dressing room. A few gulps of the pure stuff and I was out to rejoin the writhing mass.

Once basic movement had been restored and the heart rate had come back to normal, we were into the hire car, two beams of light and a big city waiting over the hill. Other than a few solitary wallaby corpses, the winding back roads to the freeway were deserted, and when we crossed the Hawkesbury River, the mangroves and oyster leases edging the water were palely visible in the moonlight.

We were alive, full of adrenalin, still pumping after the gig—and I was readying myself for a gig of a different kind. I had to get back to the city for an inaugural get-together of the members of the newly appointed Constitutional Commission, established by the Hawke government to consider how the constitution could be improved. We would be meeting at Admiralty House, the Sydney base of the governor-general.

I'd accepted an invitation from Attorney-General Lionel Bowen to serve on the Committee for Individual and Democratic Rights. Commentators had had a field day with the appointment, clearly bemused by the idea that a rock singer could add any value to the exercise. They were still stuck on a clichéd view of rock bands partying hard and destroying their brain cells. I'd said yes—after all why shouldn't an artist participate in something like this? And it wouldn't hurt to leave my comfort zone for a while to wade through the thick molasses of constitutional reform—a topic that caused many a law student's eyes to glaze over. I found out later that Bowen, who happened to be the Member for Kingsford Smith at that time, had grown tired of his teenage sons playing Oils albums late into the night and asked about the band, to be told we were serious types concerned with politics, not girls.

I was well aware that the mere mention of the word 'constitution' put many people to sleep, but it explained a lot about how our political system had evolved: it was the rulebook for governments that laid out what they could and couldn't do, and I was up for anything that might lead to improvement and updating. Sure, it's a tall order to change the constitution by referendum, requiring the consent of a majority of people in a majority of states, but this is as it should be. You don't change the foundation document of a nation on a whim. Although only eight out of forty-four proposed changes have been approved throughout our history, I think Australians have mostly got it right, even when they said no to change—such as refusing the Menzies Liberal government's plan to outlaw the Communist Party, or the Chifley Labor government's plan to nationalise the banks.

In so many aspects, we were still prisoners of the past. Australia had changed in ways no one could have imagined since the British first stepped ashore, but our thinking and our political arrangements were frozen in time. And we were captive to the constitution. It may have been the modern nation's founding document, outlining the powers and areas of responsibility for federal and state governments, but it had a number of gaps. Some of these were intentional, like leaving Aboriginal people out altogether, a glaring deficiency that was only remedied as late as 1967, although Aboriginal people were still not referenced in the introduction to the constitution, the preamble. Nor did the constitution provide protection for most political freedoms, such as freedom of expression or the right to peaceful assembly (a right that we enjoy de facto, courtesy of the way our democracy works). And nowhere in its 128 sections did it mention the environment.

The result of this last omission was that decisions about how the land was used were left to each of the states, and as the condition of the environment deteriorated this could lead to a sea of troubles. Australians who lived in the Northern Territory or New South Wales were virtually powerless to stop or influence an environmental decision taken by Queensland, even if it directly affected them. One look at the torturously complicated power-sharing arrangements needed to manage our largest river system, the Murray–Darling Basin, shows what has happened; it is a national resource but the task of ensuring its health is made more difficult because of conflicting state interests. The only recourse is to persuade the federal government to use one of its other powers listed in the constitution to overrule a law made by the state government.

This is what happened in 1983 during the Franklin Dam campaign. There had been a national outcry over plans by the Tasmanian government to build a dam across the Gordon River that would have led to the pristine Gordon-below-Franklin River valley and surrounding forests being flooded. The earth moved (metaphorically at least) when the newly elected federal Labor government of Bob Hawke stepped in to protect the river using its power under the constitution to make laws concerning 'external affairs'. Australia had signed the World Heritage Convention committing us to protecting areas of universal significance that were nominated by the national government—the region of South West Tasmania was one such area. Using the external affairs power, Hawke made a law to overrule Tasmania. This decision was narrowly supported by the High Court in the appeal that followed.

While the High Court has tended to support the Commonwealth government when it makes laws for the protection of the environment, due to the lack of a clear head of power there is no end of buck-passing and argument about who is ultimately responsible. It is neither practical nor democratic that a court should decide questions of this kind. In any case, conservative national governments persist in leaving environmental responsibilities to the states. Yet a majority of people, when asked, expect the national government to take this role. A clever country would put the environment in the constitution so the national government could specifically make laws in relation to any environmental matter. After all, the wildlife, the air and the waters of the Australian continent don't adhere to state boundaries.

These were the kinds of issues I was keen to work through when I arrived at Admiralty House, somewhat bleary-eyed after my late night in Cessnock, to meet my fellow appointees. Among them, I was looking forward to meeting Donald Horne, whose writings I admired, including the celebrated, if misunderstood, *Lucky Country*. ('Australia is a lucky country run by second-rate people who share its luck'—ouch.) Author Tom Keneally, who wrote with an Australian sensibility that had struck a chord with me growing up, would also be there. It turned out that Tom and I were on the same committee and spending time with him was a great mood lifter. Tom has always written like a man possessed. He has an impish sense of humour and an affectionate knowledge of our ways—I learned a lot hanging out with him.

Along with Sir Rupert Hamer, a former Liberal premier of Victoria, and Maurice Byers, a former Commonwealth solicitor-general,

Gough Whitlam was a commissioner. So, like a nervous school-boy, I sought him out as he stood alone at a table laden high with scones and cakes while people milled about on the verandah outside having morning tea.

'Excuse me, Mr Whitlam . . .' I began.

'Gough,' he corrected me.

'I'm Peter Garrett, son of Betty Collin. You stayed with my grand-parents in Bowral when you were at Sydney University . . .' And on I rattled, setting out the pieces that connected me to the great man.

With one eyebrow raised, Whitlam listened until the explanation finally drew to a close and then, drawing himself up to his full height, he looked at the assembled throng outside before turning back to me and saying, 'Well, it's a small world isn't it, my son?' Long pause. 'With the exception of you and I, that is.' Nice one, Gough.

I enjoyed spending time with the committee members, all of whom were decent, intelligent, civic-minded people. Along with Keneally, they included Melbourne barrister Ron Castan, part of the legal team who argued the Mabo case, and Rhonda Galbally, the fiery disability advocate who much later represented the community sector during the establishment of the National Disability Insurance Scheme by the Gillard government.

Nearly twenty years later, John Howard, as prime minister, revived the idea of a new preamble to the constitution and enlisted eminent Australian poet Les Murray to assist. Murray is an aston-ishing wordsmith—who else would riff on the emu: 'I think your story is, when you were offered the hand of evolution, you gulped it'?—but in this case ideology ruled. The resulting prose was stilted and embarrassing, a clunky ode to mateship that left everyone cold. Meanwhile, Tom Keneally's eloquent suggestions for the preamble in our committee's report are long forgotten, including my favourite line: '. . . Australia is a continent of immense extent and unique in the world and demanding as our homeland our respect, devotion and wise management.'

Among the recommendations that our committee made, many are still relevant today and one in particular stands out as urgent. This concerns the repeal of Section 51 (xxvi) of the constitution, which allows the parliament to make laws with respect to race, although an original reference to 'the Aboriginal race' was removed by the 1967 referendum. In its place we recommended enabling the Commonwealth parliament 'to make laws for the benefit of the Aboriginal people and the Torres Strait Islander people: and the making of compacts deemed necessary by the Parliament in order to recognise the ownership of Australia prior to the acquisition of sovereignty by the Crown'. (Keneally's preamble also included the line: '. . . Australia is an ancient land previously owned and occupied by Aboriginal peoples who never ceded ownership.')

This was a way of addressing the sleeper issue in our history. Despite instructions from London, and notwithstanding the usual practice of negotiating some form of treaty with the country's inhabitants during the great colonial land rush of the eighteenth and nineteenth centuries, nothing of the sort happened when Australia was claimed by the British. Righting this prejudicial wrong is unfinished business. We also recommended the repeal of Section 25, which, while not in use, provided that electorates could be determined by race. These sections are hangovers from an earlier time when the authors of the constitution specifically intended to discriminate against Aboriginal people and others of different colour.

But back in the 1980s, the work of the Constitutional Commission was doomed from the start, thanks to the shadow attorney-general, Peter Reith, who mounted a cynical attack on its activities. He argued that accepting our recommendations—which included four-year government terms, extending the right to trial by jury and freedom of religion, providing for just compensation for property acquired by government—would simply result in more power for Canberra.

It was an argument that found fertile ground, especially in the distant states where the electorate was ever suspicious of politicians from central casting. It didn't help that neither Prime Minister Hawke nor Treasurer Paul Keating actively campaigned for the changes, despite the Labor government having initiated the commission, and notwithstanding that the changes being proposed were as reasonable as the appointees who recommended them. It is a fact of political life that it's impossible to succeed in amending the constitution if one of the major parties doesn't support the proposals, no matter how necessary they might be, as members of the public often take their cue from their preferred party's position. When the changes were finally put to a referendum in 1988 they were rejected. By then the conversation had ground to a halt, and the effort to update and improve our founding document came to naught.

Since then the debate about constitutional recognition of Aboriginal and Torres Strait Islander people has been restarted a couple of times, and is now back in the national spotlight. As did his predecessors Kevin Rudd and Julia Gillard, the prime minister Tony Abbott is supporting change to the constitution, and it could happen in 2017.

There has been a big grassroots campaign by the Recognise movement and an important report from a joint parliamentary committee, co-chaired by Liberal Ken Wyatt, the first Aboriginal member of the House of Representatives, and Labor senator Nova Peris pushing the issue along. The questions of constitutional recognition of Aboriginal people in the preamble, the removal of the remaining race powers and, potentially, the inclusion of a power to specifically make laws for Indigenous Australians, are again under consideration.

It's a no brainer for this whitefella, and I know many people, including those in the blackfella community, who want it to happen. If we are to be faithful to our shared history, then what objection can there be to including the First Peoples in our foundation document? They were here long before the Europeans arrived, and their culture, language and continuing presence should be central to the modern Australian nation.

13
FORTY THOUSAND YEARS

Lieutenant-Colonel David Collins, the founding lieutenant governor of New South Wales, recalled the early days of Australia's European settlement in his book, *An Account of the English Colony in New South Wales* (1798). The following passage stayed with me long after I first read it:

> But strange as it may appear they also have their *real estates* [my emphasis]. Ben-nil-long, both before he went to England and since his return, often assured me that the island Me-mel (called by us Goat Island) close by Sydney Cove was his own property; that it was his father's, and that he should give it to By-gone; his particular friend and companion. To this little spot he appeared much attached: and we have often seen him and his wife Ba-rang-a-roo feasting and enjoying themselves on it. He told us of other people who were possessed of this kind of hereditary property, which they retained undisturbed.

By the mid-1980s, the struggle for Aboriginal and Torres Strait Islander land rights was approaching a threshold moment.

The first peoples had lived in Australia for upwards of 40,000 years, a long spell in anyone's book and a greater span of continuous occupation than any other known culture. It was only a heartbeat ago, but the historical wrong of country stolen, the 'dispossession' as it was called, had to be made right—of that I was certain.

We'd already taken a few steps in support, playing some Rock against Racism shows and hosting the Warumpi Band, a new

Aboriginal outfit from the Northern Territory, when they came to Sydney.

A quick detour a few years earlier to visit and play a stripped-back show in Numbulwar, where Richard Geeves was teaching, had made a real impact on me. It was so utterly different from anywhere we'd been, unlike anything we'd done—it was another country within the borders of a country we thought we knew. The experience had stuck; a tentative connection had been made.

In late 1985, a lawyer called Phillip Toyne, who worked for the Aboriginal land councils based in Alice Springs, sought a meeting. He wanted to know if we'd be interested in contributing a song to a film under production to commemorate the return of one of Australia's most notable locations—Ayers Rock, in the centre of Australia—to its original owners, the Anangu people. The return of the rock— Uluru by its Aboriginal name—was the culmination of a hard-fought campaign by traditional owners, who eventually took their appeal over the heads of the local conservative Northern Territory administration and direct to the federal Labor government. They succeeded, and Uluru was to be returned to the traditional owners, who in turn would lease the rock and surrounding lands back to the people of Australia as a national park.

The film was *Uluru: An Anangu Story*, and we accepted the request from the elders for some music. It says something about their smarts that people living in one of the most remote parts of the country somehow fixed on having a band from Sydney provide a song; it turned out to do the job better than anyone could have hoped. There were other tunes floating about, but 'The Dead Heart' was the obvious choice. When Rob first brought it in we had great bones to work with. Nick Launay happened to be in town, itching to be on the tools, and the song was thrown down quickly at the EMI studios in Castlereagh Street, Sydney.

It was early 1986 and I'd been stuck at the office all day, deep in conversation with Gary Morris about the next phase of our career— chewing the fat, as Gary liked to describe it—and so was seriously late, running red lights all the way down Broadway to catch up with the session.

When I walked into the studio the track was cracking, physical, reaching out of the speakers and grabbing me by the throat, with the doubled-up acoustic guitars churning like an eighteen-wheeler, backed in by a crunching snare drum sound.

I was so proud of what my partners in music could achieve: the platform that had been constructed could have held up the Parthenon, and all that remained was for me to jump in and ad lib across the breakdown and through to the end: 'the dead heart still lives here'. Jeremy Smith from pub rock warriors Hunters & Collectors—good mates of ours—was an ace French horn player. He'd flown in for the day and blew Jim's brass lines across the outro in a couple of passes— we were out before the street sweepers had started their rounds.

We were yet to venture into the desert, a trip that would change our lives and our perspective in ways we couldn't anticipate. Nor had we recorded *Diesel and Dust*, the album that detailed the journey and would see us finally break through in other parts of the world. Still, somehow, everything came together on this song, as, partly blindfolded, we aimed to deliver for a people and a culture we hardly knew.

...

The promise of the Hawke government to ensure land rights for Aboriginal people had been wound back by a cautious prime minister, although ultimately the High Court would find that Aboriginal rights to land did exist—they called it native title—and the Keating government took the huge necessary step and legislated for these rights in the following years.

Meanwhile, frustrated by the lack of public support for the claims of Aboriginal people and annoyed by his boss's backflip, Clyde Holding, the Minister for Aboriginal Affairs, was keen to get the message out.

When local Aboriginal activist Gary Foley and Gary Morris scoped a possible tour by the Oils with the Warumpi Band across Central Australia and the Top End, the Blackfella/Whitefella tour started to take shape. A plan was quickly hatched: Holding would support the Warumpi Band, we were to cover our own costs, and the ABC would send a crew to film the tour and produce a documentary to be shown on prime-time television. The bands would travel to communities through the remote Western Desert, and then up to the top of the Northern Territory across Arnhem Land, taking gear and personnel to settlements that in some cases had rarely, if ever, seen a white Anglo rock band, and certainly not an enterprise on this scale. The tour aimed to build bridges between Aboriginal and non-Aboriginal Australians, and would help us to gain a better understanding of community life. The Warumpi song 'Blackfella/WhiteFella', with its call for people to 'stand up and be counted (because) it doesn't matter what your colour, as long as you, a true fella' provided the perfect title.

We enlisted the help of didgeridoo player Charlie McMahon, known as 'Hook' on account of the metal apparatus he manipulated with wire that substituted for his right hand, blown off when a schoolboy experiment with explosives went wrong. Charlie had jumped up on stage a few times in the early days, and the sound of his growling didg became a signature part of our sound in this period. He'd also spent time in the outback, working with the Pintupi and other tribal people from the desert and knew his way around.

As camp coordinator he'd itemised the food each four-wheel drive would need to carry, including: 'self-raising flour, corned beef, dried fruit, nuts, 1 kg powdered milk, 2 packets tea, biscuits, cheese, cereal, washing scourer ... 1 sharp knife, 1 large & 1 medium billy can, 5 enamel plates & mugs, 1 wash basin'. In addition, 'each vehicle will have a 20-litre water container'. And there was a warning: 'Utensils and containers are for the whole tour—look after them.'

For most Australians, suburban dwellers used to the conveniences and tidiness of modern living, visiting an outback community is an eye-opener. The Oils' natural habitat was Sydney's inner city and suburbs, and, when working, various hotels, pubs and recording studios. We were creatures of the night, at home in the cauldron of white noise. We were now heading to the heart of the continent. At the time, I made a note about my gut feeling that if we were to get a clearer fix on where the nation sat, we had to go to the roots of our history, and so it proved. Sure, you could read about it, but once you took the step to head to a place where the wounds and the memories were as fresh as today, there were no excuses, no turning back.

So, in the midwinter of 1986, we flew to Alice Springs, picked up four-wheel drives and stores, and from there headed west along rutted dirt tracks, skirting low hills covered in spinifex grass, past rocky outcrops with desert oaks scattered over an undulating landscape that went on forever.

We slept in canvas swags, setting up camp outside the tiny settlements that usually consisted of a collection of humpies, some dilapidated houses and sheds, a store that was the central meeting place, a sports oval of hard-packed dirt, a makeshift school and, sometimes, a church. Abandoned car bodies dotted the landscape, left disintegrating in the scrub by their owners, who no longer had the wherewithal to keep them going.

Meanwhile, the skeleton crew, led by our long-time stage manager Michael Lippold, a feisty scrapper from the working-class suburbs of Melbourne, along with tougher-than-nails sound man Pat Pickett, would pull the gear from the truck and scout the landscape for a place to set up. Lippold could make just about anything happen when it came to getting the Oils on stage, but he was tested in these conditions—especially with me, Gary and a nervous film crew breathing down his neck every step of the way.

We were well out of phone range, out of sight and, it seemed after a while, out of mind as well. One time, as Charlie McMahon and I were travelling back into Alice Springs, the main town in the Centre, I had the distinct impression that we were lost. We'd been driving across ridges of sand dunes and through washouts and dry creek beds for a couple of hours and couldn't find the 'road' we had been mistakenly told would lead into town. As we consulted the only guide we'd brought—an old Reader's Digest map of the world—Charlie stabbed at a square box that encompassed about 500 square miles of the Northern Territory. 'See, Rock?' he said. 'We're here. As I told you, we are not lost!'

The only enquiry from the rest of the crew, when we finally limped into Alice well into the night, was the inevitable, 'What took you so long?'

While most of Australia's First Peoples are a diaspora, dwelling mainly in cities and towns, there are also populations a long way out who still live in or around their traditional country. For a century or so it was believed that Aboriginal people were a 'dying race', so great was the collision of cultures. Once the white sails of the *Endeavour* appeared in Botany Bay, everything changed. This was the real shock of the new: disease and displacement, alcohol and alienation.

In 1986 the people of the Western Desert had only recently been gathered up and housed in the settlement of Papunya—the home of the Warumpis—250 clicks west of Alice. For Pintupi, Luritja, Warlpiri and other clans who had been forcibly removed from their own country, it was a place of great unhappiness. Their languages and cultures were under siege, their health was failing and for some, like the Pintupi, the only way out was escape. Thirty years after the disintegration of their hunter–gatherer way of life, some of the older men simply walked home. They were followed by community members in an old truck, lumbering across some 200 kilometres of desert, eventually to resettle in the lee of the mountains at Kintore.

We were strangers in this timeless land, where the grandeur and fine detail of the landscape took your breath away, but in the same instant, the pervasive poverty and extreme conditions brought you up short, as did the ever-present sense of ennui and grief. The story of Aboriginal peoples following the arrival of white settlers was one of loss: the loss of country that sustained them and gave their life meaning; the loss of family and neighbours to the sickness that followed; and, finally, the loss of interest in living, still tragically evident in the suicide rate of young Aboriginal men.

Here in the desert we had to slow down, in the way we played, in the way we thought. In the great silence that enveloped us, we had to listen carefully—to the words that were deliberately chosen, to the long gaps in conversation, to the odd angry shout erupting in the night. Only then did we get a glimpse of the depth of the culture of those we had come to perform for, and a sense of the scale of their daily struggle.

Out there everything was different: no artificial light, massive blue skies over red earth, each community an island surrounded by an ocean of desert. Picture an indifferent camel standing at the front of a make-shift stage—actually a canvas tarpaulin in the dirt—with less than a hundred people sitting quietly, almost out of sight, as we ran through the song list with the winter wind blowing dust down our throats, the low hills surrounding the settlement turning to purple in the late afternoon. This was the world Midnight Oil now found itself in.

On arrival we'd touch base with the handful of whitefellas in the settlement: community workers putting in the hard yards as teachers and nurses and in various support roles. We'd then meet with the elders and other clan leaders, and where possible with the women as well, as they tended to do much of the work, and listen as they described the seemingly intractable problems they were all grappling with. These included how to get young people into school, teachers to come and stay longer than a month, people into work when there were no jobs, the road fixed when the grader had broken down and they'd been cut off for weeks because of sudden rain. How, even this far out, to maintain their identity in the face of a tidal wave of popular western culture—cartoons, soapies, ganja, liquor, *Penthouse*, all dished up on white bread with sugar.

After leaving Alice we went first to Uluru and then further west. By the time we reached Kintore—Walungurru to the locals—close to the border of Western Australia, nearly two weeks later, we'd found a travelling rhythm, a foretaste of making music a different way, and now and then connection. The window into another world was opening up: a world of learning and lore that preceded the arrival of the European explorers.

Johnny Scobie, a big Warlpiri warrior who was the Kintore Council chairman, decided along with other elders, including noted artist Turkey Tolson Tjupurrula, to take us to a secret location where traditional artefacts and sacred objects of great significance to the Pintupi were stored. We drove out into the desert in the late afternoon, veering off one of the many dirt tracks that surrounded the remote settlement, to visit the cultural storehouse of the Pintupi. It was a great honour; it isn't too far-fetched to say we were being shown the Pintupi equivalent of the Ten Commandments. This act of sharing enabled us to understand a little more of the real depth of their people's law and culture. It is one thing to be told about something with great meaning, and another thing altogether to see it. If part of the act of creating is a search for truth, then it was Midnight Oil's great good fortune to be invited to share Aboriginal people's truth—forever seared into our memory.

I've returned to the Centre many times since, when working on environmental issues and, more recently, in my role as a government minister. It's always confronting and I've never grown used to the bittersweet sense of estrangement and distant promise I find in these communities. There are hard choices ahead. The gaining of rights to land, important as this was, hasn't led to overall improvements in social conditions. How best to ensure young people get the education they so desperately need, and communities remain safe and healthy, is still strongly contested. Still, coming out and reconnecting means more to me than all the gold records packed away in the storeroom at home or any other emblem of success.

After three weeks in the desert we quit the vehicles and swung north in small aircraft, traversing the massed escarpments and river catchments that separate settlements across the Top End. Used to doing most of the driving, I wanted to try flying as well, so once we had a clear horizon and were in uncontrolled air space, I'd ask the young pilots for a go. Getting hold of the joystick and steering a small light aircraft through the open skies over the vast green swathes of Arnhem Land was a blast—more so for me than the rest of the Oils, who exited the Cessna muttering enough was enough.

I blamed this high-flying desire on a new set of touring companions who had joined us for the northern leg. They were the Swamp Jockeys, a knockabout group of skydivers and musicians who hailed from Darwin. They'd flown over in a couple of single-engine Cessnas with their equipment squeezed into a battered Cherokee Six. At Elcho Island and a few other locations, the Swamp Jockeys startled everybody by parachuting into an open clearing as a warm-up before we played—Top End showbiz: I doubt there's been anything like it since.

Here again the contrasts were great, and there was plenty to learn. Many of these communities—especially on the coast, where contact with Macassan traders from Indonesia and Timor had been going on for centuries—had not been removed or forced to flee their homes following the European incursion. Despite the welter of social issues they were facing—youth alienation, unemployment, alcohol abuse—there was a feeling of resolve in the air. There was plenty of food, they knew their land intimately and, while there'd been earth-shattering change, people here could work things through given time and support from governments of goodwill.

Their proud recent history of resistance to European overlay stood out. There had been a firm assertion of local people's rights, as evidenced by the first-ever bark petition calling for recognition of Aboriginal and Torres Strait Islander land and culture, which had been crafted at Yirrkala, home of the Yolngu. It said in part: 'This is Aboriginal people's place. We want to hold this country. We do not want to lose this country.' It was presented to the federal parliament in 1963.

The presentation did not succeed in making good their grievances, and neither did an ensuing High Court case, which again
sought to have the prior occupation of land recognised and compensation paid on account of a government decision taken in early 1963
to allow bauxite mining without consultation with the Yolngu. And
so the campaign for land rights was joined across Australia as other
Aboriginal clans and supporters from the wider community pressed
for recognition of their rights.

Again in 1985 at a small community festival at Barunga, near
Katherine, a statement written on bark, now known as the Barunga
Statement, was presented to Prime Minister Bob Hawke. We were
self-government from the start, it asserted, and Hawke agreed that a
treaty should now follow.

It was at Yirrkala that I first met Mandawuy Yunupingu. At that
time he was the first Yolngu man to have trained as a teacher, and
he went on to become the principal of the local primary school.
He later embarked on a second career as frontman for the band
Yothu Yindi.

Sitting in a clearing under stands of casuarinas and pandanus,
speaking in a soft voice, he described his journey so far. Little did
either of us know where it would lead, and how intertwined our lives
would later become. Fast-forward five years and Alan James, then the
manager of the Swamp Jockeys and now Yothu Yindi's manager, calls
up to say he and Mandawuy are in Sydney. He asks if I can help them
finish a new song that Mandawuy had written with Paul Kelly. The
song was called 'Treaty', and he was pretty excited about it.

They came across to the Oils office in Glebe with Paul to play the
track and right from the first listen it sounded like the business—it
was a big jump for Yothu Yindi, and had the potential to go the
distance. Later that night I dropped in to the Vault studio close by,
where we spent a bit of time figuring out how to make the phrasing
of the words match the rhythm of the music, and then I recorded a
guide, adding a few lines for a bridge section to reinforce the message.

At first 'Treaty' struggled for airplay, but following a dance-style remix featuring extensive passages of Aboriginal language, it became a hit; it was the first record to break into the mainstream with such a direct call to make good on the taking and occupying of Aboriginal country.

We later took Yothu Yindi with us to the US on the Diesel and Dust to Big Mountain tour. Later still, I worked with Mandawuy and his wife Yalmay as they, with others in their community, founded the Garma Festival in north-east Arnhem Land and fought for better health services for the region.

...

The Warumpis had kept pretty much to themselves for the desert leg of the tour, but that would change as we hit sea country, as different to them as their home was to us. From that point on we began to spend more time together. Unlike his band mates, George Rrurrambu wasn't from the desert originally. He hailed from Elcho Island, off the northern coast, and had ended up in the Western Desert settlement of Papunya after marrying a woman from that area (which also entailed breaking a tribal taboo). He'd ventured a long way from home and, used to explaining his different circumstances, was more outgoing.

It was at Elcho that George came into his own. His drinking had exasperated everyone on tour, not the least his band companions, but once back on home soil he was irrepressible; togged up in rock-star gear of tight jeans and a funky T-shirt, he swaggered through the settlement like Jagger in his heyday, with a gaggle of admiring kids at his Cuban heels.

The show that night nudged the stars, with the returning hero strutting his stuff to a crowd both astonished and highly amused by the unfolding spectacle, from skydiving to a local legend cutting it in fine style, and so they were in good spirits when we took to the stage.

The next morning a few of us got up early and, at George's invitation, went fishing at the local beach, armed only with hand spears.

Despite the shoals of good-sized fish visible near to shore, I came up empty-handed, much to the amusement of the Warumpi singer and those of his mates who'd tagged along to watch this balanda (white person) make a fool of himself. I didn't disappoint.

My fumbling attempts weren't getting us any closer to a feed, so a grinning George grabbed my spear and with one quick throw skewered lunch. The fish, still wriggling, was put directly onto a small fire lit on the sand near the water's edge. It was delicious, a real treat after days of canned food and stale biscuits.

There was one large town we hadn't yet visited, and soon we were winging our way back across the Top End to Port Keats. Located well away from most other settlements on the remote north-west coast, wedged between the mangroves and the scrub, this former Catholic mission, also known by its Aboriginal name of Wadeye, was growing quickly. Like Papunya, more than a thousand miles to the south, it was home to different clan groups, and disputes and arguments were common in its early days.

No band had ever ventured this far out. During the wet season Port Keats was often cut off from the rest of the country for up to five months at a time, with supplies either flown in at great expense or barged across from Darwin. The dilapidated hall we played in—tin roof and walls, cracked concrete floor—was packed to overflowing. Up to now, audiences had hung back, watching from a distance, though young kids occasionally darted towards the stage and performed a few lightning-quick gyrations before fleeing back to the cover of darkness, accompanied by squeals of laughter from their friends.

At Port Keats the audience seemed more animated than usual. Then, midway through the show, a tall young man wearing a pair of overalls modelled on the stage clothes we'd worn for a 'Read About It' film clip leapt onto the stage and lunged towards me. A roar unlike anything we'd heard to this point went up. Unsure what would happen next, and whether there was a hidden significance in this bold action, I just said hello and gave him a pat on the shoulder. He grinned at the audience, danced around briefly, then leapt back into the crowd—a bona fide legend from that moment on.

The young man's name was William Parmbuk, and he later came to national attention when—incensed by the impact that alcohol was having on his community—he commandeered a bulldozer and, with the assistance of a large crowd, demolished the only liquor outlet in Wadeye, the quixotically named Sport and Recreation Club. (I got to know William better when he and Tobias Nganbe, a Wadeye leader, visited Canberra to resolve a Human Rights Commission complaint Tobias had lodged after years of government inaction regarding the school in this rapidly growing community—but more of that later.)

The frantic pace of six weeks of setting up and putting on shows then moving on the next day was nearing an end as we descended over Kakadu National Park for our final performance, to be staged at Jabiru township.

Kakadu encompasses an amazing array of environments, from coastal floodplains and wetlands to magnificent rock escarpments, covered, as are many rock surfaces in Australia, with cave paintings and drawings. Giant waterfalls cascade down these rocky walls in the wet season; billabongs are a haven for a huge range of wildlife. Above all it is a living cultural landscape and home to Aboriginal people since forever. In the words of one of the region's leaders, Big Bill Neidjie:

> Rock stays
> Earth stays
> I die and put my bones in cave or earth
> Soon my bones become earth . . .
> Our story is in the land
> It is written in those sacred places.

Kakadu had been recognised as internationally significant and listed as a World Heritage area due to its extraordinary natural beauty and important cultural values, but it was also the site of three excised mining leases: Ranger, Jabiluka and Koongarra, and the Ranger uranium mine sat smack bang within the park, courtesy of an earlier government decision, which in hindsight seemed indefensible. This was a place that would feature prominently in environmental and Aboriginal politics in the years ahead, and we'd be back before too long. But for now, after weeks of living rough and playing in places we could never have imagined, we were content to end our tour, with our antennae still quivering, in one of Australia's most spectacular locations.

14

THE AUSTRALIA CARD

WHEN OUT OF the blue the Hawke government announced in 1985 that it was going to introduce a national identity card for all Australians, I decided to get involved. I was deep in Oils mode, but the idea offended me so much—the possibility of greater surveillance of ordinary citizens, with a plan cooked up by technocrats without consultation—I was determined to be part of the movement opposing it.

Decked out in green and gold, the card was to be called, predictably, the Australia Card. People would have a single identification number that could be used for Medicare, passport applications, driver's licences and so on, with all the details held in a central registry operated by the Health Insurance Commission. The card would have to be carried by every member of the population.

As in the debate concerning euthanasia, my view is that citizens should be wary about handing over too much information or authority to a bureaucratic entity. It is impossible to predict the future, but function creep is normal operating procedure in all bureaucratic systems, and the likelihood of inadvertent or intentional abuse by governments—the major source of human rights abuses, should they acquire additional power—is a given.

The principal objection to a national ID card was that it created a massive, centralised database, in a system that allowed government departments to cross-reference personal information. It may seem quaint thirty years on, with concerns about privacy ebbing away in the age of social media, but a number of individuals and civil liberties groups were opposed to the idea of the government acquiring the means to track and monitor the lives of its citizens. However, we were in a minority.

When the proposal was first mooted as a way of cracking down on tax cheats, there was hardly a murmur. But over time, as the details of the scheme became better understood, it gave rise to increasing disquiet.

A joint select committee of the parliament examined the bill that proposed the introduction of the Australia Card and found they didn't like it. Neither did the Opposition, who held the balance of power in the Senate. Bob Hawke decided to call an election in 1987, ostensibly to achieve a mandate for this and other reforms, but despite being returned to government, he failed to win control of the upper house. There was little discussion of the Australia Card in the campaign, but once the government was returned it was again presented to parliament.

The re-emergence of the legislation stirred up a hornet's nest of questions and increasing objections from privacy experts, and it wasn't long before I found myself at the Sebel Townhouse—a familiar music-industry hangout—sharing a podium with Janine Haines, a moderate slightly left-of-centre senator who was leader of the Australian Democrats; Ben Lexcen, a conservative who'd designed the winged keel on the yacht that won the 1983 America's Cup; and a raft of other strange bedfellows as the newly formed Privacy Foundation kicked off a campaign against the Australia Card.

This really was a strange crew I realised early the following week, when we met at broadcaster Alan Jones's warehouse apartment in Newtown to plot the details of a nationwide assault on the scheme. I was happy enough to be working with such a diverse group, given we had one aim in mind, but it would be an interesting journey.

Jones had a ready view on what tactics the group should adopt and how the campaign should be run but, in the end, he was more talk than action. Haines and Privacy Foundation chief Simon Davies, along with University of New South Wales privacy expert Dr Graham Greenleaf, did most of the substantive work.

Meanwhile, opposition to the card was increasing. Prominent judge and avowed monarchist Michael Kirby had gone so far as to claim: 'What is at stake is nothing less than the nature of our society.' I was inclined to agree. In Australia we were a long way from the excesses of one-party states, with their despotic leaders—Robert Mugabe, Joseph Stalin, Erich Honecker and, today, Vladimir Putin—but the slippery slope awaited. History is littered with the cruel abuses of governments, and for those in power keeping tabs on people—their movements, habits and views—was core business in each and every case. It was time for those who valued freedom to dig in. Former Communist Party member and author Frank Hardy came out against the card, as did conservative scions like businessman Hugh Morgan. Former Whitlam government minister Jim McClelland was opposed and there were last-minute rumblings in the Labor Caucus.

Meanwhile, activist lawyer Tim Robertson, right-leaning Australian Medical Association president Dr Bruce Shepherd and I took to the campaign trail. We squeezed into Simon Davies' car to drive to a meeting in Orange, a regional centre in the Central West of New South Wales, to find a river of people overflowing into the street. The locals were out in force: farmers, teachers, small business owners, families, the young and old and everyone in between.

This kind of turnout was typical. The momentum was swinging in our favour, and despite operating with few resources and even less sleep for a couple of months, our disparate crew—different in all ways other than in our view of this initiative—drew energy from the positive mood and kept soldiering on.

By the campaign's end, so many people had joined the dots that 90 per cent of the population was now opposed to the Australia Card—an incredible turnaround and a victory for people power. As historian Geoffrey Blainey said at the time, it was a eureka moment.

On its way back into the Senate, a technical glitch was discovered in the bill and the government retreated—the national ID card was dead in the water.

Since then, of course, the information and technology landscape has been transformed beyond recognition, and the bureaucracy's desire to implement a national identifier hasn't gone away. The internet is now universal and the use of social media so commonplace that the line between public and private has all but disappeared. In western countries, at least, many people don't appear to value their privacy at all. Private information is willingly shared and easily accessed, so much so that some figures in new media characterise privacy as outdated, like Facebook's Mark Zuckerberg, who then retreats to his walled estate to protect his own privacy.

The revelations, in part triggered by former US National Security Agency (NSA) contractor Edward Snowden, that the NSA had a system that could spy on everybody, sucking up data from people's phones, email and Facebook accounts, highlighted how far some governments can reach.

Reports that the Australian Signals Directorate had offered to share private information—metadata—with other nations with whom we have close intelligence ties, if true, raises very serious issues about the incursions by our government into its citizens' lives. The outcry following these revelations was limited to writers and intellectuals, who glimpsed what was at stake: our freedom to think and act without a knock on the door in the middle of the night.

A healthy suspicion about what modern governments and corporations might do if they had easy access to the personal details of citizens seems reasonable to me. There are very good reasons to keep what some have referred to as an invisible guardrail around your innermost self. Our thoughts, habits, opinions, fears and beliefs are all that we have. These are the non-material components of our character: the elements that make up the core of any individual's identity.

Surrendering these aspects that constitute an individual is a bigger step than most people think. For citizens living in a one-party state like China, where censorship and surveillance are a way of life, it's a corrosive reality.

Ai Weiwei, the renowned Chinese artist and critic of the communist state, has fought a long and exhausting battle with the Chinese government. The relentless monitoring of him and others who question the accepted party line has been a central feature of that struggle.

Recently enacted laws in Australia that give greater powers to security agencies, and those that punish whistleblowers, and the ease with which metadata records, especially those of journalists, can be tracked, already provide a barrier to the transparency of government actions.

The bottom line is that putting a white flag above the door on this issue is contrary to one of the basic tenets of our society: our inherent right to freedom of expression.

The price of liberty is still eternal vigilance, and always will be. But I wonder if we would get such a range of political opposites into the same room on this issue today, as we did when Australians first rose up against the plan for a national ID card.

15
THE TIME HAD COME

A YEAR BEFORE the Blackfella/Whitefella tour, Doris and I got married—twice: first in our backyard and then in a church. The Oils were off to South America to tour, so as an insurance policy for what we hoped wouldn't happen—revolutions, plane crashes, piranha attacks—we stood under the clothesline at our house in Fairlight, a suburb close to Manly, and exchanged vows, with my brother Matt and Louise Douglas, an old gigging friend from the Lower North Shore, as witnesses. The celebrant who presided over the ceremony asked for a reference before the ink was dry on the marriage certificate.

A couple of months later, when I'd returned from South America in one piece, we got married again. This time we exchanged our vows in the old stone Presbyterian church down the hill in Manly, with a full house of friends and band mates, and, to my eyes, my sweetheart more beautiful than any bride has ever been. We floated above the ground right through the day and into the evening on clouds of pure happiness, in love and at one with the world.

Then came the girls, in quick succession. First Emily, then May sixteen months later, and Grace followed two years after. I scribbled a few words in the diary announcing Em's arrival into the world: 'Now we are three.' Words can seem trite when trying to describe something as momentous as this: seeing the surrender to great forces that happens to a mother in childbirth, then coming face to face with the miracle of a new life arriving—it's an indelible image, one that sticks with you forever.

Of course this meant looking after the wonderful new arrivals—all in nappies, for years in a row. It was a demanding job, especially for Doris when I was away for long stretches, all the more so as we didn't have any parents or close relatives to come by and give us a break.

On the few occasions we escaped out for a meal or a movie, it was getting harder to catch our breath and share a quiet moment. More and more people were coming up to say hello and get an autograph, which was fine, and a compliment, and definitely not something to object to—except when it's your first night out in weeks and all you want to do is huddle with your wife, who you haven't seen for two months, in a quiet corner of a restaurant.

Of course it was my decision to jump onto a stage and I was up for whatever came with the job. I'm in the Sinatra camp on this: if you can't stand the heat, then get out of the kitchen. But every outing had suddenly turned into a public gathering, which wasn't much fun for the family. And given my intentionally distinctive looks, it was all but impossible to travel incognito.

Fame is something I've always found bemusing. I like the 'all of us are bloody well equal and by the way it's your shout' Aussie attitude; it helps to keep society on a more even keel. The English have their class system, and the Americans their star system, but I value the easygoing, egalitarian nature of Australians. It should go without saying that everyone deserves to be treated the same, irrespective of wealth, colour, belief or nationality, and if someone eats from a bigger table on the basis of merit and effort, fine. But that doesn't mean they're better than people who have less.

At this time we were living in Balgowlah, close to many of our early haunts and the Oils' office in Kangaroo Street, Manly. I liked being part of a neighbourhood, and we'd made some good friends in the street, including Damian Trotter, who worked for our record company, and his wife, Suzannah. I assumed, wrongly as it turned out, that people wouldn't take the Oils' newfound fame too seriously; no one close to us did. I couldn't fathom why we were put up on a pedestal simply because we'd worked hard at something we loved, got lucky and broken through. But it was increasingly clear that the family needed some kind of escape hatch. So, with the help of a couple of industrious locals, we began work on a small weekender in a patch of bush in Kangaroo Valley, a couple of hours south of Sydney.

It was as far from the thunder and lightning of my day/night job as you could get, and getting my teeth into a new project was a welcome relief. We camped in a forest glade, surrounded by eucalypts and with a permanent creek on one boundary, as we ferried tools onto the site and started building.

Constructed on the cheap, using second-hand materials we'd sourced from demolition yards and junk shops, it was an ideal hideaway.

Once it was finished, we were proud of our little corrugated-iron eco-cottage, replete with solar panels and a composting loo out the back. Doris and I could sit out on the rough wooden deck looking across the valley while the girls roamed free, content to play with sticks and rocks and a few old saucepans. In the early morning we were serenaded by birdsong, with eagles hovering above and lyrebirds scratching in the bush. During the day we'd take bushwalks under the craggy escarpment, occasionally chancing on foraging kangaroos, wallabies and echidnas, or we'd venture down to the creek to try to spot a shy platypus. In the evenings we were enveloped by stars—bliss.

I envisaged buildings like this being a model for rural housing in the future. The cottage was well off the grid, and sited to the north, with the layout based on a typical three-bay farm shed, a familiar design in farming communities. Because of the simple passive solar design, the cost of power was negligible. We used a lot of recycled materials, apart from the concrete slab, so construction costs were also low. Here was an affordable way for anyone looking to build outside the city to make a start.

Coming back into Sydney after a week away, with honking horns and high-fives at every turn, was always a reminder of how restricted our lives in the big smoke had become. Restricted—and potentially vulnerable. When a stalker left a suspicious-looking bag at the front door of our home in Balgowlah, it threw us into a panic.

It turned out to be a hoax of sorts: a weird package and some bizarre scribble from someone who was mentally ill, but the writing—in bold letters—was on the wall. We rolled down the shutters, figuratively speaking. I removed myself from the electoral roll (an action that would rebound on me down the track) and some off-duty police we knew moved into our home to keep an eye on the family, as the Oils were due to go back out on tour.

When I returned, after a restless six weeks in Europe and Canada worrying about how things were going at home, we started looking for somewhere quieter to live. We ended up buying an old house from the state government. Rowe Cottage had been used as an orphanage for decades. It was located within easy reach of Sydney in the Southern Highlands, where my mum had grown up; it was like a return to my roots.

Sitting on a gentle rise, with an oak tree outside the bedroom window and a giant eucalypt in the front garden—a mix of Doris and me that we laughed about—the original Queen Anne federation cottage had been all but obliterated by various toilet-block-style additions and bureaucratic fumblings. Inside, it was filled with broken furniture, partitions and tattered carpet tiles—all the detritus of an institution . . . but it called to us.

Before we finalised the purchase, I took my swag down, slipped in through a broken window and slept there overnight to see how much of the past had stuck to the graffiti-covered walls. The power had been turned off and I lay there in the pitch black, listening for crying in the night, but all was quiet. Unlike my old family home in Lindfield, it appeared to be ghost-free. (We later discovered that for some kids it was a refuge and, depending on the staff, a happier place than where they'd come from. For others, though, it had been like a prison, a place of cruelty and suffering.)

Here we would have a bit more space and some privacy, and the girls could have a more regular upbringing. When I was home, we could just be a family, not a sideshow. It would take a while for our new house to be repaired and made good, and for the past to be exorcised a little. In the meantime, more music was on the way.

...

Diesel and Dust, the easiest and, in retrospect, probably the most important album Midnight Oil made, was recorded at a time when several of us were expanding our families, and the thought of leaving home filled the new fathers in the band with dread. So we decided to go with Alberts, where we'd recorded our first album. They'd since moved from the city to the Lower North Shore, with the studio hidden away on the first floor of a brick office block alongside a shopping centre in Neutral Bay.

It would be hard to imagine a more modest enterprise for a label that had launched AC/DC to worldwide success. If you wanted to get out and take a breather, the only option was to walk around the leafy streets of Neutral Bay: not very rock-edgy, but highly conducive to work.

Warne Livesey came across from England to work the machines and mix. He was a low-key, music-focused producer and presided over a tight recording process. 'Peter, let's just run that again, can we? And this time, just concentrate on hitting that last note, please.'

After finishing the Blackfella/Whitefella tour we'd taken stock. Of the many things that stood out from that experience, a desire to keep it simple was one, and that meant taking finished songs into the studio and getting them down without too much fuss.

Diesel was an album where the band didn't have to strain. The anchor was the desert experience so the themes were clear. The loping, even rhythms we'd fallen into while driving across the open spaces established a base. We had too much energy to swing as a band, but it was our own kind of groove, and the songs were flowing.

It was difficult to know if we'd nailed something special, and opinions were typically varied. Yes, we could hear something in the grooves, and 'Beds Are Burning' was super-singable, memorable, but no one really knew how it would translate to the outside world. In the end, it was partly by design—getting the sound and the feel to sit right—and partly by accident, that we finally got there.

Europe had already shown some interest in the band, and that interest intensified. The pared-back songs and the bushman look of the photos and videos that accompanied the album, which was pretty much how we'd togged up on tour, proved popular among people for whom Australia was still a far-off exotic land.

In the US, 'Beds' snuck onto radio by virtue of a momentary halt in a scam that was common at the time, whereby record companies, via an intermediary known as a plugger, paid radio stations to play certain songs. Called 'payola', the practice was illegal and completely distorted the charts, and it never went away. As recently as 2005, major record companies in the US—Sony, Warner and Universal—were fined millions of dollars for this dodge. Those who could afford to bribe rarely took risks with anything that sounded or looked different, and it favoured the labels with big budgets. The lull in payola in the late 1980s saw 'Beds Are Burning' get a run in its own right. We charged through and into the bright lights. All of a sudden Midnight Oil was in the mainstream with a worldwide hit about giving land back to the Indigenous people of the most ancient continent on earth.

The success of *Diesel and Dust* saw the audience grow rapidly, although at home there was initially a degree of ambivalence about what some people saw as a preoccupation with Aboriginal issues. Once 'Beds' became a radio staple these doubts faded away. In Europe and the States, the stages and the crowds got bigger. One day we were squeezing onto the set of *Late Night with David Letterman* for the first in a series of performances, the next we were playing at an open-air show in Central Park for the UN. Getting popular in a country of over 240 million people meant we could now do a few things that might turn heads and start a conversation.

Throughout the rising tide that followed the success of *Diesel and Dust*, our peculiar polarities remained; one was the desire to stay grounded at home versus a burgeoning international career, the other, pursuing our music and issues without interference, which meant butting heads with a record company focused on exploiting our 'overnight' success. It was a set of tensions we could never completely reconcile, and over the next fifteen years the Oils morphed into a cottage industry that didn't reach the heights our manager, agents and some fans thought possible, but at least our marriages and sanity would remain (mostly) intact.

In between we got through as much touring, music-making and activism together as we could manage. There was never a question in our minds, although it was interminably asked, as to what came first—the music or the message? Of course it had to be the music. It was the juice that started the engine, the spur that got me going in the first place.

If you took a careful look, Midnight Oil's message wasn't in the songs by themselves, which varied, ranging over topics and with different expression depending on when they were recorded, and which person or combination of band members had written the particular track. The message was in joining the music and its lyrics with actions that matched what was being sung. This endeavour was a form of social/political outreach that consumed us for more than two decades. Were we earnest and self-righteous? Yes, we surely were. But we were yoked in the service of an idea bigger than success: the integrity of the work we were creating, and the legitimacy of the issues that we supported. This stance remained forever the opposite of the dream factory and infantile rebellion that was rock's constant leitmotif—this was our reason for being.

At its heart, music works primarily at an emotional level. It's obvious in jazz or classical pieces that summon up feelings without any narrative map. 'I second that emotion' is all over popular music; just think of the Crystals' 'Da Doo Ron Ron' or John Lee Hooker's 'Boom Boom'. If you have words that mesh or a story to tell or a point to make, then well and good: you've got more meat on the bone. Yet one listener relates to Dylan's 'Hurricane' as a gritty tale of injustice whereas another just likes that song about hurricanes with the great fiddle line. Once it's out in the open, floating in the ether, a song is no longer the writer's, nor is it necessarily taken as the writer intended. It's now a tiny particle in the cosmos, an infinitesimal bit of soundtrack for anyone, anywhere to feed off. But if you get out and do something concrete with it, then that adds value to the song and the issue in question.

...

Inevitably, with the release of a new album—and an album that was going gangbusters, at that—we were back on the road again. Our touring family was usually five white males (the band) and a tour manager. Sometimes we carried other players, like trombonist Glad Reed from Sydney band Just a Drummer; Charlie (Hook) McMahon, who by now had established himself with Gondwanaland; and, on the bigger concert tours that followed, Chris Abrahams on piano. Chris was a masterful keyboardist who went on to great acclaim in the Necks. I don't ever recall him playing anything approaching an off note. His phrasing was nuanced and deft, arriving at the changes at exactly the right moment.

It wouldn't have been that easy coming on tour with the Oils, at least at the start. The foundation members had already been together for so long we could go days without talking. Our characters were set, but there was a larger composite character—the band—that could answer for any of us if needed. If the collective mind was made up on an issue, then there was little need to explain. Midnight Oil talked a lot, especially about music and how to keep our nose in front, but we weren't talkative. We knew each other so well, we were, as I've said, more like brothers than best mates. Sharing a career, and seeing more of one another than our partners and families, calls for a certain kind of detachment to be sustainable. It's not about the small stuff, so long as the big stuff—the band—is still in motion.

Life on the road ultimately took its toll on Giffo, wrestling with his demons and veering to the political right; not long after *Diesel*'s release in the middle of 1987, he made an abrupt exit. No sooner was he out the door than Bones Hillman just as quickly walked in.

Originally from Kiwi band the Swingers, at the time Bones was working as a house painter in Melbourne and living with Neil Finn from Crowded House and his wife Sharon. Bonesy not only took up the bass-playing role and sang back-up without breaking into a sweat, he also brought an easygoing approach that lightened the mood in the camp. Unlike the rest of us, Bones—single and without kids— was happiest on tour. In the bus, curtains down, careering through the dead of the night after a show, he'd settle in for a movie, get out a pack of cards or play DJ with the stacks of CDs that were always flying around the galley. His pleasure at being on this self-contained ship out on the ocean, cut off from the fisticuffs of society, was only equalled by my frustration at being out of range, unable to dip into the swirl of current events washing around in a different time zone.

The others coped with touring in their own ways. I always thought of Jim and Martin—Jim whimsical and gentle, Martin dry and level—as creatures of music through and through, immersed in a parallel universe of guitars, amps and sound gadgets. They were aural architects throwing up the musical base where needed and, in Jim's case, the supplier of mountains of music: songs, extended passages, chords and textures that could turn random ideas into finished songs. This preoccupation framed their daily lives and everything the band did when we hit the studio, and when we played live.

Rob, usually tapping on something, riven by nervous energy, was always at it, reading, writing and working the angles; he was interested in the history of places and got out more to museums and galleries. And he could crack light about the various absurdities and indignities of the road when the occasion called for it.

Gary Morris rarely travelled with the band. The monotony of touring—sound check, quick bite and shower, show, after-show meet-and-greet, overnight on the bus, hotel check-in, morning radio interviews, afternoon breakfast, promo duties, sound check, show, in endless repetition—held little attraction for his restless, fertile mind.

There had to be a lynchpin, someone to coordinate and control the assembly. In our case we got lucky when tour manager Willie McInnes fronted for a US tour around 1986 and stayed almost to the end of 2002. Willie bore a striking resemblance to the cartoon character Yosemite Sam: stocky, moustache and boots, with a winning smile, and at least one bottle of bourbon stashed in his briefcase. He wore a whistle around his neck, which he used to round up the entourage and get us back on the treadmill—i.e. the bus—and, if needed, corral us like sheep and hustle us out the back door in times of strife or fan overload. Rob named his tragicomic book about the US tours of 2001 and 2002, *Willie's Bar & Grill: A rock 'n' roll tour of North America in the age of terror*, after him.

Like Connie 'Boogie Queen' Adolph, Willie had plenty of showbiz cred. He'd begun with West Coast outfit the Doobie Brothers and worked the spectrum from the Beach Boys to George Michael. He'd seen it all and more. A little out of our price range when we first met, he eventually agreed to come across to, as he put it, 'escape the A-grade prima donnas, and besides, I can't really understand what you guys are saying so that makes things more tolerable'.

Willie knew every trick of the trade, and his experience, honed over a lifetime on the road, made touring bearable and even occasionally a pleasure. With an address book to rival Bill Clinton's, he could charm a club owner, a snobby maître d' or a snarling New York cop if need be—as he had plenty of times in the past. If we were after a quiet place to play pool and wind down late at night, 'No problem.'

And if we needed to find a hotel close to bookstores and in which you could actually open the windows, or the only vegetarian restaurant in town—the kind of staples that kept us on track—again, 'No problem.'

I am often asked what it's like to be in front of a crowd of 100,000 people, all cheering and chanting your name. My answer is that, while it feels amazing, it's not about you. It's a kindred celebration between you—with your band partners—and a bigger bunch of part-time friends joining up on songs that mean something to people at the time. Of course you're elated, but the dancing on air doesn't last, and you can't take it to heart—at least that's my take.

The desire to create, to perform, to get into the limelight, draws different types of personalities. Some expel their demons every night in the glare of the spotlight as everyone cranes to look at them. This can make for irresistible entertainment. But when the demons are fuelled by drugs or alcohol, or the performer's mental and emotional state is out of kilter, then welcome to the slow-moving car crash—a tragic but familiar story.

Some performers never grow up. Look no further than Jagger, chasing ever-younger women around his various penthouses, Michael Jackson or, from an earlier era, Judy Garland. This arrested development sees these children/adults often frozen in their greatest moment, repeating their signature moves. Sooner or later they fall—or, if the gods are smiling, they push on as pale imitations of their former glorious selves. The roar of the crowd, with its truckloads of momentary unconditional love, lifts performers to dizzy heights. But it's a cruel illusion, because when the fall back to earth comes, with a bone-shaking thud, it hurts.

While I was writing this memoir, Doc Neeson, lead singer for the Angels, died. He'd been sick for a while and had gone at it hard for years, so his body wasn't as strong as he needed it to be. He was open about his troubles, which involved alcohol, prescription drugs, divorce and band break-ups. At one point, along with other supporters like former army chief and current Governor-General Peter Cosgrove, I provided a character reference to help him avoid jail for a driving-under-the-influence conviction. It worked. But I was saddened that someone who had achieved so much, a real musical force and a great stage presence, had reached this nadir. When word came through in early 2013 that a benefit show was being organised in his last months to help cover his medical expenses, I wanted to be there, even though my day job was now as a politician. On Monday, 15 April, I took a flight out of Canberra, arrived late in Sydney and changed out in the back street behind the Enmore Theatre. With Mark McEntee from the Divinyls and Jim on guitars, Rob on drums and Don Walker playing piano—quite a band—we tore through a version of 'We've Got to Get Out of This Place'.

This was the best side of the music industry, joining hands and rallying for its own. I hived off to the side of the stage to give this giant of the scene, now standing in the wings, a big hug. 'Hang in there, Doc, lots of people love you—look at tonight . . .' was all I could muster. Six months later I was among a crowd of family and music-industry friends and colleagues crammed into a chapel to bid him a final farewell.

Doc's story wasn't unusual. Lead singers seem to crumble and fall: Bon Scott, Marc Hunter, Matt Moffitt from Sydney band Matt Finish, Chrissy Amphlett, George Rrurrambu, Michael Hutchence, Johnny O'Keefe—it's a long rollcall and there are too many early departures.

I think part of the trick of hanging in there is not to get thrown off the scent: to remember to disrobe when the cheering stops. You can't take yourself too seriously, even if people around you are treating you as a cross between a prophet and a gift from the gods. It helps if you've inherited tough genes, but the privilege of popularity doesn't put off the day of reckoning. However you cut it, each of us is responsible for our own life, and everyone ultimately has to account for his or her actions. I've fallen for the fame factor a few times in the past, getting precious about little things, treating people around

the band in an off-handed way—my excuse would be that my mind
was on other things—but I needed to wake up to myself. Unless
there's someone there to remind you, or you pretty quickly figure this
stuff out, it's soon over.

...

There was no question that the Blackfella/Whitefella tour had
changed the way we saw things—you could hardly not be affected by
an experience like that.

We'd diverted some royalties to support Aboriginal reconciliation
and one result of the tour was the Building Bridges project, hosted at
our office. Other acts, like Goanna and Paul Kelly, were also making
connections with Aboriginal musicians and starting to venture into
communities. Building Bridges saw black and white bands and solo
performers come together on a joint album release, with accompa-
nying materials to make the case for reconciliation, and to show the
public the depth of talent of Aboriginal musicians.

In 1988, we took Yothu Yindi across the Pacific to America and
Canada for the Diesel and Dust to Big Mountain tour, which saw
us joined by Graffiti Man, a Native American outfit led by activist
and poet John Trudell. This was a satisfying trip, partly due to the
excitement of presenting a band made up of Balanda and Yolngu to
an audience who had no idea about this facet of life in Australia. It
was also a chance to give full recognition to the themes of the *Diesel*
album in a way that couldn't be ignored.

By the time we'd finished a second tour, the momentum for the
band was still building and we'd been invited to appear at the Grammy
Awards—a seriously big deal—but I'd committed to co-host the
Long March of Freedom, Justice and Hope, a reconciliation event that
was due to take place on 26 January 1988, Australia's bicentennial
year, and so we passed. This sent shock waves through the US record
company, who wanted to maximise the publicity that came with the
occasion, but I don't think the band even paused to discuss it.

The year started with the Australia Day march and rally in Sydney's Hyde Park of Aboriginal people and supporters who'd travelled from all over the state to hold an alternative event to the extravaganza that was going on at the other end of town. Down at Circular Quay—where the English first pitched their tents—the First Fleet re-enactment had gone off without a hitch. Now ferry races were in full swing, with fighter jets flying over the Opera House in a spectacular display of firepower as the Windsors from Buckingham Palace sat in the front row, and the public gathered in massive numbers around the harbour to take in the sight.

It was true Australia had much to celebrate. We were a successful, democratic nation with a blue-sky future in front of us and the envy of the world—not only because of our great natural endowments, but because we were seemingly young and evidently free. The gaping hole in the yarn was the unfinished business of reconciliation: the accountability for the theft of another people's country that couldn't be swept under the carpet. The secret fear of thoughtful Australians was that at some future point we would have to account for our actions, and decide what we stood for.

The ghouls of the right fed false rumours, repeated over radio, that armed mobs of Aboriginal people were converging on Sydney to wreak vengeance on the populace. When Doris and I joined the rally in Hyde Park, people were sitting quietly, listening to speakers who called for compassion and some compromise at a difficult moment when the reality of dispossession was being shoved in Aboriginal people's faces. They called too for an understanding of the past, for the proper resolution of land rights and for a positive future. The solemn quiet of the crowd was a stark contrast to the noisy celebration little more than a kilometre away.

There was no question that this was where I wanted to be, and what the Oils wanted to say. We knew whose side we were on. As the months and years sped by, we would try to pull back the white blindfold whenever the opportunity arose.

16

'WE'RE ALL GREENIES NOW'

DAYS AND MONTHS of theatres, sports halls and arenas unfolded in a blur. In the slingshot of a 747 everything is fleeting: one moment you're in America, and it's loud and tastes of sugar; a day later you're in cool Scandinavia, and there are no poor people. We were following through on an album that was making headway, but it was hard to get grounded, and exactly what it was we were chasing was less clear.

The message we were receiving from the record company *was* clear: all you have to do is get another song away just like 'Beds Are Burning', just like the one that made the charts. But chasing that particular rainbow was never going to deliver in the long run, I was certain of that. Maybe that was why I kept one of the US record company bigwigs waiting while I finished eating a meal after a late show in New York one night. We'd been told it was critical to meet this particular senior vice-president so as to get some executive support at a crucial stage of our career—something we didn't normally lose sleep over. In this instance, though, Gary was apoplectic and Rob was annoyed; the rest of the band shrugged it off as Pete being Pete.

I wasn't being intentionally rude. More likely it was psychological, me sending a message that I wasn't in thrall to the gladhanding coming our way and my mind was elsewhere.

Having spent so much time at 35,000 feet, I'd grown used to peering down at the world from this vantage point—and it put me in mind of the new perspective granted to the world when the

Apollo space missions started up. Space travel had given us a snapshot of what was at stake in a defining image of the century. There it was: a perfect blue ball, covered in flurries of white and green, suspended in space, with inky blackness all around. And visible from way up on high was the diaphanous spread of light from powered-up cities, a band of white Antarctic ice on the perimeter, a continent-sized arc of coloured coral across the South Pacific lapping our shore—miracle glimpses of life due to collide in our lifetime. The pictures from space said it all—it's small and fragile and it's the only one we've got.

Meanwhile each puff of smoke from exhaust pipes and chimneys and power plants chomping fuel keeps on coalescing. There's a big brown cloud hovering. It hangs, thickening the air—a heat blanket wrapped around the globe.

Everything seemed to be in jeopardy. Yet marshalling the will and the wherewithal to deliver a safe future was proving hard.

Coming in to land at São Paulo, Brazil, a descent that took more than half an hour over the biggest city I'd ever seen, and looking down on a spaghetti tangle of roads and shanty-town shacks and massive apartments stretching past the horizon, made me pause for breath. As did sitting in the back of the tour bus looking out on the San Diego freeway, eight lanes of unceasing, smoking, grumbling traffic extending both ways past the eyeline, a sea of cars and bulky chassis, with smog so thick I could hardly make out the prefab suburbs that lie on either side of the huge road.

All I could think at times like these was: are we at some kind of tipping point?

It seemed clear that new, fresh approaches were desperately needed to get us out of the old way of thinking; we needed to make the blue planet, not our immediate desires, a priority. But what could I do?

I could head back to the river in Lane Cove National Park where I'd played as a kid, pull some wrecked car bodies out of the bush, pick up the piles of cans and broken bottles—that would be a start.

Instead, I ended up somewhere altogether different.

...

It was only a year or so before that I'd hitched a ride with lawyer Phillip Toyne out to Warakurna in his tiny single-engine plane while on the Blackfella/Whitefella tour.

As we flew low over the Gunbarrel Highway—a thin red line of dirt snaking below us—he mentioned over the engine roar that he was thinking of applying for the position of executive director of the Australian Conservation Foundation (ACF), a big environmental organisation headquartered in Melbourne.

I thought it was a good idea. After all, he'd laboured successfully in one of the remotest and toughest spots imaginable, acting on behalf of Aboriginal people seeking land rights in the face of resistance from the Northern Territory administration and local graziers.

With the support of ACF president Hal Wootten, who had founded the University of New South Wales Faculty of Law and then become a judge, Phillip duly got the job and set about making the foundation a stronger force at a time when threats to the environment were breaking out across the country.

Now Wootten was due to retire and Phillip, along with vice-president Penny Figgis, was convinced the organisation needed to become more politically focused and extend its reach to younger Australians. In early 1989 he called me to see if I'd be interested in the position.

I figured I could work with Toyne. He was pragmatic, with a brooding manner and a sharp legal brain, but you got the feeling he'd have a go at anything if given half a chance. The ruling body of the ACF—the council—was split. The fundamentalist old guard baulked at the thought of appointing as their head someone from the world of entertainment who was younger than most of them. But eventually I got the nod and away we went. Here was something solid to get my teeth into at a time when it felt like the hourglass was running down.

The ACF had been founded in the 1960s, when the Bjelke-Petersen government in Queensland was pushing to allow oil drilling on the Great Barrier Reef. This was a bridge too far, even for some

Liberal Party supporters. The foundation was established with a bipartisan stance by, among others, the Liberal politician Malcolm Fraser, who would go on to become prime minister in the 1970s. Sir Garfield Barwick, a Liberal minister and, later, a controversial chief justice of the High Court, was chosen as president. He was followed by a procession of other luminaries, including H.C. 'Nugget' Coombs and the royal consort, Prince Philip.

Over time the organisation had grown in clout. The conservative founders had been replaced by environmentalists, many with strong campaigning backgrounds, and by the mid-1980s the ACF was on its way to becoming the nation's most respected national environmental organisation.

The 1972 decision by the Tasmanian Liberal government to flood Lake Pedder, an exquisite lake surrounded by glorious tall forests and with pristine white-sand beaches, had met with significant resistance, but the dam was still built.

Forest wars were breaking out across the country as the public became incensed by long-standing logging practices that were decimating swathes of native forests. Plans for massive real-estate development in the Daintree Rainforest in Far North Queensland also caught the Oils' attention. A new generation of activists was mobilising and the ACF was increasingly being called on to act as the public face of the environmental lobby.

In the international arena, there was a growing push to take the environment seriously. The 1987 report, *Our Common Future*, by the former prime minister of Norway, Gro Harlem Brundtland, argued the time was right for 'sustainable development', marrying the goals of continuing economic growth (to help relieve poverty) with more stringent measures to protect the global environment, now showing signs of permanent decline.

Up until this point, the ACF's modus operandi was one of measured deliberation, focused on lobbying governments and providing critiques of government policy. But now with more and more flash points around the environment forming, the foundation needed to modernise quickly, interact more closely with government and get directly involved with the issues of the day.

Elected by the foundation's members, the ACF council was a disparate collection of utopians, nature lovers, pragmatists, revolutionaries, dreamers and obsessives. It was the organisation's pinnacle policymaking body, whose work often set the standard for smaller environmental organisations. Sitting around the collection of trestle tables pushed together to accommodate the fifty or so councillors and staff who gathered when council met were prominent environmentalists of the day, including: Jack Mundey, who'd led the Green Bans in Sydney; Milo Dunphy, son of the esteemed New South Wales conservationist Miles Dunphy (father and son both indefatigable proponents of national parks); Queenslander Rosemary Hill, a key figure in the battle to save the Daintree Rainforest; and John Sinclair, who spearheaded the fight to save Fraser Island from sand mining. There were many others who were active in state or local community environmental issues, as well as future leaders of the minor parties: from South Australia there were the Democrats' John Coulter and Meg Lees, and future Greens party leader Christine Milne stopped over for a term.

The ACF relied on members' donations and small grants from government, so resources were always stretched, and resolving competing demands for limited funds, including from the membership, was a tough task—especially early on, when the council had few members with financial or marketing experience.

At times the ACF council could be a capricious and contradictory beast, and some issues, like population, were controversial and difficult to manage. As the new president, I was required to chair council meetings which had a track record of veering off topic and delivering peculiar decisions.

At one meeting, in the Hawthorn Town Hall, we arrived to find a handful of zero-population-growth activists gathered on the steps.

One, wearing a baby's bonnet, had folded himself inside a large cane shopping basket. They had come to urge councillors to support a limit to Australia's population. It wasn't easy to have a sensible debate with someone in a cane basket—did anyone say basket case?—and it didn't get any easier inside the meeting, with strident calls for the ACF to consider a policy that would have the effect of mandating the number of children a couple could have. Much like the Chinese government with their one-child policy, it would see Australia's population decline.

Meanwhile, other councillors, especially those with migrant backgrounds, took umbrage at the fortress Australia mentality that underlay the zero-population-growth arguments. A heated debate erupted and lasted all morning, by which time the meaning of life was being canvassed too, and the precious time set aside for other urgent matters had been frittered away.

Eventually a compromise of sorts, familiar to any student of politics—the agree-to-disagree option—was reached. The foundation would call on the major political parties to develop a population policy that took the environment into account, to encourage (hopefully) a mature national debate on the issue. Twenty years later, federal Labor produced such a document, but the distance between those who believe we should drastically reduce population levels, and others, especially business groups, who believe an even larger population is desirable, means we are still way off a sensible conversation about how many people should call Australia home.

Keeping the ACF ship afloat meant ensuring the organisation was solvent, and I felt it was financially irresponsible to approve a deficit budget simply because councillors kept insisting that their favourite campaign items be added, meaning a greater workload for staff but with fewer resources. Eventually I resorted to scheduling the budget as the first item for Sunday morning, confident that the furious socialising of a Saturday night in Melbourne—a rare experience for interstate greenies—would take its toll. As people straggled in, bleary-eyed and clutching cups of coffee, the budget was usually approved intact and without too much fuss.

Despite these quirks, much of the work of the council was of enormous value and, in many cases, well ahead of its time. The ACF played a prominent and constructive role in most of the major environmental issues of the period. Policy development in areas like biodiversity protection, public transport, managing World Heritage areas and national parks, sustainable use of native forests, and environmental tax reform set a template for the environment to be taken more seriously by governments and the broader community. In the case of climate change, a 1968 edition of the ACF monthly magazine, *Habitat*, laid out the consequences of increased greenhouse gas emissions and made suggestions, entirely relevant today, as to what needed to be done to address dangerous climate change.

If you wanted to learn and work with a highly motivated and experienced group of passionate environmentalists, the staff and council of the ACF were hard to beat.

···

While building our shed in Kangaroo Valley, I'd started taking the girls for day trips down to Jervis Bay, a beautiful, relatively unspoiled stretch of coast south of Sydney. The bay contained plenty of evidence of Aboriginal people's occupation, with many prehistoric rock shelters, shell middens and stone-flaking sites. The list of its environmental attributes was impressive: clean water of exceptionally high quality, healthy seagrass communities, and an abundance of fish, dolphins and penguins, as well as occasional humpback whales seeking shelter while migrating with their young. The foreshore of the bay and beyond supported mangroves and rainforest, heath and open forest, all important habitats for native species of birds and animals.

In the past, parts of Jervis Bay had been earmarked for industry, with plans for port expansion and, of all things—considering how far it was from Sydney and Melbourne—a chemicals plant. The southern side of the bay at Murrays Beach had even been chosen in the early 1970s as the best location for Australia's first large-scale nuclear reactor. While the nuclear plant didn't go ahead, a car park built for construction workers is still there to this day.

The northern peninsula was rimmed with a series of pure white-sand beaches separated by small rock platforms and outcrops. High cliffs bestrode the entrance to the bay, gazing imperiously down on the ocean. Because a section of the peninsula served as a weapons-firing range for the defence forces and was owned by the Commonwealth government, the whole area was relatively free of development. There is some irony in the fact that defence lands are often located in areas with high environmental qualities, and that these areas are therefore off limits to local and state governments, and developers. This was an important factor in the subsequent fight to save Jervis Bay, and a number of later campaigns I was involved with.

On the southern perimeter of the bay were several small hamlets, and on the ocean side an Aboriginal settlement called Wreck Bay. Here, the main threat to Jervis Bay's natural beauty was uncontrolled real-estate development through continuing land subdivisions, where adequate controls to protect significant native bushland and to stop run-off entering the bay's pristine waters were unlikely to be imposed by the local Shoalhaven Council. This body typically included a coven of redneck farmers, right-wing small-business types who saw any kind of development as a boon to the economy and, not surprisingly, real-estate agents who could stand to benefit from any decision the council might make to rezone land.

A more serious threat to the northern expanse of the bay had emerged with plans by the Department of Defence to locate an armaments depot, to store the navy's ammunition, in thick bushland on the peninsula to the south of the firing range. There were plans to construct a massive wharf at the preferred location, Cabbage Tree Point, with associated roads, concrete bays and warehouses in which to store the bombs and ammunition once they were taken off navy vessels when they returned from duty or were decommissioned.

Associated with the proposal to build this large weapons-storage facility was a longer-term plan for the entire naval fleet to be relocated from its headquarters in Sydney to Jervis Bay.

When a major threat to the environment looms, it is often local groups who respond first. These citizens are sometimes denigrated as NIMBYs (not in my backyard), but the fact is they are usually highly motivated to protect a place they know intimately and often play a key role in raising public awareness and building support for a campaign.

In 1981, the Jervis Bay Protection Committee had been formed. A small group comprising teachers, retirees and assorted nature enthusiasts, the committee had stoically countered the raft of proposals for Jervis Bay put up by successive governments—none of which appeared to take the outstanding natural values of the bay into account. But as is often the case, the local group lacked the resources of its larger and more powerful opponents. In this case, the defence department was an implacable and immoveable force, and it was committed to the move.

After visiting the area a couple of times, it had become clear to me that the only way this massive proposal could possibly be stopped in its tracks was to go national. This meant using the media to draw attention to the defence department's plans and encouraging national environmental organisations to lend their weight to the issue, to be followed by intense lobbying of key decision-makers, asking them to reconsider—a long shot in the circumstances.

I'd stayed in touch with a couple who were leading activists from the NDP period, Paul Gilding and Michelle Grosvenor. They'd been involved with the Sydney Peace Squadron, a gung-ho group who'd protested the presence of nuclear weapons on visiting American naval vessels by taking to Sydney Harbour in small boats and canoes, and on surfboards. Paul's background was very different to mine. He'd left school early and ended up living and working in Aboriginal communities in Queensland, spent some time as a union organiser

and then served in the air force. He was self-taught and had a determined, practical air about him—over time a good friendship grew
between us.

We set about establishing the National Save Jervis Bay Campaign,
with Paul, who was at a loose end, taking on the position of national
coordinator. Barrister Tim Robertson provided legal advice and,
with support from the Oils—who were happy to see their lead singer
usefully occupied—and operating out of our office in Glebe, we
were set to go. Inaugurated as a national coalition, the campaign
included the local Jervis Bay Protection Committee, the Wreck Bay
Aboriginal Council and other like-minded organisations who could
be persuaded to join.

As the new ACF president, I was keen for the foundation to get
more involved, but the first few council meetings had alerted me to
the problem of the ACF taking on too many issues. A strong case
would have to be made for involvement this late in the day. In the
end, though, the arguments for the bay's protection were unassailable,
and this, along with the local branch's history of involvement in the
issue, supported by ACF members in Canberra, saw the foundation
join up. But little could be provided in the way of resources, so along
with the Jervis Bay Protection Committee and a few volunteers, Paul
and I, for the most part, worked alone.

We were convinced the proposal was flawed and hadn't been thought
through properly. Scientific reports showed the risks that were likely
with a facility of this scale, especially the impact massive dredging
would have on the healthy seagrass beds that hugged the foreshore.

Covering a pristine stretch of the bay with concrete would also
change the character of the area substantially, and degrade what had
been a popular retreat for holidaymakers and local families.

As well, locating a huge arms depot, and then the fleet base, outside
Sydney placed a substantial logistical burden on the navy. If the move
went ahead, vessels would have to transit up and down the coast from
existing bases just to store their weapons, and then ensure they were

safely secured, and later move offices, personnel and myriad support services to an isolated location that, surprisingly, turned out to have only one access road.

I was confident that once these points could be put to someone at the top of the food chain, sanity might prevail and the proposal would be quashed. Reasoning that there might be senior officers who held reservations about the cost and inconvenience of having what amounted to another naval base built well away from Sydney, I sought an opportunity to put the case to the officer corps at HMAS *Penguin* at Mosman, a picturesque suburb situated on Sydney Harbour. After laying out the technical objections, I asked the officers if they would really be content to give up this fabulous location, twenty minutes from the centre of the city, close to good schools, hospitals and restaurants, to relocate three hours south to a place where the nearest town, Nowra, had a population of fewer than 20,000 people. From the polite chatter that ensued after I'd finished speaking, I guessed that some officers might be having second thoughts, although no one went so far as to express them.

Whatever misgivings were held by the admirals and commanders, however, there was no wavering by the defence department or the government. Everyone, it seemed, was resolved to push ahead.

I travelled to Canberra to meet Robert Ray, an influential leader from Labor's right faction who was soon to become defence minister. I got to know Ray a little better when I later entered parliament, and came to appreciate him as an astute tactician with solid Labor values. At the time of our first meeting, though, I must have appeared to be an anti-American, anti-nuclear activist, who had somehow been chosen to head the ACF and was now arriving at the eleventh hour to demand that the defence department abandon a decision that was the result of years of careful planning—a decision that he happened to support.

Ray heard me out, feet on desk, with barely concealed contempt. 'There's no way we're pulling out of Jervis Bay,' he grunted, then added, just in case I hadn't understood, 'Over my dead body will a bunch of greenies stop the Australian navy from doing what needs to be done.' With that, the meeting was over.

Paul and I mulled over our predicament. We needed an out-of-the-box manoeuvre to push Jervis Bay into as many faces as possible, to signal that we were prepared to dig in and fight. Up to this stage, the campaign had delivered reports and petitions, lobbied politicians, built strong community support, and now included most of the leading national and state-based conservation organisations. We'd ticked off most of the tasks that need to be done in a campaign of this kind, but there was still no sign of a change of heart or mind by anyone of consequence and time was running out. In the end, we concluded that the only course of action was to directly confront the Department of Defence.

When the firing range was due to be used it was closed to public access as fighter jets from the air force and navy screamed low over the peninsula doing target runs with dummy ammunition. On 5 June 1989—World Environment Day of all days—the range was scheduled to be used for joint exercises called Tasmanlink, and forces from New Zealand and the US were joining in, which would attract larger numbers of aircraft and personnel than usual.

The plan was simple. Under cover of darkness, just before the range was declared off limits to the public and the training exercise started, a group of activists would hide out on the bombing range. The whole enterprise would then have to be delayed, and the resulting publicity would launch Jervis Bay into the national media spotlight.

The action went off without a hitch as around a dozen people, including Diana Lindsay from the Oils office, snuck into the bush and dug in. Well camouflaged, wearing dark colours and covered with branches, they were all but invisible from the air.

At first light, an hour or so before the joint exercises were due to start, and with navy ships gathered outside the entrance to the bay and crews preparing aircraft for flight, Paul Gilding made his first phone calls: to the range commander to inform him there were a dozen human shields on the firing range, and then to national and local media in quick succession.

Astonishingly, despite having state-of-the-art equipment and plenty of army and navy personnel at their disposal, the authorities were unable to find anyone hidden on the range. The jets that flew overhead trying to spot the infiltrators appeared to be moving too fast for anyone to see clearly; either that or their fancy gear wasn't working properly. The ground searches, in which soldiers and sailors actually had to hike through the scrub, were half-hearted affairs.

Most of the activists remained out on the range for nearly a week; a few even snuck out at night for supplies and returned before daybreak. To our amazement, six days later the entire Tasmanlink exercise was cancelled.

The action made the nightly news bulletins for most of the week and we kept pressing hard on the back of this lift in media interest for the plan to be abandoned. Every day more and more people were questioning why such an unspoiled part of the state should be turned into a heavily industrialised military port.

We held public rallies, including one extraordinary gathering on the brilliant white sands of Cabbage Tree Beach (adjoining the wharf site), where protesters formed a human chain that spelled out 'Save Jervis Bay' for the television crews. As helicopters raked the beach, a pod of dolphins materialised right on cue to add some colour to the television coverage.

In the lead-up to the 1990 federal election, Jervis Bay was at last elevated as a priority environmental issue.

Finishing the last leg of a European winter tour at the end of 1989, I was caught in a fog of fatigue, constantly on the phone to Australia while everyone else slept.

I'd been joined by Doris and our girls for the last few shows in Paris—madcap, over-the-top affairs during which I struggled to talk to the typically excitable crowd in poor schoolboy French—and we decided to drive down to Spain to take a breather before coming home. There, hunkered down in a two-storey stuccoed house on the coast owned by the business arm of the Jesuits whom Doris's mum had worked for, we could see the coast of North Africa. It was the off-season, with a smattering of locals our only company.

I swam a couple of times in the chilly Mediterranean Sea, but it was singularly depressing. Above the waterline everything appeared normal, but below the surface it was a rubbish tip. I dived down with a snorkel to check out the sea floor and scout for fish but found nothing: just old bottles and cans, bits of plastic, rope and twine, broken buckets and assorted detritus that had fallen, or been chucked, off fishing boats. There wasn't a single living thing in sight.

I couldn't bear the thought of losing Jervis Bay: it was so healthy, just bursting with life in comparison. So I redoubled the calls to Australia, hassling Paul, Phillip Toyne, the office of environment minister Graham Richardson, journos who might be willing to cover the issue, anyone I could think of who might take an interest. It was frustrating to be so far away, and after my melancholy swims, I was intensely aware of how high the stakes were.

I finally heard back from Richardson early one morning when the rest of the house was still asleep. Despite our past interactions, we'd always had a professional relationship and he was undoubtedly an effective environment minister. He'd spoken to Hawke, he told me. Kim Beazley, the defence minister, had been rolled. Labor would go to the election with a promise not to move the Sydney naval fleet. For the time being, Jervis Bay was saved.

I felt a wave of relief breaking over me and slept soundly for days after.

A couple of weeks later, when we'd returned home, I travelled to Melbourne to join Bob Hawke as he opened the new ACF head-quarters located in an old factory in the grungy suburb of Fitzroy.

Hawke was in an upbeat mood when he arrived, which persisted, despite me leading him by mistake right into a large broom cupboard during a tour of the premises. The two of us stood shoulder to shoulder in the dark, with a few muffled voices calling 'PM?' from outside.

Inside the cupboard, I said, 'Sorry, Bob.'

'A-a-ah, no worries, Peter.'

Once out in daylight again, the prime minister announced that the government was 'no longer disposed' to move the navy to Jervis Bay. The cheering could be heard up and down the eastern seaboard.

In his speech, Hawke reflected that 'with greater information coming to light about the global threats posed by greenhouse gases and CFCs, concern for the environment has spread from the preserve of a relative few, seeking to protect a local river, beach or forest, to occupy the minds of people all around the world who would have never considered themselves to be greenies'.

As we were 'all greenies now'—an expression that would be used by John Howard when he became prime minister in 1996—Hawke went on to commit the government to working up policy on ecologically sustainable development (ESD) in partnership with the ACF and other environmental organisations, the forest, agricultural and mining industries, relevant ministers and the chief scientist.

This was a world first, with the environment being recognised as deserving a place at the table of high-level decision-making. The ESD process offered the first substantial opportunity for government, the conservation movement and industry to sketch out how Australia could continue to grow in a way that didn't run down our natural assets. Picking up on the *Our Common Future* report, which aimed to square the circle on economic growth and a healthy environment, the participants eventually delivered a suite of recommendations for government that reset policy in ways less harmful to natural ecosystems. Finding areas of agreement proved a difficult and time-consuming exercise, but it was a good start and provided a platform for change.

Along with the leaders of most of the groups participating, I travelled to a roundtable meeting with the new prime minister, Paul Keating, in Parliament House, to press the case. Once the reports were made public, the prime minister and cabinet and other government departments had run a mile. Those recommendations that hadn't already been neutered were simply ignored, and it became apparent that Keating had little appetite for this kind of reform. He'd been dismayed by Bob Hawke's unilateral decision, when Hawke was still prime minister, to reject the siting of a mine at Coronation Hill in Kakadu National Park, despite the majority of the cabinet being in favour. Phillip Toyne and I had pushed hard, and the ACF's entreaties, along with those of the traditional owners, helped scupper the project. This was a bridge too far for Keating, who was then treasurer, and for a number of other senior ministers. It was the first and only occasion on which Hawke directly overruled the cabinet, and it was the beginning of the end of his highly successful leadership.

Ironically, the Coronation Hill decision was characterised as a win for conservationists. The blowback from the business community was intense, and was used by Finance Minister Peter Walsh and others to rebuff what they saw as the insidious influence environmentalists had over the government. The narrative was taken up by a gullible press gallery; Labor was now in thrall to the 'greenies'. Yet the Coronation Hill decision was primarily about Aboriginal interests; the destruction of specific sacred sites of the Jawoyn people was considered sufficient reason to knock back the proposal, notwithstanding the environmental significance of the Kakadu area.

The relationship between the ACF and Labor had been a constructive one. It was built on a reasonable degree of mutual trust that had built up over time. This didn't prevent the ACF advocating for policy change without fear or favour, nor did the government readily acquiesce to the ACF's demands. And there were many areas in which it was difficult, if not impossible, to make ground. But at the least the door was always open, and in politics getting a foot in the door is often the hardest task.

In the background was the decision by national conservation organisations, including the ACF, to direct their members to consider preferencing Labor in the 1990 federal election—a decision that helped return the party to government. In the 1987 election, the ACF council voted specifically to endorse Labor in the House of Representatives, despite Toyne and president Hal Wootten disagreeing with the tactic. In the following years, my advice would echo theirs. It made sense to point out the strengths and weaknesses of all the parties, but endorsement of one was self-defeating. It jeopardised the capacity of the ACF and the conservation movement to work with the government of the day, irrespective of its political persuasion.

Rather than affirming the importance of environment issues to voters, the 1990 result, along with the Coronation Hill decision, seemed to convince Keating of the need to create distance between green groups and Labor to reassure big business that the party wasn't beholden to environmentalists. It's been mainly uphill ever since. The need to protect the natural environment—including national parks, when conservative governments hold sway—never goes away. Serious environmental reform always demands national leadership.

In the case of Jervis Bay, a skirmish had been won, but there would be plenty of battles ahead. And even for this jewel of the South Coast, managing the demand for housing, maintaining the marine reserves and limiting sewage run-off so as to protect the integrity of the bay are live issues to this day.

Since that time I've tried to get down to Cabbage Tree Point at least once a year to spend a couple of hours wandering along the beach, snorkelling over the wavy seagrass, watching the stingrays and schools of fish grazing in brilliant clear water. Boats anchor off the beach and families traipse down onto the blinding white sand, as seabirds soar over the bay. It's a way for me to recharge the batteries, to take a moment to reflect, and to toast all those—especially the brave handful that occupied the firing range—who made this victory possible.

17

ONE PLACE LEFT IN THE WORLD

THE BREAKOUT OF the environment as a critical issue had rounded off the 1980s. There was a lot going on and inevitably my focus, as ACF president, skewed from music to the raft of issues I needed to get my head around. With a dramatic rise in public awareness of the environment, we'd reached a stage where real progress could be made.

The preservation of the Antarctic—the last and only great wilderness—stands out because of its international significance. Locally, increasing attention was being paid to the fate of Australia's native forests, whether in Tasmania, in Gippsland, Victoria, in the southeast of New South Wales or on Fraser Island in Queensland. The state of our eroded, salty soils and stressed river systems, especially in times of drought, was crying out for action, as was air pollution and the increase in greenhouse gases in the atmosphere—the biggie. We needed to address the growing mountains of waste that were clogging up our cities and to ensure that World Heritage areas like the Great Barrier Reef stayed in good shape—and there was plenty more.

The developing relationship between the federal Labor government and conservation groups, particularly the ACF, had been aided by this increasing public concern and the environment started to rate highly as an electoral issue. A number of other highly motivated professionals, some with activist backgrounds, started to take up key positions in government. Simon Balderstone, a former *Age* journalist who worked briefly for the ACF before joining Graham Richardson's staff when

Richardson became environment minister (Balderstone later served as an adviser to Hawke and Keating—some kind of record), had a solid grasp of green issues and worked well with Phillip Toyne. As did Penny Figgis, the ACF's first national liaison officer, who brought a strategic sensibility to lobbying, an increasingly important tool in the campaigner's toolbox, especially in the nation's capital.

Along with Balderstone, Gregg Borschmann and Janet Willis served on Richardson's staff. Michael Rae from the Wilderness Society spent a lot of time in Canberra in this period. Judy Lambert, also from the Wilderness Society, and up-and-coming bureaucrats Warren Nicholls and Tony Fleming all worked for Ros Kelly when she succeeded Richardson. Sue Salmon, a former ACF national liaison officer, with Fleming and Peter Hitchcock, an outstanding advocate who'd worked in academia, advised John Faulkner when he subsequently took the role.

The influence that green preferences had on the 1990 election was real. But it is the record of what was achieved at the time that is most striking: the Franklin Dam decision, which saved the Franklin and Gordon river valleys; protecting the Queensland Wet Tropics; extending Kakadu National Park; protecting native forests in south-west Tasmania and south-east New South Wales; preserving Shelburne Bay in Cape York; establishing Landcare; safeguarding Jervis Bay. This high-water mark of Australian conservation—saving special places for generations to come—hasn't been equalled since.

I had a bird's-eye view of the Antarctic campaign: a many-layered tale, which started with Australia, following the age of Antarctic exploration typified by the stoic endurance of explorers like Douglas Mawson, claiming 42 per cent of the continent—some 6 million square kilometres—as Australian territory. Of course we were not alone there. Other countries had asserted sovereignty, including the UK, France and Argentina, and there were nations that disputed these claims and subsequently sought involvement in Antarctica, like Malaysia and India and, later, China.

The Antarctic Treaty, strongly supported by Australia, envisaged the pristine, white continent as being used for strictly peaceful purposes for all of humanity. When pressure was brought to bear by a number of countries, among them the US, for a minerals convention to be signed to allow access to the huge resources potential of the Antarctic, and with even the Department of Foreign Affairs in favour, this was seen by many to be undermining the treaty and was strongly resisted by conservation organisations, including Greenpeace and the ACF.

A handful of campaigners, among them Lyn Goldsworthy and Jim Barnes, formed the Antarctic and Southern Ocean Coalition to raise awareness of the threats to the Antarctic. They were so few in number it is said they had their first meetings squeezed around a kitchen table. Their efforts paid off as the issue gained more prominence, helped by the famous French oceanographer Jacques Cousteau, who was pressuring his government not to agree to a minerals convention at the same time as Bob Hawke was being lobbied in Australia.

Success, as the saying goes, has many fathers. Hawke deserves credit for persuading President François Mitterrand and the French government, led by Prime Minister Michel Rocard, to join with Australia and refuse to sign up to the convention. If one of the founding signatories to the Antarctic Treaty opted out of the convention, this meant that it was dead in the water. The federal Coalition in Australia had signalled that it, too, was opposed to the planned convention.

Yet it is unlikely Hawke would have been so emboldened had it not been for the efforts of the early movers who got the campaign off the ground. From the Antarctic and Southern Ocean Coalition to the Greenpeace activists, who at one stage set up a base camp in the Antarctic, to the persistent ACF staff, who relentlessly badgered the bureaucrats who sat in the negotiation process, everyone played a part. In the final stages, Phillip Toyne's role was crucial. At a key juncture, when it seemed that Australia was retreating and Hawke was convinced he couldn't get a decision across the line, Toyne pulled a rabbit out of the hat. With the assistance of Hawke's environment adviser, Craig Emerson, who later served in the Gillard cabinet, he managed to get in to see the prime minister and show him a short film (excerpts from a *Four Corners* episode), narrated by ABC science broadcaster Robyn Williams, which illustrated Antarctica's phenomenal beauty. The pictures were worth 10,000 words and more.

Around the same time, Hawke and his wife Hazel had invited our family over to Kirribilli House—the prime minister's Sydney residence—for lunch. It was a rare opportunity to get in the prime minister's ear at a critical time and turned out to be a visit we would never forget—for reasons that had nothing to do with politics.

We'd dressed smart casual for the occasion and were greeted at the door by Hawke himself, in shorts, bare feet and a sports shirt—only in Australia.

It was a glorious Saturday afternoon with the harbour at its shimmering best, but Hawke, a keen punter, was constantly checking the racing guide as I tried to steer the conversation to the environment. I'd brought a boom box with me and insisted on playing 'Antarctica', an Oils track that had been worked up late and ended the *Blue Sky Mining* album. It was a haunting, softer piece, featuring the refrain 'There must be one place left in the world'. Get it, Bob? I don't claim the song made any difference to the eventual decision, but it was certainly a full-court press.

Along with a few members of the prime minister's family, we went across to the swimming pool at Admiralty House, next door, to continue the discussions. A lilo was floating in the pool and while everyone was chatting, May, aged two and a half, toppled in without anyone noticing, and was floating underneath the lilo out of sight. It must have happened in seconds; we later speculated that she may have tried to step on it and fallen in.

There was a sudden shout as Hawke's son-in-law, Matt Dillon, who'd spied Maysie sinking, leapt fully clothed into the pool and fished her out. We held our bedraggled bundle of joy upside down as water poured out of her nose and mouth. Mercifully, she was breathing again in seconds. It was a heart-stopping moment, and recalling it still gives me the shakes. Doris and I are eternally grateful for Matt's quick action, and whenever I've found myself around a swimming pool with kids since then I can't relax.

There was a happy outcome for the Antarctic, too. Hawke, along with Rocard, held the line, and with Australia and France in lockstep for the time being at least, the frozen continent, like the northern reaches of Jervis Bay, was safe.

The resulting agreement, called the Madrid Protocol, commits nations to ensure the environmental protection of the continent. This is consistent with the original vision, very much driven by Australia, that the Antarctic remain a natural reserve devoted to peace and science. The Antarctic occupies a unique place in global ecosystems. It is the canary in the coalmine in relation to atmospheric changes, where the evidence of increased levels of carbon dioxide, as well as radioactive decay from nuclear testing, can be detected and measured. As global sea temperatures increase, the disintegration of West Antarctica glaciers makes the rise of the sea level inevitable. The only question is, by how much?

Unfortunately, there has been increasing activity by nations that do not necessarily share the goals of the Antarctic Treaty, nor respect the territorial claims of Australia. A number of countries, notably India and China, have increased their Antarctic programs—in China's case, erecting a number of research stations, as well as a weather station that sits on the highest peak in Antarctica, located within the Australian Antarctic Territory. This creeping utilisation of a resource that Australia, along with other claimant countries, holds in trust for the rest of the world carries the possibility of the base being used not only for research—the single legitimate purpose under existing Antarctic Treaty law—but also for communications which, in the future, may have a military purpose.

The pronounced role of the Chinese is an issue I took exception to as a government minister, as the record should show in twenty years, when the cabinet papers are released. I remain convinced China is playing a double game: paying lip service to the treaty, but working to maximise its access to the Antarctic's minerals. Recent talks aimed at creating marine protected areas were not supported by Russia or China, and Ukraine has openly canvassed the minerals promise that the Antarctic holds.

The arrival of new entrants onto the Antarctic stage has coincided with Australia in some instances playing down its involvement, and an overall levelling out of research activities. It is imperative that we commit sufficient resources and increased diplomatic effort to make sure the founding principles of the Antarctic Treaty System and Australia's early and sovereign interests are preserved.

...

The backstory to the rush of environment issues onto the national political stage lies partly in the collision between unfettered economic growth and nature, and partly in the collisions of cultures—European and Indigenous—that played out as the white settlers adapted to the physical character of Australia.

Unbeknown to the settlers, the park-like appearance of much of eastern Australia that featured in many early colonial paintings was the result of active large-scale landscape management by Aboriginal people, who lived directly off the land, carefully modifying the vegetation mix with the judicious use of fire. European Australians were slow to awaken to the reality that Terra Australis was far removed from their mother country not only in distance, but in every other way imaginable.

Not only is it hotter than hell at times, but the local trees breathe fire and most don't appear to produce any edible fruit. The rivers run all over the place, sometimes in flood, more often dry. In many places the soil is thin and, with much tree cover removed, easily blown away.

Rocky escarpments, arid plains and vast deserts make up much of the continent, and regular droughts continue to take their toll—and there will be monster dries ahead. Notwithstanding that, eco-ignorant politicians still talk about drought-proofing the country.

In their desire to harvest the riches that this new continent offered—gold, wool and wheat, and numerous minerals—the newcomers to the country set about taming the bush in order to grow crops and graze livestock but ended up trashing the land. I'd seen some of this degradation from the road and the air as Midnight Oil sped from city to city. Close up, the facts were depressing: a big decline in native species, the disappearance of wetlands, spreading dryland salinity—all evidence that the early path chosen was often the wrong one.

Living near the coast, and buffered from the harshness of the inland climate, many people had only a limited idea of the scale of problems faced on the other side of the Great Dividing Range, and benumbed farmers pressed on. It was only due to repeated ringing of the alarm bell by scientists, environmentalists and occasionally individual farmers that the rural community and political parties started to take seriously the parlous condition of many agricultural landscapes.

For an organisation like the ACF, aware of the havoc that farming practices like intensive land clearing had caused to the habitat of native plants and animals, a positive relationship with the rural sector was desirable, and fortunately, the stars were coming into alignment. Like the ACF with Phillip Toyne, the peak farmers' organisation, the National Farmers' Federation (NFF), had appointed a new executive director, Rick Farley. Farley had grown up in northern New South Wales and had been a hippie in his youth; importantly, he was open to breaking old paradigms. The two young directors hit it off and managed to persuade their organisations to work in the face of mounting evidence that across the country things were crook.

This alliance meant ignoring the city–country divide. I'd spent some time on rural properties while still at school and felt at ease with people who made their living on the land. In our first tentative meeting, NFF president Graham Blight and I found plenty to talk about. Later I was able to develop constructive relationships with Ian Donges, a rangy wheat and sheep farmer, when he was elected president, and then Peter Corish, a cotton grower from New South Wales, throughout the 1990s decade of Landcare.

This national decade of Landcare was a partnership between farmers and conservationists, the first time such a union had been forged in Australia, if not the world. After intense negotiations, the NFF and the ACF agreed on steps to repair the waterways and landscapes by seeking significant government investment, based on best-practice principles, to achieve a healthier environment and ensure the future of agriculture. Allied with increasing support from government came a more developed ethic of caring for the land, utilising not only the government's resources but also volunteers as local Landcare groups were established.

Previously, the two groups had had an antagonistic relationship, and the likelihood of either securing big sums to fix degraded lands, let alone agree on the priorities, was slim. Now, standing together, it was win-win: with the farmers' close links to the Coalition and the environmentalists' links to Labor, the bipartisan push was impossible for governments to resist.

As is often the case, setting aside existing preconceptions was the biggest barrier to change; the main obstacles were not political or financial, but cultural. Farley and his president needed to bring a very conservative organisation to the table, many of whose members had contempt for 'city slickers' and saw environmentalists as the enemy.

Correspondingly, Phillip and I had to persuade the ACF's council to agree to a partnership with a sector of society that was partly responsible for the very problems ACF had been arguing for years needed fixing. Getting senior government figures and the media on side proved easy; getting the council to agree to the new partnership less so. But following numerous meetings, discussions and phone calls, agreement was reached inside the organisation and the program was launched with great fanfare by the Hawke government in 1989.

There was always a sizeable rump in the farming community that was resistant to change. While they were willing to accept additional investment on their farms, self-interest ruled as many farmers opposed measures that restricted them in any way, such as caveats against the clearing of native bush from their properties. This remains a sore point today when conservative state governments relax existing native-vegetation controls, despite the weight of scientific evidence showing that such measures are necessary to slow the decline in our biodiversity, the full suite of plant and animal species.

The large-scale problems that the Landcare program sought to address required big money. At one stage, the estimate ran to nearly $4 billion at a time when the health budget was $24 billion and defence about $18 billion. Protection of river frontages, plantations for salinity management, fencing for remnant vegetation, environmental flows for stressed rivers—all these measures come at a cost. But while repairing damaged natural ecosystems costs money, doing nothing comes at a greater cost, one that increases over time. At some point we needed to start investing in the environmental health of the country, and Landcare, with its well-articulated plan of repair and recovery, was the down payment.

Landcare was mainly confined to the south-east and south-west of the country, where landscape change had been greatest and the problems were most acute. It wasn't so long ago that farmers had been paid to chop down trees to clear their properties, so it shouldn't be a surprise that around 40 per cent of our forest cover has gone. When John Oxley explored the inland rivers of New South Wales in the early days of colonisation, flocks of waterbirds blocked the sun, and lagoons abounded with fish and fowl. Now, nearly every waterway in south-eastern Australia is in poor health.

Yet across the north, from Cape York to the Kimberley, rivers run free, there is plenty of clean water, and there are big stretches of country still in good shape. On my increasingly frequent visits to the Top End, I was struck that here was an opportunity to do things differently. I wasn't alone in thinking this way. European populations were sparse and while there was never any shortage of plans to develop the region—a constant stream of ideas was trotted out with increasing frequency by governments of all persuasions—surely, by working closely with local communities, who knew the land intimately, the mistakes of the past, so evident further south, could be avoided. It was exciting to think that we didn't always have to follow the same script, that previously untried ideas and outcomes were possible in this extraordinary part of Australia. This was a project that could really set the pulse racing, and one to which I would try to devote more time as the months and years unfolded.

...

The ingrained habits from old Europe were in clear view at Sydney Cove, the site of first occupation, where the direction was set early.

Chosen on account of its sheltered anchorage and supplies of fresh water, the site hosted the colony's first dwellings clustered along the little Tank Stream that flowed into the harbour at Sydney Cove, now Circular Quay. In no time it became an open sewer as soldiers and convicts alike threw their rubbish, and shat, into the stream.

So rapid was the Tank Stream's demise, that despite successive governors issuing laws to punish the polluters, it became a major source of illness in the fledgling settlement. Finally, in the 1830s, Governor Macquarie prohibited its use and instructed that water be sourced from the nearby lakes and Botany Bay swamps. The stream of precious water that flowed falteringly down to the 'finest harbour in the world', as British officers proudly asserted, had lasted less than fifty years.

Fast-forward 150 years and, with 12 million people living on or near the Australian coast, history was repeating itself on an industrial scale. Now, huge pipes carrying untreated sewage were pumping the muck straight into the ocean. It was lazy engineering and negligent in its failure to take account of the impact on the health of the marine environment.

I was one of thousands angered and puzzled that I had to swim through turds and rubbish at our much-loved beaches, especially if I'd ducked down to Manly on a day when the wind was blowing onshore. Even the apolitical surfing community decided they'd had enough, and the rumble of discontent quickly built to turn back the tide.

So began the marches and concerts organised by People Opposed to Ocean Outfalls (naturally enough called POOO), joined by local environment groups and a new organisation, the Surfrider Foundation Australia, supported by a few of the big names in surfing at the time like Mark Richards, Wayne 'Rabbit' Bartholomew and Nat Young.

I'd first come across Nat when I inadvertently dropped in on a wave he was carving up when I was bodysurfing at North Narrabeen. He was a former world champion with the nickname Animal, and didn't take too kindly to this breach of surfing protocol, particularly from a lowest-of-the-low body basher. Despite a few heated words, with neither of us giving much ground, we became friends.

Nat Young wanted to give the surfing community a louder public voice, and get the beaches cleaned up in the process, and soon after our collision he decided to run as an independent for the northern beaches seat of Pittwater in the New South Wales parliament. Along with a handful of local activists, and a few of his friends, I joined in to help get this last-minute tilt at political office underway. Nat ran a boisterous campaign attacking all and sundry and making a splash with scandalous posters featuring the outrageous cartoon figure Captain Goodvibes, riding a giant wave through canyons of office blocks and smoking an oversized joint. In spite of the salvoes he polled well, but still ended up missing out, probably a good thing for him and the electors of the northern beaches. Nat was a restless spirit,

Blackfella/Whitefella tour, Northern Territory, 1986. RAY KENNEDY/*THE AGE*

With Gary Morris on the Blackfella/Whitefella tour. RAY KENNEDY/*THE AGE*

Leaving the church on our wedding day, Manly, 1985.

At Palm Beach, Sydney, with our firstborn, Emily, 1986.

Just warming up on the Blackfella/Whitefella tour, 1986. RAY KENNEDY/*THE AGE*

Doris and I at the 'other' Australia Day rally, Hyde Park, Sydney, 1988. PETER POYNTON

Diesel and Dust. KEN DUNCAN

US *Diesel and Dust* tour, 1988, featuring Rob's corrugated iron tank as an extra drum.

SUSAN ALZNER

Filming 'Blue Sky Mine', Kalgoorlie, 1990, with the fire brigade lending a hand.

KEN DUNCAN

With Prime Minister Bob Hawke
at the opening of the new ACF
headquarters, Melbourne, 1989.
MICHAEL POTTER/NEWSPIX

Protest gig outside the Exxon Oil
building, Sixth Avenue, New York,
1990. CHUCK PULIN

Blue Sky Mining. KEN DUNCAN

Filming 'Forgotten Years', Verdun, France, mid-winter, 1990. YOURI LENQUETTE

Band and crew pulling over to look at snow, some of us for the first time, Canada, early 90s.

A Glen Preece painting to
commemorate the successful
campaign halting a dam on the
Fitzroy River, near Broome,
Western Australia, 1999.
GLEN PREECE

Doris and I backstage with Sting
after one of his rainforest concerts,
Sydney, early 1990s.

Greenpeace launch of *NRG*, a solar-powered recording (various artists), Los Angeles, 1994. ANDREAS SMETANA/GREENPEACE

Preparing the ground for a new reserve at Broadmeadows, Victoria, 1991. JAMIE DAVIES/NEWSPIX

Stills from *Shoalwater: Up For Grabs*, a film by David Bradbury, Shoalwater Bay, 1992.
PETER SOLNESS

On the shoot for the Australian version of the 'Truganini' film clip, 1993. JOHN VELLA

Performing at the Clayoquot Sound protest site, Vancouver Island, Canada, 1993.
MIDNIGHT OIL ARCHIVE

'In the Valley' film clip, Broome, 1993. JOHN VELLA

A 1993 promo shot for *Earth and Sun and Moon*. ANDRZEJ LIGUZ

inclined to speak his mind regardless of the consequences. I couldn't
see him sitting still for too long, which is de rigueur in state politics.

Rabbit was another former surfing champion with ample energy
who helped organise competitions for the group Surfers Against
Nuclear Destruction (SAND). A grassroots initiative by Gold Coast
surfers, with local solicitor Denis Callinan driving it along, SAND
ran competitions through the 1980s and got the word on nuclear
issues out to a new generation of surfers.

The Surfrider Foundation Australia was established around this
time with a specific focus on the health of the coastal environment and
threats to local surfing spots. I spent some time with Surfrider early
on. The interesting question was whether the huge constituency of
surfers and beachgoers around Australia could be mobilised. Given the
right information and some encouragement, this group could become
a formidable political force. But in the main, surfers, especially the
younger brigade, are a hedonistic, anarchic bunch and their potency
as a pressure group has never been fully realised. Just like the volunteers who always show up for community fundraising work, those who
labour in the Surfrider Foundation are few in number but big of heart.

The task of stopping the idiocy of pouring raw sewage onto the
beaches meant taking on the various water boards and local councils,
where authorities were wedded to an engineering solution for treating
waste and struggled to get their heads around reuse and recycling. The
public campaign came to a head on Good Friday, 1989. A quarter of
a million people marched down to Bondi Beach to support POOO.
Midnight Oil played on a rudimentary stage at one end of the beach,
along with Dragon, Noiseworks, Rose Tattoo and a bunch of others.
I could see across to the gentle waves of one of Australia's most notable
tourist attractions as we sang our hearts out. There wasn't a place like
it anywhere else in the world that I knew of: a panorama so fetching,
yet so close to millions of city dwellers.

The concert marked a turning point of sorts as governments
promised to deliver cleaner beaches. But undoing a hundred years of

engineering and short-term thinking will take time. Heavy metals still end up in the ocean off our cities and after a big downpour Sydney's beaches can be unsafe for swimmers for days. Still, the upsurge of community sentiment that peaked on that day saw partial progress, as secondary treatments became the norm and rubbish traps were installed at the ends of the giant stormwater drains that emptied straight into the sea up and down the coast. The water utilities and governments were on notice that the habits of the Tank Stream era were over.

Ultimately, a bigger transformation in the way we treat water will be needed. We know hotter days and tougher droughts will hit the continent hard, so water use in our cities and suburbs needs to be properly priced. And instead of losing millions of gallons through the deep ocean outfalls, built to reduce the pollution levels on our beaches, more of that water should be captured and recycled for the future when it will be more precious than ever before.

18
BROOME TIME

THE TUG OF war between the Oils' overseas career demands and the siren calls of home had been temporarily settled when the band decided to take 1991 off (prompting the industry to ask: 'Are you trying to shoot yourselves in the foot again?').

The answer to that question was no. We were merely applying some self-preservation thinking to the career. We'd gone out to give the seventh album, *Blue Sky Mining*, a decent shot, and it did well, surpassing *Diesel and Dust* in the end, but we were longing for family and familiar neighbourhoods, and jumping off the conveyor belt was one sure way of getting home.

The title track, concerning the effects of exposure to asbestos dust, and the fact that the companies mining and manufacturing the material knew it could kill people, had been one of the last tracks to go down. Based on a demo called 'Dust' that Jim had brought in, it got the marriage of music and lyric right.

Up to that time there was a lot of strong material already recorded, but much of it was evenly paced, with careful vocal harmonies and layered keyboard parts that didn't set me on fire. At one point, coming in to see how the sessions were faring, I amped up, convinced we needed something that sparked, and so work started on a more up-tempo tune.

I'd sit downstairs in my study trying to stitch the verse, playing it over and over again on the same old crappy mono cassette player I'd always carried around with me, while fending off requests for ACF to jump into new hot spots. This was typical and unexceptional; the juggle between music and politics was a fact of life for me. But if we were going to actually experience our kids growing up and share at least some of the joys and tribulations that went with it, we simply had to stop at home for a while.

Part of the success of both albums was due to the series of film clips that accompanied the singles and found their way on to the screen at a time when music on television, in particular the MTV channel, was a dominant marketing force in the US and Europe.

The clips for 'Beds Are Burning', directed by Andrew De Groot, and 'The Dead Heart', directed by Ray Argall, featuring us interacting with Aboriginal people in outback scenes enhanced by the great Australian light, were different from anything else that was showing at the time. They were expertly made, and we were lucky to have the services of a group of highly creative and committed local filmmakers, including directors like Argall, John Whitteron, Paul Elliot, Tony Stephens, and Claudia Castle, who filmed 'Blue Sky Mine'.

Shooting the 'Blue Sky Mine' film clip in Kalgoorlie saw half the town turn up to dance in the main street as the fire brigade showered us with water on a day that was so hot the runway at the airport had started melting.

But it wasn't a case of relying only on exotic Aussie locations. Claudia Castle, with her sister Jane on camera, also directed Rob's anthemic plea, 'Forgotten Years', which sits with Eric Bogle's 'And the Band Played Waltzing Matilda' and John Schumann's 'I Was Only Nineteen' (recorded with Schumann's band, Redgum), as one of the great anti-war songs of our generation. We filmed it in the middle of winter in a sea of white crosses at the huge war cemetery in Verdun, France. The images embellish the message and cleave to the music, adding another dimension to the song, which is what you hope for in a clip.

···

Towards the end of 1991, I visited Broome for what was advertised as an informal bush meeting. It had become increasingly evident that while continuing to campaign on issues the membership deemed important, like native forest protection, the ACF had to build its capacity and develop stronger relationships in the remote north. As it turned out, much of the foundation's involvement in these distant areas would be initiated during my second stint as president, in the late 1990s. It was then that we launched the Northern Project specifically to address environmental issues across the top of Australia.

The purpose of this early bush meeting—which included representatives from the Yawuru Aboriginal Corporation and the Kimberley Conservation Group—was to sit with local Aboriginal people to follow up on a resolution that had been passed by the General Assembly of the World Conservation Union—the UN equivalent of an international environmental organisation—recognising the 'relationship between living Aboriginal culture and the Kimberley landscape'. The resolution had been sought by long-time Wilderness Society campaigner Peter Robertson, and detailed the ecological importance of the region and the lack of participation by Aboriginal groups in decision-making about land use. It identified the need for conservation reserves and protected areas, and renewed involvement of Aboriginal people in active management of their country.

As a rough rule of thumb, the further away from the axis of political power and the concentrations of population in the south-east you travelled, the more opportunity you had to adopt sound conservation practices and keep country in good condition. But it wasn't just the notion of a fresh start that drew me to the Kimberley, even though I had a strong attraction to remote and unspoiled places. Even though my western eyes couldn't easily see the many layers of history that had impregnated the land, I knew people had been here for a very long time. Here you could breathe deeply, dream and sense the possibilities. Maybe the future wasn't bound to follow the brick-and-tile

pattern, the beaten-field past. Maybe there could be practical reconciliation in the real sense of that term. People might get moving
with a new vision. In Broome, the landscape wasn't drained—it was
still singing.

Here is what I saw for the first time: massed gorges and mountain
ranges, wide savanna grassland plains, a profusion of plant life,
including the distinctive boab tree (that featured so heavily in Baz
Luhrmann's film, *Australia*), and a coastline of exquisite beauty. After
the wet season, huge waterfalls cascaded into the gorges, sending
great pulses of water rushing into hundreds of creeks winding down
through stone and sandhill country. The mighty Fitzroy, the main
river that flows north-east to west, would rise by up to ten metres,
spewing billions of litres every hour from its mouth into the sea near
Derby. Immense volumes of this precious liquid would spill into
wetlands and billabongs pulsing with birdlife, native fish, freshwa-
ter crocs and yabbies, replenishing the aquifers below ground that
continue to seep ever so slowly, resurfacing as mound springs that
extend to the drier desert country further away from the coast.

In the past Europeans had travelled north from Perth, bringing
cattle to the Kimberley. However, the extremes of weather and the
vast distances made it difficult to establish viable enterprises. And
there was resistance to the early European forays by Aboriginal clans
living in the region. One notable figure was the Aboriginal warrior
Jandamarra, who fought a valiant three-year guerrilla campaign
against the European incursion. On the coast, the saltwater people—
referenced in the song 'Saltwater Cowboy' by notable Broome
identities the Pigram Brothers—lived peacefully, enjoying plentiful
resources with which to feed their families.

The town of Broome itself, with two long beaches splayed out to
the north and south, a collection of turn-of-the-century cottages, a
tiny Chinatown and the Kimberley region at its back door, set my
imagination alight. A long way from anywhere and cut off in the
wet, its isolation could send you mad, but Broomites were creative

to the core and the town had a well-developed cultural scene. There were great musicians, including Jimmy Chi, the songwriter who'd written the musical *Bran Nue Day*, and Scrap Metal (who, as the Pigram Brothers, would later feature in the film clip for the Oils track 'In the Valley' from *Earth and Sun and Moon*). Magabala Books, a local publishing house, promotes local writers and illustrators, and Kimberley painters such as Rover Thomas and Jimmy Pike were conjuring works of great power and beauty, rendering their stories and country on canvas to great acclaim.

Broome seemed more tolerant than most isolated places I'd visited, due to intermarriage between local Aboriginal people and the Malaysians, Chinese, Timorese and Japanese who'd come in the early 1900s to work as indentured labour in the burgeoning pearl industry. That Broome was also awash with itinerant people—some from the desert, some from the coast—was a reminder of how recently a way of life common across Australia had been uprooted. Forced removal of Aboriginal children from their parents led to terrible misery for many in the local community, compounded by the many grog camps that had sprung up in the area, and, tragically, youth suicide was approaching epidemic levels.

There were so many ifs: if the Kimberley clans and local leaders could assert their authority and chart their own course; if the cultural and natural inheritance of the region was protected; if young people gained a full education, thus increasing their chances of work . . . If these aspirations could be brought to fruition, then Broome's future as a vibrant fishing and pearling centre, and increasingly a must-see destination for tourists, was gold-plated.

Like much of Western Australia, parts of the region were also rich in mineral deposits. Judiciously exploiting these resources, and providing long-term benefits to the local people without spoiling the Kimberley's intrinsic beauty, would require great care. For this to happen, active participation in decision-making by the Aboriginal community and the locals of Broome—often one and the same—would be necessary. Dictating policy and exercising control from Perth and Canberra wasn't going to serve the region well, a fact that had long been communicated to both sides of politics by prominent Aboriginal leaders like Patrick Dodson and Peter Yu.

I have a map given to me by Paddy Roe, the custodian of the Goolarabooloo clan, who I met on my first trip to the region. It shows the dreaming path that bisects Cape Leveque, north of Broome. I kept this map as evidence of the long-standing ties people have to their land, and as an important reminder that any exploitation of the area can only happen with the full cooperation and consent of traditional owners. In the event, it wasn't until 2010, following a long hiatus, that a land-use agreement between government and the local clan group, the Yawuru, was finally concluded, providing a role for the Yawuru in future development and setting aside areas for conservation and residential use.

I would return to Broome and the Kimberley many times after that first bush meeting. A year later, the Oils appeared at the open-air Stompin' Ground concert with our old mates the Warumpi Band and Scrap Metal, who'd previously toured with us on a few legs back east. And that bush meeting proved to be a precursor to the campaign that sprang up twenty years later to oppose the siting of a gas hub at James Price Point on Cape Leveque, just north of Broome, a project vigorously pushed by the Western Australian premier Colin Barnett and one that split the harmonious town in two. In one of the many instances of synchronicity that I experienced while environment minister for a time, I ended up with carriage over the approvals process for the siting of the plant.

The trip that had the greatest impact, though, was the one I took with my three daughters in July of 1991. Mindful that high school wasn't far off for Em and May, and with Doris back at university studying to become a psychotherapist, I took the girls out of school, packed my swag, a small tent and some basic supplies into a four-wheel drive, and set out to see the country at a slower pace.

We headed north-west, on a 4000-kilometre drive—after a slight detour to Geelong, 1000 kilometres south, to fulfil a long-standing speaking engagement (a detour that had the girls scratching their heads once they'd looked at a map!). We crossed into South Australia and tracked up to the Centre, with a night in Coober Pedy. We made a brief stop in Alice Springs, where the low arms of the MacDonnell Ranges stretch either side of a small gap in which the town is situated, then we set off across the Tanami Desert with extra fuel and water and, I noted in the diary, enjoyed 'untroubled sleep on the road'.

I exulted in the freedom, and loved the fact that the girls all took to the rough and tumble of travel off the beaten track without any qualms. It was a time of great happiness, exploring, singing and chatting as we went. In two days on the Tanami we saw only one other vehicle, a couple trundling along in a Kombi van—brave souls. There were long driving days, singing along to music to pass the time: Harry Nilsson, Aretha Franklin, Paul McCartney, the Jayhawks, Scrap Metal (in preparation for Broome), Crowded House, the Pretenders, the Hoodoo Gurus—a bagful of melodies in a landscape that went on forever.

The girls each kept a journal detailing things of interest they spotted along the way: the huge expanse of flinty, treeless plains that make up the Pitjantjatjara lands; crossing the border as an albino dingo scurried behind the 'Welcome to Western Australia' sign which was covered in graffiti and surrounded by abandoned car bodies; a sole Japanese cyclist wearing a rising-sun bandana—not an especially wise choice of headgear—completely covered in dust and sunburned deep red, in the middle of absolutely nowhere, saddle bags swaying as he pedalled along in the dirt. Whatever my daughters decided to do with their lives, I hoped rough jaunts like this would go into their memory banks to be drawn on, if only for a laugh, in the coming years.

There's good light in Broome, according to Warumpi Band guitarist Neil Murray, as I'd come to appreciate on my earlier visits. The scale of the town felt right to me, as Broome sits on the rim of a massive desert and gorge region. On an unhurried holiday its charms seemed even more radiant, although we weren't the first to appreciate its delights by any stretch. Only five years before, English property developer Lord McAlpine, who doubled for a period as a political adviser to Margaret Thatcher, happened on the Kimberley and returned, armed with a sizeable piggy bank, to build hotels, buy up houses and drag the picturesque outpost into the spotlight. Now Broome was being discovered, as tourist promotions and double-page spreads in newspaper travel sections extolled the town's delights.

We hooked up with Damian Trotter and his son from the Balgowlah days. Dames then worked for Sony, which had taken over CBS Records. He was a laidback, wry travelling companion who came armed with a swag of new music. Our now overloaded vehicle lurched up to Cape Leveque as we explored the coast and tried out a few of the locally run camping grounds. It was so low key we almost disappeared off the map. The slow rhythm of the days—a giant meditation on family and place—meant our sojourn was turning into one of the best trips ever.

Eventually we quit boab country, farewelling Damian, and drove across to Darwin, on the way checking in at one of the leading tourist spots, Katherine Gorge, in Nitmiluk National Park. In rugged sandstone country, Katherine is one of the best-known and biggest of the water-filled gorges that dot the Top End.

Up to this point, I'd usually managed to find a quiet out-of-the-way spot in which to throw down the swags, but increasing numbers of fences and 'Private Property—Keep Out!' signs meant the official camping ground was the only option. I'd been cramming in the sights, wanting us to see as much as possible, and so by the time we arrived at dusk, the area set aside for camping was chock-full of grey nomads, retirees taking their time to potter across Australia. Trailers, multi-roomed tents and swish caravans, some with TV aerials, had claimed nearly every inch of space, and so we ended up on a low piece of ground in a far corner—exposed and vulnerable if it rained. In the background, the hum of generators, partly masked by the bland lilt of muzak, drowned out the calls of the park's unique birdlife.

The atmosphere was contented, friendly, as lavish—to our eyes—evening meals were prepared on state-of-the-art barbecues, and small groups gathered to chat and compare travel notes. I closed my eyes for a moment. The sound of clinking glasses took me back to the Pymble Golf Club, caddying for my dad and sitting at the clubhouse once the round had finished. There, in the spiritual heart of the North Shore, genteel matrons and their businessmen husbands sipped their wine and beer after a day on the course. Back then, they alone would have been in a position to travel widely and enjoy retirement. But here in this camping ground I was witnessing an Australian success story: an economy that, with only a few blips, had remained strong, with ever-increasing house prices giving the downsizers a great launch pad for their senior years. Add to this the benefits of the Keating government's superannuation reforms—what bounty. Now many more working people were in a position to enjoy the fruits of a lifetime in employment, and by the looks of it a fair number of them were taking the opportunity to travel around Australia. I was glad to see it, but at the same time had the worrying thought that this was what the Kimberley would face ten years hence, magnified ten times over.

If Broome could manage the pressures that come with intense growth and development, I pondered, then perhaps the south could learn something from this tolerant and vibrant northern outpost we left behind with much regret.

This meant recognising without reservation that it was Aboriginal people's country, shared now by subsequent waves of visitors and settlers bound to respect the First Peoples.

It meant accepting that the area shouldn't be worked over as though it was a southerner's dream location or a miner's feasting ground.

It also meant getting the nuts and bolts of planning right and making certain the locals benefited from the latest mining boom—whatever its size or duration—as people worked through the trade-offs that came with big numbers and big dollars.

These issues are not exclusive to Broome. They arise in different shades in many parts of the country, especially in the north. My hope was that here people of the land could build for a future that served their interests, not those of the powerful, nor the central planners in a distant city building making decisions from the comfort of their air-conditioned offices.

Meanwhile, taking the time to experience the sweep of the country, as people we bumped into along the way were doing—including families like us, with young children and their blotting-paper minds—could only help to deepen our appreciation of what was at stake.

We'd swum in swimming holes, creeks and oceans, camped in the desert, walked through wetlands and into caves covered in rock art, hung out with locals as our kids played together, heedless of colour or station. I tried to help my daughters understand the backstories of the towns and people we met. And we laughed and sang along the way.

When we finally got back to Mittagong, Doris and I planted three plum trees, clustered together in the front garden. Easily seen from the kitchen window, they blossom early, with a shimmering mauve that fades in a few short weeks. They sing out that spring is coming, with bursts of fresh growth that remind us of our daughters, who mean so much to us, who are always there in the still inner reaches of our hearts.

19
UP FOR GRABS

A BIT OF downtime had given me some space to think through some of the bigger questions that were lurking underneath the covers, but I needed clear air to chew on them.

When Emily and May were still very young, I'd push them in a double stroller up the hill to a tiny Uniting Church in Balgowlah. We'd sneak in after the service had started, filing into the back row, and the girls would play on the floor with a few random toys while the congregation got a dose of earthy common sense from a minister who'd grown up on a dairy farm and wasn't there to judge anyone.

Stephen Hawking's remark that 'Now I understand a little of how the universe works, but I still don't know why' raises a big philosophical flag, but I never thought the 'why' was about escaping damnation. Over time I moved away from formal churches of any persuasion. There was an exclusiveness and punitive dimension to formal religious practice that turned me off. And the monstrous failings of church leadership, especially the Catholics and Anglicans, to protect children in their care—as would be revealed in years to come—made me furious. I had read and thought a lot about the early Christian church. The energy of its mission was an incredible enterprise, but the institution had drifted away from the core precepts, as evidenced in Jesus' life and teaching. Better for me to give little thought to tomorrow, but rather to try to live each day with as little enmity and as much focus as I could muster. Aiming for love in the true sense of the word, no matter how difficult, wasn't naïve, it was the only way.

As to the why in Hawking's question, I was convinced part of the answer lay in the purpose to which you addressed your life. Charles Birch, the eminent Sydney-based Christian philosopher, had written a great book about the subject. It was the act of living faithfully, diligently in the moment that counted. And then asking, what is happening to my neighbour? What is happening to the creation? And what, if anything (and there is always something) can I do to help? Not to advance my own interests but because I believe (and this can come through belief in God) that this is what humans are meant—'called' in the Christian tradition—to do. It might sound trite but when the act of cleaning your shoes is as satisfying as buying a new pair, and you make an effort to help people who can't afford shoes at all, then I believe you can experience deep-rooted happiness.

...

Meanwhile, after a year off, it was time for Midnight Oil to get back to the long and winding road. Occasionally, though, we'd go the short route, for one-off events. In one instance, in early 1992, we ventured forth to play a major concert in Boston to coincide with Earth Day and the lead-up to the Rio Earth Summit. The meeting in Rio was the first major gathering of world leaders—joined by more than 15,000 members of civil society—aimed at reaching agreement on steps to help the world's environment. Expectations were high for this hallmark event, which, among other things, established the United Nations Framework Convention on Climate Change that subsequently became the Kyoto Protocol. Paul Keating, now prime minister, was a no-show, which sent a worrying message about the new Labor government's priorities.

We arrived in Boston on a freezing gloomy April afternoon to find that a huge crowd, undeterred by the weather, had gathered outdoors in the Foxboro Stadium. It was a national event and a squadron of broadcast vans was crammed into the loading dock—music and mainstream media lurked in every corner.

The long trek from Sydney meant getting everyone to the Northern Hemisphere was a costly, complicated exercise, no matter how important the cause. I was the last-minute man, impatient with the time it took to get there and then set up, the fiddling with gear that was a mandatory part of tour preparations. I was usually still catching my breath, trying to tie up the loose ends of other projects. And I liked to keep things fresh. If this meant flying by the seat of our pants, I could wear the odd mid-air collision. It gave the shows more edge, and even if I wasn't being totally fair to the crew in expecting everything to be honed to perfection, it was preferable to doing things the same way every night.

Earth Day saw us huddled in a makeshift tent at the side of the stage, grey sleet turning the ground to frozen sludge. We were desperately trying to warm up, having arrived late and still jetlagged, as the patient crowd turned numb in the twilight.

We'd done only one manic warm-up the night before but could usually rise to the occasion. A lifetime of touring in all kinds of weather, often with our backs to the wall, was solid insurance for shows like these. As with many events of this ilk, it had been a long day. The audience had already been treated to Willie Nelson, the Violent Femmes, Joan Baez singing with the Indigo Girls, and Steve Miller rocking out in mild guitar-hero style.

We pushed our way through the set, full of longish songs about the state of the planet. As we finished, four skinny little figures in charcoal and black zoot suits tumbled out of a limousine and leapt straight onto the stage, wired up and speeding like Formula One race cars. The Kinks blew the gig away. In rapid succession, ten three-minute radio classics were delivered at hyper speed, including 'You Really Got Me', 'All Day and All of the Night', 'Waterloo Sunset' and 'Lola'. The crowd, growing warmer as each hit smacked them in the face, loved it. The wily old popsters then departed in the reverse sequence of their arrival without a word to anyone.

Somehow Willie McInnes had managed to get clam chowder delivered to our tent, which now resembled a tattered piece of North Pole infrastructure, and there we sat warming our lips and tending our wounds. We were rarely blown off the stage in nearly thirty years of touring, but Ray Davies and his band took the prize that afternoon without raising a sweat.

It was a relief, a week later, to return home from the icy wastes of north-eastern US. Back with my sweetheart, whose smile made me forget I'd ever had a bluesy moment, spending time with my daughters, and within spitting distance of mates and the ocean, I could repair my body and restore my sense of equilibrium—and my sense of purpose.

Midnight Oil were gearing up to record the *Earth and Sun and Moon* album, but before starting in the studio I pitched in on a new campaign thrown together with my old uni friend, filmmaker David Bradbury.

There were only two locations on the east coast where defence forces could conduct air, land and sea exercises. One was Jervis Bay, the other the Shoalwater Bay training area, some 2000 kilometres north. The Shoalwater Bay area is massive, nearly 4500 square kilometres of the largest undeveloped tract of coastal ecosystem south of Cape York. It was in pristine condition, too, with a multitude of wetlands, mangrove estuaries spreading out from small creeks and, importantly, a series of vegetated parabolic sand dunes that run from north to south on the landward side of the bay.

When viewed from a distance, the dunes appear as a low forested mountain range. They'd been undisturbed for around 700,000 years and acted like giant water filters, in the wet season absorbing rainfall that eventually fed a small stream flowing from the southern perimeter of the hills and providing a year-round supply of clean drinking water to the coastal town of Yeppoon, fifty kilometres south. The entire area had been placed on the Register of the National Estate, a list of outstanding areas with high environmental values. Despite this, Graham Richardson, while still environment minister, had approved the issuing of mining leases over parts of Shoalwater Bay, including the sandhills.

I'd noticed the area while flying up to Cairns on a Midnight Oil tour. 'Suddenly, a huge chunk of green and blue appeared below, nearly twice the size of suburban Sydney,' I later noted in a press release, issued to alert people to the bay's assets. The ACF had Shoalwater Bay on its watch list and, before moving on from the foundation in 1992, Phillip Toyne sought meetings with the new environment minister, Ros Kelly, to discuss its future.

As is often the case, a local community group had been trying to draw attention to developments at Shoalwater, but drumming up interest was all but impossible. The media in the nearest major centre, Rockhampton, were more interested in monitoring cattle prices than the antics of a small group of protesters a couple of hours' drive away. And while there had been calls for the ACF and other national groups to get involved, the conservation movement was already occupied on a multitude of fronts. The issuing of the leases, after a number of false starts, was seen as a fait accompli, notwithstanding some dubious business deals that accompanied the process.

As it turned out, the threat of sand mining was worrying the commander of the training area as well. Major Sam Hassall was an unlikely ally who had come to appreciate the natural qualities of the lands and water for which he had responsibility. Crucially, he could facilitate access to the Shoalwater Bay training area. But how to derail the imminent arrival of men and machines set to denude the oldest undisturbed forested sandhills on the face of the globe?

David Bradbury was already well established as a documentary filmmaker; he wore his politics proudly on his sleeve, and was used to operating on a shoestring budget. His previous films—including his earliest, *Front Line*—had received numerous awards. He'd been made aware of the furore that was erupting in Central Queensland and, with researcher Helen Stickley-Thompson and editor Peter Scott, his small team was chafing at the bit to make a film to highlight what was at stake.

I agreed to come on board to push things along and help write and narrate the film, provisionally titled *The Last Frontier*, which we hoped would provide a powerful campaigning tool and alert a much wider audience to what was happening up on the Central Queensland coast.

Bradbury had secured funding from the Australian Film Commission with back-up from actor Bryan Brown if he blew the budget. But the film would have to be made quickly, given Richardson had already issued the leases. The only hope was that the Keating government could be persuaded to reconsider the decision before the project got off the ground.

A week after the film's funding came through, I found myself at Rockhampton airport with a group consisting of a world-weary Sydney film crew, a young Aboriginal activist from the coast who'd been invited to provide a local perspective and a couple of committed volunteers. We were heading into the unknown, with half a script and even less of an idea about how the film would turn out. But in many ways the documentary made itself. Like Jervis Bay, or any other area with significant natural values, there was a backdrop of images of pristine environments that would translate powerfully to the screen.

An old fishing trawler, the *Pearl Bay*, had been hired at bargain-basement rates to enable the crew to film from the water, and we launched a runabout from the boat and set about exploring, filming as we went. It was hard work for the crew but for me idyllic: doing my pieces to camera, the days warm and still, the nights clear. And wherever we looked there was rampant life: rainforest thickets alive with birdcalls, mudflats and mangroves teeming with crabs and worms and tiny insects.

Despite its occasional use by the military, the bay was one of the healthiest waterways I'd ever encountered: crystal clear, with ample seagrass beds in the sheltered coves and inlets that were ideal hideouts for prawns to spawn and dugongs to feed and calve. It was gloriously free of any permanent moorings, with no run-off, waste or rubbish. The treasure trove of fish species explained why local fishing groups, usually no friend of the conservationists, were also trenchantly opposed to the sand mining.

By the time we finished filming from the boat we were knackered, running short of time and due to return south to Yeppoon. As the afternoon cooled, out of nowhere a gale blew up and strong winds raked across the bay where we'd moored. The temperature dropped abruptly—bad weather was on the way.

'Should we stay or should we go?' the ghost of Joe Strummer crooned in my ear as I sought out the skipper. I found him, a burly, unshaven fisherman in his mid-forties, slumped on what passed for the bridge of the *Pearl Bay*. He was listening to crackly weather updates on an old radio, periodically glancing up at the threatening clouds and then at the smallest radar I'd seen on any boat.

'It's blowing pretty hard and it's meant to get worse,' he offered before I could say a word. When I queried the seaworthiness of his distinctly ramshackle vessel, he just shrugged his shoulders. 'It's been through worse, Pete. I reckon we'll be fine.'

This wasn't how most of the film crew saw the situation. After days of tramping along numerous creeks, through mud and sand, carting gear on and off boats and up and down hilly, heavily timbered ranges, with minimal breaks and catering that consisted of stale sandwiches, bottles of water and health bars—all of which they'd endured in good humour for a good cause—the increasing howl of the wind, whirring and screaming through the mast and fittings, had cast a pall over the team and a minor mutiny erupted. There was a 'meeting', followed by an announcement. Some of the crew wanted to stay in the relative calm of the bay, never mind the schedule and the extra cost. Besides, did we really trust this decrepit captain and his equally decrepit-looking boat? Were Bradbury and I really prepared to risk everyone's lives by taking to sea in conditions as bad as these?

Our answer was equally brief—yes. As the more experienced hands might already have guessed, we couldn't afford to stay. Hiring the trawler for an extra day or two simply wasn't in the budget. And we had to trust our captain. If he was really in fear of his life or concerned for his vessel—most likely uninsured—then no doubt he would have expressed some reservations. He hadn't. We were going.

We chugged out of the bay and rounded the point into open water, as the evening went gloomy and black and the wind blew louder.

It was a wild ride as the shallow waters in this section of the coast meant the big swells were hard to breach head on. Waves reared up at all angles, sending torrents of water across the bow. The captain, however, seemed oblivious to the trawler's heaving and crashing, and to the uneasy mood of his passengers.

I knew I'd be sick if I stayed below deck and so stood at the stern, hanging on like hell as we pitched through the night, occasionally shouting out to the skipper: 'Here comes a big one! Look, over there, there's another one coming!' But he just grunted and ignored me as we continued to smash through the swells. The voyage seemed to go on forever.

We eventually motored in past the breakwater at Yeppoon before midnight and jumped off the boat, swaying on our feet, giddy with relief. We reached the motel to find it in total darkness, but the owner had thoughtfully left the keys in each door before retiring for the night.

Lying in my room I couldn't sleep; my head was still swimming after our gut-churning voyage and the wind continued to rage outside. Had this actually been the last-ever voyage of the *Pearl Bay*, I wondered? Other than the skipper there had been no crew, and I couldn't recall any markings on the vessel nor any life jackets—or was I simply delirious? Still, we hadn't blown the budget and we had the makings of a memorable documentary with some great footage under our belt—not to mention a hair-raising adventure to tell our friends about.

...

Back in Sydney, I joined the Oils, who were by now ensconced at Megaphon Studios in St Peters, near the airport, to set about recording *Earth and Sun and Moon*, again with Nick Launay. The album took forever to make, but we didn't get too bogged down and the mood was even. It helped that the studio, a laidback folksy affair, was run by mates and we could get home at night.

What the record lacked in urgency it made up for in feel. But by this point the expansive songs that we were recording—like 'Now or Never Land' and 'Outbreak of Love'—were at odds with the raw sounds of Seattle grunge that were the next big thing. In the absence of the kind of radio-friendly song that the overseas record company believed was essential if we were to capitalise on the exposure we got from 'Beds Are Burning' and a couple of the *Blue Sky Mining* tracks, our progress was stalling.

This was always going to happen. The chart success we'd enjoyed in the past had been as much by accident as design. It wasn't the raison d'être of Midnight Oil, even if sometimes we aimed for it. It was our 'spiritual crisis', as Jim called it, for we weren't really a singles band by temperament, and yet it was individual ear-worm songs that propelled a career and marked you out from the pack. When we'd done the big European summer festivals sharing the bill with Bowie and Dylan, Bob remarked that a band could tour forever on 'Beds Are Burning'. I wasn't there to respond; I'd baulked on going backstage to say hello, as I didn't want to break the spell Dylan songs had over me by meeting their creator, though I'm sure he would have been charming, enigmatic or maybe just Bob Dylan. In the end, roundabout discussions about which singles should go to radio and the size of film-clip budgets tested our relationships with one another and with senior record execs of the alpha-male persuasion, like Don Ienner, in the US.

Gary Morris and our long-time Sony contact in North America, Mason Munoz, were increasingly locking horns with Ienner, the label boss—a career-limiting exercise for all concerned if it went on for too long. To its credit, Sony in Australia, with CEO Denis Handlin, senior execs Chris Moss and a host of others, remained loyal to the Oils, but the writing was on the wall—implacable artist meets immoveable corporation—and so we set about playing where it suited us, ignoring the stalemate that had arisen in New York, and pursued the things that interested us.

We were still together, weren't we? And we'd managed to get another album done and it wasn't too bad either. I wasn't going to lose any sleep over not getting into the top ten.

...

Meanwhile, Channel 7 had agreed to screen the Shoalwater film, but the program manager got cold feet and parried every suggestion that was made to maximise its promotion, citing concern about its 'political' quality.

Bradbury was indefatigable; used to drumming up publicity from a standing start, he organised for leaflets to be handed out at Beach Boys concerts, then taking place in the big cities, and harassed Channel 7 past the point of usefulness. We planned a special phone-in and fundraising drive on Triple J radio and, wearing my ACF president's hat, I sent a memo to all the national conservation groups asking for support—the only time I ever took that step.

Retitled *Shoalwater: Up for Grabs*, the film rated well enough and delivered the publicity boost needed. Now was the time to try to rescue the situation. All we needed was an opportunity to persuade the government to revisit the decision. In a timely twist of fate, Prime Minister Paul Keating was due to visit Rockhampton after we'd concluded filming, and I'd suggested to his office and any minister I could reach that the prime minister's VIP aircraft take a quick detour over Shoalwater Bay so he could see what all the fuss was about. If that happened, I was confident there would be a chance of a reprieve. If not, the last resort would be to take the matter into the courts, a messy and expensive exercise.

Shoalwater: Up for Grabs had gone to air on 29 November 1992. In the first two weeks of December, National Party senator Ian Macdonald from Queensland peppered the government with questions in parliament about the documentary and whether the claims we'd made were true.

In reply, Senator Bob Collins, representing the environment minister, pointed out: 'The area includes habitat for a number of species that are listed as endangered or vulnerable . . . [including] the humpback whale and the loggerhead turtle . . . The area also includes habitat for the dugong, which is listed by the International Union for the Conservation of Nature as vulnerable to extinction.' No more needed to be said.

On 21 December 1992, the Keating government's environment statement announced that a commission of inquiry would undertake a full and proper assessment of the environmental and economic values of all the Commonwealth lands within the Shoalwater Bay area. Two years later the inquiry made its recommendations. They included that sand mining be prohibited at Shoalwater Bay and the area be listed for further protection. Now it was decision time . . .

In the lead-up to the decision there were frantic rounds of lobbying, and John Faulkner, the next person responsible for the environment portfolio, was doing all he could to help. The omens, for once, were good. Keating, who'd famously said that if you weren't living in Sydney you were camping out, and having now flown over the region, had later remarked to a Tourism Taskforce conference in Sydney, '. . . if you ever see it [Shoalwater Bay] it will never get off your list. It's one of the most beautiful places on the coast.'

His government accepted the inquiry recommendations. Sand mining was formally excluded and conservation given equal status to the training purposes of the area. Shoalwater Bay came off our watch list.

In the ensuing years, the training area has increasingly been used, not only by the Australian Defence Force, but also by the US and other countries from the region, to conduct joint exercises. At one point, concerns were raised about the presence of depleted uranium in US weapons, but the defence department insisted this was not the case, and that the sensitive areas of the bay had not been significantly impacted.

In the future, the original vision of the local community should be honoured by the defence department working in concert with the environment department. The area should not be allowed to become a de facto military base. Those whose job it is to protect the nation must also do their bit to protect one of the nation's outstanding environmental assets.

20

AMSTERDAM AND BUST

OR THE PREVIOUS four years, I'd been doing two jobs, as musician and activist, and in my mind they'd been equally important. But I also had a growing family and I was anxious to spend more time with my wife and daughters: time we all were missing out on, time we could never get back.

Like Phillip Toyne, who had finished up at the end of a packed five years, after the Shoalwater Bay campaign I was ready to move on from the ACF. I felt I'd done all I could for the foundation, from council and executive get-togethers and public meetings to endless lobbying and fundraising.

My old friend from the Jervis Bay campaign, Paul Gilding, had gone on to become the executive director of Greenpeace Australia, and he soon raised the organisation's profile with a series of confronting actions aimed at chemical companies still discharging toxic waste into waterways. This led to his selection as head of Greenpeace International at a time when that body, after a period of rapid growth, was reviewing its operations and direction.

It was a big leap to take and, knowing I was spending more time in the Northern Hemisphere as the Oils toured in Europe and North America, he asked me to join the board, both to provide a Southern Hemisphere perspective and to give his leadership some support.

Looking back, I can't believe I took on the position. I was fine with finishing up at the ACF. They had been fast and furious years, but a lot had been achieved and I felt the organisation was in pretty good shape. At this point I should have paused, as I'd intended, and given more time to Doris and our marriage, but I failed to appreciate how necessary this was at the time. She was the light of my life yet I wasn't around enough to kindle the flame. Some downtime to allow space for creative thinking to sputter back to life wouldn't have gone astray either.

But I was drawn to what I felt was a profoundly important cause. Greenpeace was a global force for the environment. Its reach was on par with the biggest multinational companies and it was flattering to be asked—I was sucked back into the vortex. To my way of thinking, the organisation had got stuck in recent times and I had a view about how it might regain its mojo. Maybe this was a chance to influence its direction. The clincher was the opportunity to work with a friend who found himself in different and difficult circumstances. I've always enjoyed teaming up with people I feel share the same take on the big questions, colleagues I feel are in it for the right reasons.

My relationship with Gary Morris was a bit like this. I loved him like a brother, and we'd been through a lot together—getting the band out the door, keeping that intangible quality of 'Oil' intact. From the start Gary had an instinct about what was right for the band, and flashes of inventiveness that were breathtaking if we could make them work. But he was so headstrong that at times it was plain exhausting. The story of one of my daughters picking up a toy phone and saying, 'No, Gary, no, Gary, no!' wasn't apocryphal as many people assumed, it was true.

The result of saying yes to Paul (and to Gary) made for a manic journey in the years that followed. Coming from the back end of a tour, sleepwalking through Schiphol airport and into Greenpeace meetings in Amsterdam, then back to play, off to a Greenpeace office in some other country, then overnight to Australia, a few weeks of follow-up activity at home and then I'd be gone again.

There was no pause button in view and so Doris and I decided to move the family to a tiny village in Germany, near the Dutch border, so we could see more of each other. Everswinkel, with its rows of near-identical houses that backed on to neatly tilled fields, was so quiet that whenever I spent a night there I couldn't sleep for the sound of tinnitus—the muso's curse—in my ears: the leftover hum from planes and trains and automobiles and loud rock music.

In the small apartment we'd rented, Doris set up a makeshift classroom in the cellar where she could homeschool the girls. It was a workable arrangement. She was closer to her family and old friends, and I was able to cut my travel time down by days. I wasn't someone who took great pride in the number of flying hours I was racking up, but there wasn't any alternative if I wanted to have a go at doing my jobs properly.

I identified with the Greenpeace ethos that was forged in opposition to nuclear testing when the first Greenpeace yacht sailed into the impact zone off the coast of Canada in the late 1960s. It was in the spirit of the Gandhian tradition, taken up by Martin Luther King during the civil rights struggles in America's Deep South, continuing through to the peace movement that had re-emerged under the shadow of the nuclear arms race.

Greenpeace had done brave work and, with a highly recognisable name, was capable of turning an issue around very quickly. At the same time, the organisation was effectively controlled by a handful of affluent European member states that dominated the politics of the central organisation, which in turn licensed the right to operate as Greenpeace to groups in other countries. It was a long way from the membership-based ACF, with its constitution and genuine community representation.

The potential of the organisation to be a potent global force was obvious and new Greenpeace offices were springing up in a number of developing countries, where environmental campaigning was still something of an anomaly. I visited Brazil briefly to look in on their work and see whether it would be possible to organise a joint concert with Sting at the Manaus Opera House in the middle of the Amazon rainforest—the lungs of the earth. At that time, the Amazon was an epicentre of global environmental concern, with thousands of hectares of rainforest being clear-felled each day. Cattle barons had taken control of the lands and were forcing the local Indigenous tribes to retreat—this battle is still raging.

The concert never got off the ground, but the enthusiasm of the Brazilian activists, working with very limited resources and often up against entrenched hostility, corruption and physical threats, was phenomenal. No matter how tough things seemed, they never lost their joyful approach to life—dancing, singing and eating with abandon before charging back into the trenches.

The Oils later toured Brazil and reconnected with some of the Greenpeace crew, including staging a silent protest—faces covered with gas masks—against air pollution at one of the busiest intersections in São Paulo. There was plenty of local media coverage, but the traffic didn't pause for a second. I put that down to the exuberant Latin approach to life; slowing down was not an option.

Back in Amsterdam I was a blow-in, the new executive director's rep on a governing board that included some of the early Green-peace principals, who were in constant conflict with the powerful European offices. Gilding and other newly recruited staff were intent on reforming the organisation, improving governance and financial management, and devolving power to offices in other countries campaigning on the ground.

Despite some on the board agreeing this was a necessary path, there remained a sizeable rump, influenced from the wings by the former chairman David McTaggart, determined to resist. They were people who'd accomplished a great deal in a brief period when audacious direct action by Greenpeace broke the mould. But it was hard for them to let go of their baby, and although no one said it out loud, they didn't fully trust newcomers to faithfully acquit the Greenpeace ideal. Relinquishing power is never easy—just think of the United

Nations Security Council, or political leaders who stay on past their use-by date. Uncertain about the merits of the changes in the wind, the chair scheduled a board meeting in Washington DC 'to discuss the executive director's plans'.

The writing was on the wall and everyone followed the script to its logical conclusion—stasis. After nearly two years with the organisation I departed, and Paul finished a couple of months later.

The environment was coming in from the margins, and was increasingly seen as a mainstream issue, and with politicians and business wanting in, the opportunities to make gains were great if you got the strategies right. At a time when there was a growing sense of urgency around the issue of global warming, and with the rapid growth in newly developing countries placing immense stress on their environments, Greenpeace International struggled to evolve and accommodate the new world order. It lost much of the following decade trying to do so.

Whether it would have managed better with the continued involvement of the Australians and the new guard I can't say. Nor can I say whether it would have made a difference to its effectiveness. Perhaps the conflict was an inevitable part of an activist group struggling to adjust to its issues gaining mainstream acceptance. Still, despite this failure on Paul's and my part, give me a Greenpeace any day. Some twenty years later, they continue to run some great campaigns with some of the world's most creative campaigners. The world needs all the help it can get. The stakes are getting higher and the clock is ticking.

...

I'd come to value working with conservation leaders like Paul Gilding and Phillip Toyne, and with groups like the ACF council. There was always a serious focus around this work. No one did it for the money and people could be wrung dry and burn out badly, but if you succeeded, the legacy was immense.

Being on stage night after night, trying to keep each other's musical psyche joined up, sorting and sifting through the decisions that bands need to make and then jumping across into activism, which sometimes involved working with people who didn't share the same cultural assumptions or political values, had reinforced for me the power of collaboration. It was similarly the collective nature of Midnight Oil that gave the band its strength and purpose. We were rarely more effective than when we were rowing together in the same direction.

I knew my extracurricular activities were at times frustrating for the band. But it had been like that for a long while, and we'd got through. They constructed the musical bed and I took our subject matter out into the political domain. We had become a power-ful partnership and my musical instincts were anchored in one place only.

When Rob announced in 1990 that he was going to make a solo record and sing his own songs, we reached a turning point. I could understand why he wanted to do it. Artists are restless creatures, compelled to follow their guiding light wherever it leads, and he fancied himself a chance, having penned some of the Oils' biggest songs. We would survive the breach, for a while at least. But I had the feeling that the five-against-the-world bond had been dented, and things would never be quite the same again.

21
WRONG MINE, WRONG PLACE

Y STINT AT Greenpeace now over, two years later, to my surprise, the ACF approached me to consider a second term as president. We'd returned to Australia in 1994 and I was looking forward to spending more time based at home. Working with Don Henry, the new ACF executive director, would be a good use of energy, and Melbourne was a much easier commute than Europe, so I said yes.

The election in 1996 of a conservative federal government led by John Howard saw new approaches evolving to respond to the environmental crisis. They included putting a value on natural assets, making protection of ecosystems a priority, and supporting low-carbon industries and renewable energy. But, other than an ill-fated attempt to get more water back into the Murray–Darling Basin, none of these measures would be actively promoted in the Howard government's plans or policies.

Plenty of Liberals saw active environmentalists as the 'enemy', part of a collectivist conspiracy that wanted nothing less than the end of the free-enterprise system. (Ironically, front-line environmental activists could just as easily be seen as true conservatives, given they are trying to preserve what is already in place and has served society well up to now.)

In this atmosphere, any individual or organisation that contested Howard's ascendancy was in for a ride on Bleak Street—and eighteen months into his government's first term, that's where I found myself.

I had an early meeting with one of the friendlier senior Liberals, Robert Hill. He was an accomplished environment minister, who, despite the hard-line position of his colleagues, got a few things done, including introducing new environmental legislation that would swing the balance towards the national government taking more responsibility. Hill was bemused that I would consider taking on the position of ACF president a second time given, as he freely admitted, that the opportunities for a conservation agenda would be limited. And I'd already 'done it'—true.

I expected little ground to be made during Howard's reign, but banging my head up against that wall—as opposed to a stack of speakers, as was the habit of some music fans—was going to be a fact of life as far as I could see.

A broader civil-society coalition, including conservation and community groups (some of whom were pretty isolated), the academic sector, churches and other willing parties, was needed to counter the conservative offensive. In addition, Don Henry and I knew that forging stronger bonds with Aboriginal and Torres Strait Islander people would be crucial, as would bolstering relationships with those in the business and farming sectors who understood the importance of maintaining an environmental bottom line. The agenda had grown: getting water back into the Snowy River, addressing widespread salinity, advancing new thinking in environmental economics and halting a series of dam proposals for WA's Fitzroy River had been added to an already long list.

By early 1998, a pressing issue had arisen concerning the fate of an existing uranium-mining lease called Jabiluka, which by an accident of history—along with the Ranger mine, and a lease at Koongarra—was located within the Kakadu World Heritage Area.

One of the first decisions by the newly elected Howard government was to overthrow Labor's three-mine policy, which restricted the number of uranium mines in Australia thus preventing any new mines. The new government instead gave the go-ahead for a second uranium mine—Jabiluka—in Kakadu, a clear message from the Coalition about their priorities and values, and the decision was immediately controversial. Following this, Robert Hill determined that a low-level environmental assessment of the project would be sufficient.

The mining company, Energy Resources of Australia (ERA, now majority-owned by Rio Tinto), wasn't prepared to pause and discuss the proposal with the Mirarr, the traditional owners of Jabiluka, who were opposed to the mine. Instead, they announced that site preparations would commence as soon as possible.

For the traditional owners, many scientists and environment groups, and particularly the ACF, which had a long-standing interest in the region, Jabiluka was a make-or-break issue, given its location within Kakadu, our largest national park. The existing Ranger mine had commenced production in 1980 with claims of coercion of Aboriginal traditional owners by the Northern Land Council. Both Ranger and Jabiluka were sited close to the Magela wetlands and the protected environment of the park, which for some elders was seen as a transgression of their culture. Toby Gangale, the father of current traditional owner Yvonne Margarula, had opposed the Ranger mine, but had received little support from the recently established Northern Land Council, which was under intense pressure from the Fraser Government in Canberra. The lobbying of traditional owners and political manoeuvring was unrelenting. In the end Fraser introduced changes to the Aboriginal Land Rights (Northern Territory) Bill which specifically removed the veto rights the Mirarr traditional owners would have held. When the bill became law in 1976 it entrenched this denial for the Mirarr people of a legal right all other traditional owners in the Northern Territory enjoy to this day. Two years later, on 3 November 1978, the details of the mining arrangements were finalised. Tellingly, on that day the Kakadu National Park lease was also executed, the Fraser government having linked the execution of the park lease to securing the mine. Sadly, and not for the first time, land rights had been cynically used to secure mining development.

No amount of money can make up for the impact of the existing Ranger mine whose giant tailings pond, a cocktail of radioactive sludge, dominates the landscape in this part of Kakadu. Accidents have been a too-frequent occurrence at Ranger. In extreme wet conditions, which are common in the tropics and more likely in a force-fed climate future, the giant pool of slurry threatens to overflow, and on some occasions the unthinkable has happened, with radioactive water leaking into the surrounding wetlands.

Locating another mine here was like putting an open-all-hours bottle shop in the chancery of a church—but, needless to say, the company didn't see it like that. It was primed to go and, following the breakdown of meetings between Hill and conservation organisations, the minister signed off on the mine. The resources minister, Warwick Parer, subsequently watered down the conditions Hill had included to minimise the risk of polluting the surrounding environment, and with work on the new mine site due to start, the only remaining option for opponents—a blockade of the site—was quickly organised.

Remote, blisteringly hot in the dry and tricky to access in the wet, Jabiluka was as difficult a place to campaign in as could be imagined. It was a four-hour drive from Darwin, with minimal services and, once the blockade was announced, a throng of people who needed access to water and toilet facilities began turning up in increasing numbers. Local groups and the two campaign coordinators—firebrand Jacqui Katona, who worked for the Mirarr, and ACF councillor Jayne Weepers—kept the blockade functioning while they conducted a media campaign from a demountable hut and Jabiluka fast became a household name. Yvonne Margarula, too, was steadfast in her opposition. Since the Oils had played in 1986 at the Jabiru township near the mine site, I'd been back a couple of times and had come to greatly respect Yvonne, who at that time was working as a housemaid at the Kakadu resort, and showed great resolve in calmly opposing a second mine.

By the middle of 1998, with the blockade in full swing, there had been over a hundred arrests, with many activists refused bail. For these people and the growing number of supporters of direct action, it was simply the wrong mine, in the wrong place, with the wrong product.

At a time when fatigue was starting to set in and sprits were running low, I paid a visit to Kakadu with Tom Uren—the former Labor minister and anti-war activist. At dusk, in a dry clearing in Kakadu, we were surrounded by about 300 people clustered in the savanna on blankets and sleeping bags. Young forest activists with braided hair and beads, white-haired grandparents . . . people from all backgrounds had made the trek. A handful of Mirarr sat at the back, listening carefully. The young protestors stared blankly as Tom, now in his eighties, stood to address the crowd. With a lifetime of speeches at public meetings, at the dispatch box in parliament and on the streets, balancing on the balls of his feet like the champion boxer he once was, Uren galvanised the assembled crowd as he exhorted them to stay strong.

The large number of people who had flocked to Jabiluka—a great proportion from Melbourne, over 3000 kilometres south—contradicted the idea that Australians were an apathetic lot when it came to the environment. Mass poster runs in the capital cities featuring the Jabiluka symbol had raised public awareness, and once people came to understand what was happening up there their verdict was clear. By the time the Oils returned to play a dawn concert with Regurgitator and Coloured Stone, and then march across the boundary of the mining lease in the pink morning light, we were thousands strong, and Jabiluka was squarely in the national spotlight.

One of the great natural and cultural wonders of the world, the giant rock escarpments that surrounded us, bore silent witness to the quick-burning fuse of spreading mass protest—a political backdown was on the cards.

When it came, months later, it smelled of bad faith, and was only a conditional concession. The protests had succeeded to the extent that the company would not proceed with the Jabiluka mine without consent of the traditional owners, as should have been the case from the beginning. But in 2013 ERA stated that the Jabiluka deposit was 'still under consideration to be developed to the benefit of all stakeholders'. Since then the ground has shifted a little. ERA has now said the Ranger mine cannot be expanded underground unless the mining lease is extended, while Rio Tinto, its majority shareholder, has indicated that the existing mine should not continue beyond its current time frame, thus reducing the likelihood of a second mine at Jabiluka. Notwithstanding this, the pressure on Yvonne Margarula and her family will continue until this question is settled and until Jabiluka is incorporated into Kakadu, but I'm certain they'll stay strong.

The Mirarr can take heart, too, from the stance of Jeffrey Lee, the traditional owner of Koongarra, the other remaining lease in the area that could have been utilised for uranium mining.

Situated adjacent to some of Kakadu's most striking landforms, including Nourlangie Rock, Koongarra encompasses around 1600 hectares of country, and the case for it remaining undisturbed was strong. So long as it remained outside the boundary of the park it was a potential mine, although, as with Jabiluka, the consent of the traditional owner would be required.

I'd run into Jeffrey, a softly spoken, gentle bloke who worked as a ranger at Kakadu, when I first visited the Jabiluka blockade. He was adamant that he had no interest in the money that would come from exploiting the uranium ore body at Koongarra. His wish was for the area to be protected forever.

It wouldn't be too long before there was a chance to help make that wish come true.

22

I SEE MOTION

THE DIGITAL TRANSFORMATION of the world was accelerating in the mid- to late 90s—most notably the rise and rise of Apple and Microsoft, and the birth of Google—and the initial stirrings of China were a taste of things to come, but in popular music most of it was of little consequence. The dominance of dance music didn't give way, as many observers—me included—had predicted would happen, and the grunge movement that had predominated in the early years of the decade had fragmented into subgenres overnight. Alternative music was swallowed by MTV, and easy access to free downloads over the internet would soon put a hole in the music business model. The only light on the horizon was hip-hop starting its rumble. The Oils couldn't remake ourselves with a new image, as artists like Bowie constantly did, even if we wanted to—which we didn't. Our headspace was too serious. We'd cast the die many times: choosing world music over grunge, the multicultural vibe in preference to Budweiser-sponsored teen rebellion by going with Peter Gabriel on the WOMAD tour instead of joining the increasingly popular Lollapalooza circuit.

In addition, locking horns with Sony in New York had left all parties bruised. A band that had never capitulated to record company edicts, and had dug its heels in, could simply be ignored. So we were now stuck in a holding pattern. We could relax and go along for the ride. Or we could rebel and strike out for new pastures, which was my instinct.

A warts-and-all move having been ruled out by different members at different times, instead we focused on doing the shortest possible tours in the most compressed periods. We were making it hard for ourselves. It was one thing to be reminded by loudspeaker when you landed at LAX—yet again—to stay 'visually connected to your luggage', another altogether to remain visually connected to your audience if you kept leaving town. When we were in Australia, Sydney was still the epicentre of our work, so I was constantly driving up the freeway from our home in Mittagong, to the city. No matter how late I'd worked, I always tried to make the run for home. To stay awake I'd wind the windows down, crank up both the air-conditioning and the radio, chiming in on 'More Than a Feeling' and creaming the high notes. Across the dial my friend—radio, the child of Thomas Edison—rarely let me down: I was learning something I otherwise would never have discovered on ABC Radio National, unearthing scintillating new songs on Triple J, swooning to Dvorak on the classical station, or back to Triple M or 2WS for a pump up with big rock.

If I drew a blank I'd throw on Dragon's greatest hits and revisit a favourite hymn like 'Age of Reason', or just dip into the big box of blues CDs I had stashed in the car. God knows what the Campbelltown koalas thought as I flashed past the corridors of scrabbly wattle shouting, 'The blues had *another* baby and they named it rock and roll!'

After nearly twenty years on the road, I'd do this run anytime, even from gigs as far away as Newcastle, four hours north, just to wake up in my idea of heaven: my own bed.

Barely an hour or two later, half awake, I would faintly hear the girls getting ready for school, playing and chattering over breakfast as the early-morning sun poked through the oak tree in the front garden. I could easily forgo all the MTV Awards and platinum records—these snatched moments made my world go round.

...

By the middle of 1998, we'd finally finished recording *Redneck Wonderland*. We actually recorded it twice, at considerable expense, as we couldn't agree on the final mixes of the first version. The lyrics on *Redneck* were a sharp rebuke to the rise of One Nation and the indifference to nature that seeped out of the pores of the establishment, and the music was scarifying in places, even if some people had stopped listening.

We even ended up with two versions of the same song, 'Cemetery in My Mind', having failed to nail down a single that sat right. The 'true believers' version, like odd assortments of Oils' work over the years, was eerily prophetic. It combined the original chorus with a spoken-word intro, 'I'm on a barge without a river in a room without a door, there's not much time for true believers to be seen'—indeed.

I still didn't know where I'd find myself a few years hence, although one could make a pretty fair guess. Looking back, the words paint as good a picture as any of the time I subsequently spent in the Labor Party.

In 1998 Australia sweltered through the hottest year yet on record, as the ACF ramped up efforts to get water back into the Snowy River with the formation of the Snowy River Alliance, which included local farmers; the independent member for Gippsland East, Craig Ingram; and the New South Wales-based Total Environment Centre, led by highly experienced campaigner Jeff Angel.

The Victorian Liberal government of Jeff Kennett had been swept from power, and Ingram's win had been crucial in raising the stakes on the state of a river that occupied such a prominent place in Australian folklore. The alliance succeeded in getting the states to the table, although the federal Coalition environment minister, Robert Hill from South Australia, had derided the campaign to get water into the Snowy as a 'romantic notion'.

The truth was the Snowy desperately needed environmental flows just as much as the Murray River did, and we'd thrown everything at the campaign, with Tim Fisher from the ACF producing a comprehensive portfolio detailing our case and enlisting sympathetic media drawn to the iconic status of the river, and it worked. In 2002, during my second stint with ACF, I travelled to Jindabyne with New South Wales premier Bob Carr and Victorian premier Steve Bracks. We were there to commemorate an agreement between the two state governments to get at least 21 per cent more water back into the Snowy, which in some seasons was down to a mere 1 per cent of its original flow. This victory was one that the pundits typically predicted couldn't happen, but the alliance never doubted the rightness of its cause, nor that it would prevail. Our 'doubts are traitors, and make us lose the good we oft might win, by fearing to attempt', Shakespeare wrote, and he was right.

The Oils also lent a hand, via some benefit shows, to the East Timorese politician José Ramos-Horta as he argued the case for independence for the tiny country that had been there for Australian troops in World War II.

Throughout, I was pushing for the establishment of what eventually became the Mittagong Forum: bringing together the established environmental movement—big national organisations and state-based conservation groups—to look at ways of working more effectively. It made sense for the groups to cooperate and even share resources when the situation demanded it, and there was a strategic opportunity to build on the recent growth of the movement—which could wax and wane—if there were strong joint campaigns.

I also got involved with the Jubilee Debt Campaign. This was a powerful initiative, bringing together aid organisations and churches, that had been championed by Bono and special adviser to the UN Secretary General, Professor Jeffrey Sachs, among others. It had a practical and a moral dimension: the practical was that, without some reduction in debt, poor countries were never likely to be able to lift their people out of poverty. The moral component spoke for itself and ultimately led to the forgiveness of big debts in very poor countries.

If I was at home, the days went by in a chaotic rush—ceaseless phone calls, a quick lunch, snatched conversations and a folder full of plans—as I ploughed through all the requests and activities that presented themselves. If we were away, then I'd be constantly looking over my shoulder to home.

From a distance, one thing stood out sharply: the appetite for reconciliation was growing.

At first blush, reconciliation appeared to be a tokenistic word, without any tangible goals. John Howard's government played to this impression and instead supported what the prime minister termed 'practical reconciliation'. But if you looked closely at what was intended by the expression 'reconciliation', it was nothing less than a wholesale reappraisal of relations between Aboriginal and Torres Strait Islander people and the rest of us, through a public education campaign aimed at deepening understanding and enlarging our values. And hand in hand with reconciliation went a series of steps to address political recognition, social justice, land rights and, ultimately, some form of compact or treaty.

I saw reconciliation as a stepping stone to righting past wrongs that were a fact of history, and now, as the movement grew stronger, the Oils wanted to be around to provide support. This meant connecting with Reconciliation Australia leaders like Pat Dodson and Shelley Reys and trying to fit in events with them where possible, and hooking up with old surfing colleagues like Rabbit Bartholomew and Mark Richards as they pushed the cause by staging the Billabong Indigenous Surf Festival.

Ultimately this surge in public awareness reached a zenith with the bridge walks for reconciliation held in capital cities and towns throughout 2000. Hundreds of thousands of people participated—with the notable exception of most conservative politicians.

Howard's obduracy in refusing to countenance the claims of Aboriginal people stemmed the surge. He was like King Canute trying to hold back the waves, claiming at one point that reconciliation in the form of a treaty could lead to large payouts to Aboriginal people from the public purse. It was an utterly immoral position and futile to boot, considering the clarion call for acknowledgement and justice the previous prime minister, Paul Keating, had made in his historic speech in Redfern Park in 1992.

Seven years after the bridge walks and a host of associated events, when I was an MP, Prime Minister Kevin Rudd took a positive step towards reconciliation with an apology to the Stolen Generations in the first year of the new Labor government. Despite my long association with Aboriginal people and the reconciliation movement, Rudd didn't bother to include me in any of the meetings and proceedings that surrounded the event. I was bemused by the oversight—deliberate or otherwise—as I'd already served as shadow parliamentary secretary for reconciliation. This was a common trait in the parliamentary wing of the Labor Party: you don't advantage a colleague unless you owe them, they bully you, or because the factional position they occupy means they have to be accommodated. I contented myself with handshakes and hugs with the elders I knew who had been invited to sit in the House of Representatives chamber, where alongside former prime ministers Whitlam, Fraser, Hawke and Keating, MPs listened to a speech that was the best of Rudd's leadership by a country mile.

The symbolism of these reconciliation events was important. They were visual, collective strikes into the popular consciousness, while the hard work continued in the background: processing native title claims, ongoing efforts to improve Indigenous health and education, creating space for economic activity and jobs, and, crucially, adding measures that would enable a greater degree of self-determination and local control.

• • •

The struggle in Australia to achieve reconciliation at the end of the millennium echoed a struggle for justice that had played out earlier in the decade as we watched and hoped and agitated for a safe transition to a multiracial democracy and the end of apartheid in South Africa.

At the height of the struggle, I went with friends to hear the African National Congress leader Oliver Tambo address a crowd of fervent supporters at Sydney's Trades Hall. Asked to explain the success of the campaign for equality in such difficult circumstances—armed struggle, riots, leaders jailed—Tambo replied with three words: 'Organise, organise, organise.'

So determined and inspiring from afar were those campaigners—most conspicuously Nelson Mandela—that not even the most stubborn conservative politician could hold the gates closed on a multiracial polity forever. Still, like British prime minister Margaret Thatcher, whom he greatly admired, John Howard, before he secured the prime ministership, refused to support sanctions against the apartheid regime and did virtually nothing to bring it to a close.

The Oils finally visited South Africa towards the end of 1994, following Mandela's election as president. It was a time of both exhilaration and sober appraisal of the task that lay ahead.

I stood for hours at the window of my Cape Town hotel looking across the harbour to Robben Island, where Mandela had spent much of his twenty-seven years of imprisonment. Sixteen floors below me, black taxi drivers sat on crates and boxes playing cards, as the lights twinkled in the gated estates nestled under Table Mountain. Having organised, the new government would now have to 'educate, educate, educate', to give the many impoverished young South Africans any chance of building a new life at all.

Meanwhile, the concerts, some with Sting and Johnny Clegg, a prominent South African singer-songwriter and advocate, were joyous affairs. For the first time, local audiences, both black and white, were listening to performers whose music they knew well (though they had never before had the opportunity to see them live) and who had, in some way or other, expressed support for a multiracial South Africa.

Along with millions around the world, we'd been waiting for this moment to come. In the mid-1980s, the Special AKA had released a single, 'Free Nelson Mandela', which went top ten in the UK. Following this, Steven 'Little Steven' Van Zandt, from Bruce Springsteen's band, called to ask if I'd do some vocals on a track he'd written called 'Sun City'. The chorus—'I ain't gonna play Sun City'—referred to a casino-hotel complex in South Africa where international acts were paid big money to play to select audiences as a way of legitimising the whites-only stance of the regime. It was a con, and yet performers like Queen and Rod Stewart had played there, giving the racist government a fig leaf of legitimacy.

The Oils were transiting through LA at the time so I took a detour and drove up to Jackson Browne's house in the Hollywood Hills mid-afternoon, said hello to his girlfriend of the time, Daryl Hannah—sans make-up and famous-actress airs—and squeezed into his tiny home studio for a couple of run-throughs.

Van Zandt had asked numerous artists, including Browne, to perform and Run DMC, Springsteen, Bob Dylan, Lou Reed, U2, Bonnie Raitt and Miles Davis were already on board. There were only two lines of verse to sing plus a bit of scatting over the outro and, as sometimes happens when you're fresh and you get lucky, it went down in one take. It took ten minutes, but could have been a lot longer if I'd missed the first pass.

The engineer was still sorting the mix and phoning New York to play it to producer Arthur Baker as I headed out the door to catch a plane home. With the fate of Nelson Mandela, then still in jail, starting to make front pages everywhere, I hoped this noisy declaration would push the temperature a little higher.

...

It may seem like an obvious thing to say, but I've always lived and loved music. I feel a stirring in my gut when the notes ring out, when the rhythm locks in and a song begins. At the same time, I don't believe that music, by itself, changes the world. It's people who make the changes—for better and for worse.

Music can be the soundtrack for the big issues of the times. It can be a powerful partner, providing the callout that a greater mass can respond to. Music can provide an emotional touchstone that sums up a mood or inspires a change in thinking. But by itself music doesn't do the job of getting on the right side of history. While a world without music would be a barren, soulless place, it is people, through their sweat and commitment and sacrifice, who make the difference. Mandela didn't have a tape recorder in his prison cell. He had a conviction he was prepared to die for, and those who worked with him, both in South Africa and in exile, along with supporters in other countries, spent long, difficult years bringing that issue home. The musicians' efforts were an opportunity to join in and lend a voice to a worthwhile cause. Of course it helps to have songs that hit the mark, songs that you can sing along to, but music by itself doesn't do the hard yards.

And so we found ourselves on the back of a truck on the streets of New York, interrupting the lunch hour in Midtown Manhattan with 'Midnight Oil makes you dance, Exxon makes us sick' after the *Exxon Valdez* ran aground on the Alaskan coastline in 1989, spilling millions of gallons of oil in one of the worst environmental disasters in history. People poured out of office blocks to see what was happening and stayed for the entire performance. The streets were closed, while the blinds were drawn in the Exxon building opposite.

Or deep in the forests of British Columbia at Clayoquot Sound, where several hundred activists had blockaded a clearcut. With a backdrop of amputated giant cedar and spruce trees, we played a concert that was broadcast uninterrupted across Canada.

As we were leaving the forest clearing, crossing over a small timber bridge, a group of burly loggers surrounded our van and started rocking it from side to side. Luckily they lacked either the strength or the resolve to tip us into the ravine below. Bones was filming the panic from inside the van on a hand-held video camera, and maybe that or the increasingly shrill cries from Jim's wife of 'Stop it, stop it! We're going to die!' gave the loggers pause.

Eventually a new Native American Indian forest company instituted a much lighter cutting regimen, and in 2000 Clayoquot was declared a UNESCO Biosphere Reserve.

And then at the closing of the Sydney 2000 Olympics . . .

Years of culture jamming meant we were well prepared for this one and we were united in wanting to give expression to what, by our reckoning, was a giant log stuck in the eye of the leader of the nation.

We now knew a bit about the past, that the time for a fresh start had come. There was at last a growing movement for reconciliation with the First Peoples of the country—not on the scale of the struggle against apartheid maybe, but in our part of the world, equally important. Yet we had a prime minister who couldn't bring himself to apologise for the hurt that every single Aboriginal person had suffered, to make space for some healing.

We ended up hightailing it back out to Papunya, in the Western Desert, where Warumpi Band guitarist Sammy Butcher lived and where, as a band, we'd last visited fourteen years before. Gary came too, and we camped on the side of a stony hill, looking out across the purple MacDonnell Ranges, sitting around a fire—out of range and out of mind—and talked through how to get it done: which words to use, which song to sing, what to wear, how to prepare and keep the surprise action under wraps for the night.

On the way back we played a wild night at the Todd Tavern at Alice Springs with local band Nokturnl. The audience was delirious with grog and excitement, and after logging thousands of kilometres in three days, we were delirious too. The smell of bodies—black and white, some of which hadn't seen a shower in weeks—dust and beer and desert air clung to our clothes all the way back to Sydney.

I called Mandawuy Yunupingu to touch base. Yothu Yindi would also be at the closing ceremony, performing the hit song 'Treaty', a potent attack on the failure of an earlier prime minister, Bob Hawke, to honour his promise to begin treaty negotiations. They may have thoughts about how they wanted to present themselves and a view about the Oils' proposal, and they did—'Go for it!'

We would be playing to over 2 billion people, at that time the largest global audience in history, so it was critical everything was in place before the lights went up. We expected the director of the TV broadcast, David Atkins, would probably guess the Oils would try something on, and so the outline of the plan would have to be shared with him—the cameras had to come in close. Otherwise it was a closely guarded secret.

The dress rehearsals were a simple matter. I was away at the time and the band showed up in black overalls and went through the motions, accompanied by much official head-nodding.

On a balmy Sydney evening in October 2000, the Olympic complex was alive with an expectant crowd. Our stage manager, Michael Lippold, blocked the dressing-room door as we geared up, first one pair of black overalls emblazoned with 'Sorry', sewn in white in different places, and over those overalls a second plain pair. We did a quick undress rehearsal and timed how long it would take to get the second pair off—about ten seconds.

As we stand in the race with a loud hum coursing through the building and around the stands, the Olympics official party, with President Juan Antonio Samaranch in their midst, sweeps past, all smiles—the Sydney games have been judged a success. But there's just one thing.

'Midnight Oil, one minute!' shouts the marshal. After silently counting down for 50 seconds we start undoing the buttons, casually. I step out of the first pair of overalls and hand them to the unsmiling detective assigned to keep an eye on us, standing next to me in the race. 'Can you mind these for me, please?'

And then out we jog, across the sports field and onto a high stage, with the giant props—goolies, cartoon figures, weird space ships—made by Reg Mombassa (our old touring comrade from Mental as Anything) swaying over us.

The boys are miming in case the wind blows an amp over, but the vocals are live. I glance across the massed spectacle as the first three chords of 'Beds' sound out: E, G, A.

Athletes from all around the ground charge towards our stage, waving their national flags and jigging furiously.

There's a split second of calm as the sound revs up, the giant screens flicker to life and then, with a roar, the entire crowd is on its feet.

Everyone, that is, except Prime Minister John Howard and his wife, and the governor-general, Sir William Deane, and Mrs Deane; Deane, one of our most compassionate elders, is obliged to sit solemnly alongside one of the worst deniers of our history while a stadium full of people dance and sing around them.

Back in the green room we caught our breath, towelling ourselves dry as the hubbub died away. On the opposite side of the room other performers were sitting quietly having a drink. Slim Dusty, still wearing his Akubra bush hat, was there with his wife Joy and a few members of his band. They had also been part of the closing ceremony's entertainment. He looked across, nodded his head slightly, and then gave the double thumbs-up—we'd passed the Slim test at least.

We'd decided that I wouldn't go out the next day and add to the gesture with endless media interviews, unless it was needed. In the event it was, but only for a brief rejoinder to Howard. The prime minister made it clear on morning radio that he was 'disappointed' by the performance. This wasn't an occasion for mixing politics and sport, he chided.

The last time Australians heard these words was during the apartheid era, when the South African rugby team came to play. When people spoke out against the tour they were criticised for mixing sport and politics. Twenty-three years later, Nelson Mandela was elected the first president of a multiracial South Africa.

23
INTO THE RING

THE ANSWER TO the question of which was more important, the music or the politics, had, up to now, been easy to answer—they came together. I'd poured into both as much energy as I could summon. Enervating, exasperating, exhausting—strapped into the rocket, the journey had been a blast.

Now, in the music world, we were in a state of suspended animation. When we came off the road to activist politics, by contrast, there was a lot happening and it looked like things would only speed up from this point on. It wasn't as if I was torn between the two vocations; rather, the gravitational pull of requests, new campaigns, ACF business and associated work just kept getting stronger.

The 2002 run Midnight Oil did around Australia before I finally said goodbye to the band distilled some of the elements of my predicament.

Returning to venues we'd played twenty years before—Revesby Workers' Club, Manly and Parramatta leagues clubs, the Darwin Botanic Gardens—was a reminder of how tricky it can be to keep things fresh when the setting is so familiar.

Activist groups setting up in the foyer of a big room we performed at in downtown Perth, and then crashing backstage to continue the conversation about the future of Ningaloo Reef, the home of the Great Whale Shark.

Flying across from Emerald to Rockhampton in Central Queensland in a tatty twin-engine aircraft, only to discover later that Gary had asked for the 'cheapest' charter.

Launching the new Northern Australia office for the ACF the night after a steamy Cairns gig in another blighted footy club full of pokies. There, pressed against the stage, was Margaret Thorsborne, the seventy-year-old conservationist who'd fought off the developers near Hinchinbrook Island and was now in danger of getting trampled by the young men around her. I spent half the night willing them to notice her.

Nearly walking on water at the Forum in Melbourne as we lifted off, and went higher than ever before, and the sound was so ripe you could taste it and it made you swallow hard, and the crowd, the names and faces of the front row as familiar as extended family, which was what they'd become, refusing to let us leave the stage.

I'd already told the Oils I wanted to move on. I wasn't the only one who'd considered getting out—just about everyone had countenanced pulling up stakes at one point or other—but I'd been holding back, acutely aware of the weight of a decision that would affect a lot of people and bring something too special for words to a halt. It ended up happening by phone, which was not the best way, but no one would have been surprised.

We played our final two shows at Twin Towns Services Club, on the border of New South Wales and Queensland. At the last minute, Jim and Martin decided they would do the set lists. We would play two songs from each album, starting at the 'Blue Meanie' (the name fans had given to the first album, because of the LP's blue cover). I managed to record the experience in a few lines in the diary, noting that it was 'still exhilarating to hear the brash explosiveness of the early songs, compared with the more steadied craft of the later'.

It's an iron law of rock that fans say: 'I like your old stuff better than your new stuff.' Except this judgement isn't about the quality of the songs; it's about memories. 'Star of Hope' from *Breathe* or 'Concrete' from *Redneck Wonderland* are of equal weight to 'Back on the Border-line' from *Head Injuries* or 'Bullroarer' from *Diesel and Dust*. Except they don't carry as many associated experiences for listeners because they arrived when everyone, band and audience, had a few more years under their belts. When you're young and chafing at the bit and you fasten on to a song, nothing a band does later will come close. That song partnered your salad days, when you were experiencing the tribulations and ecstasies of growing up, and it will always sound better than anything that follows. Your memories are vivid and you still want to hear that song years from then, and remember—that's an iron law of getting older.

On the final night we finished a four-song encore with 'Redneck Wonderland'. What more was there to say? The audience was morose, confused, and the two *Capricornia* songs marked for a possible second encore remain unplayed—'A metaphor for the career,' said Jim. Afterwards, we hung around till late, talking and drinking beer.

The next day I flew down to Melbourne for ACF executive and council meetings, while the band flew back to Sydney and the crew, with trucks full of gear, wended their way down the coast for the last time.

I knew I would miss the freedom that I'd had up to now, the dressing-room rituals, the suspension of time deep in performance and the core group of people who had been there for the long haul: Gary, Michael Lippold, our street-smart publicist Paula Jones, the Office team, with Arlene Brookes a constant presence. I knew the rest of the Oils would be sad, angry, pissed off, anxious, relieved and any number of other emotions. I had plenty of mixed emotions too, but relief was the strongest; I just had to let it go.

At the same time I suspected it wasn't completely finished. How could it be? The character of Midnight Oil was bigger than any single member. The band had decided they would continue to play and keep it going in some shape. I later heard they chased around for a female vocalist without unearthing a candidate, eventually re-emerging as a surf instrumental band called the Break—how ironic to have a soundtrack for surfing after all those years.

As a group of people for whom being together on stage made perfect sense, this band could always do it again if the reasons stacked up, as happened when we played benefits at the Sydney Cricket Ground for those affected by the Indian Ocean tsunami on Boxing Day, 2004, and later at the Melbourne Cricket Ground for victims of the 2009 Victorian bushfires.

'I love ya, big man,' Bones had said when we parted ways at the airport, and the feeling was mutual. But then, he'd been through a break-up before. For Jim, Martin and Rob, Midnight Oil was just about all they'd known—it had to hurt.

. . .

The calls started coming almost immediately. The first two were from Phillip Toyne and Bob Carr, wanting to know when I was going to join the Labor Party. Carr had already hinted at a spot as environment minister in New South Wales, and was coming back for a second bite. Phillip, now heading up the Bush Heritage Trust, was, as usual, thinking upstream and keen to see someone with a strong conservation background in mainstream politics. In the days and weeks that followed, there were plenty of other calls, including from Tom Uren, Bob Brown, John Faulkner and a host of mates. There'd be plenty of time to follow them up later on, but for now I just wanted to catch my breath and spend more time on the home front. The girls were growing up in front of my eyes, turning into spirited, sensitive, funny young women, filling up the house as teenagers do. Grace, no longer a baby, was now playing piano, Em and May were out on the sporting field on Saturdays, and I wanted to be there as much as I could.

Besides, my presidency of the ACF still left me with plenty to do for the present, especially with the foundation moving to refurbished offices in an old three-storey building in Carlton in Melbourne that was intended to showcase the best energy- and water-saving technologies and sustainable building methods.

Dubbed 'the ACF Green Building', this project got me excited, and was a stellar example of leading thinking from the council and its previous president, Professor David Yencken, who had long argued for the ACF to walk the talk in its own premises. Located at 60 Leicester Street, the renovation project was designed as an affordable fit-out that could be easily replicated. It had been made possible by a generous donation from a charitable foundation called the Poola Foundation, operated by Eve Kantor (Rupert Murdoch's niece) and her husband, Mark Wootton.

While ACF's Green Building features a number of sustainable elements, like generous rainwater storage, waterless urinals—always a good talking point—and an ingenious heating and cooling system that relies on an automated system of louvres that track the sun, it was the behavioural elements of the approach that turned out to be most important. The enthusiasm of the people working in the building to extend their tasks to monitoring the temperature, sharing workstations and always turning off the lights when they go home ultimately provided the biggest energy-saving payback. With its six-star energy rating, the Green Building became a showpiece, demonstrating that low energy and water use could be business as usual, but it was the workers' willingness to change a little that made the biggest difference.

It wasn't only environmental issues that took my attention. I was appalled by the decision of the Howard government, in early 2003, to commit Australian troops to the war in Iraq, and spoke out against the war, including at a large rally at Federation Square in Melbourne. It was clear that the invasion was illegal, as the relevant Security Council resolution on Iraq did not expressly authorise the use of force, and I was encouraged by Labor's clear opposition to the war in the parliament. It was a reminder of the power that principled oppositions can have and I took note. It was also a reminder of the

need for the parliament, not the executive, to determine whether the
nation should go to war.

At ACF we were focused on a redesign of the economic system so
it didn't operate counter to ecological principles and society didn't
have to fight for the natural world at every turn.

In June 2003 I addressed the National Press Club, a venue that
provides a unique opportunity to talk directly to the nation's media.
John Connor, the new ACF campaign director, executive director
Don Henry and I spent a lot of time preparing a speech that we hoped
would reset the compass. It laid out a template for environmental tax
reform and a new approach to natural resource management that
would help reverse the decline in the health of Australia's precious
ecosystems. But the gallery's mind was elsewhere and the appeal fell
on deaf ears.

I remained in touch with the then Labor Party leader Simon Crean
and others in the party as we attempted to green the party's policies.
But the absence of anyone willing to stick their neck out and go to
the wall was telling, and I began to think that if the opportunity
arose to influence policy from inside the parliament, I would take it.

Simon Balderstone visited me in Mittagong and we scoped out
possible scenarios. Discussions intensified when Mark Latham
became Labor leader. Doris and I had hosted Latham and his wife
Janine and their kids at our place, and I found him serious, interested in policy and forceful to boot. There was something about his
showing up at old-style town hall meetings and arguing the toss with
all and sundry until everyone went home talked out that appealed
to me. That he was a bona fide maddie, and could explode at any
moment, I didn't recognise at the time.

People whom I'd confided in about possibly throwing my hat in
the ring thought I was tending to mad as well—but it goes with the
territory. Doris knew that, having come this far, I would have a go
if the chance arose, and she was supportive. Again, I can't overstate
her generosity. If it came to pass, it meant a lot more time apart,

a state neither of us liked, even if our relationship was strong enough to withstand the absences.

In the end, nothing would have happened if the member for the Sydney seat of Kingsford Smith, Laurie Brereton, hadn't resigned very late in the day, leaving open the possibility for the new federal Labor leader to request that a candidate be selected without going through a bitter rank-and-file process, there being no clear-cut contender in the electorate. Accordingly, Latham struck.

Once a Labor leader has made a call like that, the party could be expected to fall into line, but it wasn't that straightforward. The blur of calls and meetings to prepare the ground was now accompanied by a growing media frenzy over whether or not I was about to make an announcement. And there were plenty of Labor insiders who didn't like the idea at all.

It was pretty simple when you boiled it down. I wanted to make a difference. After years of heading to Canberra to get some attention and make the case for change, why not go and see if things could be taken further? Until now, I'd always worked as an outsider. I'd written and commentated on issues. I'd done time as the talking head with a quote for the day. I'd been on the front line pushing and shoving to get issues on to the agenda, and I'd campaigned for change. It was time to get into the ring.

I knew my decision to enter formal politics would put me offside with a raft of people: conservative voters generally, the rebels and purists who saw me as selling out, Greens party members who felt I should have joined them, ALP members who thought I was getting a free ride. And for those closest to my roots, the legion of Oils fans— who yearned for us to keep doing what we had always done—here I was really walking away from the band.

I'd watched politics closely over the years and seen that idealism and pragmatism have to reach a balance in successful policy-making. You want to aim for the best possible result, with the best chance of making it work, and that means bringing dreamers and idealists together with managers and the technically skilled to see if you can get a project up to create change that lasts. I was willing to try to find that sweet spot in the endeavour of government.

At the same time, I was too much of an economic dry and too allergic to utopianism to side with the Australian Greens. When leader Bob Brown had asked me to consider joining, I spent some time in discussions with him and his adviser, Ben Oquist. Oquist, one of the next in line, was willing to make way for me in the queue for a Senate seat. Later on, he was rejected by the New South Wales Greens as a candidate, which was a pity. He is smart and principled and would have made an outstanding representative.

Sanctimony sucks, and while there were a number of people involved with the party whom I liked and had worked with in the past, including Bob, I couldn't envisage years of playing a dishonest song to the bleachers, promising a nirvana that couldn't be delivered and castigating everyone else as moral inferiors. There was another factor, too, and that concerned the flirtation of the Wilderness Society with the Liberal/National Coalition when Labor had been in government in the 1980s. From the luxury of opposition, the conservatives had promised greater environmental gains that, sure enough, once Howard came to power, were never realised. It was a characteristic position of the Wilderness Society and, later, the Greens, that they would deal with either of the major parties, having equal contempt for both. In their eyes, Labor and Liberal were indistinguishable from one another, characterised as 'laborials', different in name only. As a way of slicing votes, particularly from inner-city electorates, it was effective rhetoric, but a long way from the truth. On environmental issues like climate change, the differences were great, which explained why, in nearly all cases, the Greens would exchange preference votes with Labor, the party they spent most time attacking. They preferred Labor to stay in power but they also wanted to enlist the support of left-oriented Labor supporters—it was a deft double act but not one in which I wanted to participate.

By the time I left parliament it was impossible to identify a single environmental gain that the Greens, even when part of a minority government, could credibly lay claim to.

Strange as it may sound, I also respected small business, having spent more than twenty-five years in a partnership generating income, paying taxes and employing people. I knew how hard it was to keep productivity going up, which was the only solution to the inexorable demands on the budget, especially for social services that had to be paid out of the public purse.

When I sat quietly to consider my future, I knew that the Australian Labor Party, despite its flaws, was my natural home. I'd grown up with Labor and many of its values rang true for me. I believed a fair reading of Australia's modern history showed that our social and economic progress was due in no small measure to the ALP: centralised wage-fixing, saving the Antarctic from mineral exploitation, supporting the formation of the UN, establishing Medicare and compulsory superannuation, legislating for native title, and there was plenty more. And while it was, and still is, in danger of becoming a closed-door club for careerists and union hacks, to date Labor had been a major source of positive reform going back to its formation in the dawning days of our democracy.

I knew a number of senior Labor figures well—John Faulkner, Warren Snowdon, Kim Beazley, Bob Carr, Ros Kelly, Steve Bracks, Susan Ryan—and appreciated the serious intent they applied to the calling. I'd got to know others, too, like Simon Balderstone and Sam Mostyn, both of whom had worked in Keating's office. They believed the values of Labor best matched the values of young Australians and were supportive of me getting on board.

No matter what lay ahead, I was genuinely animated by the thought of representing an electorate in parliament. This notion was one that some of my peers, and even strangers I ran into in the street, couldn't get their heads around. Why put yourself through the endless school speech nights and sporting events, accessible to all and sundry day and night, with precious little time for family and the finer things of life, to be Mr Everyman in the suburbs?

My answer, and one that had the cynics gagging, was that I believed in this aspect of democracy—it was real, for a start. I valued the service a diligent local member could bring to their electorate and was proud to do that job regardless of what else might eventuate. I happened to think the grist of politics is better for the fact of physical representation—eye to eye with the decent as well as the deranged— and I liked people, liked to be in the place they lived, bound by the weave of family and community life. I didn't see it as a chore.

...

I travelled to Sydney at the beginning of June 2004 to sign the ALP membership papers as the factional deliberations were settled by John Faulkner representing the left, and right-wing state MP Eric Roozendaal (who became embroiled in corruption allegations later on) at Faulkner's home in Sydney.

The right were far from happy, and having examined the electoral roll and discovered I wasn't registered, someone close to head office chose their moment and, once the announcement was made, leaked it to the media—welcome to the Labor Party.

I'd voted in every election, and assumed, since the stalking incident in Balgowlah years earlier, that I'd been on the silent electors roll. The media firestorm that followed was a taste of things to come. No one really doubted that I was genuinely interested in politics and had always fronted on election day. There was even a photo of me voting at the US consulate in New York, and friends, including Todd Hunter from Dragon and his wife Johanna Pigott, had been with me at the polling booth at the previous election and were willing to testify on my behalf.

The whole incident left a sour aftertaste. I knew that it would require a big dose of stamina and some deep breathing if I was to survive going over the falls in the months ahead. There was choppy water wherever you looked and the rollcall of those who'd dived in late and foundered included: former Australian Democrats leader Cheryl Kernot, a late addition to the Labor Party (beleaguered and abandoned in tears at Hobart airport); rugby league great Mal Meninga ('I'm buggered' two minutes into his first radio interview); Australian Olympic hockey coach and medico Ric Charlesworth (stranded on the backbench); and, later on, ABC journalist Maxine McKew, after one all-too-brief term ('It's all their fault!'). Their fate was a reminder there were no lifesavers around here.

...

The months preceding my decision to run for federal parliament passed in a flurry of activity as I tried to square off existing commitments.

Don Henry had proved a positive leader, successfully shepherding the ACF through the operational changes and maintaining a close focus on Cape York and national and global climate change developments. Always cheerful, Don was impossible not to like: beneath the smiling exterior he was a determined advocate who never wavered in trying to win the day for conservation.

We'd only just launched an important new paper, 'Natural Advantage: A blueprint for a sustainable Australia', with the Governor-General, Sir William Deane. It was a thorough set of policy ideas to try to match environmental protection with economic growth, a reboot of the principles of ecologically sustainable development (ESD). Despite some strong corporate endorsement, however, it failed to excite any interest from the Howard government.

We'd also begun a dialogue with Labor's shadow cabinet, and new leader Mark Latham's office, about repositioning the environment around a low-carbon economy and finally cracking the code on the long-running Tasmanian forests dispute. After I departed the ACF, the discussions on Tassie forests continued all the way through to the 2014 election. At the time, Latham was clear that he wanted, as he put it, 'to be bold'. Don and I kept pushing at the policy, aware that at long last there was a chance to go right over the Maginot Line that had separated the warring parties for so long.

The result has gone into political folklore, but without much perspective. Labor's announcement, when it came, of significant increases in areas of protected old-growth forests, was a campaign disaster in 2004. John Howard had sensed the enmity that many in the powerful forestry union, the Construction, Forestry, Mining and Energy Union (CFMEU), had to an ambitious environmental agenda and he outflanked Latham by appearing at a union rally, promising to save timber workers' jobs and offering some modest proposals for forest protection. Amazingly, the unionists cheered Howard, their natural enemy, blinded by the hatred that coursed through the veins of most Tassie workers for the 'greenies', who in their eyes were blow-ins, nothing more than a rent-a-crowd of ratbags, intent on taking timber jobs away while squatting on the dole. Of course, once re-elected, Howard cynically abandoned his promise to add substantially to the conservation estate and the forestry industry continued to struggle and shed jobs. It wasn't until much later, in 2013, under the Gillard government, that a proposal to save significant areas of Tasmania's tall native forests, along with a restructuring package to assist displaced workers, was accepted by both governments, the conservation groups and most of the unions and industry, although subsequently the Abbott government torpedoed the agreement. It was remarkably similar to the policy put up by Labor a decade earlier.

In Tasmania there was an irrational fear of taking a leap and doing something positive for the environment, despite the kudos that had come with the successful Franklin Dam campaign thirty years earlier. Everything was viewed through a prism of fear and loss, in this case shared between the opposing forces of organised labour on the left and industry on the right. It showed up as a footnote as my entry into parliament was mooted.

To Coalition environment minister David Kemp, I was a 'rogue ideologue'. And to prove the assertion, he pointed out I was even opposing the Australia–United States Free Trade Agreement. (On firm grounds, as it turned out, given the lack of real benefits that have flowed since—and the fact that it freezes the quota for Australian music at 25 per cent.)

The CFMEU, for their part, predicted 'a massive backlash' within the Labor Party if I was ever elected. This was highly unlikely, and there was one thing I could confidently predict even then: if elected, I would show more loyalty to the ALP than had been on display from this angry rabble.

Ironically, Michael O'Connor, who headed up the forestry branch of the union and had been for many years a trenchant opponent of the ACF, was sitting on the national executive of the ALP when it sanctioned my selection as the ALP candidate for Kingsford Smith.

Following Latham's captain's call, I had to travel to Canberra to meet with this key administrative body so my candidature could be formalised. Sitting around a big table were some familiar and some not-so-familiar faces that I would get to know a lot better in the coming years, including politicians like Victorian left warlord Kim Carr as well as CFMEU boss O'Connor.

During the course of the interview, O'Connor aggressively questioned whether I would use the party to further an environmental agenda.

My reply was that I would be a team player, but I'd argue strongly for better environmental policies every step of the way. Labor should be proud of its past record of achievement, but there was much more to do.

...

I raced around, trying to get the groundwork done so I could make the transition to a new career as a federal politician, and in a brief window I took the opportunity to visit East Timor. I'd wanted to get there for some time. Since Midnight Oil had done benefit shows for the East Timorese, I'd come to know José Ramos-Horta, the recipient of a Nobel Peace Prize in 1996 after years of trying to draw attention to East Timor's plight. The Oils ended up doing two songs in support of the cause: one, Jim's thundering denunciation of Australian complicity in East Timor's history, 'Say Your Prayers', featured on one of the few EPs we released; the other, 'Kolele Mai', was an arrangement of a traditional Timorese folk song.

I had a long-standing invitation to visit from Kirsty Sword Gusmão, an Australian married to Xanana Gusmão, Timor-Leste's first elected president. Gusmão was a resistance leader who, after years of struggle—including time in Indonesian jails—was now wrestling with the enormous task of getting the country back on its feet. Kirsty asked me to come for a concert they were holding to commemorate East Timor's independence. The idea was to spend some time with local musicians and politicians, and get a better sense of the issues this tiny new nation was facing.

I journeyed up to the president's residence to have lunch and hear from Gusmão about the current situation. The Gusmãos lived just outside the capital, Dili, in a modest bungalow that wouldn't have looked out of place in any sea-change town along the Australian coast. His was a dire report. The infant nation was struggling; they were in good spirits but lacked the bare essentials: schools and hospitals were rudimentary, in some areas non-existent, and they were facing difficult tasks on every front.

In 1975 Indonesia had invaded East Timor and a brutal war followed. At the time of the invasion, the population of Indonesia was around 140 million, whereas East Timor had a population of about 700,000. During the course of the conflict and subsequent declaration that East Timor was part of Indonesia—a declaration recognised by Australia alone—it was estimated that nearly 200,000 Timorese had been killed, with many more displaced.

Violence, beatings and rape were common throughout this

period and human rights activists, and some sections of the Catholic Church—notably Carmelite nuns and the Sisters of St Joseph of the Sacred Heart (the order founded by Mary MacKillop)—had worked hard, and eventually with considerable success, to bring the plight of the East Timorese to the attention of the Australian public.

At the same time the realpolitik of not upsetting a powerful regional neighbour had been central to the thinking of the Department of Foreign Affairs and successive governments since Whitlam. My predecessor in the seat of Kingsford Smith, Laurie Brereton, as Labor's shadow foreign minister, had, against this ingrained view, moved to strengthen Labor's support for the East Timorese. I discovered later that this task was made more difficult by the activities of a newly elected ALP member, Kevin Rudd, who coveted Brereton's position. Rudd worked in concert with the Howard government's foreign minister, Alexander Downer, to undermine Brereton, including secretly briefing the US embassy in Canberra against Brereton on the issue of national missile defence. Even by the standard of politics played hard, it was an act of cold betrayal and once exposed should have sent warning signals about Rudd's character to the Labor Caucus, the collection of members and senators who choose the leader of the party.

In the end, a decision by Indonesian president B.J. Habibie to allow the Timorese a plebiscite on independence, supervised by Indonesian forces, brought events to a head. The Australian prime minister, John Howard, supported this decision, but in fidelity to the elite view wrote to the Indonesians indicating Australia would accept Indonesia retaining sovereignty.

The Timorese showed great courage, with nearly 80 per cent voting in favour of nationhood, and Australian forces played a substantial role in the UN-led peacekeeping mission that followed.

On my final night in town, I joined Paul Kelly, Paul Stewart from Melbourne band Painters and Dockers, and local musician Ego Lemos for a concert held in a ramshackle part of Dili's downtown.

If any country deserved to succeed, Timor was surely one. I hoped they'd get there, but Australia wasn't making it any easier. For a successful fresh start, they required a fair share of royalties from the oil and gas reserves located in offshore waters close by, a substantial portion of which was claimed by Australia. With a reliable source of income, the country's leaders could invest in health and education and in the infrastructure needed to raise standards of living without having to meet the crippling debt repayments that many less-developed countries had been saddled with in recent decades.

Timor's fair share was never entirely realised, although some royalties now flow into Dili. The original agreement Australia signed with Indonesia, which effectively denies Timor access to a large part of its oil and gas reserves, is under challenge. Even though a subsequent agreement saw the East Timorese parliament approve that arrangement, recent events, including instances of Australian government espionage in East Timor, have reopened the issue.

...

One thing that stood out after decades of touring was the fervour of audiences south of the New South Wales border. Melburnians are among the most loyal supporters around. I don't know if it's because of the weather, or it's a facet of their culture, but they stick with their favourite footy teams and their causes through thick and thin.

It was in the Melbourne suburb of Essendon that I saw my first, unforgettable, AFL game. There I stood shoulder to shoulder at the club's old ground, the aptly named Windy Hill, on a freezing, wet afternoon, with the full sweep of Melbourne society: well-dressed matrons, mongrel sons and daughters, toffs and working people of all ages, shapes and sizes, many togged up in scarves and beanies in the Dons' colours, red and black.

The crowd was screaming at the top of their lungs as the ball was punted up and down the ground and players lunged into the air for a catch or threw themselves into melees to retrieve the precious pill.

The shouting extended to the umpire when he made a questionable call—'Ya mug, ump!'—and across the ground to tease rival supporters for good measure. The smell of pies and beery breath and sweat seeped through the crowd. And it was like that week in and week out. I've followed the Bombers ever since.

There was good reason to be a Bombers fan during the period when Kevin Sheedy was coaching. He was a social pioneer and encouraged Aboriginal players in the sport. The 'Dreamtime at the G' fixture between Essendon and Richmond, which celebrates the contribution Indigenous AFL players have made to the sport, was a stand-out initiative.

When it was first mooted I got behind the event—at last, a focus on the big picture; black players had made a huge contribution to AFL—and always tried to get down for the game. When I got back from Timor, it was to join Shane Howard, Paul Kelly (again), Archie Roach and Ruby Hunter at the G for a sober version of Goanna's 'Solid Rock'.

On another occasion we marched to the ground with Michael Long, the former Essendon great, who had just walked from Melbourne to Canberra—a real long march—to put pressure on the 'gutless' (his word) Howard government for not making Indigenous issues a priority.

I'd called him up on the way in to see how he was going after walking 500 kilometres. He was characteristically low key. 'It's been all right,' he said. 'But I need a new pair of shoes.'

Wearing out shoe leather was about to become a fact of life for me as well, although not quite on the scale of Long's arduous trek.

A decade of tramping around the streets and through the corridors of power was just around the corner, and I had little idea what lay ahead. The only thing I knew for sure was that when it came to the governance of my country, the time to stand up and be counted had well and truly come.

24

NO TIME TO WASTE

IN LATE JUNE 2004, I took the train from Mittagong to Sydney to move a few essentials into the small flat I'd rented until we had a chance to get something bigger for the family in the electorate. The margin in favour of Labor was running around 8 per cent, so I could expect to win the seat if I waged a strong campaign. The country was still in the grip of a big dry. As the train emerged from the last of the rock cuttings that accommodate the railway line before Camden, the miserably thin soil line stuck out like a sliver of gold in a rubbish tip. Rattling into full sunlight, there in sharp relief, was empty dam upon empty dam, squatting at the bottom of bleached grey paddocks. This drought was at last concentrating people's minds on water, or the lack thereof, with rivers slowing to a trickle and the threat of bushfires building. And hopefully it was making us rethink climate change too. For we couldn't keep stumbling along this barren path to another blazing inferno, could we? It was a good time to be going to the nation's capital; there was serious work to be done.

A short-term lease on a shopfront—formerly a Thai restaurant—along one of the shopping strips in Maroubra, in the centre of the electorate, provided premises for the campaign team. Kate Pasterfield, a former staffer from Laurie Brereton's office who'd left university early and worked with various Labor MPs while still a teenager, had been employed by head office to help coordinate. We were joined by a slew of fresh faces—local party members tired of the rote politics of the machine, keen to shake things up—and a few media tagging along to file celebrity politician pieces, or better still to catch a stumble (though none were forthcoming just then).

The vexed issue of celebrity meant that I was still considered a rock star of sorts, even if I didn't see myself that way, and sitting astride the fame-o-meter with a suit and tie on would make me fair game. Sure enough, an early report referred scathingly to the 'well-cut suit' I was wearing, as if the normal mode of dress for a politician was somehow confirmation of my lack of integrity in exiting the stage to make a run for parliament. Scurrilous snippets appeared suggesting all wasn't well in my marriage—a descent into the dirtiest gutter that made me feel sick. I'd never paraded my family around; it was enough that we had to manage long separations without dropping them in it head first. Anyone with a smidgen of decency, and a background check under their belt, would have known that reports of marital strife simply weren't true.

These were petty examples of journalistic practices that weren't exceptional. There were a few good journalists who stuck to the facts, didn't take sides and delivered credible media. But it looked like the bar would be set high for me and I'd be granted a slimmer margin of forgiveness for the inevitable mistakes to come. In time, I just had to accept there would be judgement by prejudice, not fact, and often from the projections of a cohort who got their steer on events from anonymous whisperers and talk-show blowhards. I wouldn't be the only politician who was set up and then assaulted in the docks. It happened on a greater and more damaging scale to Julia Gillard when she was prime minister: she had to wear a relentless negative and palpably misogynistic media campaign. It says a lot about her fortitude that she persevered without displaying any bitterness at the treatment she received.

Our political system might still be a method of finding proximate solutions for intractable problems (as American commentator Reinhold Niebuhr has observed), but it's usually a messy business of incremental change, often with two steps forward and one back. Only rarely is there the big flash of light and a great leap ahead. Yet it seemed as if some expected a hero who would suddenly ride into the middle of a pitched battle they had been waging forever and carry their flag to victory—if only. I never bought in to the hero myth tied to success or notoriety. Real-life heroes are those who risk their lives in war, natural disasters and emergencies when no one else will step up to help. The sense of disappointment that some felt at my joining Labor was a projection of people's assumptions about me rather than a reflection on what I actually said or did; in these instances, it wasn't about me at all.

In the meantime, in comparison to any number of ego-driven airheads that infect our culture, the politician has become the modern-day bogeyman, infinitely attackable, a locus point of envy, animosity, cynicism, disdain and world-weariness. While there is no shortage of politicians who are deserving targets, tarring every politician with the same brush is inaccurate and lazy. Still, when New South Wales Labor turned toxic, having shown bad faith with the public and genuine party members by allowing crooks and thugs to inhabit the party, people understandably treated any politician they came across as a punching bag. It was a strange sensation to be warding off these attacks while at the same time being told not to take it personally.

Some have it that voters are hypocrites, who complain that there are too many laws, then immediately want another one to fix something that's wrong in their lives. But this is too harsh. Voters act both rationally and emotionally, and the picture of people's responses to politics as a consequence can be confusing. It is rational to expect governments to enforce laws that protect children or to object to a politician breaking a promise. It is not rational to expect that governments can legislate for better behaviour, or that politicians will keep every promise they make if conditions change markedly in the interim. People's view of my role wasn't always rational, but that didn't mean it wasn't genuinely felt, and I still encounter the conflicting responses to my decision to step into politics to this day.

...

The slogan I chose was 'Energy—Action—Commitment', having discarded the predictables: 'Our Area, Our Voice' and 'Working with You'. It was as good a summary of the approach I wanted to take as we could find.

Initially, our modest campaign headquarters were a magnet for anyone with a barrow to push. At the start of the campaign, to the surprise of Kate Pasterfield and the team, much time had to be spent handling these incursions, aimed at elevating a personal grudge or pet issue into the spotlight.

One memorable media stunt, and a sign of things to come, saw the Wilderness Society hire a front-end loader and dump several tonnes of woodchips on the footpath in front of the office, preventing anyone from getting in or out, accompanied by signs saying: 'Garrett has to save the forests now!' This was well before the election. After the camera crews had taken their shots and left, one of the activists returned and sheepishly asked if he could borrow a broom to sweep up the mess—a request that was politely denied through gritted teeth.

During the campaign I travelled a little with Latham and tried to satisfy the entreaties from other Labor candidates for photo-op visits, but mainly I stayed on home turf as much as possible. I was pretty sure electors didn't want to see their putative local member on TV; they wanted to see him in the flesh, and I was determined to stay put.

Election day 2004 came upon us in what seemed like minutes, not months. The day itself was one rush of continual movement— visiting each polling booth, as was the practice, to thank party members who'd turned up, while the team made sure everyone had a coffee and a feed at some point. No one had time to sit and catch their breath until all the votes were in. Then the business of getting out early to catch the commuters, walking the streets, visiting clubs, schools, Saturday-morning sport, anywhere there were people, all the while responding to scuttlebutt and incoming attacks from the other parties, abruptly stopped dead.

On the morning before the big day, I'd stood with a team of volunteers at Maroubra Junction, handing out leaflets to passers-by. Some were forthcoming about our prospects. It was clear we weren't going to win: they didn't like Howard, but they didn't trust Latham. In Kingsford Smith, though, the party had rallied; the angst about the method of my entry had vanished in the heat of the campaign. The tribe was out in force, and in greater numbers than our opponents: there was a seat to win.

Two days later I was the new member of parliament for Kingsford Smith. I stood in an empty office on the top floor of a six-storey medical centre, watching a line of international flights descending into Sydney's Kingsford Smith Airport, as flickering TVs blinked back at me from the rows of houses and flats in the streets below, catching my breath after a contest that was already sliding off the radar and marvelling at the bizarreness of it all. And then it was time to get to work as we started to draw up a list of actions for the coming year.

The idea was simple. I wanted us to operate like I felt the church up on the hill should: open to help all comers, regardless of rank or affiliation. I'd come into the party without any faction behind me and I wasn't intending to join one now. The existing system of favours, the counterbalancing of various personal debts and credits that was part and parcel of political office, and essential to the upward climb of most members of parliament, wouldn't have purchase here—much to the chagrin of the local heavies.

I was grateful for the loyal branch members who attended the early fundraisers, and for the generous support that had flowed my way from outside the local party apparatus, including from cricketer Mike Whitney; soon-to-be state Opposition leader John Robertson; my old pal Simon Balderstone; Paul Gilding and his wife Michelle Grosvenor, who were great contributors; and Michael Ward, a long-time Labor Party member, who'd previously been CEO of Ecos Corporation, a green-energy company established by Paul, and who had rallied many of his colleagues to our cause.

Also there were my brother Matt and his partner Brett and many long-time friends, including Doddo, who by now had written a successful book, *Beds Are Burning*, about the Oils; comedian Angela Webber and Stuart Matchett from Double J; Pam Swain, an original Double J staffer; film producer, director and actor Jeremy Sims; Greig (H.G. Nelson) Pickhaver; artists Peter O'Doherty and his wife Sue; Stephanie Lewis, who'd worked in the Oils office in the 80s; lobbyist Gabi Trainor; musician Chris Latham, and a host of others—a diverse collection from arts and business and activism who showed up to munch on rubber chicken and buy a few raffle tickets, the staple of any Labor Party fundraiser. A smattering of new colleagues came as well, including Tanya Plibersek, the member for Sydney, whom I came to know better once we got to Canberra.

These 'normal' people were in stark contrast to the team of younger party apparatchiks, sharply dressed and constantly fingering their mobile phones, who had descended on us by now; their self-important air broadcast the message: 'Don't forget me, one day I will be a member of parliament, and not long after that, prime minister.'

Kate Pasterfield, despite having experienced the strangeness of campaigning with an ex-rocker and activist, organising how-to-vote cards and mass autograph signings at the same time, had chosen to stay on. But inside the tent, and despite all hands having been on the pump on election day, we were mostly friendless.

…

Not long in, and before I'd even given my maiden speech, I decided to have a quick early-morning swim at Maroubra. The ocean had always been a healing force; I figured a surf would help to clear away the sour lemon taste of the last few months of carry-on.

Treading water out the back, I felt my body start to go numb and my head wonky. I thought I'd been stung by something nasty and just managed to heave myself onto a wave as the shapes of the surfers around me started to smudge and go out of focus.

The wave was a long time breaking but I hung on till it surged across the shallows. With great effort, my knees by now scraping on the sand, I crawled out of the ocean and promptly blacked out. My last thought as everything faded to black was, assuming I survived, what state would my brain and body be in?

When I came to in the emergency ward at Prince of Wales Hospital, hooked up to all manner of life-saving apparatus, the cause of the blackout was still a mystery of sorts. The medical team could see *what* had happened, but couldn't definitively say *why* it had. Still, they got me going again and by week's end I was back at work.

Misreported as a surfing accident, the puzzle was only solved after I received an email from an Oils fan working as a specialist in rare allergies in California who'd read the media reports and wondered if I might have developed an allergy to cold water.

The professor of all things allergic at Royal North Shore Hospital confirmed the diagnosis. Her verdict was sobering: the condition could be fatal, so I needed to carry an EpiPen at all times. This implement was filled with adrenalin to kick me back into gear in the event I fell overboard or encountered cold water in my travels and my system shut down. (Keeping track of the EpiPen proved too difficult, however; I promptly lost the first one, and several others are now strewn across the country.) Medical science has, as yet, no answer as to why this reaction materialised overnight, but in the majority of cases it isn't expected to last more than eight or nine years—at the moment it's still going, but hopefully not forever.

...

While the work of serving a constituency could now get underway without too much fuss, adapting to life in Canberra, where the federal

MPs met and internal politics was a blood sport, was going to be, to use one of the bywords of politics and political speeches . . . 'challenging'.

It is the way of the ALP that you sit in a room full of 'comrades', most of whom are ensnared in a web of IOUs and silent handshakes that go back twenty or thirty years, to the deep well of young Labor or the union movement or both. As a newcomer, you are a comrade in name only, unless you have friends from the past whom you can trust to tell you what's actually on their mind. I was lucky to have a handful of those, and over time made a few more.

This phenomenon is not confined to the Labor Party, even if it is more pronounced there. I was surprised to find myself walking out of the House of Representatives one evening with National Party leader and deputy prime minister John Anderson, departing after his valedictory speech. 'I never really understood this place,' he said mournfully over his shoulder to the empty chamber—a sentiment I heard expressed on a number of occasions, even from long-termers.

From the point you go in, to the day they drag or throw you out, it's an exercise in losing skin, an apt expression that sums up the after-effects of heated contests inside the party, as people jockey for position, and outside, as you spar with your political opponents.

There were strange moments that did my head in a bit early on, such as when Coalition treasurer Peter Costello had fun mimicking my dancing style in question time. One thing that stood out in Canberra was that none of the political class had any shame or, with a few exceptions, any sense of style—or, in Costello's case, rhythm. The press saw the performance as a funny jape, but it reminded me of private school boys' jokes, where it doesn't matter how stupid you look, if you're mocking someone your gang agrees is deserving, it's a riot. This kind of stunt might be what made Costello an effective parliamentary performer in his day, but it was low-rent stuff, one of the reasons the public saw parliament as a circus.

Foreign minister Alexander Downer made similar sport with Oils song lyrics, until his escapades in approving illicit payments to the

Australian Wheat Board during the illegal war in Iraq forced him to turn his mind to more serious matters.

Two weeks after opining that I'd make a welcome addition to the front bench, and even, God forbid, a good leader, Bob Brown was telling the Senate I was a 'sell-out' after I campaigned vigorously in the inner-city seat of Melbourne in the state election, urging a vote for Labor—what treachery from a new Labor member! Bronwyn Pike, formerly a Uniting Church activist, ultimately won the seat for the ALP and went on to serve as education minister in the Bracks government.

For their part, various Labor colleagues pressed me to join the unofficial members' choir, known as the Parliamentary Poets, who assemble every year for a sing-off against the press gallery choir at the annual charity event, the Federal Parliamentary Press Gallery Midwinter Ball.

The journos had more time to practise and a common opponent to inspire them, and they usually performed better. Sailing above the fray, without a thought that they too might deserve the occasional brickbat, they delighted in carrying on their daily occupation of pin-pricking politicians—from prime ministers down the food chain to gaffe-prone backbenchers—into semi-witty musical putdowns.

They were beatable, but not so long as my choir mates, without a hint of self-awareness, continued to instruct their new star recruit and de facto choir leader in how we should sing. Most struggled to hold a tune, so what we needed to do was practise, plain and simple. Yet, strangely, people would rarely make themselves available for rehearsals. I eventually gave up on this harmless yet surreal extra-curricular activity.

On a more serious note, the centre-left faction, balanced between dominant left and right factions, had lost some steam, and senior members sounded me out about joining. 'The left is your natural home, but there's a traffic jam of people,' was the pitch— I declined.

Likewise I declined South Australian premier Mike Rann's invitation to join him and Clare Martin, chief minister of the Northern Territory, on a joint ticket for the rotating presidency of the Labor Party.

I had a lot of time for Rann; he had an eye on the future. He was trying to get on top of climate change, was driving a modern innovation agenda in his state, and he wasn't factionally aligned. Still, it seemed premature, as I'd only just landed in parliament. I wanted to sit on the backbench, put my head down and learn the ropes, start working on policy and rise or fall on merit, not the fame factor.

Following the election, Mark Latham's leadership had gone up in smoke and Kim Beazley was back as leader after an earlier five-year stint. I respected and liked Kim a lot, although we differed on many issues. Worryingly, as he freely admitted, he didn't have a green bone in his body. Plenty of effort would be required to produce a solid environment policy by the time the next election came round, and given the maximum term for national governments is a ludicrously short three years, there was no time to waste.

25
MAD DANCE

B Y EARLY 2005 I was finding my feet and getting used to the strange new political arena I'd entered, but more than anything I just wanted to get to know Kingsford Smith better.

At the southern end of Sydney's eastern suburbs, the coast is the pulse point of the electorate, with its collection of surf beaches, inlets and expanses of rocky cliffs, leading from the well-heeled suburb of Clovelly on the northern perimeter down to La Perouse, where many Aboriginal people lived. Homes and apartments, many with supersized windows and glass sliding doors to take in the sweep of ocean, crowd ever closer together on the steep hillsides that lead down to the water.

There is never a time, day or night, when someone, somewhere, isn't diving in for a quick dip, walking, fishing, playing, socialising or misbehaving along the ocean paths and beachside promenades.

And there was never a time when the streets were free of real-estate propaganda. Sydney, including the eastern suburbs, where premium water views were dream booty, was trapped in the grip of a massive real-estate boom. Every weekend the auction signs would dot the suburbs; every week the notices of the next sale and information on the latest round of record prices would be slipped into the letterbox. Sydney's real estate was now among the most expensive in the world, jobs were plentiful in this part of Sydney and no one was pausing for breath.

During the long-forgotten hard days of the 1930s depression, a special building program to generate employment saw scores of concrete and rock outdoor swimming pools built next to Sydney's beaches. These were marvellous public assets and, if properly maintained, they promise to endure as long as the Roman baths and aqueducts across France and Germany—at least that was how I saw it.

One of these pools, known as Wylie's Baths, had been built below the cliffs south of Coogee Beach and so faced directly out to the open sea. It was spectacular in any season and in its early days was a favourite haunt of some of Sydney's best-known artists, including Arthur Streeton.

The Oils had shot a clip for 'Surf's Up Tonight', from the album *Breathe*, there. It was typically mayhem. Every film shoot I've ever been involved with had run behind schedule, and so did this one. The main problem was that part of the clip featured us in Wylie's Baths, sitting on lilos and watching surf footage with the open sea a couple of metres away, held back by the pool wall. Things were going swimmingly until the tide started coming in—a predictable event that hadn't been factored into the schedule. Waves started spilling over and into the pool, threatening to wash us, the crew and all their gear out to sea. The shoot finished pretty quickly after that.

Wylie's features quaint timber walkways, and with the rock embankment of the pool now restored—thanks to the foresight of one-time mayor Chris Bastic—is a haven for locals and in-the-know tourists alike. It was here that one of Kingsford Smith's most enduring eccentrics, academic and sculptor Eileen Slarke, had single-handedly raised funds to create a bronze work featuring painters from the thirties, which now sits overlooking the azure Pacific from atop the cliffs.

Eileen was a regular visitor to my office. Although approaching her mid-seventies, she usually dressed like a sharp, mall-prowling teenager, in long track pants, state-of-the-art runners, some modest bling and up-to-the minute hairstyling. She quivered with the mad energy of a creative soul and was impossible to ignore, in contrast to the morose, mousy hordes of retirees, bussed in free by the South Sydney Junior Rugby League Club to feed money into the gaping maws of the club's ranks of brightly coloured poker machines. There were some livewire characters among these crowds, as I came to appreciate, but from a distance they resembled lemmings at a state-sanctioned picnic.

I hadn't experienced a moment of uncertainty about the move to this area. In fact, I felt very much at home. Selina's—pub rock central—was close by; so too was the University of New South Wales, where I'd scrambled to finish my law studies. Even the Regent Hotel, where the Oils, venturing over to the south side of town, played one of our first-ever gigs, was in my new electorate.

And much of my life had been spent in the orbit of politics, thinking about it, breathing it and acting on it. This was about being Australian faithful, with a lengthy list of admirably high-level areas I wanted to work on jotted in the diary, including: 'rejuvenating democracy', 'true sustainability', 'empowering and educating Australia' and 'a real settlement with Aboriginal and Torres Strait Islander people'. In retrospect it looked ridiculously ambitious but these were the issues I felt needed attention. I agreed that history's clues were clear: the centre must hold and the spread of wealth needs to be wise or strife will follow. This was Labor's true course and I was willing to join.

I spent much of my first month as Kingsford Smith's new member visiting party loyalists and explaining my position to them. My message was simple: I would try to do my utmost for Labor, and I wasn't going to play games or abuse the position. By the time I'd put in a few years of attending branch meetings and doing the rounds, quite a few had come around, and I ended up with a coterie of solid supporters. This meant a lot to me, for they were the true believers—a hackneyed phrase, maybe, but it still evokes those who are the heart and soul of the Labor Party. I cherished these diehards who could be relied on to staff election booths when the opinion polls looked bad and the weather even worse, who would turn up to fundraising events with their wallets open and even volunteer to come doorknocking on the few occasions I took this route to meet electors. They cared about politics, had no time for the Coalition parties they contemptuously referred to as 'the Tories' and felt that Labor was the only viable outfit to mount a reform agenda. They were both faithful and fatalistic, living in hope that things would improve. By the time I arrived, they were, tragically, a diminishing force, but they never wavered in their commitment to the Labor cause.

One of my early tasks had been to get down to La Perouse, on the shores of Botany Bay, to make contact with the Aboriginal community living there.

'La Pa', as it is commonly called, is a site of rupture and sadness, still torn from earlier times, with long-standing unresolved grievances and the community divided along family lines. It is on the slow road to health but the shadow of the past hangs heavy over its dilapidated bungalows.

In my judgement the best help we could give was simply to be there for people where possible, and support those trying to make a difference in trying circumstances—as is the case in many Indigenous communities.

Europeans had been bumping into Australia—the Great South Land—since the 1600s. Other seafarers from the north, of whom there are no written accounts, doubtless came even earlier.

The Dutch mariners tracking across the Indian Ocean to the East Indies (the Indonesian Archipelago) had sighted landfall off Cape York in 1606 in the *Little Dove*. One quick look and they, like others who followed, decided the continent was too inhospitable, impassable and incomprehensible to justify exploring further.

Captain James Cook's arrival at Botany Bay in 1770, followed by Frenchman La Perouse eighteen years later—hence the name of the suburb—is one of the earliest written accounts of first contact.

As we approached the shore they [the natives] all made off, except 2 Men who seemed resolved to oppose our landing . . . We then threw them some nails and beads, etc., a shore [sic] which they took up, and seem'd not ill pleased with, in so much as I thought that they beckon'd to us to come ashore; but in this we were mistaken, for as soon as we put the boat in they again came to oppose us, upon which I fir'd a musquet between the 2, which had no Effect than to make them retire back, where bundles of their darts lay, and one of them took up a stone and threw at us . . .

This was how it began.

As the tentacles of the real-estate boom spread ever outward, even long neglected La Pa was under siege, as newcomers, taking advantage of the relatively cheap houses and bedazzled by the water views, bought in.

The makeover of the first permanent settlement of Aboriginal people in modern Australia was underway.

. . .

I'd often get up early on a Saturday morning, do some shopping (a good way to rub shoulders with voters), grab the papers, then drift past the beaches: Clovelly, Coogee, North and South Maroubra, to see the hundreds of nippers—kids getting their junior lifesaving qualifications—clustered, like swarms of stick insects, on the sand. The lifesaving movement, with women and people from different cultural backgrounds increasingly included in its ranks, glues young and old together. It is uniquely Australian in expression and provides a service to the community no government could easily replace.

I was excited that the area was home to leading researchers at the University of New South Wales, including Dr Martin Green, who with his colleagues had developed one of the world's most efficient solar cells, and Professor Matthew England and the team at the Climate Change Research Centre, experts on the science and impacts of global warming.

An economic system that penalised pollution and facilitated renewable sources—sun, wind and ocean—could help stabilise the planet's temperature. The innovative ideas and technologies that made this happen could be the industries of the future. This was the vision—a virtuous circle of fixing the environment and creating jobs—that Labor subsequently pursued, and then years later strained to put into practice.

...

The fabric of the community—and the rents within it—came into clearer view as race-based issues swept across the electorate.

The riot in 2005 by young surfers and locals from the predominantly Anglo Sutherland Shire, about forty minutes south of Kingsford Smith, exposed deep animosities still lurking in the Australian psyche. Australia Day had already taken on a quasi-fascist flavour for some, who, draped in the flag and with a belly full of beer, were only too ready to abuse anyone who appeared different.

The 2005 incident followed the assault of two young lifesavers at North Cronulla by a gang of Middle Eastern youths, and stemmed from incidents of sexist and often aggro behaviour from some young Middle Eastern men who frequented the beach in summer.

Across Sydney, the airwaves crackled with the outrage of those who resented sharing the beaches and the public spaces of the city with crowds of the recently arrived. The division between 'us' and 'them' was fostered and encouraged by right-wing radio shock jock Alan Jones, whose tirades later saw him fined for breaching the radio code of practice.

The night following the assault, after an ugly mob attacked and abused groups of Middle Eastern men around the beach at Cronulla, came reprisals by Lebanese groups from the south-west of Sydney. A church in Auburn was torched and cars trashed as far away as the beachside suburb of Maroubra, in my electorate.

Here the 'locals only' culture was deeply ingrained, personified by the Bra Boys, a gang led by local surfers the Abberton brothers, whose notoriety had seen them feted in the surfing and Fairfax media. They too weighed in, threatening to storm the mosque in Lakemba before relenting and offering to make peace with Muslim youth— culminating in a staged photo op that sucked the media in yet again.

In this climate of hysterical claims and festering racism, I feared the situation could easily get out of hand and escalate further. My office had kept in touch with the local police area command, and the following evening I joined young officers as they patrolled the shabby shopping strip and 1960s apartment blocks on the Maroubra foreshore. Here a smattering of locals were now arming themselves with cricket bats and assorted weapons stored in garages and hidden under bushes in nearby parks to repel foreign invaders—many of whom had attended school only three suburbs away to the west. Fortunately, it turned out to be a quiet night, but the atmosphere was deeply unsettling.

Next morning, all the staff collected in the office for urgent discussions. I was intent on us mounting some kind of response in our area to a festering boil that needed lancing. Members of the public, unhappy with the way events were unfolding, had called in offering to do something, anything, positive. Following discussions with a larger group of constituents, including film director Rowan Woods, we decided to hold a march called 'Wave of Respect'. The idea was simple: to broadcast a positive message and provide a counterpoint to the hate-filled hype from extremists on both sides. We would try to persuade as many well-known faces as we could to join us in order to generate media coverage for our theme of inclusion.

A series of quick calls to friends and sympathetic celebs was answered with a rollup, only two days later, of around fifty, including rugby league great Mario Fenech; singer Jimmy Barnes; comedian Anh Do; part owner of the South Sydney Rabbitohs Peter Holmes à Court; actors Claudia Karvan, Bryan Brown and Cate Blanchett; and a host of others, decked out in Wave of Respect T-shirts courtesy of Remo. The march was well covered by the media—as it deserved to be. At the least, a marker had been laid down showing there were people in this part of Sydney who believed in respecting one another, regardless of how anyone looked or how long they'd been in the country.

Sad to say, racism was hardly a new issue. Despite our success in building a modern nation based on immigration, Australia was not immune to the welling-up of racial hatred, seen in the recent past by the rise of the far-right One Nation party and lately in the outbreak of mass booing directed at Adam Goodes, the Indigenous Australian footballer. The Oils had had a go at One Nation and all that it stood for when we recorded *Redneck Wonderland*. To kick off the *Redneck Wonderland* tour, we ventured north, where the vote for One Nation was highest. In a Queensland state election, it had ratcheted up to around 28 per cent. In the 1996 federal election, party founder and star candidate Pauline Hanson had ended up with a seat in the House of Representatives, so we headed to the town of Ipswich, where she had famously launched her career. We searched far and wide for someone who'd voted for Pauline, without success. The bubble had already burst. As a local said to me, 'She got all big-headed when she went to Canberra to play with the big boys.' As far as he was concerned, Hanson didn't represent the people of Ipswich at all.

In the next federal election, Labor won the seat back. Hanson, after failing to win a Senate spot and with the party in disarray, then had a shot at the New South Wales parliament. Despite some serious campaigning in the Sutherland Shire, she failed again, receiving only around 2 per cent of the vote. Whether this was a testament to Australians' underlying decency, or simply the fact that Hanson's stance had been appropriated in soft focus by John Howard, who famously refused to condemn her outright, is a question that can be argued endlessly. But either way, our system was still mainly operating as a bulwark against ideological nastiness.

How long would this continue to be the case?, I wondered. Early in the morning of 25 April, I stood in a side street off the main road leading through the suburb of Matraville, there for the first of a number of traditional Anzac Day services I would attend that day. A handful of local politicians and a small cohort of ageing returned servicemen— and a smattering of women—all bedecked in medals, marching to the beat of a lone drummer, stepped out onto the main road. A single police car was parked across three lanes to halt occasional traffic, but it was a public holiday and, so far, reasonably quiet.

Two hundred metres up the road we paused at the Catholic church, where we were joined by a small group of children from the parish school, to listen to an address through a tiny, crackly speaker. It was turning into a glorious autumn day and the neighbourhood was starting to venture out into their gardens, or head off to the beach or local parks.

Much of what the priest said about the nature of sacrifice was drowned out by the hum of an increasing numbers of cars on the move behind us.

Across the road, in one of the flats above the shopping strip, two bare-chested young men with dark skin sat on a blistered concrete balcony sipping cans of beer—the sky a fierce blue backdrop.

They'd fired up the ghetto blaster—thudding bass beats, angry rap—in preparation for a day's hard partying, and were looking across to the head-bowed crowd opposite. They must surely have known that this was one of the most important days in the nation's calendar—the fact is hard to escape—but what they made of the procession as it trundled back out onto the road, I couldn't imagine.

Did they see it as a reminder of a war waged nearly a century ago in a faraway place, a place perhaps which these young men's own families might have come from? Perhaps they should have been invited to join us?

We headed to the final destination, the RSL Club, another 300 metres further along. By now the muffled rhythms of the ceremony were all but overwhelmed as the Last Post echoed across the suburban air, already thickening with engine fumes and party music, as Anzac Day came alive.

. . .

Bands wear black. A *Rolling Stone* cover shot, 1993. ANDRZEJ LIGUZ

Extended family, back row, from left: me, Matt, Lyndall, Doris and Andrew. Front row, from left: Em, May, Darcy, Grace, Maude and Jack.

The family in Amsterdam, 1992. From left: Emily, May and Grace.

From left: May, Em and Grace, back in Australia, 1994.

Doris and I at the Kangaroo Valley shed, 1989.

Trying something different, Sydney, 1996. ANDRZEJ LIGUZ

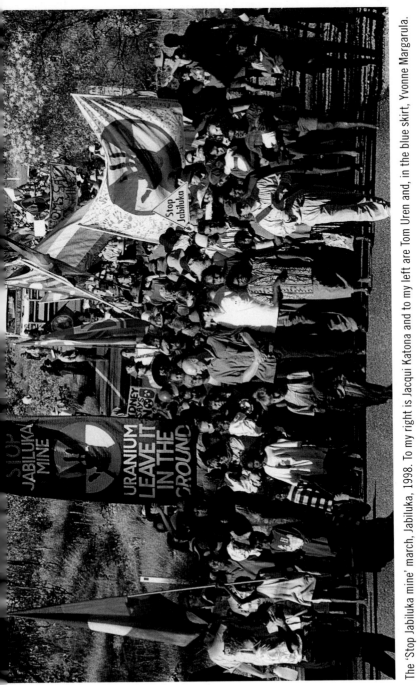

The 'Stop Jabiluka mine' march, Jabiluka, 1998. To my right is Jacqui Katona and to my left are Tom Uren and, in the blue skirt, Yvonne Margarula.

Closing ceremony, Sydney Summer Olympics, 2000. RICK STEVENS/FAIRFAX

Jabiluka blockade, Kakadu, at the height of the protests, 1998. BRENDAN FITZPATRICK

With José Ramos-Horta, Diplomacy Training Program, University of New South Wales, 2001.

With Gough Whitlam, Mick Young Charity Race Day, Randwick Race Course, Sydney, 2004.

With Mark Dodshon (left) and Damian Trotter, between Docker River and Kintore (Walungurru), 2003.

With Dames (left) and Doddo on the beach near Shelburne Bay, Cape York, 2006.
Glen Preece was behind the camera.

With, from left: Tim Freedman, Gough Whitlam and Bob Hawke on Gough's 90th birthday, 2006.

How Can You Sleep When My Ice is Melting

Greeted by protestors outside a restaurant, Hobart, 2007. RAOUL KOCHANOWSKI/NEWSPIX

At the despatch box, House of Representatives. GARY RAMAGE/NEWSPIX

Global Warming rally, Sydney, 2007, from left to right: Don Henry (ACF), Tanya Plibersek, John Connor (Climate Institute), George Newhouse, me, Anthony Albanese, Alec Marr (The Wilderness Society), Bob Brown and Cate Faehrmann (Nature Conservation Council of NSW). LISA WILLIAMS/NEWSPIX

With Prime Minister Julia Gillard at Parliament House, Canberra, during the Gonski school funding campaign, 2013. GARY RAMAGE/NEWSPIX

With William Parmbuk, Wadeye settlement, Melbourne, 2012. AARON FRANCIS

Taking a lucky catch at the Big Bash Celebrity Twenty20 cricket match, SCG, for the
Victorian Bushfire Appeal, 2009. GREGG PORTEOUS/NEWSPIX

With my one and only.

With the girls, from left: Grace, May and Emily.

Sometimes, for change to happen, all it takes is for enough people to say out loud that they've had enough; this was the principle behind the Make Poverty History movement for debt relief, along with the Jubilee Debt Campaign, both of which aimed to force the developed nations to forgive a chunk of the crippling long-term debt some small poor countries owed to organisations like the World Bank.

In support of a Make Poverty History concert organised by World Vision, in 2006 I headed down to Melbourne where, at an over-flowing Myer Music Bowl, big-name imports Pearl Jam, along with Bono and the Edge from U2, hooked their way through Neil Young's 'Rockin' in the Free World'.

Bono had agreed to do *Lateline*, the ABC current affairs program, to publicise the cause. So with World Vision supremo Tim Costello in tow, we drove out to the studio, offering up statistics and a steer on the local political context. Tony Jones, a smart and sharp journalist, was interviewing, so the advice was simple. 'He'll fasten on to you like a kelpie on a sheep's back leg,' we told Bono.

Croaky voice from the back seat: 'And what's a kelpie?'

'Anyway, just ignore the same question repeated over and over, and try to get the message out,' we advised.

We needn't have bothered. Bono was not about to be derailed by the inquisitorial Jones, who in any event handled the overseas talent more gently than he normally did locals (plus he clearly had some sympathy for the cause). The Irish gifts of oodles of charm and talking with conviction were on full display.

Driving back we cranked up a freshly recorded 'Beautiful Day', and bellowed into Fitzroy for a late-night meal and a catch-up with Eddie Vedder and a group of passionate young anti-poverty campaigners. We then escaped into the night just as the first wave of fans descended to be photographed with the Seattle and Dublin vocalists. I enjoyed these get-togethers; occasions like this would be few and far between in the long days and nights that were just around the corner as we geared up for a federal election the following year.

...

I had signed up early as an ambassador for White Ribbon Day, which had been established to take a stand on violence against women, an issue that deep down nagged away at me. As a father of three daughters, I wanted them to grow up free of the fear of violence. In addition, my electorate office in Maroubra was staffed mainly by women. As is often the case in the Labor Party, women hang tough and hold the 'show' (as the party is colloquially referred to) together, no matter what else is going down at the time. Kate Pasterfield, with Jenny Hunter doing local media and Sandi Chick dealing with constituent issues, typified this loyalty and they stuck by me for the long haul. If they worked back late, as was often the case, the question of whether they could get home safely would have to be taken into account.

An additional reason for joining the White Ribbon campaign had to do with some of the attitudes I'd encountered since I was elected.

Perhaps because they'd grown up seeing me on TV or listening to Oils songs, people often opened up on meeting me as if we'd known one another forever. The most intimate information about my constituents and their families would be revealed to me—details of a recent domestic argument, for example—often as we stood surrounded by a crowd in a shopping centre or other public space. And I'd discovered something that initially surprised me: many older men's attitudes to women still sucked. Given that in the majority of cases violence against women is committed by a man the victim knows, and that men are responsible for much of the violence that besets the world, I tried to confront these views whenever the opportunity arose. If humanity was ever going to make peaceful relations standard operating procedure between neighbours, countries and religions, it had to start at home.

In the first few years of the campaign I mainly visited shopping malls to hand out White Ribbon Day material and chat with whoever we happened to bump into. Over time, as the campaign picked up speed, more local schools became involved, as did the local services: police, fire and ambulance. White Ribbon Day was increasingly well supported by the media both locally and nationally, and this made a huge difference. Within ten years of its inception, the day had grown into a major community event as representatives from all tiers of government, a phalanx of local service personnel led by the police, and members of the public marched through the suburbs and down to a large park near the Coogee waterfront to make a public pledge in support of a violence-free future for women.

At last domestic violence has been dragged out from under the covers and is now on the political agenda, although the statistics are horrendous. It seems as if we are only seeing the tip of the iceberg at present; much more heavy lifting, including a massive education program and more effective regulation of the perpetrators, will be needed to quell this scourge.

...

During my first term in parliament, I discovered that in the winter break many parliamentarians would head overseas on what were euphemistically described as 'study tours'. In reality, they were soft travel rorts, and it was rare for politicians to learn anything of use to the taxpayer.

I wasn't interested in signing up to this masquerade, but the slowdown gave me the opportunity to bring together a group of close mates and head back to the Western Desert to connect with some of the Blackfella/Whitefella communities, whose progress I'd tried to keep abreast of over the years.

Just before entering parliament, I'd joined with my old mates from Warumpi Band, George Rrurrambu and Sammy Butcher, to open a small recording studio—built with support from World Vision and other NGOs—at Papunya. I was keen to get back to see how it was going. There was no shortage of talent out there, but equally no shortage of dust and debris to clog up the complex equipment.

Sammy was aiming to encourage younger musos, getting them in to rehearse and record in a setting as far removed from the slick facilities of Sydney or LA as one could envisage. George was returning to the scene of earlier triumphs; now sober and always sartorially splendid, his was a magnetic presence around the town.

These kids had to handle a lot, and the songs, compared to the overwrought clichés that keep reappearing in western pop, were potent to the core. The Little Orphans, a group made up of young boys aged around ten or eleven, played a song they'd written for the occasion. Loosely translated, it went: 'Brother's sniffing petrol, sister's on marijuana, Daddy's on the grog and Mummy's gambling. Who do I talk to?' There was no question these settlements were still beset by a range of social ills, some more than others. But singing it loud and still proud could only help build confidence and self-esteem, and maybe, at a very long shot, start a career.

As we trundled and bumped further out to Kintore (Walungurru) and then back to Alice, I found the experience bittersweet. Communities were variously trying to make a go of it—organising health programs, getting people out on country, maintaining cultural sites and seeking out bush tucker—although the employment opportunities were still limited.

The maverick Northern Territory politician Alison Anderson, who hails from Papunya, makes the point that there is a vast amount of unrealised human potential in these communities. In a stinging rebuke to *Utopia*, a documentary made by expatriate journalist John Pilger which derided the notion that any progress had been made in remote Aboriginal Australia, she said, '[People] do not wake up in the morning and think to themselves, "How dysfunctional I am, how bad is life!" They wake up and think, "How lucky we are to be living on our country in full possession of our language and culture and to be a little removed from the madness, pace and poisons of the mainstream world."'

Other than being home with Doris, or getting out with the family in tow, these trips into the Centre were my greatest solace. Here, with a group of friends—Doddo, Paul Gilding, Dames, artist Glen Preece, Richard Morecroft and others—along for the ride, we could camp undisturbed, surrounded by desert oaks, illuminated by the open fire, under the massive southern sky. And yet I was more than ever aware that my pleasure at travelling rough was as nothing compared to the sense of a world adrift still lingering in the subsoil of many of these remote settlements.

...

In 2005, a year after I'd entered parliament, Kim Beazley gave me the role of Parliamentary Secretary for Reconciliation and the Arts.

A few months later, the Howard government introduced additional anti-terror legislation, automatically supported by Beazley but containing, as it happened, a worrying bit of overreach. This was a provision for the offence of 'sedition', a crime in which political language or actions can be interpreted as an intention to overthrow the state. The definition was arguably so broad that it could easily include political opinions and acts of free expression, including by artists.

Prime Minister Howard's mantra that 'we will decide who comes to this country, and the circumstances in which they come' was a restatement of necessity by a sovereign leader, but the second part of the phrase (deciding 'circumstances') marked a hardening of attitude to the plight of asylum seekers. The timing caused much grief for Labor, as it reflected the opinion of many Australians, who were swayed by Howard's determination to use the issue of refugees—a growing number of whom were arriving by boat—in an election campaign. The problem lay in the solution for maintaining control: establishing offshore detention centres at great cost, and keeping children in detention.

It is the case that any national government should exercise the authority to control its borders, but it is an ugly step from that proposition to demonising people fleeing their own country, treating arbitrarily those who arrive, leaving children vulnerable in other countries and confecting a larger patriotic storm around the genuine threat that terrorism poses—all in the name of national security.

Once governments start to enlarge the legal and political apparatus of the state, this in turn restricts democratic freedoms, leading, as was the case with the sedition provisions, to potentially crushing all dissent.

Naturally, the Coalition government had no intention of removing the offence of sedition from the legislation. We commissioned an opinion from a senior Sydney barrister, Peter Gray, who advised that, as I suspected, the proposed legislation could indeed encompass artistic expression. The relevant Senate committee examining the proposed legislation concurred. After some public campaigning and political wrangling it was removed—a small tick on the board.

Early on in my new role, I floated a proposal to Chris Evans, who was shadow minister for Indigenous affairs, that we consider approaching the government to offer the mechanism of a joint working group made up of ministers and shadow ministers to try to find a common position on advancing reconciliation. It was the kind of initiative that would take time and trust to develop—both were in short supply—and events moved too fast for the idea to take hold. Similar proposals are around today, and offer one way through the mire; if we can take the partisanship out and consult closely with Indigenous leaders to agree on some basic principles upfront, then there's a chance that reconciliation, and the programs and positive actions that should go with it, can be achieved.

...

Developing new election policies was a crucial but tedious exercise while in Opposition—undertaking the hard thinking and extensive consultations with interested parties so that, in the event of victory, you can actually do something constructive when you get your hands on the steering wheel. I was struck that party politics seemed to attract plenty of people with a surprisingly bureaucratic mindset, so there was a welter of committees and review processes in place, intended to refine the process but, in many cases, making it more cumbersome.

Still, as the 2007 federal election drew closer, so the task became more urgent. In this period, Kevin Rudd's ambition to lead Labor was palpable; it was as if he was possessed by a demonic force. At the time, like many others, I saw that this energy and focus might just dislodge the incumbent. Howard was now vulnerable, weakened by community backlash against his industrial legislation, known as WorkChoices, and his intractability in the face of growing scientific alarm around global warming. He appeared to be a man out of sync with the times. Rudd—unlike Beazley, who'd previously failed to best Howard in the 1998 and 2001 elections—looked like the person who might get Labor over the line.

I made my share of mistakes over nearly ten years in parliament, but in light of the trail of destruction and abandoned policy Rudd left as a two-time leader, supporting him was certainly the biggest. Yet the result of his successful challenge for the party leadership was my elevation to the shadow ministry, with added responsibility for the environment, including climate change, and the arts—such are the quirks of politics.

We worked like fury to get Labor in shape for the election.

Priority one was dogging Malcolm Turnbull, then environment minister, with constant reminders of Howard's neglect on climate change.

On the first day of parliament in February 2005, following Labor's loss, Howard had told the house that 'the jury was out' on the connection between global warming and greenhouse emissions.

By March, the United Nations' leading scientific body on the issue, the Intergovernmental Panel on Climate Change (IPCC), stated it was 'unequivocal' that humans were contributing to climate change. Later that month, record downpours saw massive floods in the Kakadu wetlands, just as the IPCC modelling suggested could happen.

By June, Turnbull was still insisting the Coalition had the most comprehensive plan in the world to address the problem, even as his ministerial colleagues continued to question the science.

An important part of the debate was using this science to buttress the arguments, as we made the case for profound change to a public increasingly anxious about global warming. This meant highlighting the potential impacts on the environment the punters were now seeing, as Australia was still in the grip of severe drought—again, consistent with the scientists' climate change models—that saw drying rivers and baking landscapes featuring regularly on the television news.

It is rare that there is unanimity on new policy in political parties, and this was the case with climate change for both of Labor's terms. The argument to embed a renewable-energy target of 20 per cent, a target that had in-principle endorsement, was intense. Shadow resources minister Martin Ferguson was one of a number, including the so-called economic rationalists, who wanted this measure struck out, but it was a case of digging in to make sure a decent target prevailed. It was an important stoush to win and the policy proved more successful than anyone had expected. I needed the support of senior left colleagues, including Chris Evans and Anthony Albanese, to get the commitment inked as we finalised our pre-election promises, but it was a satisfying day when it happened.

The overall climate, environment and arts policies we put up were radical and far reaching. By the time the election was called, there was daylight plus between us and the Coalition, with opinion polls showing that on the question of who was best placed to lead the country when it came to the environment and climate change, Labor led the Coalition by a factor of two to one. And although Rudd would later hand climate change responsibilities to South Australian senator Penny Wong, the policy was now in place to secure one of the most significant economic reforms and the most significant environmental reform the country had ever attempted.

As my three years in Opposition drew to a close, I put the protection of Malabar Headland back on the agenda.

In another example of the colliding worlds that kept cropping up in my parliamentary term, the headland at the southern end of Maroubra Beach was the last remaining tract of undeveloped land in the electorate, and still under the control of the Commonwealth government. Comprising 180 hectares of coastal heath and rare native bushland, it had been a defence site from the early nineteenth century, complete with gun emplacements facing out to sea, intended to repel Russian warships. One section was now used as a rifle range, another by horse-riding clubs, and the western and eastern sections for local bushwalking.

Labor members, state and federal, had long promised that the headland would be returned to NSW and turned into national park, but progress had been so slow that many in the community had given up hope that this would ever happen. Complicating the issue was the fact that under current zoning arrangements, the westerly portion of the site, with sweeping views over the coastline, could be sold off at great profit for housing, which was the long-time fear of local residents.

If I succeeded in doing nothing else locally, I wanted to resolve the future of Malabar Headland. I'd long campaigned on issues like this from the outside. Now I was on the inside, and potentially in government, surely there was a chance to secure this special place. The commitment to return Malabar Headland to NSW, along with a parcel of other policies, including those on climate change and renewable energy, and energising the arts sector, were now in black and white. If we prevailed at the election, and took government, then these commitments could become law. That was the whole point of stepping off the soapbox and the stage for a while—to see what could be achieved in the mad dance of power and policies that passes for politics in our part of the world.

26
ON THE INSIDE

THE MORNING HAS already turned laundromat-warm by the time we emerge from the moderately sized white bungalow with gardens and acres of lawn leading down to Lake Burley Griffin. It's 3 December 2007, and I'm at Yarralumla, the official residence of the governor-general, Australia's head of state.

Only nine days before, John Howard's government had been turfed out of office, with the sitting prime minister himself losing his seat, such was the public's appetite for new faces.

Time, moving in mysterious ways, lay waiting in the wings, and picked its moment to sneak up and shape-shift my memory. Walking in through the front door of Government House an hour earlier, it didn't seem so long ago that I was hooning around on a motorbike just over the fence a few hundred metres away, with my mate Doddo. And here I am, waiting my turn to be sworn in as, one by one, each ministerial appointee is called forward by the leader to approach the small desk at the front of the room where the paperwork is co-signed by the governor-general, retired military officer Michael Jeffery.

The last chore is to stand with the governor-general on the front steps of the residence for the obligatory photo op. Like polite lady bowlers queued up for lunch, a long line of white government cars wait to ferry freshly minted ministers back to Parliament House. We are a mixture of grizzled veterans and ambitious newbies: union officials, long-time staffers, former members of Young Labor, lots of lawyers and men—I'm guilty on the last two counts. Most of my colleagues have waited all their lives for this moment. I'm the only one to have arrived just in time for the great adventure. This is the pick of the litter from our side of the political divide. In the new cabinet are seventeen men and four women—smart and hardworking, indefatigable opponents—who have proved to be the most adept at climbing to the top. For better or for worse, the prospects of the eleventh federal Labor government rest squarely on our shoulders.

On the way back into Parliament House that morning, Stephen Smith, who'd been the Minister for Foreign Affairs for half an hour, remarked that after you'd done just one thing—and for me that meant something the 'tories' wouldn't dream of doing—then even if a bus fell on you tomorrow, it would have been worth it.

Agreed. No matter what stuff-ups ensued—and there turned out to be one or two—very few people get to occupy high office, and not many stay long. You had to make the most of the opportunity.

...

The road to the ministry hadn't been without its obstacles. Despite now having done time in Opposition and in the bleachers, I was still the outsider with the inside run, and there would be no free kicks or rescues in or out of the parliament.

Towards the end of the 2007 campaign, I'd bumped into right-wing shock jock Steve Price in the Qantas lounge at Melbourne airport while chatting with Nine's entertainment reporter, Richard Wilkins. In response to Price's query about the election I told him not to worry, 'We'll change it all'—humour, irony, an off-the-cuff remark, jocular even (which was the nerdy word I later used to describe the incident), but by the time I reached the hotel the dogs of war had been let off the leash.

Price had immediately phoned my quip through to his Liberal mates, and the private conversation was now news. The right-leaning press went into overdrive; Peter Costello weighed in claiming that this was yet more evidence of Labor's radical plans. Rudd and his office panicked and blocked me from going out and cleaning it up a day later, as one normally does with a gaffe, even one manufactured in the heat of an election campaign. I wasn't at my sharpest at the time, and with a rabid pack leaping on the comments, the initial press conference was less than satisfactory. But I'd always disliked the dog-ate-my-homework excuse-makers and I wasn't prepared to blame my slip of the tongue on a brain snap or an off day; I'd simply repeat the expression with a smile and note it was no big deal. But I never got the opportunity, and by the time we reached the campaign launch in Brisbane a couple of weeks later, demonstrators lined the road leading to the Convention Centre holding placards saying: 'If Labor is elected, they'll change it all.' The only people to emerge from the episode with their reputations intact were Richard Wilkins, who stated honestly what had actually happened—namely that it had been a chance remark, no more, no less—and veteran political reporter Laurie Oakes, who reported the incident straight.

But blips like these were forgotten as we were swept into office. The incoming Labor government wanted to make Australia a better, fairer place, with a serious plan to overcome the dead hand of denial and finally do something about impending climate chaos.

Yes, the new government was hobbled by its ambitions, but isn't this the way it has always been? Labor charts reform, and aims to improve the lot of ordinary Australians. The Coalition parties usually resist in favour of retaining the status quo. Our ambition in the first decade of the new millennium was great.

Here was the opportunity to establish an insurance scheme to cater for the needs of people with disabilities, who'd been shamefully ignored up till now.

Now we could have a national broadband network that took all Australians, wherever they lived, into the era of high-speed digital communications.

At long last there would be a decent, properly indexed pension system for older citizens who'd done their bit for the country.

After years of declining performance, there would be more investment in education and skills to benefit young Australians—regardless of how well off their parents were—from the crucial early years through to university.

The critical transformation of our old, polluting nineteenth-century economy into a low-emissions, planet-friendly exemplar was finally at hand. This was the paramount reform: escaping our dependence on shipping dirt and ore, and generating a raft of employment and investment opportunities in a low-carbon economy to set the country up for the future.

These initiatives weren't trifles. The last had been a prime reason for me to take the step into parliamentary politics in the first place. Together they would make a big difference to people's lives, if only we could manage to nail them down.

The to-do list in the environment and arts portfolio for which I now had responsibility was head-spinning.

We would create an emissions trading scheme, partnered with a range of policies to increase energy efficiency, the cheapest and most effective way to reduce greenhouse pollution.

With help from the Renewable Energy Target, solar power—the sleeping giant in a land of abundant sunshine—would be encouraged through solar hot-water rebates and incentives for rooftop solar panels.

We would establish solar cities, with smart grids that provided instant feedback on individual energy use and put decisions about using energy back in the hands of the consumer.

Look out the car window and in many places the land is pummelled and tired. Along 3000 kilometres of the east coast, you couldn't find an unpolluted river south of Cooktown. It was our intention to refashion natural resource management programs with Caring for Our Country, with ambitious plans to increase the size and number of national parks and reserves that make up the National Reserve System. On top of this, we would triple the funding and create additional Indigenous Protected Areas: tracts of land owned or controlled by Aboriginal people to be managed with a strong focus on the environment and sustainable land use. These steps would provide more conservation corridors across the continent, linking areas of high ecological quality and, hopefully, increasing the resilience of natural landscapes Australia wide.

We had a well-resourced plan to improve water quality for the Great Barrier Reef, the greatest of our natural treasures and a major source of perpetual income. Called Reef Rescue, it gave farmers incentives to reduce the nutrient load on the inshore waters of the reef to increase its capacity to deal with stress in the face of other threats, including climate change.

We wanted to protect breathtaking environments like Ningaloo Reef in Western Australia, Koongarra in Kakadu, and the Kimberley, as well as making sure Australia's vast ocean estate stayed healthy by creating new marine national parks.

Back on land we envisaged a national waste strategy with the introduction of the first e-waste recycling scheme, covering old computers and televisions.

We would advance the cause of whale conservation, along with two other measures that went to the heart of strengthened environmental decision-making. The first was to use the full powers of the powerful *Environment Protection Biodiversity and Conservation (EPBC) Act*— the key environmental law—while reviewing the legislation to look at improving its effectiveness. The second was to establish a set of national environmental accounts that would provide up-to-date information about the state of health of all the nation's ecosystems. If we didn't all know how our environment was faring, then how could we plan to improve it, and monitor progress?

This was the bulk of the work plan for three years, and by the end of the term most of it had been achieved. Some energy efficiency measures had foundered along the way, and other initiatives flowed into the next term; many were controversial.

In the early days it was decisions under the *EPBC Act* that attracted the most attention. These laws gave the minister the power to approve large-scale developments—like a mining operation—by considering its effect on matters of national environmental significance, such as threatened and endangered animal and plant species. The minister would consider the information supplied by the environment department, and he or she could also call for extra reports or research that might help to inform their decision.

This power could be seen in vastly different lights, depending on where you sat on the political spectrum. Coming as I did from a background of environmental activism, the right feared what I would do and the left feared what I wouldn't. For the business and rural communities and their cheerleaders, the anxiety was that I would use the power I had as 'the most powerful environmentalist in Australia', as the Greens described me, to use the environment as an excuse to halt any activity in its tracks. For any community wanting to stop a proposal that might affect their local environment, the fear was that I wouldn't immediately step in because I was now a Labor politician and thus fatally compromised. Added to this was the false assumption that in every case a minister could do pretty much what they wished.

Our political opponents simply had a bet each way. Some days I was selling out because I wasn't seen to be taking strong enough action. Other days I was threatening to wreck the economy. In one instance of overblown rhetoric before he lost office, John Howard claimed Labor's promise to put a price on carbon pollution meant a 'Garrett recession' was just around the corner. A front page from *The Australian* warned of 'Garrett's six-billion-dollar solar bill' as a consequence of promising rebates for solar hot-water systems—a fudged figure that didn't provide an accurate reading of the real cost and benefits of the scheme.

The truth about what a minister could and should do was, as ever, more complex. For starters, decisions under the legislation to approve or deny development had to be made by the minister alone. A decision couldn't be made simply as a consequence of a cabinet decision or as a result of direct influence by colleagues.

Second, even though opportunities for legal challenge had been unnecessarily limited by the former government, any decision could still be appealed to a higher court, and so had to be made properly, not on a whim. On more than one occasion I was left with the unenviable task of remaking decisions, including approving McArthur River Mine in the Northern Territory and the exploitation of Christmas Island phosphate reserves already underway, which had been sloppily made by previous Coalition ministers and were subsequently overturned in court. I later refused the next application for mining on Christmas Island.

Third, under the Australian Constitution, state governments still had powers over land use and the environment. Unless a specific action infringed on those activities listed in the Commonwealth act, a federal minister's power was limited.

I may have been an occasional student at law school, but I knew this much: the whole system of public trust and political account-ability would break down if ministers turned into Dr Strangelove and started making it up as they went along. You had to operate within the legislative framework, and if it needed changing, then get about that task as well.

But this bigger picture was irrelevant to the public debate, in which the narrative of a high-profile minister mired in conflict or under pressure for alleged compromises was irresistible to the press.

The centrepiece in creating big corridors of healthier natural land-scapes was an extra $180 million for the National Reserve System, which would significantly increase its scope and lift the funding from a paltry $2–$3 million in the final Howard years. It was one of our first announcements, and represented a hefty injection of funds along with a more ambitious approach.

At 9.30 a.m. early in the New Year, I was raring to go at a national park close to Canberra. Very few journos showed up for the presser ('Too early in the morning,' one office wit remarked) and the coverage was risible—as it would remain for the next three years: outside of whaling, *The Sydney Morning Herald*, for example, barely covered any announcements in the environment portfolio at all. The exception to this lack of interest was a front-page headline, accompanied by a suitably unflattering photo, from leading rural newspaper *Stock & Land*. The caption read: 'This man wants to increase the National Reserve System by 25 per cent—and he has your farm in his sights.'

When it came to decisions under the *EPBC Act*, the in-tray had been stuffed with explosive devices and hospital passes so we strapped ourselves in for the ride.

The issues generating the most public interest, and hate mail in both directions, were the ongoing sagas around the fate of a proposed pulp mill in Tasmania being pursued by Gunns Limited, and the plans by the Queensland government to build a dam—called the Traveston Dam—on the Mary River, inland from the Sunshine Coast. There were plenty of others waiting in the queue, including: the expansion of the Beverley Uranium Mine; proposed development around the lighthouse at Nobbys Head in Newcastle; dredging in Port Phillip Bay; the Gorgon gas project on 'Australia's Ark', Barrow Island; and a proposal by Waratah Coal—owned by Clive Palmer, who later bankrolled himself into parliament—to build a railway line across a vast tract of undisturbed native vegetation and rainforest, including the southern part of Shoalwater Bay.

In the case of the pulp mill, many people saw this as an opportunity for me to flex some ministerial muscle and break the ugly nexus between industry and the unions that had kept destructive native forest logging afloat in Tasmania. There was one major problem: in a novel approach, Malcolm Turnbull, the Howard government's environment minister, had split the project into a series of modules—representing stages from site clearance to mill construction—each to be dealt with on their individual merits. As a consequence, the project was already partially approved. It would require extreme circumstances and rock-solid reasons to withdraw this approval, or the Commonwealth would be taken to court and likely lose.

During my time at the ACF, I'd come to believe we should value-add from our timber, so I wasn't automatically opposed to a pulp mill, so long as it didn't draw on environmentally important forests or pour toxic chemicals into the adjoining waters of Bass Strait. It was ridiculous that Australia simply clear-felled and woodchipped its forests, selling the raw material overseas only to buy it back again as processed paper at much higher prices. As long as we protected native forests with high conservation values, and carefully used other forests and plantations as feedstock for building materials and paper products, then more employment could be generated in rural areas and Australia's balance of payments would get a boost. Utilising forests carefully could help combat climate change. In housing construction, for example, it is better to use a renewable resource like trees for timber walls and floors instead of concrete and steel, major sources of greenhouse emissions. The best course of action, unless the mill project fell over altogether (as ultimately happened), was to set the bar for approval as high as possible, while encouraging another company with first-class green credentials to get involved.

Yet none of these arguments washed with opponents of the mill, who were aghast at the prospect of a large industrial facility being built close to the farms and bays of the Launceston region. And the odour emanating from Gunns was rotten-egg gas plus; I could smell it from Canberra. The company's reputation for logging pristine forests, and an unholy alliance between Gunns and Tasmanian politicians—including a highly compromised former Labor premier, Paul Lennon, who'd pushed legislation favouring the company through the state parliament—added more fuel to the fire.

Matters came to a head when, on a visit to Hobart, I attended a dinner marking Labor MP Duncan Kerr's twentieth anniversary in parliament.

With Kate Pasterfield acting as media adviser, I arrived at the hotel where we were staying to find an angry crowd milling outside. We set out on foot along the road opposite Constitution Dock on the way to Kerr's celebration, trailed by a growing swarm of protestors demanding loudly that the mill be stopped. A couple of burly union officials joined us as we stepped up the pace, hoping to shake off the uninvited guests.

When we approached the entrance of the restaurant, a bevy of cameras rushed out to film the spectacle. On cue, the mob, by now increasingly agitated, upped the ante by throwing handfuls of wood-chips and pouring boiling wax over us. As party tricks go it was a little extreme, but certain to make the evening TV bulletins. (It also succeeded in seeing off our amateur security detail, who promptly headed for the back door.) Fortunately, with a bit of ducking and weaving, Kate and I managed to make our way inside relatively unscathed. Almost immediately I was hounded by a wild-eyed activist with a camera crew in tow, offering me a plate on which were two small round chocolate cakes covered in coconut icing, with the sign 'Mr Garrett's balls' attached.

Even staffers accustomed to the rough and tumble of Labor politics had never seen anything like this. In part it was a classic set-up, in part a local overreaction to a national malaise. People no longer had any faith in political processes—and considering how shonky Tasmanian Labor politics had been, who could blame them?

In time, I added conditions that applied civil and criminal penalties if the mill exceeded its environmental limits, and a sunset clause that denied any company the opportunity to proceed unless they could show the mill wouldn't damage the marine environment. At the very least, this meant installing the world's best tertiary treatment equipment; the expense would be significant, making agreement a true test of the bona fides of whoever wanted to operate a pulp mill. At the same time we entered into discussions with a Swedish

company which was committed to world's best environmental standards in pulp and paper manufacturing.

Later, there was a new minister and events moved in an entirely
different direction. While my successor eventually approved the final
modules, in line with the higher bar that had been set, Gunns went
into receivership and, despite the efforts of the state government and
others, the mill remains unbuilt. Only the memory of Kate's singed
hair, my stained suit and flushed, angry faces remains.

Two thousand kilometres to the north, the Traveston Dam decision
was a different kettle of fish. The Queensland government had spent
hundreds of millions of dollars planning the project, including going
so far as to resume people's properties, with the aim of providing more
water for South East Queensland, still reeling from a severe drought.

The dam was to be constructed at the lower end of the Mary
River, in relatively flat country, and a visit to the site revealed it would
have generated a large shallow pond of water rather than a deep pool,
as is normally the case with a dam. More problematic was the fact
that any dam would impede the breeding cycle of the endangered
and rare Australian lungfish and the Mary River turtle, for whom the
river was prime habitat.

Some colleagues were less than impressed with the way the issue
was shaping up, especially as a number of National Party members
who'd never met a dam they didn't love were opposed to Traveston
simply because it fell within one of their electorates. Even the Senate
became involved and, spotlighting the major flaw in the Queensland
government's case, passed a resolution calling on me to explain how
the spawning grounds for these species would be protected if the dam
went ahead. The intricate system of fish ladders designed to allow
fish to get over the dam wall had been proven unworkable, so I was
pleased to confirm this unhappy fact.

In the final days before the decision I went to the Sydney Opera
House wharf to accept a petition of thousands of signatures that had
been collected by kayaker Steve Posselt, who'd paddled more than

1000 kilometres from the mouth of the Mary River to deliver the document. My acceptance of the petition was seen as a provocative act by supporters of the dam, including the office of the Queensland premier, Anna Bligh, who felt I was prejudging the issue. The query came down from Rudd's staff: what is he up to?

On the face of it, this proposal was yet another example of a government and a powerful bureaucracy steamrolling small-town people in order to fulfil a political imperative, regardless of the consequences. I didn't like it, but that wasn't a sufficient reason to reject the plan. My eventual decision was never in doubt. In this case the advice and the science were crystal clear: the effect of the dam on endangered native fish would be fatal.

I refused to approve the project, and flew to Brisbane to broadcast the announcement from a crowded conference room at the Commonwealth Offices. Cue cheers and tears from the locals watching the press conference from the Kandanga Hotel in the Mary Valley, and howls of outrage from *The Australian* and some right-wing Labor types like former Queensland premier Peter Beattie, complaining about the process. *The Age* newspaper claimed it was 'the biggest decision made by an environment minister in ten years of national environment law'. The speaking notes issued the following day to ministers, known as round the worlds (RTWs), offered that Rudd used to love swimming in the Mary River—turning a negative into a positive, Queensland-style.

Travelling back to the airport, I asked the driver to turn up the music; Chisel's classic 'Flame Trees' was on his iPod. My advisers Jack Smith and Ben Pratt joined in as we sang along to this heart-of-the-country tune—a way of letting off a little steam after the compressed intensity of the past forty-eight hours.

The local community's joy was understandable. The dam had been poorly conceived, and flooding farmland and the small hamlets in the valley would have permanently changed their way of life. But their relief was a by-product of a decision to use the Commonwealth law in the way it was designed to be used: namely, to protect the nation's environment, and the native plant and animal species that make it up—no more, no less.

...

In the midst of these high-profile cases, my office continued to work towards having the Koongarra mining lease incorporated back into Kakadu National Park. Jeffrey Lee, the traditional owner, was keen— the original decision to exclude it from the park had been made without the consent of his family—and long-time ACF campaigner Dave Sweeney had never wavered in his efforts to make it happen.

It took a good deal of pushing and shoving before we were able to announce in August 2010 that the government would move ahead. The correspondence from Julia Gillard, as acting prime minister, confirming the course of action we proposed was one of the most welcome letters I received. Eventually the incorporation of Koongarra into Kakadu was finalised by Tony Burke when he became environment minister.

Jeffrey Lee came down to Canberra that day to see the bill brought into parliament, and we greeted him like the Australian hero he surely is.

The opportunity to draw a line and secure Koongarra, now a part of Kakadu National Park, was a validation of my decision to enter formal politics. It was one of the positives that could be deposited in the vault, and was very difficult to undo. You walk on air for a second or two when decisions like this happen. In distinct contrast, the request to approve the expansion of an existing uranium mine at Beverley in South Australia was the most difficult decision I faced. Here I suffered pangs of conscience colliding with ministerial duty in a way no other matter affected me during my time in parliament.

I could rationalise making a decision that came through my department's assessment process with a positive recommendation— one that imposed rigorous conditions, buttressed by two additional scientific reports I'd sought that reinforced the department's view—for a mine that already existed, in an area that was not overly sensitive to the mining process. I was as certain as I could be that every aspect of the decision was correct, if you accepted that the mine was already legally in place and bound to remain. But I was emotionally torn and, at the same time, dogged by the public perception—fuelled by Labor's political opponents on the left and right—that I was fatally compromised, given that I'd opposed uranium mining in the past. The fact that I continued to oppose uranium mining throughout my time in government didn't count for much in the heat of the moment. This included subsequently leading the debate on the floor of the ALP National Conference, arguing for the party not to relax its vexed three-mine policy—an argument that was narrowly lost.

In the case of Beverley, I had three options. I could refuse the department's advice, which in this instance was sound, thus provoking the company to mount a legal challenge that could succeed, leading to a political fight with no prospect of victory for the anti-uranium constituency. I could resign and go to the backbench (a prospect that didn't appeal; it wasn't clear what purpose would be served and, besides, I wasn't the resigning type). Or I could treat the matter on its merits and take the action that was required, as ministers do every day when applying the policy of the government they have sworn to uphold.

I chose the last course of action, and don't regret the decision I made. Of course it didn't turn me into an apologist for uranium mining; in fact, it reinforced my existing view, and I applied extensive conditions relating to water management to prevent any long-term impacts from the enterprise.

Approving the expansion would have sent a message to my colleagues, and anyone who thought seriously about the political system, that I was willing to put my responsibilities ahead of my personal feelings, in this case at least. But it was a painful step to take, a reminder of what a double-edged sword the environment portfolio was for me.

It was as if one half of the country expected me to wave a magic wand over every single issue, regardless of its history or circumstances, even if that meant breaking the law, while the other half were fearful that I'd stop at nothing to advantage the environment. I wanted to be the best minister I could in the circumstances, and I was certain I could make a better fist of it than most, if not all, of the alternative candidates. I was fine with being judged on the criteria of the substance of the decisions I took and the policies I brought to the table. But my rock'n'roll and activist past well and truly caught up with me at this time. Perception was everything and people wanted fireworks every step of the way.

There was a welter of proposals on the table for energy projects in the Kimberley, with a number to be sited on the pristine coastline, posing risks to the environment, and a contentious one, a gas hub at James Price Point, which drew opposition from across Australia, as well as locally. Part of the solution was to enable a strategic assessment for one area only (something that hadn't been tried before), thus confining the impact of any development. In fact I hadn't forgotten the note I'd received years before from Joseph Roe, one of a group of Aboriginal traditional owners opposed to the industrial facility being constructed on their land. I'd taken the opportunity when visiting Broome to remake the point that James Price shouldn't go ahead if traditional owners weren't onside and there was significant impact on marine species, but the media were short-staffed that day and the comment went unnoticed. Not long afterwards the project was halted on legal grounds as public opposition reached fever pitch.

A chance remark from a senior official as I pushed to get work on a set of national environment accounts underway put the job in perspective. 'We'll do our best,' he said, 'but as you know, Minister, the average length of time someone spends in this office is less than eighteen months.' The message was clear: we've seen the occupants of this office and their brave new plans come and go. So, Mr Hyper Driven Greenie Muso, just remember we'll outlast you.

It was a tart reminder that in this place you never knew what lay around the corner, and it caused me to drive my staff and myself even harder. So off we went, running through airports, dashing from meeting to meeting, and staying up till the early hours to wade through legal advices and numerous reports in order to get decisions out the door. There's nothing unusual in this scenario for anyone working in government. I could only look back in wonder to the time when I could spend a few hours sitting poolside working on a song list, or taking a few days or, in one case, a year off to recharge the batteries. They really were the good old days.

27

ART FOR EVERYONE'S SAKE

WHEN IT CAME to the arts portfolio, I was among friends, on the surface at least. I was an artist and had a bit in common with 'cultural creatives', estimated to comprise around a quarter of the population.

Disenchanted with consumerism, caring about social justice, operating in the middle of a web of coalescing social movements, this was my milieu. I still had blisters on my hands from climbing the rocky slope and knew how difficult it could be for practising artists to get started. I also knew they frequently felt their contribution in what often seemed like a country besotted with sport was underappreciated. I recognised that the creative act happens across all art forms—from the heritage offerings of opera and ballet ('heritage' being a term the practitioners hate) to digital installations and street performance. What was needed was an injection of government resources to rev up the sector.

We'd consulted with the arts community before the election, and the central policy—realigning the funding system to give more support to young and emerging artists—was launched at Parramatta to signal the new direction. Plenty of artists made the journey west, but very few journos. We wanted to better assist Indigenous artists, including by legislating for a resale royalty scheme for painters, and also work more closely with the local film industry. Despite an abundance of world-class actors and technicians, it took a fair slab of public money. But audiences, with the exception of the odd breakthrough movie, were paltry.

There is immeasurable value in the insights and lift the artists of Australia could offer our national life, but I believe the role of government is to lay the groundwork for the arts to flourish, not to pick winners or support favourites. I also don't believe that simply calling yourself an artist means you can automatically expect taxpayer support. And I don't think that popular music, prior to the age of the digital download, needed much in the way of direct government assistance. As a band we never had our hand out, nor should we have.

Governments have a role to play in supporting non-mainstream arts, new work and the national institutions that display the best of Australian creativity and provide performance opportunities and training. If they are concerned about the vitality of the nation's cultural life, governments need to get the 'settings' right—tax arrangements, subsidies, loans and grants—to give artists a decent crack.

Contrary to the impression that artists working the popular avenue sometimes give, I respect output that has stood the test of time and spoken across centuries. This is the heavy weight of the canon; it had lasted the distance, and left much of the confused output of the postmodern era, overly influenced by academic theory, for dead.

At the same time, the existing arts budget was heavily skewed towards perpetuating these classics, through opera, classical music and dance. If we were going to produce more Australian work that spoke to current generations, and for the best of that work to, in time, become part of our canon, the budget needed to support new work, not simply recycle the old. Consequently more money, both public and private, would have to be found to reach this goal.

It wasn't the minister's prerogative to determine the specifics of who received funding, even though it was frustrating at times to see what qualified for a dollar. I'd come from a very different world, where bums on seats ruled and competition was tough. It had to be as good as you could make it from the get-go or you quickly ended up as a footnote in a fanzine.

There was plenty that was good, and some—like Cate Blanchett doing *A Streetcar Named Desire*, or the Canning Stock Route exhibition curated by Aboriginal artists, or the Australian Youth Orchestra ripping up a symphony with the impudent energy of the young—was great. When I saw work that fell short, or simply copied someone else's success, I usually made a note not to recommend it to friends and left it at that.

One night I attended a post-concert supper at the Sydney Opera House after the Sydney Symphony Orchestra had performed with their visiting conductor, the world-acclaimed Vladimir Ashkenazy. With a twinkle in his eye, the conductor asked me directly, 'as a musician', what I had thought of the performance.

I replied, 'As a musician? Well, not too bad, but it would sound better if they got themselves in tune and everyone played in time.'

More eye-twinkling from the super-energetic maestro as he responded, 'Exactly.'

There are a lot of moving parts in an orchestra, and even though the players, skilled musicians all, simply have to alight in unison on the black notes, I knew it wasn't that easy. But before we could discuss how Ashkenazy would lift the performance bar (which he subsequently did), a crowd descended, showering the diminutive conductor with praise and proclaiming the concert one of the best ever.

Much of the contemporary visual art I saw was freighted up with cultural commentary and insider allusions and often struck me as cold, yet it was crucial that people kept at it—even Bill Henson.

Henson found himself at the centre of a storm when the police seized his photos of barely clothed underage children to investigate accusations that they were child pornography, forcing the closure of his exhibition. The next day, on morning television, Kevin Rudd fanned the controversy when he said he found the photos 'revolting'.

The arts community demanded Henson be defended and Rudd's comments criticised. My response—to defend the artist's right to create work, but not to breach existing laws, thus avoiding criticising the prime minister at the same time—was way too legalistic for some. Journalists hyperventilated, with David Marr claiming in *The Monthly* that I had 'nothing to say' about 'the biggest art controversy in half a century'. In hindsight, despite plenty of discussion with the arts community, I should have said more, namely that while I found some of Henson's work with teenagers creepy, and his habit of soliciting young children to model for him questionable, I would continue to defend his right to make photographs . . . as long as he didn't break the law.

Good luck to artists if they found an audience; many jewels could always be discovered among the dross. Apart from Australian literature, which I'd always enjoyed and managed to dig into from time to time, including trying to read all the finalists in the Prime Minister's Literary awards, theatre was the stand-out form. While not averse to recycling the classics, it balanced this by delivering new work and featuring Australian playwrights like Maxine Mellor and Campion Decent, whose play *Embers* had a lasting effect on me. Theatre is so in your face it can't easily escape or pretend to its audience.

I did manage to find a few spare moments to run some master classes in vocal performance for the final-year students at the National Institute of Dramatic Art (NIDA), which happened to be near my electorate office. I suspect I got more out of it than they did. The pent-up energy of these students sizzled through the rehearsal room like a high-tension wire in a swamp. They responded to the class with so much verve that I left the sessions alive and kicking.

Supporting Aboriginal and Torres Strait Islander arts where possible was also an immediate priority. The painting, especially from remote areas, embodied a sense of the country unlike anything I'd seen, with stories that deserved a wider audience. One of the most remarkable outpourings of creativity in the twentieth century was taking place in every corner of the continent, pulsing out of the desert lands and the unconquered north—it was nothing short of remarkable. I knew the paintings could be appreciated internationally.

As recently as 2006, attendance at an Emily Kngwarreye exhibition in Japan had matched that of an Andy Warhol exhibition held at the same time.

Indigenous artists, living on the edge of poverty, often painting in the dirt, were producing art of great power and beauty, earning income for themselves and their communities—and they deserved help. This meant making sure there was a resale royalty scheme in place, consistent funding for arts centres and a workable code of conduct for Indigenous art (the fakes and mass-produced work flooding the market were a growing problem).

Above all, across the portfolio the funding mix had to be changed, and that included seeing where genuine savings from other areas of the budget could be found.

And find them I did, though I was to discover that hell hath no fury like the spoiled having something taken away from them without warning; so it was with the decision to restructure the Australian National Academy of Music (ANAM).

The academy is headquartered in Melbourne with a brief to provide first-class tuition to young classical musicians from across Australia. The organisation was struggling and was after more money, despite already receiving large dollops from the Commonwealth, but I demurred. My department's advice, accepted by the Department of the Prime Minister and Cabinet, was that the academy should be co-located within the University of Melbourne, and a new board be put in place to sort out the mess, with a brief to draw less on government funding and to cast a wider net for students.

The outcry was immediate and the decision subject to a barrage of criticism, led by eminent composer Brett Dean, who was the ANAM artistic director, with the backing of Richard Tognetti, artistic director of the Australian Chamber Orchestra, and many of my colleagues in the music community.

Looking back, it is clear the decision was poorly executed, without sufficient consultation and preparation. I felt the department and my chief of staff had let me down, but the ultimate responsibility was mine. We wore the catcalls as the Melbourne establishment took up the campaign, leading to Terry Moran, the secretary of the prime minister's department and a Melbourne arts aficionado, edging backwards and weighing in at the same time—a dangerous sign.

Still, I stubbornly pressed on, with some compromise around logistics and location, while trying to get people to understand the issue, including meeting with a delegation of students who came to Canberra to press their case. When I pointed out to the assembled group—middle class and plummy rude—that well over 90 per cent of ANAM's funding came from the government (even Opera Australia wasn't on that good a wicket), that there wasn't a bottomless pit of money in my budget and, finally, that there were other deserving artists who could do with a bit of help, no one so much as blinked. The culture of entitlement had a firm hold over these young players. They were adamant that the government had 'no choice' but to fully subsidise their learning in this privileged location.

When, on the eve of the 2010 election, an old bloke from out in the sticks replied to a reporter's question about what he was looking for from government by saying, 'I've got me hand out for more of those handouts,' he neatly summed up the prevailing zeitgeist. These students had grown up with the special pleading that typifies modern politics. They'd seen industry, farmers and unions all engage, some with more success than others. Now it was their turn, and in their minds their cause was just. Bob Hawke, Paul Keating and John Howard managed to root out some subsidies that had no economic or enduring social purpose but instead imposed an unnecessary charge on the public. But Howard and his treasurer, Peter Costello, also took budget surpluses from selling off public assets and then provided more middle-class welfare to people who didn't need it, and so a sense of entitlement spread across the electorate—it's still there.

We persevered with the changes to ANAM long after the fracas had died down, and when I met with representatives of the new board some time later, the transition was complete and the organisation is now in better shape, 'thanks to the minister'—no worries, everyone.

Always back the horse named self-interest, New South Wales premier Jack Lang famously said, and this episode, and the assault by the mining and resources sector on Labor's plans for an emissions trading scheme, showed again, as if anyone needed reminding, that self-interest knows no bounds and has no shame. The extensive, and expensive, series of ads in which the industry attacked the government's plans across all forms of media raised doubts in the public mind, and emboldened the Opposition to scream ever louder about the sins of pricing pollution; the rationale for the scheme didn't get a look in.

On a much smaller scale, self-interest was on ugly display in the opposition to our plan for a Resale Royalty Bill.

The principle was simple. A resale royalty for artists was a long-time Labor promise, and had previously been recommended by Melbourne businessman Rupert Myer, who later went on to chair the National Gallery of Australia, in his *Report of the Contemporary Visual Arts and Craft Inquiry* (2002). This legislation would create a scheme under which visual artists—painters, printmakers and sculptors—would automatically receive a small percentage of the sale price (5 per cent of the total) every time one of their works was resold on the secondary art market. The examples of Aboriginal artists in particular—who were often paid a couple of hundred dollars for a painting only to see it resold for tens and sometimes hundreds of thousands of dollars without them receiving a cent—was reason enough to have this scheme. But this scenario wasn't confined to Indigenous artists; it was a feature of many outstanding artists' careers. Music composers and authors had copyright that extended beyond their lifetime, so why shouldn't artists have a similar right?

Despite its obvious merits, the bill was strenuously opposed by the Coalition arts spokesman, Liberal senator George Brandis, and by a number of private auction houses and some galleries, on the basis of unworkability and extra costs. Given that the record-keeping requirements were modest, my suspicion was that some sections of the art world didn't want the transparency and greater accountability that the measure would bring. Their ally Brandis appeared comfortable sipping champagne and siding with Sotheby's and the professional dealers association, even if this meant denying the poorest people in the land some extra income. The critics fumed that the costs of running the scheme would eat away at the meagre royalties expected in the first few years, and once in government Brandis ordered a review of the scheme and threatened to repeal the legislation.

In fact, after four years of operation the resale royalties paid to visual artists exceeded early estimates and will grow over time. The scheme already pays for itself and is achieving what it set out to do. This joining up of culture and creativity offers a solid platform for expression and livelihood for people in the future—as long as the free-enterprise zealots don't tear the house down.

28

DAY OF RECKONING

THE MOST PERPLEXING and ultimately dangerous feature of Labor's first term was the disconnect between established climate science and the ongoing refusal of sections of the media and the conservative forces in the country to take the issue seriously.

I found the debate around the issue utterly repellent, the balance sheet really was breaking up the sky, and the evidence was everywhere and mounting. Delegations of Pacific Islanders, now climate refugees, visited Parliament House to present the facts and press the case for action. Yet resource and manufacturing interests, and a large portion of the right-wing political classes, remained in a state of constant denial.

And when it came to pass that terrible bushfires ravaged the land, woe betide anyone—like the Australian Greens' Adam Bandt, the federal member for Melbourne—who dared suggest that pushing ever more coal-fired pollution into the atmosphere might have contributed.

In 2009, the Black Saturday fires centred on the Victorian towns of Kinglake and Marysville, exacerbated by four consecutive high-wind days over forty degrees, had seen serious loss of life and hundreds of thousands of hectares of national park and farmland burned out.

Parliament resumed three days later and question time began with a condolence motion for the victims. The first speaker referred to the numbers of deaths now standing at 107. By the time the speeches had finished, 135 deaths had been recorded and the toll was still rising. (The final number was 173.)

Along with Victorian premier John Brumby, I visited Kinglake to participate in the first remembrance ceremony; the locals were still numb with grief and in shock, lucky to survive but really hurting. There wasn't much we could do but listen and console people. I'd been asked to sing 'Advance Australia Fair' with Ross Buchanan, who'd lost two members of his family in the conflagration. I wondered how he would hold it together after what he'd been through. Ross made it, showing yet more bravery in a town where plenty had been on display.

Driving up to the ranges on the way to Kinglake had brought us up short. There was no sign of life as far as the eye could see. A week earlier, green swathes of eucalypt forest, myrtle, great mountain ash, wattles and orchids had covered these hills. Now, thousands of burnt black sticks stood on hills that resembled an abandoned battlefield. Sure, summer bushfires were a part of Australia's weather pattern and the forest should bounce back in time, but it looked like an alien landscape, and I feared for the future: hotter days, stronger winds and bigger, meaner fires.

There was an incredible outpouring of support for those who'd been affected by the fires, such was the scale of the loss of life. When Steve Waugh called to invite me to play in a charity cricket game at the SCG, I jumped at the chance—not only to be a part of something that was going to help those who had suffered, but also to experience the hallowed turf where my great-grandfather had thrown down a few curly ones.

One look at me poking away at a few balls in the nets saw the skipper relegate me to number eleven in the batting order, and the one over I bowled couldn't finish quickly enough, as our opponents scored freely. Mark 'Tubby' Taylor, a big John Howard fan, was the opposing team captain and came to the crease determined to make inroads on the score.

I'd been dispatched to the outfield, out of harm's way, when Tubby, having dug in for a long innings, took a swing at a slow ball from boxer Anthony Mundine and skied it. It ended up coming my way under a blaze of lights. 'Catch it!' shouted my teammates, and Mike Whitney, who was umpiring close by, yelled out, 'Run, Pete, run!'

I fastened my eye on the ball, ran as instructed and managed to hold it—no matter if I fell, I was determined to clutch that red bullet.

After the game, Taylor seemed miffed and didn't shake hands—a surprise, but then again maybe he didn't like the look of the score-card: Taylor (Australian captain, Liberal supporter), bowled Mundine (champion boxer, Aboriginal man, Muslim identity), caught Garrett (Labor politician, green activist).

The Oils geared up when approached to play at Sound Relief, a fundraising concert for the bushfire victims and their families organised by Michael Gudinski and the Melbourne music crew. We'd be sharing the bill with some good mates, Split Enz and Hunters & Collectors, as well as contributing to the cause. We had an affinity with the Melbourne-based Hunters, who had morphed from a uni student art band into a thundering, blue-singlet pub rock band. They blasted out big singalong anthems, underpinned by John Archer's rumbling earth-shaking bass, fleshed out by a brass section that included Jeremy Smith and trumpeter Jack Howard, who went on to play in the Break. We toured Europe together in the early 90s, and with seven band members interested in a wide range of subjects, from the latest injury count for the Bombers through popular culture to quantum physics, they were sterling companions. I liked singer Mark Seymour; he was intense—a trait we shared—and worried away at things, including politics, which showed up in their songs. On one of the rare nights that I went out with them and tore up the town—Frankfurt, as it happened—he was good company till sun-up.

I'd need to shake out the cobwebs, so I reacquainted myself with the Oils' albums while flying back from a ministerial meeting in Papua New Guinea—'So that's what we sound like.'

On the way in to Canberra I swung past Jim's place to catch up with the band so we could run through some songs on acoustic guitars. But we ended up talking the afternoon away, just catching up and seeing how everyone's kids, originally called the Baby Oils when they travelled with us years ago as toddlers in little Oils T-shirts, were faring.

With much inane speculation over whether the band would play 'US Forces' (we did), we then swung through a couple of warm-up nights in Canberra. By the eve of the first show, we'd still had no time to rehearse. But the reason for playing—doing something for others—was the driving force, so it didn't really matter. Michael Lippold couldn't get down for the shows, but most of our long-time road crew—including production manager John 'Ozzie' Vasey, lighting engineer Nick Elvin, monitor engineer Ben Shapiro and sound engineer Colin Ellis—had materialised for the warm-ups. They would make sure the wheels were firmly bolted back on.

The boys had kept at it—playing, recording and producing—so it didn't sound too flabby. Bones was a revelation. Having by now spent a couple of years as a session muso in Nashville, his bass was stronger than ever. Once we got out in front of 80,000 at the MCG, with Melbourne's strong community spirit ignoring the rain and filling the stadium, energy from every quarter propelled us over the line. The night was a gladdening reminder of the power of music to bring people together.

The Kinglake senior constable Cameron Caine, who'd been smack bang in the middle of the conflagration and witnessed too much trauma, asked me to return after the media circus had moved on, and so I visited again a year or so later.

While the slow pace of rebuilding was frustrating some locals, it was the time the emotional scars were taking to heal that was the hardest thing to cope with. In Australia, governments provide a fair level of support for people after natural disasters, and there was plenty of evidence of that in Kinglake, but the sadness was palpable, a black cloud hanging between the hills.

After leaving parliament, I was invited to go back again and spend some time at the Kinglake Football/Netball Club. I travelled up to the hills to see that much of the razed and blackened forest had, almost miraculously, come back to life after a few seasons of good rains. The lives of the residents, however, were still in abeyance, with outstanding legal cases and insurance claims unresolved. Many had rebuilt and moved on, some had moved out, but for others the wounds were as raw as yesterday. Discussion veered to other topics. People didn't want to be defined by the tragedy, and who could blame them?

...

After a natural disaster like Black Saturday, or hurricane Katrina in New Orleans, the urgent need to face up to dangerous climate change was indisputable. Yet once Tony Abbott was elected leader of the Coalition by just one vote in 2009, he went on a mission of national destruction, repeatedly lying about the effect pricing greenhouse gas emissions would have on the economy: the towns of Whyalla, Port Pirie, Gladstone and more were to be wiped off the map, he asserted, and at one point the Coalition claimed the price of a leg of lamb would rise to $100.

As soon as he won office in 2013, Abbott moved immediately to repeal the existing 'carbon tax', replacing it with a policy that made taxpayers, not polluters, pay for emissions reduction. He prepared to wind down the Climate Change Authority, cut funding to the CSIRO, ceased support for the Climate Commission and signalled his willingness to do the same for the solar roofs program, and later the Renewable Energy Agency, while reducing the Renewable Energy Target. Fashioning himself as the infrastructure prime minister dedicated to building new roads, Abbott retreated to an 'asphalt economy', a grotesque and costly public policy failure. Meanwhile, the multibillion-dollar revenue stream from Labor's scheme, which was funding new low-emissions technologies and businesses, was gone. So too was the income source that enabled Labor to deliver tax cuts and pension increases so low- and middle-income households were not negatively impacted by the price on carbon.

The scheme Labor ended up with was a levy on big polluting industries, as well as a limit on pollution from around 60 per cent of the economy. Unfortunately, the decision by Rudd's inner circle to focus on the price rather than the pollution limit, on the economy rather than the environment, turned the debate technical, and the Opposition's cliché factory went into overdrive. Yet the 'cap and trade' emissions trading mechanism Labor delivered was backed by almost all economists as the cheapest way to start bringing planet-heating emissions down. And it unambiguously worked: contributing to the biggest-ever drop in Australia's emissions, with a reduction of 40 million tonnes and a cost-of-living impact of less than 1 per cent following the introduction of the carbon laws. It will take a lot of time and money to recover from the black hole of the Abbott years, however long they last.

The perverse nature of the climate change debate in Australia was striking, but for the incoming Labor government, managing its dynamics was equally vexed. At the time the government, especially Prime Minister Rudd, was trying to keep business and the hypercritical *Australian* and News Corporation tabloid newspapers onside. It was a fruitless exercise and many ministers knew it, but the flow-on effect was to weaken the government's resolve as climate change committee meetings were cancelled and the policy constantly reworked. The doubters in the cabinet were always dropping dissent to the press gallery. Having opponents in the ranks like Joel Fitzgibbon and Martin Ferguson didn't help.

As recorded by accounts of the period, there was a window of opportunity for bipartisan action. During that brief period of time the Opposition was led by Malcolm Turnbull, who was willing to take action on climate change by supporting a full legislative package.

However, Rudd was intent on inflicting political pain on the Coalition and on Malcolm Turnbull in particular, and drew out the negotiations seeking support from minor parties in the Senate with the aim of denying Turnbull the opportunity to take some credit. Meanwhile Greens party leaders Bob Brown and Christine Milne wanted to do the same to Labor by refusing to support the proposed scheme on the basis the emissions targets were too modest, thus denying the government the achievement.

One day after finally agreeing with the government to pass the legislation, Malcolm Turnbull was deposed as leader and the Greens voted with the Abbott-led Opposition to defeat the Carbon Pollution Reduction Scheme. The nail in the coffin for the original scheme as we envisaged it in Opposition was the ultimate failure of conviction by Rudd and those close to him at the time, who were opposed to it going ahead in the aftermath of the disappointments of the 2009 Copenhagen Climate Change Conference.

Rudd's eventual decision to delay the bill wasn't communicated to the cabinet before being made public. In walking away from the Carbon Pollution Reduction Scheme, which by then had been rejected by the Senate twice, thus setting the ground for a double dissolution election, he missed the opportunity to take the issue back to the people, still willing to see strong action on climate change.

It was always an uphill battle to sustain the first flush of ambition for an effective emissions trading scheme. The climate change subcommittee had initially canvassed limiting permit allocations to 30 per cent of the most affected businesses, a figure that was then lifted to 60, and finally ended at 90 per cent, and this pattern was repeated ad nauseam across most aspects of the proposal. I should have seen the about face coming, having argued for a bigger cut in emissions in the original scheme, only to find myself friendless in cabinet. Having famously declared climate change the greatest moral issue of our time, Rudd—aided and abetted by the bloody-mindedness of the Greens, who were willing to sacrifice the good for the perfect—squibbed it.

The remarkable opportunity that the 2007 election outcome offered to introduce effective emissions trading into a high-carbon economy was squandered. It was a body blow to everyone who'd worked so hard up to that point and a calamity for the nation, given how daunting the issue is. The bitter irony was that now conservative parties in other countries were adopting or championing policies diametrically opposed to their Australian counterparts. David Cameron in the UK, German chancellor Angela Merkel and even Arnie Schwarzenegger in California promoted carbon-pricing mechanisms and other clean-energy policies. And we've since seen the emergence of carbon-pricing or emissions trading schemes in South Korea, South Africa and China.

I visited the US early on to assess the progress of energy-efficiency programs in states like California as we planned an ambitious rollout at home. In that state, Republican governor Arnold Schwarzenegger was delivering policies aimed at curtailing greenhouse emissions in the eighth largest economy in the world.

We met in the state capital, Sacramento, and when Schwarzenegger learned I wasn't leaving till late the following day, he asked me to lunch at his home in the Los Angeles hills. The customary practice is for visiting dignitaries to exchange small gifts when they meet. Due to Australian sensitivities about politicians receiving any gifts at all, our offerings were usually modest, verging on tokenistic: a coffee-table book on Australia's outback, or a native timber business-card holder were typical examples. In this case, the 'Governator'—as Schwarzenegger was dubbed—handed me a smart boxed collection of famous American films, including a few of his that I'd never seen and probably wouldn't have made the critics' top-ten list, but it was an appropriate gift.

Unusually, and luckily, I'd brought a collection of Oils CDs, just in case I bumped into someone in LA who'd appreciate them. So the koala tiepin was shelved and a more appropriate exchange took place.

The next day we wended our way up to Arnie's place, my adviser's jaw dropping as we surveyed the length of the movie star-cum-politician's driveway.

My view on LA hadn't changed—too much smog and self-promotion for my liking—but perched on the top of a hill high above the San Fernando Valley with the Governator dishing up steak and swapping yarns, it felt relatively benign. We were safe from evil crime lords and at last there was someone prepared to take on vested interests, including those in his own party, and go out on a limb on the great moral issue of our time.

Once Greg Combet was appointed Minister for Climate Change and Energy in 2010, he was able to engineer a constructive process, as the second-term Gillard government legislated a price on carbon pollution. But by then climate change had gone from a political asset to a millstone around the government's neck. Much of the government's political capital had drained away and the scheme we ended up with was a weaker version of the original proposal.

···

The sad fact is that Labor in power lacked the internal discipline to smoothly shepherd reforms as big as this one out the door. Even though it's a truth universally acknowledged that in politics, as in marriage, disunity is death, this didn't prevent selfish and ultimately self-defeating acts of sabotage and disloyalty from infecting the Rudd/Gillard governments from day one.

All the members of the Labor Caucus would have been aware that the Whitlam government's rocky tenure owed much to monumental instances of disloyalty and ill-discipline. The Hawke and Keating governments fared better, as tighter factions worked to impose some discipline. Even Keating's leadership push, which might have knocked Labor off balance, was out in the open and hardly relied on dirty tricks to see him prevail. But in the period leading up to Kevin Rudd's ascension as leader breakouts were common, and with multiple changes of leadership, undermining and backgrounding had become de rigueur.

This kind of behaviour is not exceptional, nor confined to the Labor Party, but under Labor in these two terms it was endemic. Irrespective of the party or the circumstances, despite voters saying they want to hear politicians speaking plainly, once conflict is out in the open they shy away in droves.

In peace or war, depression or prosperity, one important element of stable government in our political system is the principle of Cabinet-in-Confidence. The discipline of cabinet solidarity, meaning that once the cabinet has made a decision then ministers and the Caucus lock in behind it, is crucial. If a minister feels they can't support a decision, they can always resign.

Without this assurance of confidentiality, anyone could use the media as an auxiliary propaganda arm to attack or defend a decision, or to advance their own position. The result is that the government's internal travails, not the reforms it is attempting to secure, become the story, and the underlying untrustworthiness of politicians is communicated to the press gallery journalists, who in turn report it to their readers. One way of understanding the Rudd/Gillard years is through this prism. Rudd was a chronic feeder of information to favoured journalists, although he was by no means alone.

The possibility of reading, even in code, what you'd said behind closed doors meant the level of trust required to have open discussion was absent. Other than in my portfolio areas in cabinet, I would contribute where I thought I could add value, and speak out strongly on propositions I opposed, such as the offshore-processing arrangements for refugees on Manus Island. But that was where the discussion should have ended. I never believed it was right to subsequently broadcast my view, nor leak cabinet decisions to the media.

People often ask how it is that the Rudd and, later, Gillard governments struggled with aspects of governing. A big part of the answer lies in the nature of Rudd's leadership. The new prime minister turned out to be a poll-driven control freak who couldn't bring himself to delegate and who surrounded himself with overconfident, inexperienced advisers. The business of government quickly became paralysed as he tried to micromanage national affairs and an ambitious reform agenda around the twenty-four-hour news cycle. His treatment of senior bureaucrats and colleagues was laced with contempt. Rudd liked to cite the modern saint Dietrich Bonhoeffer as a model, but he was more like Brute Bernard, the 1960s professional bad-boy wrestler, except that the Brute was just play-acting, whereas beneath his chirpy exterior, Rudd really was a brute.

Another part is that the senior leadership group—Faulkner, Gillard, Swan, Albanese, Conroy and others—didn't put ministers (starting with Rudd) and backbenchers sufficiently on the spot when destabilising behaviour raised its ugly head. They may have undertaken this task individually, but the collective will to stamp out destructive behaviour was lacking. Nor did they make sure the leader stuck with the strategic direction agreed by cabinet and insist on the discipline to see it through.

It was a frustrating experience for someone new to the party. I would keep my own counsel, but I was often left scratching my head at the tolerance of errant behaviour, particularly from the leader. The absence of order at the top meant we would just have to concentrate on getting on with the job. In those lunatic days and restless nights, what else you could do?

29

DYING LIGHT

A N UNEXPECTED PART of my new role turned out to be the moving encounters I had with people, some at the end of their lives. Whether it was an intimate brush with mortality, or a throwaway conversation in a plane with a stranger about the hopes they had for their kids, these interactions underscored for me how crucial it was to cement positive things in place now that we were in government. Actions that would outlast me, and hopefully endure.

Through late 2007 I took some time to get the hang of being a minister, all the while hankering to get north and roll out some decent dollars into additional Indigenous Protected Areas (IPAs).

Along with arts centres, the Indigenous ranger programs that had been established to look after these newly acquired areas had proved to be durable organisations, especially during the period of the Howard government's intervention in the Northern Territory. The rangers were a great success story. Their on-ground knowledge was unmatched—passed down by older community members who'd walked their country for a lifetime and cherished it as a library—and was now invaluable when it came to managing the land, as well as giving people a reason to stay in touch with their country. Their tasks were diverse: controlling feral invaders, fire management, and tracking and monitoring endemic species—all part of a day's work. Rangers needed to acquire a variety of new skills in order to take on these tasks, from motor repair to logistics and planning, and over time some ranger programs had grown into highly professional, effective organisations, crucial to increasing the number of young locals in work.

One of my first trips was to the Northern Territory. Landing at Darwin airport, the visitor is met by a giant mural of mythical stick figures in the landscape—a symbol of the Top End. It was painted by Bardayal 'Lofty' Nadjamerrek, one of the great clan leaders of western Arnhem Land. Lofty was a noted artist who'd lived for a time in a cave in the stone country east of Kakadu, while the filament of his culture burned dimly because his people didn't have ready access to their homelands.

Our decision to deliver two connected IPAs, Warddeken and Djelk, in the Arnhem Land region meant this part of Lofty's struggle was over. Together, the two IPAs comprise over 20,000 square kilometres of sandstone gorges and pristine rivers.

The hand-over ceremony was held at the base of a display of spectacular rock art, near the tiny community settlement of Kabulwarnamyo. Lofty, by now blind and ailing, was pushed to the site in a wheelchair and afterwards lay on a camp stretcher under a lean-to as family members and well-wishers came and went.

When the official proceedings were over, I went across to sit with him for a while. He'd seen a lot, this old man. He'd been awarded an Order of Australia, his delicate bark paintings had been exhibited far and wide, and like Moses he'd led his people out of Darwin and back to their homeland. Now, in his dying days, the means to care for this country had finally been returned to them—but it shouldn't have taken so long.

...

Out of the blue, I started receiving phone calls from Warumpi Band singer George Rrurrambu, at all times of the day and night. I tried to take his calls, unless I was sitting in question time.

George, back on his feet and with a successful one-man show under his belt, had great plans for continuing his work mentoring young

Aboriginal bands, teaching them the ropes and the pitfalls, most of which he'd experienced firsthand, but he'd been struck down by illness.

The first time he rang he said, 'I'm sick, and I'm going to die,' adding in a soft voice, 'Don't worry about that.'

I was gutted to hear the news, although not altogether surprised. Life expectancy for Aboriginal men is well below the national average, and George had played pretty hard. He was stricken with cancer, yet had found some sort of peace in this, the final predicament he would face.

'We're brothers,' he said of his reason for ringing. 'I wanted to talk with you before I go.'

I don't know if he made many calls like this or only a few. Surrounded though I was by constant interruptions—phones ringing, and the incessant jawboning that was integral to life on the hill—George's news turned my emotions on their head. I closed the door to shut out the noise and we talked about the past. He was now looking ahead to being reunited with his totem once he'd drawn his last breath.

George's funeral took place in winter out on Elcho Island. It was still balmy during the day and his body, dressed in his stage clothes and covered with flowers, was laid out in a donga on the hillside overlooking the sea, kept cool by an air-conditioning unit turned up full blast.

We gathered on a gentle rise leading down to the water's edge. Various dignitaries had flown in, including the Northern Territory chief minister Paul Henderson, and my pal the NT administrator and folkie Ted Egan, as had George's ex from Papunya and his current wife.

There was some debate as to who should be granted the position of chief mourner in the official seating area. The first wife sorted it pretty quickly by thumping the newcomer.

There was special ceremonial dancing and song, numerous and lengthy speeches, and then bands played into the late afternoon, as the

event took on a dreamy, party-like atmosphere. The contrast between
the serious and sober farewells of other funerals I'd attended, including those of my parents, and this explosion of laughter and ceremony
couldn't have been greater. It was plain to me that this was a better
way to go. Just put the music on and dance like there's no tomorrow.
No breast-beating or self-pity, no howling at the moon. Keep me
close to my girls and scatter my ashes across the water. Leave a few
morsels for the bush, but no sombre, sad funeral for me, please—and
don't forget to have a laugh.

…

At long last my lifestyle had become predictable. As the Oils frontman
I'd kept strange hours at all points of the globe. In the environmental
activist years I was covering as much ground as possible while fending
off crises, both real and manufactured. Now, as a parliamentarian,
my activities were clearly prescribed—determined by parliamentary
timetables and extended obligations to the government. It was a
strange feeling for an instinctive freewheeler—swell's running, let's
go—which was how I'd previously operated.

Parliament sits for about half the year from Monday to Thursday,
and each day every member has to gather for questions without notice
at 2 p.m.

The atmosphere, when the House of Representatives was full,
was a heady mix of bravado, conviction and the aftertaste of age-old
enmities renewing the battle. Many of the adversaries, including Julia
Gillard and Tony Abbott, had cut their teeth in student politics, and
the verbal jousting was incessant.

The noise of debate would swell like massed cicadas in song, filling
the people's house, as the combatants—jeering, shouting and even
laughing at witty interjections—engaged in verbal battle.

I knew if I was ejected from parliament in my first few years
it would confirm the image of me as an angry radical that the

conservative parties were doing their utmost to create, and so I kept my cool. As time went on, I grew tired of the petty and undignified outbursts that often earned a send-off, as I suspect many people watching or listening to parliament did too. That didn't mean I wasn't taking proceedings seriously, just that I was taking the institution seriously too, unlike the former speaker Bronwyn Bishop, whose rulings were so one-sided I doubt I would have lasted a week without expulsion.

In the first term I sat next to Lindsay Tanner, then the finance minister, easy to recognise by the old-style double-breasted suits he favoured. Tanner was bowerbird bright, and a big music fan with a prodigious storehouse of rock trivia. Keeping one ear on proceedings, he would throw out the occasional gibe across the chamber designed to get under the guard of our opponents, as we shared lists: top-five desert island discs, best four-piece bands, ten most overrated guitarists, to keep ourselves amused.

In the second term I shared space with Tanya Plibersek, who managed to combine grace with combativeness, firing commentary back at her opposite number while checking her phone for messages. Question Time was a ritual, until the spotlight fell on you and the eyes of the press gallery swung your way, and then you had to have your wits about you. But nowadays it's usually the two leaders who slug it out, and the focus on them is unremitting. As a consequence everyone in the joint multitasked: preparing for surprise questions, doing correspondence, tweeting, chatting and, importantly, reminding ourselves why we were sitting there—because if we weren't occupying this space then those across the table would be, and the future of the country would be at great risk.

I'd arrive in Canberra on Sunday evening and spend time preparing for the week. All over the capital, often coming in to Parliament House, other ministers and advisers, almost unrecognisable in their civvies, were doing the same thing. I'd taken a room in the home of Warren Nicholls, whom I'd met when he was on the ACF executive and who'd previously worked for Ros Kelly in the Hawke era. He lived close by, and he and his wife Jo were gracious hosts, putting up with me leaving very early and getting back late. I'd have a Commonwealth car drop me half a kilometre short of Warren's house and walk the rest of the way through the leafy streets of inner suburban Canberra to clear my head while catching up by phone with Doris to see how things were going, but really just to hear her voice. I've always walked, especially at night on tour—the back streets of Las Vegas, the docks of Hamburg, the tourist quarter in New Orleans, even the old colonial suburbs of Rangoon. But here it was incredibly quiet and I rarely saw another person.

...

The more predictable the political argy-bargy, the more I rejoiced in the flashing spark of life when it happened to shine across my path.

I could see that the effervescence that explodes out of children— and made school visits so enjoyable—wasn't that far below the surface, no matter how many years a person had on the clock.

I'd had little to do with nursing homes before entering politics, but they were a sober fact of life, the abstract phrase 'Australia's ageing population' made real. On my first visit I found the experience shocking: row upon row of beds and chairs, each holding men and women whose life force appeared to be draining away, everyone behaving like dull decline was normal. It wasn't the smell of decay but rather the abject loneliness of many residents that pulled me up short.

It made me ponder the ethics of euthanasia, family ties, the way we organise our last years, how we relate to death and lots more besides. In an earlier time you might have been relegated to the back of the family home to see out your days, but at least the soundtrack of your life would still be playing—doors opening and shutting, the voices of loved ones preparing meals in the kitchen, the ebb and flow of the peak hour, early-morning currawongs, even some early Stones—familiar and reassuring. Here in these institutions, everything is muted: conversation, the TV and the colour-coded pill container. If there is any relief, it comes from food and, for the lucky ones, regular family visits. Yet the spark of life isn't completely extinguished; it just needs some kindling, someone with a match.

One nursing home that had recently opened in my electorate had extended a standing invitation to visit. The operators were keen to show off the facility, and some of the extra effort they claimed was being made for the residents. 'Come on Friday afternoon, if you can. We always have a party then, and sometimes there's music.' By the end of the week it was usually the last thing I felt like doing, but eventually I went.

The facility—modern, flat-roofed and close to the coast—was brighter and breezier than most. The windows were open, letting salty air blow through, and there was plenty of natural light. We headed to the dining room where about sixty residents—the majority of them women, some in wheelchairs—were sitting around waiting for proceedings to start. Tables and chairs had been cleared away, leaving an open space in the centre of the room. Small groups clustered in corners, most of their members gazing vacantly out the window or studying their shoes—it was apparent that dementia had struck down many in these parts.

I felt the nursing-home blues descend as staff appeared with trays full of glasses of pink champagne mixed with lemonade; no water, no tea, a Maroubra special. Some residents reached eagerly for a glass, others ignored the offer. There was little noise or movement, apart from a few of the younger crew—who looked to be in their mid- to late seventies—but at last the party was sort of underway.

Suddenly a large woman in her late fifties, dressed in a super-tight black blouse and matching skirt, burst into the room. Behind her came the manager, dragging a small sound system, which he proceeded to set up in a flurry of activity. 'Carla's here!' he called out excitedly, to little response from the dozy crowd.

Unfazed, Carla, adjusted the speakers, picked up a microphone and shrieked, 'Hi, everybody!'

Silence.

She tried again. 'Why, hello, darlings—you look fabulous.'

Still no response.

She paused then cried gamely, 'It's soooo good to be here. Are you ready for a good time?'

There were a few nodding heads but the room stayed mainly contemplative as a white-headed gran came up to me and whispered, 'Isn't she a nice girl?'

I'd been up since 5.30 a.m., had flown down and back to Melbourne for a special arts announcement we'd been working on for weeks, then plunged straight into a series of meetings once we'd returned. My energy levels were flagging, the day wasn't over, and I was due at another event in fifteen minutes. I wanted nothing more than to be home sharing a glass of wine with Doris, the pair of us downloading on our past week. But I just nodded in agreement while musing on what Carla's opening number might be. Whatever song she chose, I was sure she would murder it. I didn't know whether to laugh or cry. I was too tired to do either.

Then Carla hit play and music—loud and lilting—filled the room. There was some shuddering as people started in their chairs. Then she launched into a song made famous by Engelbert Humperdinck, 'Release Me', skilfully acting out the lyrics with large hand gestures.

I instantly took back my earlier misgivings with a tinge of shame for my scepticism. Carla was proving to be a pretty good singer. In fact, by halfway through the verse it was apparent that she was a showbiz trouper par excellence—a soul sister, in fact. I now found myself silently urging her on.

Then, out of nowhere, came an unexpected miracle. Like the petals of a flower unfolding, the frail bodies around me began to stir. The staff now moved among the residents—some dressed smartly, others in their pyjamas—inviting them to dance. Heaven poured into the room, as bent backs straightened and the residents swayed onto the makeshift dance floor, some singing in pure, thin voices, others just humming along.

'Who'd like to dance with Mr Garrett?' Carla called between verses, and so I took the hands of one of the dears who'd waved and we waltzed into the crowd, as she clung on to me with dry bony hands as a drowning woman might cling to a rope, and tears welled up in my eyes.

I've always believed that humans are born to sing, to make music, to dance, to tell stories, to paint pictures in order to celebrate life and to try to make sense of death. My visit to the nursing home was a reminder of how deeply the yearning for creative connection is embedded in our being. A lifetime's exposure to soap opera and sport can't erase it altogether; music and song are triggers that unlock memory and the shared experiences that make us human.

A population grounded in literature and music, dance and theatre, film, painting, sculpture and art in all its forms of expression has a great reservoir to draw on in the lottery that is life.

Politics, with its limited reach, is only part of the story. While I was able to persuade education ministers to include the arts in the national curriculum, helped by an enormous lobbying effort by many cultural organisations, including the Music Council, it was one of many subjects being shoehorned into the learning schedule and is still a long way from being a priority.

Its inclusion was a good starting point, a way of giving young people the opportunity to experience the stuff of creativity and try it for themselves. And when I grabbed some extra funds to increase support for the Artists in Schools programs we'd started in the first term, there was another small avenue of employment for highly skilled, but always underpaid, artists who could give so much to young people at a crucial stage in their intellectual and emotional development.

I can hardly think of a single downside to supporting the arts other than a few scarce tax dollars being spilled. The upside is huge.

In hospitals and special schools, music therapy is used to help treat those suffering illness or disability. Singing in school choirs has been linked to improved academic performance, giving kids a sense of achievement and assisting in addressing behavioural problems. Life without a sweet song or a soaring soundtrack is a dull imitation of the real thing, because music, like laughter, is medicine. With ever-increasing numbers of people experiencing mental and physical ill health, especially as they age, there's a simple prescription: liberate the mind and the body with heaps of art, and lots of music.

I hadn't witnessed my parents growing old, and so had nothing with which to compare these intimate exchanges I was experiencing as a minister. Yet I sensed that once a life—in whatever conditions and context—was stripped bare, it was love, of family and place, alongside the inner yearning to give full rein to our creative expression, located in each one of us, that gave some meaning to the journey.

30
THE FALL GUY

I'D TRIED TO heed Goethe's warning: 'The things that matter most must never be at the mercy of things that matter least.' This meant ignoring the irritations and getting on with the job, but early in Labor's first term in office there arose a bigger and more difficult issue than any of us could have anticipated—one that would nearly finish me off and contribute to Kevin Rudd's downfall as well.

In 2008, an economic downturn in the US featuring a credit crunch and falling house prices became a full-blown recession following the collapse of banking giant Lehman Brothers; the effects spilled into Europe and across other parts of the world, and suddenly there was a real possibility that Australia might get dragged into what was soon dubbed a global financial crisis.

In the event, we didn't go under and, luckily, due to prompt action by Rudd and Swan, Australia was among the few nations that managed to weather the storm. The advice from Treasury head Ken Henry was to 'go early and go hard', and so measures were put in place to stimulate the economy. The 'stimulus package', as it was known, was designed and coordinated by a special high-level task force, headed up by senior public servant Mike Mrdak, and chaired by the Department of the Prime Minister and Cabinet. The package included an enormous nationwide program to build new facilities in schools—such as science laboratories, libraries and halls—and a

large-scale home-insulation program, for which my department had
day-to-day responsibility.

The government wanted the insulation scheme rolled out quickly
and into as many homes as possible, and the final design offered
full rebates for the cost of the insulation. Almost from the outset,
the program—which was good for the environment and reduced
people's power bills, as well as protected us from the effects of the
global financial crisis—was pilloried by *The Australian* as expensive,
wasteful and riven with failings. It wasn't long before the rest of the
News Limited stable joined in the criticism. Yet when the OECD
found that Australia's increase in unemployment was lower and
increase in GDP higher than those of comparable countries, and that
due to the 'Nation Building and Jobs Plan' we had avoided a recession, there was hardly a squeak from the media, and certainly no
acknowledgement of how the government's quick actions had led to
us successfully riding out the financial storm.

In the latter stages of the rollout, four young installers lost their
lives—one in New South Wales and three in Queensland—and the
criticisms intensified. That young people involved in a government
scheme had died was a tragedy that stopped my office in its tracks,
and from the first death my bones felt heavy when I got out of bed
each morning.

In the New South Wales case, a young man had stupidly been
allowed to go into a roof cavity in forty-degree heat with only a sports
drink to relieve his thirst. Even now it's hard to find words to describe
how futile this death was, although it could hardly be said to be the
government's fault.

In Queensland, three young men died when stapling insulation to ceiling joists with metal fasteners that came in contact with
wiring in the roofs. In one instance, there was a pre-existing electrical
fault in the ceiling. One of the men had undertaken the training
program for installers and done over a hundred jobs, but had still used
metal fasteners, which I'd banned months earlier, following advice

that this measure would improve safety. In each of the Queensland cases, the employers were found to have ignored the scheme's guidelines and a number were subsequently found guilty of negligence, and in one case of perjury, and fined. They'd clearly failed in their duty of care to their employees, but—understandably—for the families of the young men who'd died, none of this mattered.

As the program was ramped up we devoted more time to monitoring progress, taking advice from the department and meeting regularly with the insulation industry, looking for ways to make the program as safe as possible. When that advice was presented, or on the occasions when I requested extra measures be considered, they were put in place immediately. Ultimately, they included nearly sixty measures designed to increase safety and reduce fraud: we banned the use of metal fasteners in order to prevent electric shocks; made the use of downlight covers compulsory; implemented a 'name and shame' register of installers who had breached the rules and been deregistered; established a national training scheme; and required a risk assessment of the job before putting people in ceilings to install the insulation.

The speed of the rollout and the fact that occupational health and safety was a state responsibility—although only South Australia had specific regulations in place for insulation—meant the program relied on the companies and individuals involved to do the right thing. Most did, but some, including those involved in the fatalities, didn't.

By early February 2010, with the four fatalities uppermost in people's minds, the program was under pressure and it was clear that something had to give—the question was what that 'something' would be. According to Opposition leader Tony Abbott, by then making a career out of overreach, I was in 'electrocution denial' and guilty of 'industrial manslaughter'. As a man who had stated, in a 2002 address to the Queensland Industrial Relations Society (titled 'In Praise of Bosses [and the jobs they bring]', that '. . . workplace safety is a shared responsibility between employer and employee . . . [and] we should also be aware of the tendency to be wise after the

event and seek scapegoats rather than solutions', his hypocrisy was
breathtaking.

Abbott showed no restraint: the program was a disaster and I had
blood on my hands, he thundered; accusations that hurt, especially
when picked up by members of the public.

Greg Hunt, Abbott's environment spokesman, led the charge
outside parliament by simply repeating that I should have somehow
predicted every one of the program's problems before they eventu-
ated. This line was taken up with relish by the radio shock jocks
whom Hunt fed on a regular basis. These bleaters seemed perfectly
happy to ignore the reality that, whether or not there was a home-
insulation program, any one of their listeners could install insulation
in their own roofs without any kind of training or minimum requirements. Hunt claimed that both Rudd and myself had received ten
direct warnings about the dangers in the scheme and that these had
been ignored, and further claimed that Rudd had specifically ignored
warnings that I'd sent him.

He was wrong, as subsequent reviews, including the Abbott
government's royal commission into the scheme, would show. I'd
written four letters to Rudd, detailing issues concerning the insulation scheme that he answered over time. (To my surprise, when I
left parliament I received a card from Greg Hunt that said, 'I regard
you as one of the people with the highest integrity in the parliament
and an outstandingly decent person.') But by now anyone with a
by-line, a blog or any other kind of bully pulpit was slavering to have
a go. The pattern was set: a groundless accusation from the Opposition or a mischievous claim from an unnamed member of the public
was made, and reported breathlessly as fact, without any attempt to
examine the truth of the allegation and what, if any, actions had been
taken by the government as a consequence. The final ignominy came
when I was secretly filmed early one morning in my tracksuit pants
letting Woody, the family dog, out for a pee. *The Daily Telegraph*
photographer hiding behind a row of parked cars chose his moment

well—they aren't called snappers for nothing—and the front page screamed loser.

Much of the media, including senior ABC journalists like Chris Uhlmann, swallowed it hook, line and sinker. After a barrage of headlines from News Limited papers, and already convinced that all politicians were liars, most journalists had come to the view that, if not guilty, I was at least culpable. The mud would stick for some time to come.

The press gallery hacks were so convinced of my imminent demise that a press conference to report on the scheme, convened in the Blue Room, in the ministerial wing of Parliament House just prior to question time, was a full house. The journalists turned up expecting my resignation and more than one let my media adviser know how disappointed they were when it didn't come, such was the pack's blood lust.

Desperate for the ultimate prize in political combat—a minister's scalp—the Coalition now applied what is euphemistically described as the blowtorch, and the attack in parliament escalated. I faced question after question, and censure motions, considered one of the most severe mechanisms for criticising a government, rained down.

Yet in the midst of the fury I was reasonably calm, desperately sorry for what had happened, but certain that I'd done everything I could to deliver the government program and to make it as safe as possible in the circumstances.

Midway through Wednesday of the second week of haranguing, having failed to come up with any new angles, the attack on me faltered and the Opposition started aiming its sights on the prime minister. We'd been well prepared, including having a relay team running material into the house when needed, and the questions to me suddenly stopped.

A few old hands passed down notes saying, 'Well done, you're through the worst of it.' As it turned out, I wasn't.

We still had Senate estimates to contend with. While one of the most useful exercises in the parliament, where the government can be questioned in detail on the budget and any specific programs, it is also an opportunity for political point-scoring around contentious issues. In the preceding fortnight, not confident that all the available information about the program had been funnelled up through the bureaucracy, we did a document dump, checking every email and letter, to make sure we knew what had been communicated to my office on each day since the program started. All my senior staff and advisers (Ben Pratt, Peter Wright, Matt Levey, David Blumenthal, Kate Pasterfield, Andy Palfreyman and Jack Smith) were pulled off their existing duties and worked through the night going through the thousands of emails and documents that had come from the department.

Satisfied that we had a robust case and a clear understanding of what advice had come to us and when, I then asked Robyn Kruk, secretary of the Department of the Environment, Water, Heritage and the Arts, whether the various measures that had been put in place to address safety could guarantee there wouldn't be further injuries. Robyn had been recruited from New South Wales and was an able, experienced bureaucrat. But she too had been let down by inexperienced officials struggling to manage the volume of insulation activity and not reporting up to her sufficiently. Her advice was clear: she couldn't guarantee the program didn't still contain significant risks. Indeed, how could she?

The estimates sessions hadn't uncovered any additional glitches, but I'd requested written advice to confirm Kruk's assessment that there could still be problems lurking, and material was prepared for a decision to be taken by the special budget committee of cabinet that oversaw the program. During this period, the Department of the Prime Minister and Cabinet and Treasury were sending signals that the program should be kept open. Emissaries from Rudd's office called to discuss the issue but eventually his deputy chief of staff,

David Fredericks, a straight shooter whom I respected, agreed that the position we'd arrived at, to suspend the program, should come before the committee as soon as possible, and a meeting was scheduled for Wednesday, 17 February 2010.

I had an uneasy feeling that something wasn't quite right when I showed up in the cabinet suite to find Terry Moran, the head of Prime Minister and Cabinet, hovering grim-faced in the corridor. There was a problem, Fredericks told me: we didn't have agreement.

I assumed 'we' could only mean the officials from what is called the central agencies—Prime Minister and Cabinet, Treasury and Finance—or Rudd, who was absent. I still went into the meeting determined to press for a suspension.

As Fredericks had indicated, the committee didn't support me. There was discussion about the impact on businesses and jobs, and whether some hybrid of the scheme could continue. Instead of reaching a decision, they sought additional advice about the state of the program. Despite Rudd's chief of staff, Alister Jordan, assuring me, 'We're not going to hang you out to dry,' this was the kind of manoeuvre that could buy time for an exit strategy to be decided— or it could create space to allow a scapegoat to be identified, either departmental or political. Whichever way it played, and given how feeble support from the prime minister's office had been up to that time, I had a strong suspicion that I was being set up for a fall. Either that, or the bureaucrats involved were trying to work out how to cover their backsides.

I pressed into the gale of negativity, urging that the matter be resolved as soon as possible, and a further meeting was scheduled for two days later.

In the interim we continued our arguments that the program needed to cease, including through Robyn Kruk speaking directly to Moran.

Despite the fact that the government was now under intense pressure, with calls for my resignation growing louder, when the meeting reconvened I was aghast to find the prime minister's office and the treasurer still arguing against closure. Andrew Charlton, a young economist from Rudd's office, was the most emphatic. Which rock had he been sleeping under?, I wondered, as he and others argued against stopping the rollout, and sought to argue the issue on the grounds of the effect on insulation businesses and the economy as a whole.

Notwithstanding this eleventh-hour stalling, the sound of the enemy cavalry galloping up Capital Hill and into our offices was by now so deafening it couldn't be ignored, so eventually realpolitik prevailed and it was agreed to suspend the program.

Rudd had chaired the meeting but there'd been so much toing and froing it ran behind time. The announcement dribbled out late on Friday evening and immediately added impetus to the Opposition's case.

Back in parliament the following week, they renewed their attack on Rudd—who, incidentally, was also seeing his personal approval ratings slide. At one stage, without warning, he headed out of his office solo to confront a small anti-government demonstration, including some angry installers, at the front of parliament. Notebook in hand, he took details from the crowd, promising to look into their complaints and fix their problems, saying, 'I get it, we get it.'

That night these comments were highlighted unfavourably on some evening news broadcasts and the next evening, when Rudd appeared on the ABC's *7.30 Report*, he was belittled for this lapse by the interviewer, Kerry O'Brien.

Both Rudd's and my offices had agreed on the government's response, but live on air Rudd left the door open for an additional comeback, though, confusingly, he remained vague about what that might mean. It was a bizarre performance that hinted at extra steps that could be taken, presumably actions that included me.

I knew then that, whatever else happened, my long-term political career was grounded. I also knew that the leader of the country, and the only boss I'd ever worked under, had completely lost the plot, but that didn't really help.

When pressed about my position, Rudd had said, 'I stand by the minister as I did last week, as I'll do next week.' This was a sentiment he also expressed in the regular Caucus meeting, which was greeted by applause from Labor members.

By the next week I was dead meat. Rudd's office had called on the Thursday when parliament broke to say he wanted to see me in Sydney the following day.

On Friday, 26 February, I flew to Sydney with Kate Pasterfield and Ben Pratt. There I met with Rudd and Jordan in the Commonwealth Offices in Bridge Street to be told that 'once the smoke has cleared', there would be additional roles pre-election—as if. And, to add insult to injury, they suggested that, after the election, I would be given more responsibilities around renewable energy, which all and sundry knew was one of my prime obsessions. For now, though, some parts of the portfolio would be handed over to others. It was a demotion, notwithstanding Rudd telling me it was about 'perceptions', not performance. An hour and a half later he gave a press conference announcing the decision, during which he omitted saying he had any confidence in me as a minister.

Of course Rudd didn't need to dump me, and you would like to think a leader with any sense of loyalty or spine, like P.J. Keating, wouldn't have. Whatever damage the government had suffered, the matter had run its course. And in yet another piece of irony, the weekly polls showed the government increasing its low standing by one percentage point.

A few months before, an article had appeared in *The Daily Telegraph* detailing the beginnings of Rudd's loss of personal popularity, particularly among western Sydney voters who, because of the large numbers of seats, can determine an election. In fact, Rudd's artificially high figures were simply returning to normal territory, but for someone who craved public appreciation and had designed his politics around playing to public perceptions, this trend was poison.

Also reported were pre-Christmas conversations canvassing my ministerial position, between Rudd and numbers man Senator Mark Arbib, a leader of the New South Wales right faction who'd recently come into the senate. Rudd owed his position to Arbib, who had been placed in charge of the whole of the stimulus package but took little interest in its problems. I'd ignored the rumours that were generated by the reporting of the Arbib/Rudd conversations, but it was clear the sharks were circling, even if they hadn't quite figured out what to do.

In the wash-up of the scheme's closure, respected former head of the defence department Allan Hawke was commissioned to review the insulation program and found my responses were 'appropriate and timely'. The auditor-general subsequently stated that 'the former minister received incomplete, inaccurate and untimely briefings' and that bureaucrats had withheld information from my office, as I was by now well aware.

The fact was that the home-insulation scheme had become one of the symbols of the government's alleged failings. The narrative was so strongly repeated it became folklore, accepted by people within the Labor Party as well as outside it. Only a handful of journalists, like Radio National's Fran Kelly and *The Australian*'s Peter van Onselen, Laura Tingle from the *Financial Review*, Barry Cassidy from ABC's *Insiders* and the Sky News team of David Speers and Kieran Gilbert, continued to report events in dispassionate terms. The ABC's Virginia Trioli was among the first to call out publicly what had become increasingly clear when she asked in the midst of an interview about whaling: 'You've ultimately then been made the fall guy, haven't you, for the fact that you properly informed your prime minister?'

Only a rare few members of the fourth estate, including Bernard Keane and Alan Austin from *Crikey* and Jack Waterford from *The Canberra Times*, chose to step back and analyse the program in detail. In an article published on 3 September 2014 ('Pink batts commission hands Abbott four explosive problems'), Austin came to the view that the government's achievement in avoiding recession had been virtually ignored, as had the fact that insulation had been installed in nearly a million homes at a greatly improved safety rate. In fact, contrary to the water-cooler chatter, the program had saved young Australians from the unemployment queues and the misery that accompany a recession, and, drawing on CSIRO research, it was clear that building and installing insulation was now safer than before the scheme began. Responsibility for the program's failures lay primarily with the central agencies—Prime Minister and Cabinet, Treasury and Finance—that designed and supervised the scheme. These observations were obscured by Tony Abbott's need for a political scalp, and the press gallery's appetite for controversy.

The problems the scheme was facing fed into a broader narrative of government dysfunction that was impossible to shake. It is the case that the program was rushed, but that was necessary; if it hadn't been done quickly, it wouldn't have achieved its economic purpose. But it did mean mistakes were made. It was too open to shonks, and the environment department struggled to administer it in such a way as to reduce risk even further.

My view was that the government should take responsibility for this program, but not solely. Everyone seemed to forget that before the scheme there were no mandatory skill requirements in the insulation industry, and no agreements between the states that this was necessary. The states and their safety regulators, the companies involved and their work practices, and individuals exercising care for their workmates all had a role.

But the notion that in every instance any government can and should be able to prevent bad things from happening set a standard no future government could ever hope to meet. A roads minister could hardly guarantee there wouldn't be any deaths if people ignored traffic lights. It was a perverse manifestation of the culture of entitlement in overdrive—with Tony Abbott leading the charge.

I hadn't sought to apportion blame, despite the scheme originating in the prime minister and treasurer's offices, and I certainly wasn't going to make the government's position any worse by pointing fingers in the middle of the brawl. In the end I took one for the team, because I came into parliament understanding this was what joining a team meant. As the minister with responsibility for the program, it was the right thing to do.

I held this position right through to the 2013 Royal Commission into the Home Insulation Program that Abbott had instigated once elected. Intended to cause Labor political damage, the inquiry was a waste of public money. Despite having unparalleled access to cabinet documents and government communications (a serious breach of the outgoing government's cabinet deliberations being off limits), some of which I'd never seen, it had failed to uncover any 'smoking gun' in relation to Rudd's actions. The commission, while critical of the former government, delivered no adverse findings against myself or any other Labor minister, and found that I was not specifically advised of any risk of injury and death before the first fatality occurred. At the same time, the commissioner, Ian Hanger, went so far as to criticise the Abbott government for failing to hand over documents or suggest any possible witnesses, not even bringing forward 'any evidence of its own volition'. After all the sound and fury the Coalition had generated on this issue, with Liberal senator Simon Birmingham from South Australia at one stage claiming that 'the greatest threat to the safety of many Australian families' had been the home-insulation program, the Abbott government provided no additional material for consideration to the $20 million charade it had initiated and funded. Nearly $7 million was redirected by the Attorney-General George Brandis from the Royal Commission on Institutional Responses to Child Sexual Abuse.

Of all my regrets from this period, my assumption that employers and workers would take proper care of those under their charge is the greatest. That and expecting that senior members of the government, especially the prime minister, would back me instead of hanging me out to dry. Individual members of Caucus and the ministry were supportive, but in the initial flurry of controversy many in the leadership team, with the exception of Nicola Roxon and Gary Gray, were silent, and cabinet committee members, other than Julia Gillard, were reluctant to shut down the program, even though it had a fixed spending limit which was fast approaching.

...

In the week following the scheme's closure, Barack Obama announced a large-scale home-insulation program to help American households reduce their energy bills and lower greenhouse gas emissions, and it was reported that Tony Abbott had got lost hooning around in the Northern Territory on a quad runner—he was just having fun.

I headed down to Ruby Hunter's funeral in the Riverland of South Australia. Ruby was singer Archie Roach's partner, and along with Archie had come off the streets to forge a durable music career and inspire a generation of young Aboriginal kids to believe. I sat with the girls from the band Tiddas, Shane Howard and Paul Kelly as we mourned this feisty woman—only just past fifty when she died—and I licked my wounds, only too aware that four young kids for whom I bore some responsibility hadn't made it.

Then the drought in Queensland broke, and over Easter a Chinese ship carrying coal ran aground on the Great Barrier Reef. Life was returning to a semblance of surreal normality.

...

The first term ended in a flash. Looking back, I can see we managed to sprint through a lot more than people realised. The crisis period that reached a climax at the beginning of 2010 had, ironically, provided cover for a range of other important decisions we could just get on and make.

The conservation estate was much bigger than when we switched on the lights on day one, and not a single major decision had been overturned—the environment laws worked if a minister was willing to use them. And even the work to construct a set of national environment accounts hobbled along, although the numbers men and women of Treasury continued to resist. The Kimberley region was now subject to a national heritage listing that would supply more reasons for protecting its extraordinary beauty and give the local community a greater stake in its future. And I'd persuaded Western Australian premier Colin Barnett to finally agree to jointly seek World Heritage listing for Ningaloo Reef, which came through a year later.

We stopped Clive Palmer's Waratah Coal in its tracks; in one of many micro decisions an important area of cassowary habitat at Mission Beach was now protected for the first time; and Newcastle residents didn't have an eyesore on their most prominent headland.

The marine bioregions planning process was well underway, with a declaration of a conservation zone, east of the Great Barrier Reef Marine Park, covering nearly a million square kilometres of the Coral Sea, and now a number of marine national parks were ready to go.

The largest ever roll-out of solar panels at homes and schools had begun, lifting the solar industry to such an extent that it would never look back, transforming the energy landscape right across the country.

We'd revived the system of grants to community groups that had been stopped under the former government and established a national recycling scheme for televisions and computers.

A new direction for the arts had been set with healthy budgets—later hacked into by the Coalition. There were artists in schools and suburbs reaching out, exciting the creative instincts of young people, and Aboriginal and Torres Strait Islander artists were supported more than ever.

There was a bundle of other things we got out the door—the unreal business of being an activist in a suit—and I wished I'd had time to do more. There were times when I felt I had fallen way short, like I was wading through wet cement and the world was willing failure, but we'd survived. One night I had a strange dream about The Dakota building, where John Lennon was shot and the world stopped in a frozen moment. When I woke up I knew I just had to press on to that wide open road.

31

GREAT BIG SINGERS

M Y DEEPEST FEAR was that, in the blink of an eye, 500 million plus years of evolution was coming undone.

Humanity's is a supercharged history, one that, when I think about it, is both exhilarating and worrisome. I was elated by the triumphs of the incredible journey so far, distressed about where it might end if we didn't get our act together.

The oceans—where life on earth began—had once teemed with fish: the enormous cod migrations through the North Atlantic, the masses of tuna, swordfish and mackerel that swam in cooler waters. There were literally billions of shrimp and krill, and tinier organisms still, all part of a giant food chain that has at its apex the biggest animal that has ever lived: the great blue whale. Traversing whole oceans, covering vast distances, whales create intricate songs to assist their courtships and guide their way.

Massive, gentle, slow-moving: once handheld spears gave way to the mechanised explosive harpoon, they were all too easy to kill and so were slaughtered in huge numbers. By the late 1970s, a perfect storm of dwindling stock numbers and looming extinctions darkened the horizon. Would one symbol of humanity's progress be a museum exhibit with the inscription: 'Here rests the last of the greatest sea creatures the world has ever seen'?

Not yet, as it turned out, for a campaign to halt commercial whaling, begun by Greenpeace and soon joined by other environmental groups, captured people's imagination and quickly reached a climax.

Earlier efforts to contain the industrial slaughter of whales had proved ineffective, so an international body—the International Whaling Commission (IWC)—was set up in 1946 to supervise commercial whaling while 'providing for the proper conservation of whale stocks'. Whaling for the purposes of Indigenous subsistence was also permitted. Over time, most countries with an interest in whaling joined the IWC, and the result of the anti-whaling campaign was a limited moratorium on the commercial killing of whales considered to be in danger of extinction. The moratorium was championed by Australia, where the last whaling station had closed in 1978, and was given effect by the Fraser government in the early 1980s. More and more countries signed up, and the moratorium came into law through the commission in 1986.

At the same time, IWC members were allowed to establish their own scientific whaling programs, which saw a handful of whales taken for research purposes by some countries, including, at one point, Australia. Over time an uncomfortable truce emerged, with the Japanese instituting a large program of so-called 'scientific whaling'. They eventually targeted over 800 minke whales and fin whales, and reserved the right to take humpbacks as well. Japan argued that whaling was a cultural practice, but national pride played a part too (no one tells us—a fishing nation that relies on the sea for our livelihood—what to do) and, importantly, the fear that a precedent would be set that might see other 'fish' similarly protected.

And so Japanese ships would steam into the Southern Ocean off the tip of Antarctica—closer to Sydney or Auckland than Tokyo—for the annual whale hunt. There was no real science involved, and the cultural connection between Japanese domestic whaling and hunting down whales in Antarctic waters was non-existent. In any event, scientists can study whales without killing them, as is the case with other animal research. But the membership of the IWC included nations that had little direct connection with whales but backed Japan, which in turn supported them with sweetheart trade arrangements, soft loans and bribes.

Successive Australian governments, from Fraser's onwards, had opposed commercial whaling, while holding back on taking additional steps for fear of harming relations with a country that happened to be one of our most important trading partners. Meanwhile, IWC members kept bickering, and during the term of the Howard government, when Malcolm Turnbull was environment minister, the number of whales targeted by the Japanese had doubled.

By the time the Rudd government was elected in late 2007, the issue was in stalemate. In Opposition, we had strengthened the Labor position, promising to consider taking legal action in the International Court of Justice (ICJ)—something I'd called for in 1994 as president of the ACF—along with sending a vessel to scrutinise the Japanese whalers and collect information for any potential legal case, and also appointing a whaling envoy to ramp up our diplomatic efforts in the IWC.

Rudd, ever alert to the public mood, was aware that a large majority of Australians consistently opposed whaling, and he was prepared to go further than previous Coalition governments, which had shrieked loudly but done little. Thus, immediately following the election, with Japanese whalers again en route to the killing fields, the decision was taken to dispatch an Australian customs vessel, the *Oceanic Viking*, to monitor the fleet—a move that would signal to both the Australian public and the Japanese that we were serious. An Australian government aircraft would fly overhead and also relay data back to the mainland. This caused significant disquiet in diplomatic circles, especially considering the closer economic and political trajectory the two countries were on.

I drove down to Canberra on a blustery day in January 2008 to meet officials in the Australian Customs Service monitoring suite. Here, images uploaded via satellite from the *Oceanic Viking*, tasked with shadowing the Japanese vessels across the wild reaches of the freezing Southern Ocean, were downloaded, and the exact location and activities of the fleet could be easily tracked. The graphic images confirmed that the operation was all about hunting whales and had nothing to do with science. We had all the evidence needed for a court action. Would the final step to launch a case against one of our most important allies now be taken, and, if so, what were the chances of victory?

In the meantime, the ground needed to be prepared for a new approach for the IWC. I envisaged the whaling commission as a conservation-focused organisation with the management and conservation of all whales and dolphins (cetaceans) as its primary function. This new template would be informed by non-lethal research and developing policy around whale watching as a legitimate economic activity, as opposed to killing whales for commercial purposes. It was an exciting vision. Senior officials in the environment department were encouraged to bring forward their best thinking as to how we could get it to stick. This was the moment when the new government should do everything possible to turn the issue around.

Within twelve months, we had launched the inaugural Southern Ocean Research Partnership, a multimillion-dollar initiative, driven by our view that the IWC should move from regulating the whaling industry to being an organisation that 'stands for the recovery and conservation of global cetaceans'. Australia hosted the world's first international workshop on non-lethal whale research in Sydney, with a good rollup, especially among Latin American nations.

The IWC was holding meetings between sessions as officials tried to find a way through the deadlock between anti- and pro-whaling forces, and Australia had lodged a substantial paper outlining what a reformed IWC might look like. At the same time, a proposal had been floated through the US, New Zealand and others that would see Japanese coastal whaling accepted in return for an end to 'scientific whaling'.

This was never going to be acceptable to me, although other departments, including the Department of Foreign Affairs, didn't exclude it as an option. I'd always been clear that a Labor government would never support a return to commercial whaling in any guise, and that we weren't ruling out the possibility of taking legal action at a later date. Still, I was determined that Australia should stay in the tent—a tactic that led to accusations of compromise by the Sea Shepherd Conservation Society and others—and continue discussions at the next IWC meeting. Our position never changed, but participating in the talks bought us some time in which to gather support from other like-minded countries for the reform package.

The hardest task was to prevent discussion going off the rails, for the commission was actually closely balanced between anti- and pro-whaling nations, given that any country could join the IWC if it could pay the membership fees—or its fees were met by another member nation, as was suspected in some cases. The efforts of the Japanese in courting small Caribbean states and tiny countries like Nauru ensured they could be relied on to vote with Japan and against our proposals. At this stage, it was all but impossible to garner the three-quarters majority needed to make a change of the magnitude we were proposing. In fact, we would have to strive like fury just to bring a simple majority along with us, so compromised were some countries by their relationship with Japan.

The situation was further complicated by the fact that two of our allies, the US and New Zealand, were playing a double game. Both nations had always been strong members of the anti-whaling camp, and still were, but they had grown tired of the stand-off and were desperately searching for a means of breaking the stalemate. The Americans were chairing the special working group set up to find a way through, and former New Zealand prime minister Sir Geoffrey Palmer, who'd served as an IWC commissioner and was well respected in whaling circles, bought in with a paper aimed at delivering a short-term solution. The US was pushing an option that would enable Japan to begin coastal whaling, which would have sent a green light to other pro-whaling nations like Russia and South Korea to scale up their operations. The compromise variation offered by Palmer provided a ten-year period of limited commercial whaling in the Southern Ocean in return for a cutback in the number of whales targeted by the Japanese. This would have effectively ended the moratorium on commercial whaling that, until now, had held whaling nations at bay.

I was aghast: it offered far too much for nothing in return, while acquiescing to a position we'd long opposed. The officials in charge of our negotiations agreed. Not surprisingly the chief Japanese negotiator described Palmer's contribution as 'a courageous proposal'.

The omens were not good. A concerted campaign was underway to undercut Australia's position and convince other countries and NGOs that the compromise proposal was the only sensible option. At one stage, two major environmental organisations, Greenpeace and Pew Charitable Trusts, under immense pressure from the Americans, had expressed qualified support for the proposal. Some of the groups we could usually rely on to stand firm were wavering.

And so began a period of intensive whaling shuttle diplomacy, with whaling envoy Sandy Hollway, Australia's whaling commissioner Donna Petrachenko and myself travelling to the far reaches of the globe to push our case.

The government's appointment of Hollway, a former senior bureaucrat, as our first Special Envoy for Whaling meant wide coverage was possible in our diplomatic efforts. He was smart and well versed in diplo talk, and kept discussions going as long as needed.

My office and key officials made sure the line was held internally and with IWC members. I made numerous calls to environment ministers, travelled to Europe and twice visited the US. My first trip, in September 2009, was to communicate Australia's reasons for rebuffing the compromises and to explain why we were seeking a new course for the IWC. Key US officials, including Under Secretary of State for Civilian Security, Democracy and Human Rights Maria Otero and Lisa P. Jackson, head of the Environmental Protection Authority, listened politely—but they were unmoved. The push-back from the Americans continued unabated. In October they were claiming the IWC was 'coming unstuck'. By December the new options were described as a 'normalisation' of the IWC. We were now entering the familiar Orwellian realm of word warfare I dislike intensely, but it was a sign our opponents were pressing home their campaign.

It was around this time that we received the first of several letters sent by US Secretary of State Hillary Clinton, aimed at blocking our charge. The letter said in part: 'We urge all IWC member governments to remain engaged in this process and not take precipitous actions outside the IWC that would compromise the chance of a diplomatic solution.' It seemed to be a clear warning to Australia not to take the Japanese to court. The communication set off senior bureaucrats in the Department of Foreign Affairs and the Department of the Prime Minister and Cabinet, and a flurry of emails and meetings followed. But I just noted the content of the letter on the ministerial brief that came through and we kept ploughing the same furrow.

My next trip to the US, in December 2009, was ridiculous—forty hours of travel by commercial airlines for twenty hours on the ground—but necessary. The occasion was the fiftieth anniversary of the Antarctic Treaty, to be marked with a ceremony in Washington. Australia had been a founding signatory and placed great store in the treaty, and it was important to register our ongoing commitment by attending.

At lunch following the meeting, I had a cordial conversation with Hillary Clinton, who was hosting the event. The two nations had worked well in relation to the Antarctic and whaling in the past, but now some differences had emerged. We were not for turning, was my unambiguous message.

The issue would now come to a head at the June 2010 meeting to be held in Agadir, Morocco. In the meantime, we maintained the arguments, and moved ahead with the non-lethal research program that was already making good progress. The early findings demonstrated what most people suspected intuitively: that harpooning large numbers of whales and dragging them, often bleeding and in distress, onto factory ships was not in any way scientific. There were non-lethal research techniques that could be used, like taking blood samples by dart. Allowing this mass slaughter to continue was making a mockery of the IWC.

I visited whale-watching enterprises in Australia and New Zealand to highlight the case for the economic benefits of keeping whales alive. This became an unexpectedly hazardous activity, as along with the mysterious arrival of the cold-water allergy, I'd now developed chronic seasickness, which materialised at the first hint of motion once on a boat. I could only wistfully recall my time as a teenager, sailing in catamarans with a friend around Pittwater. Then it was a case of the wilder the better. Now I longed to get back to dry land, while struggling to keep from vomiting—which no doubt would provide an amusing yarn for the press corps who often tagged along for these scenic trips.

As it happened, a dirty tricks campaign was now running in the media, a sign that our opponents really meant business, and a reflection of the utter bastardry that infects sections of the fourth estate. Typical was a story in *The Sunday Telegraph* alleging I'd spent a record sum on overseas jaunts to do with the whaling issue. Politician's travel expenses are a no-brainer for the press, and sometimes the criticism is justified. But the figure seemed way too high, and for a reason. It included the travel costs of most of the officials and our IWC commissioner as well—but there was no opportunity for comeback.

We stayed the course, pushing hard to get Conservation Management Plans, which clearly outlined how whale populations were to be protected, accepted at a previous IWC meeting. They provided a great example of what the IWC could do in the future, as well as established a precedent for conservation-based action. Nearly half a million blue whales had been slaughtered in the period of industrial whaling, and even since the moratorium these peaceful giants of the sea were at less than 2 per cent of their pre-whaling numbers. It was in this context that the core parts of our reform initiative needed to be advanced. I specifically wanted civil society—the NGOs that had long led the campaign—to have greater access to IWC processes and better communications with government too.

We had initiated a series of regular meetings with conservation groups such as Greenpeace, the International Fund for Animal Welfare, the Humane Society and Pew, and invited representatives of these organisations to the government's daily meetings when the IWC met. These were long-term players that worked hard in public outreach and behind the scenes. Despite lacking the resources of government, I knew they could always be relied on to show up and put the case, although Pew and Greenpeace's support for the compromise had taken me by surprise.

Sea Shepherd didn't participate, as they'd been banned from the IWC meetings. Instead they mounted an attack on anyone they perceived to be inside the tent, even those organisations and countries that were vigorously opposing the pro-whaling nations. Leader Paul Watson would lurk in the hotel lobby, demonising the meeting and the participants as sell-outs. This was the sum total of the Sea Shepherd contribution, other than sending protest ships to harass the Japanese fleet every year. I had always publicly supported direct action—and still do—but, like most of the NGOs who'd been working on the whaling issue for decades, I was far from convinced that in this case it would deter the Japanese from sending their fleet to hunt whales.

There was no doubt that getting in the way of the whaling fleet could disrupt the kill, and confronting Japan on the high seas was dramatic stuff and came with great images—Watson always had a camera in tow—which provided a terrific fundraising platform for Sea Shepherd. ('We are the only ones with the courage to take on the Japanese, so support us!') But neither their rhetoric nor their actions could deliver a long-term solution, no matter how many nail-biting docos they made for *National Geographic*. And there remained the very real risk of harm to activists—whose motivation was never in question—so far from land and in such a treacherous stretch of ocean, who would need to be rescued by 'sell-out' governments if things went pear-shaped. The final irony, which seemed lost on most people, was that Sea Shepherd's last resort was to call on these very same governments to do something: institute trade bans, send a ship, arrest Japanese seafarers, whatever.

At the height of the skirmishes in the 2009–10 season, a radio announcer on the high-rating Melbourne station 3AW put it to me that I could make myself 'the most popular politician on earth' by declaring war on the Land of the Rising Sun. By now, after years of effort spent trying to resolve an issue that I'd long cared about, and now as environment minister, I would have done just about anything to bring this campaign to a close—short of going to war with one of our most important regional neighbours, with whom, especially given the rise of China, we shared an increasingly close relationship.

While I wouldn't advocate going to war, I was all in favour of taking the battle to the ICJ. I'd sent a paper to cabinet outlining the state of play and arguing for that step, but it took forever to emerge. At the end of the day, it would have to be a joint cabinet submission from my department and the Department of Foreign Affairs, which kept gnawing away, mounting rear-guard actions to prevent what they saw as an unnecessarily imprudent and uncertain course being taken. The Crown law officers were similarly unconvinced, despite the urgings of some ambitious academics, so I hunkered down with advisers to hone our understanding of international law.

I then spoke to the solicitor-general, Stephen Gageler, to get his steer on the proposed action. As you'd expect from a future High Court judge, he was cautious, and pointed out the uncertainties that accompanied taking a case to a court that had more than a dozen judges from different countries sitting at any one time.

I lobbied for the support of the lugubrious attorney-general, Rob McClelland, whose department was still nervous about taking what it described as the nuke option. I also pressed the case with Stephen Smith, the foreign affairs minister. In private a fan of all things dark and loud, and a Bad Seeds tragic, in public he was dapper and chipper—qualities not usually found in a typical Australian politician—and he had a wry take on the vagaries of political life, having been a player for many years. He would argue his department's case till the writing was on the wall—as in this instance, with Rudd still willing to press the case, it eventually was.

Despite the misgivings of colleagues, I felt it was crucial to persevere. There were many reasons: we'd already promised we would take legal action if the Japanese persisted; we needed to have a fallback in the event the IWC fell apart; we couldn't allow any country to continue flouting the rules in this way; and, finally, the times had changed. This last reason was in some ways the most important. The natural world and all living things were now more valued, and more in jeopardy, than in the past. Perhaps the international court would reflect some of that changed global thinking as well.

The eventual cabinet submission was delayed, sent back on several occasions, but finally agreed, with Rudd, Smith and me left to sort the details. To my horror, the decision was instantly leaked to a Fairfax journalist, which would have taken away the impetus of a statement, but didn't make the splash the coward(s) intended.

As this was going on, behind the scenes the US and New Zealand had continued side discussions with Japan. Their aim was to reach some form of agreement that could be put forward at the upcoming IWC meeting and thus circumvent the need for any legal challenge. In the absence of any change in position from Japan, which throughout showed no willingness to compromise, their ambassadors mounted a last-minute appeal to the Department of Foreign Affairs and Trade on 24 May, focusing on the importance of the two nations' relationship with Australia—to no avail.

A week later, on Friday, 28 May 2010, Stephen Smith and I announced the government's decision to take legal action in the ICJ against Japan. This was only the second time Australia had taken such a step. The previous occasion had been in 1973, when we challenged the French over nuclear testing in the South Pacific.

On the same day, a paper arrived from the Americans seeking a delay—it was too late. In two weeks I'd be at the next meeting of the IWC with the strongest position yet any government had presented against whaling.

The following Monday I met with the ambassadors of Brazil and Argentina to thank them for their support and to discuss tactics for the upcoming meeting. A day later formal court documents were lodged at The Hague in the Netherlands, home of the ICJ.

Before leaving for Morocco, I dropped in to see Lou Reed, in town with his partner Laurie Anderson, who was directing the Vivid festival in Sydney. I was relieved to be back in a hassle-free zone, if only to pause for breath, as Reed, who was filling in time doing a radio show from the Opera House studios, back announced and discussed obscure New York garage bands with his friend, American producer Hal Willner. Eventually, Lou asked me what I'd been up to.

It was difficult to know where to start, but I launched into a précis of my recent walk on the wild side.

Lou listened thoughtfully for a minute, and then said very slowly in his New York drawl, 'Amazing. You're actually *in* the government?'

'Yes, that's right,' I replied.

Lou shook his head, clearly bemused as to why on earth anyone would want to work in politics. Then we shook hands and I headed out to the airport. A few years later he was gone.

...

Quite why officials had decided to gather in the sleepy seaside resort of Agadir on the eastern shores of the kingdom of Morocco, in a part of the world that is virtually whale-free, took a while to fathom.

But it was hard to escape the suspicion—voiced by my ever-vigilant media adviser Ben Pratt, who'd spotted various spouses and relatives in attendance from other delegations—that for some it was a junket. Why else were most meetings held in such exotic locations?

Our task, on the other hand, was serious: we needed to strengthen the anti-whaling coalition and try to embed a new conservation-based vision for the IWC. At the same time, it was critical that some version of the weaker compromise floated by Sir Geoffrey Palmer, with support from the Americans, didn't grow legs. In addition, we wanted to prevent a walkout by the Japanese and other pro-whaling nations that had been angered by the provocation of Australia's announcement of legal action.

It was likely to be a bruising affair that would need deft handling, all the more so when our position was laid out: that all whaling should be brought under control of the IWC and 'scientific whaling' immediately ended; that no new whaling be allowed; that the quota for taking vulnerable species be reduced to zero; and that all forms of whaling be prohibited in IWC-recognised whale sanctuaries. We argued for better mechanisms to be developed for monitoring, compliance and phase-outs, and for improved governance. We pushed for the IWC to agree that principle-based science determine policy, with climate change impacts on whale and dolphin populations now being taken into account. There was more, but the effect of this declaration was to drive undecided nations into one corner or the other.

The US and New Zealand proposals started to lose steam as the conference ground on. This was due in no small part to the marathon efforts of several leading environment department officials, in particular the secretary, Robyn Kruk, and our representative on the IWC, Donna Petrachenko. Along with Antarctic chief scientist Nick Gales, this issue had become a labour of love as well as their job.

My experience in the international meetings I'd attended was that Australian officials were usually highly competent and diligent. Most delegates who attend meetings of this kind are skilful bureaucrats, often in the diplomatic service, but here at Agadir some were simply going through the motions. Not so our team, who had war-gamed every possible scenario. I can't recall receiving a more thorough brief on any other issue. Our officials believed in what we were trying to achieve and it showed. And ultimately it worked.

Strong backing from the Latin American bloc and the UK, which had long held anti-whaling positions, helped as, in a blitz of last-minute lobbying—with as much personal contact with ministers as could be managed, and with significant pressure applied by their domestic NGOs—we received welcome support from the leading European nations, Germany and France.

At one point, with the Japanese team swapping restaurant tips with their allies from Saint Kitts and Nevis, and Kiribati, I accepted a petition from over a million people worldwide, which reinforced Australia's position. It was a substantial expression of public will and, along with the displays and side events scheduled by the NGOs to sway conference delegates and media outside the main meeting room, kept the anti-whaling wheel turning.

By the second last day of the conference, Australia was starting to drive the agenda. I was pleased we'd got this far and naturally keen for people at home to know about it. Far from running up the white flag to the Japanese, as our political opponents were fond of claiming, we'd presented a new path to an international body mired in an old way of thinking. And we'd backed it up with real programs, proper science and clear thinking.

It had been a hard-fought struggle and, even though we weren't claiming total victory, at a crucial juncture the IWC had abandoned a compromise plan that would have ended the moratorium on commercial whaling. We'd well and truly avoided the predicted defeat, and laid a much stronger foundation for the next stage in the battle to save the whales.

Due to the time difference, I was due to speak to Tony Jones from the ABC's *Lateline* program just as the day was coming to an end.

Ben Pratt and I were standing outside the conference hall, waiting for the interview to begin, when suddenly Ben's phone started ringing. He ignored it, but it kept going off.

A day before we'd received calls from some members of the press gallery we knew well; something was starting to bubble. An hour or so earlier, I'd received a call from Alister Jordan, Kevin Rudd's chief of staff, that confirmed it. He was trawling for likely numbers in the event of a leadership spill.

It was a very short conversation with Jordan. My position was straightforward, I told him. 'As a cabinet minister, I support the prime minister, but I won't vote for Rudd if there is a challenge, and you should know that. I'm 10,000 kilometres away and need to get back to this meeting.' Click.

By the time I was ready to begin the *Lateline* interview, with a small microphone stuck in my left ear and a voice from another hemisphere whispering, 'One minute, Mr Garrett, you're going live,' Ben's phone was beeping furiously. I'd put my own mobile on silent, but it was vibrating madly in my trouser pocket.

I could hear the animated voices of delegates as they poured out of the conference into the dry heat of the late Moroccan afternoon. It had been quite a day, even compared to the highly charged atmospherics that were the norm in the IWC.

Jones devoted the first half-dozen questions to the leadership challenge that was currently underway in Canberra, an event I couldn't participate in, and one I'd given little thought to in the blur of the week's frantic activity. I was likely the only cabinet minister in front of a camera at this moment, and had no intention of setting off a hand grenade from Morocco, much as I wished to see Rudd out of the leadership, but the spill hadn't happened yet. Added to which I needed to make clear the government's position at the conference to lock in our allies' support, and let people at home know the state of play.

So many people cared about these creatures and how they were treated, and they had a right to know what had happened on this day.

So many people had fought hard to get the issue to this stage and they deserved to relish the moment.

A lot of time, effort and resources had been spent to make good ground and I felt the government, at last and at least, deserved some credit.

But it was not to be. We'd left Canberra with one prime minister in charge and flew back in to find another, Julia Gillard, had taken his place. The leadership stoush—as it always would—completely over-shadowed everything else. On days like this, politics really is the pits.

On the way back to Australia I dreamed about vast pods of hump-backs and southern right whales making their way along the Sydney coast, swimming south for the summer. In my mind's eye I could see crowds clustered on Malabar Headland, watching the sea erupt as massive, shiny flanks breached the surface, with giant tail flukes slapping the water and sending rockets of white spray shooting into the blue air.

We'd successfully rebuffed the push to kill more whales, and at long last, the question of whether these animals could be indiscriminately killed in the name of science was now in the hands of the court.

...

Nearly four years later, in 2014, word came through that the judges were ready to bring down a decision. The arguments by the Australian legal team had been convincing, but there was always a question of how far the court would go. The ICJ was really part court, part tribunal, and scoring international disputes of this nature can sometimes deliver messy results. The most I was hoping for was a ruling that Japan's so-called scientific whaling didn't conform to IWC rules. This, at the least, would bring the issue back to the commission for further discussion and be a moral victory for Australia.

I was home alone in the evening, with the laptop set up on the kitchen bench to monitor the judgment as it came down live. I could see the packed courtroom, with a sizeable Japanese contingent, and

Australia's legal team sitting quietly at the front. As the chief judge started reading the decision, I couldn't quite believe what I was hearing: the court, by a clear majority, had accepted most of Australia's arguments. We had won the case convincingly, and the judges had taken the unusual additional step of issuing orders to Japan to stop scientific whaling.

The Japanese delegation studied the floor intently, the Australian team shook hands and smiled, and I whooped with joy. I'd never expected the decision to be so clear-cut. For the first time in a hundred years, no whales would be taken in the Southern Ocean, and the wind is in the sails of all those who have worked to make the preservation of whales a successful global environmental issue.

For Australia, the world is watching. Having got this far, one only hopes we won't back down at the final hour—although the initial signs aren't encouraging. Under the Abbott government, Australia's diplomatic efforts have slackened on the whaling issue, and the Japanese have gone back to the IWC to get approval to renew lethal Antarctic scientific whaling beginning in 2015–16. They intend to target more than 300 minke whales over ten years with a proposal designed to meet the test for scientific whaling laid down by the court; and this proposal has now been adopted in IWC rules.

Australia should play a leading role in analysing the proposal and developing a strategy to counter it, otherwise a majority of countries might support Japan. The court decision has given anti-whaling nations and the NGO community a rock-solid campaigning tool to ensure this doesn't happen. This is now a litmus test of the willingness of our political leaders and diplomats to press home to the Japanese that sham whaling activities are no longer acceptable, but it will require a substantial effort to make sure Japan doesn't win the next round.

Some of the most wondrous creatures on earth are depending on us to hold the line, as is the future course of nature conservation on our planet.

32
THE MIXMASTER

THE 2010 ELECTION turned out to be a dog's breakfast. Having announced the date eight months out—in truth, not a real surprise—early on Julia Gillard had decamped to the western suburbs of Sydney to get in touch with the people. It was a bad move.

Voters expected their leaders to work hard in Canberra or at home, and some resented the pariah status that was implied by this tokenistic stunt. At another time the tactic might have worked, but so skewed was Sydney's *Daily Telegraph* against the prime minister it wouldn't have mattered what she'd done—every headline dripped vitriol.

When the campaign formally began, the Labor Party's re-election narrative was disjointed, dominated by the debate over how to manage increasing numbers of people arriving by boat to seek asylum.

More damaging was the dam full of leaks covered in the fingerprints of former leader Kevin Rudd. These appeared regularly, a gift to the press pack that created such turbulence Gillard's campaign could never ascend into clear air.

Added to this, the climate change policy quickly went off the rails. During the campaign, the prime minister announced that there wouldn't be a carbon tax, a position she qualified late in the day by adding that, if re-elected, the government would aim for an emissions trading scheme—the qualifier was lost in the hubbub. In the absence of a 'carbon tax' a proposal for a citizen's assembly to 'consider' the issue had been mooted. Business groups loved this do-nothing idea, but what was meant to happen next was never made clear and the thought bubble was quickly discarded. Even more vexing was the string of bizarre comments from Tony Abbott, who at one point had stated the world wasn't warming; this from a man who had already distinguished himself by declaring a year earlier that 'the climate change argument is absolute crap'. Former Opposition leader Malcolm Turnbull added to the wackiness by stating that his own party's climate policy was a farce. By the time of the official campaign launch, the environment didn't rate a mention at all and there was only a passing reference to climate change. Most of the potential opportunities for spending commitments had been diverted into marginal seat campaigns, many of which were in western Sydney.

My last election task had been to fly up to Far North Queensland for the day to campaign with local Labor candidate Tony Mooney, a former mayor of the region's major city, Townsville.

Delirium caused by sleep deprivation was setting in as I tried to make sense of the news of the day. The new British prime minister, David Cameron, had given his first major foreign policy speech, which predictably didn't mention Australia—that was one for the monarchists.

The Daily Telegraph had a major puff piece on Australia's most prominent supporter of the royals, Tony Abbott, portraying him as a blend of Mussolini and Obama—that was subtle. Titled 'Yes we can', the profile was accompanied by testimonials from up-and-coming rugby league players, one quoted as saying that he wouldn't be voting for Gillard because of her 'whiny voice'—never mind the policies.

A *Sydney Morning Herald* columnist, Elizabeth Farrelly, was already dreaming of a government run by Malcolm Turnbull and Bob Brown—so much for female solidarity and logic.

Meanwhile, in Townsville, fishing groups had taken out full-page ads featuring a small boy standing on a beach fishing, with the text claiming this would no longer be possible as a result of Labor's new marine parks. In fact, the waters of the proposed marine parks—called bioregions, which research showed were necessary for healthy fish populations—were at least five kilometres offshore, so no one would be prevented from recreational fishing on the coast. Whatever happened to truth in advertising?

Along with a gaggle of advisers and media, I duly fronted for the pre-election press conference at a nondescript site in the Townsville suburbs with the candidate. Halfway through my introductory remarks, having welcomed Mooney, my memory kicked into gear as it dawned on me that the person I was now endorsing was someone I'd actually opposed, from a distance, years earlier for his staunch anti-environmental views. I hadn't recognised him straight away, although I should have been familiar with his name. Mooney had previously been investigated for allegations of branch stacking. As the mayor of Townsville a decade earlier, he had forcefully pushed an anti-green pro-development agenda. I wasn't too disappointed when he failed to win the seat, despite his campaign receiving $5000 from a company connected to the corrupt former New South Wales Labor MP Eddie Obeid. Afterwards I learned that Mooney went on to work as a consultant to a coal company and had been appointed by Tony Burke to the board of the Great Barrier Reef Marine Park Authority.

After a day with a candidate like this, I was ready to chuck it in.

Meanwhile, back home, Kingsford Smith had been overrun by Liberal Party volunteers recruited on air by Alan Jones from radio station 2GB. Jones, who was manically campaigning against Labor MPs and a host of other dangerous left-wingers, including North Coast independent Rob Oakeshott, effusively championed my opponent, ultimately without success.

A rare bright spot during the campaign came with the long-awaited announcement that Malabar Headland would become a national park. This announcement was a high point, made with the prime minister on the crispest of winter days at Maroubra Beach—glistening aqua fresh, magnificent. Having finally got this commitment out the door, along with some much-needed money for rehabilitation of the site, on this day I knew that my being in government had definitely made a difference to the electorate I was representing.

Having spent most of the preceding month in a fit of pique, leaking and undermining the government, displaced leader Kevin Rudd sent a message to local members of parliament the day before the election to convey his and his family's very best wishes. It spewed out of the fax machine late in the day, ending face up on the floor as scores of busy volunteers and fatigued staff walked over it without pause.

···

I'd always enjoyed election days, and with jasmine on the breeze this one was no different. Small groups of mums and dads arrived early to set up sausage sizzles to raise funds for their schools that, on this day, doubled as polling booths. Volunteers engaged in affable banter across political lines, while fixing the coloured bunting and posters of the candidates and party leaders to fences and power poles.

Democracy still happened in Australia, and this was its finest day.

By late afternoon, streams of locals had fronted to perform their democratic duty. The banners were by now drooping, the skewed posters of candidates with their fixed smiles gazed down at the detritus of the day scattered across the footpath: ribbons and balloons and party leaflets and scrunched-up paper serviettes with tomato-sauce lipstick stains. A last-minute rush of pissed punters from Randwick racecourse shouting, 'I'm gonna vote for the Sex Party!' closed out the day.

The post-mortems from the party faithful got underway quickly. With long experience in reading the public mood, and after ten hours of standing at the entrance thrusting how-to-vote cards at every voter, the verdict was in: the mob had turned against us.

Abbott's scare campaign, based on three simplistic slogans—Stop the Boats, Scrap the Tax, End the Waste—had proved effective. But the saying that Oppositions don't win elections, governments lose them still held true. Fed up with the infighting and disturbed by the last-minute leadership change to Gillard, repulsed by the mediocrity of NSW Labor and its procession of premiers and corrupt ministers, confused about what the key issues were and disappointed that, when prime minister, Rudd had walked away from an emissions trading scheme, the voters had turned against Labor in droves.

As predicted, there was a strong swing away from Labor, most noticeably in New South Wales and Queensland, but along with similarly placed Labor members, I held my seat, though the national result was uncertain, with neither of the major parties winning enough seats to form a majority government. As it happened, Julia Gillard proved an adept and more trustworthy negotiator than Tony Abbott, and after seventeen days of discussion she reached agreements with the independents—Tony Windsor and Rob Oakeshott from regional New South Wales—and the Australian Greens to form government. This was Gillard's greatest achievement, from which other achievements could be realised. However, the high levels of ignorance about our democratic system fuelled public antipathy towards these arrangements, and no amount of actual legislation passed by the new parliament could temper the public's residual aggro.

The first term of government had been a bruising three years. Despite the siren call of song and action that I could faintly hear from my former world, and my recent moment of what-am-I-doing-here angst in Townsville, I was determined to hang in and see what transpired. It might sound self-serving, but I had tried to live out the values of discipline and loyalty that I believed were essential in politics. Unlike any other minister, I had no praetorian guard to protect me. Building constructive relationships across the ministry and the Caucus helped, but my strategy to hold a line and not play games, and with Kate Pasterfield on the alert for mischief, meant we'd repulsed the mini assaults that came from within. In spite of being hung out to dry, we'd managed to maintain the calm, and got a few runs on the board. Now I was up for whatever came my way, be it isolation or warm embrace. We would just have to wait and see.

33

IT'S EDUCATION, STUPID

M AYBE IT WAS always going to end this way.
 After the election, I happened on a draft speech I never got around to giving when environment minister.

One part read:

> Now more than ever nations will rise and fall on their capacity to ensure shared natural ecosystems are not degraded and that people—their most important resource—are equipped to work in the future economy: driven by services and innovation, focused on low-carbon technologies and featuring mutual cooperation. That is why education is central to Australia's future.

It was a straightforward observation, obvious even, but what I didn't fully appreciate then was the scale of the schooling problem we were facing.

Our education performance had been sliding backwards. Many Australian students were not doing as well as their counterparts in other countries, including a number of our Asian neighbours. Serious steps were needed to halt this downward spiral.

In its first term, Labor, with Julia Gillard as education minister, set out to remedy the problem with an 'education revolution'. This major makeover aimed to address deficiencies in the early years of school, presenting more information on students' progress, beginning with the introduction of the My School website and NAPLAN testing for numeracy and literacy. The next step was to propel improvements in teacher quality, roll out a national curriculum and, to cap it off, introduce a new funding model for school education.

Once Gillard became prime minister, the question of how this complex, multifaceted revolution would be advanced was as yet unanswered.

I'd by now been through a few cabinet reshuffles and become used to the strange feeling of being part of the inner circle and out of it at the same time. How the various paybacks and factional advancements would be determined in this new term of government was well outside my realm.

The chief of the dominant New South Wales right faction, Mark Arbib, called to say, 'Mate, you're a superstar.' He told me that they were backing me for a cabinet role, which made me feel a little uneasy. Since coming to Canberra I'd religiously steered clear of pub microphones and karaoke bars. I held my own band in too high regard. An endorsement from political vipers like this could mean anything.

I'd retained the portfolio of Environment Protection, Heritage and the Arts in Julia Gillard's first ministry. Before the election, one of my final decisions in the environment portfolio was actually a non-decision. I'd hit the pause button and deferred the approval of two major proposals by British Gas and Santos, for coal seam gas and liquefied natural gas projects, which would include a major port upgrade at Gladstone in Central Queensland. I suspected it was difficult, if not impossible, to manage the impacts of large-scale dredging on the waters adjacent to the Great Barrier Reef Marine Park.

There was another issue that warranted further consideration. The contamination of groundwater by the extraction process—a growing problem for coal seam gas projects—needed to be fully explored, and the advice from Geosciences Australia had been unambiguous: 'The impact of coal seam gas development on the Great Artesian Basin is not sufficiently addressed.'

But as was usually the case, there was intense pressure for an announcement that would have strong headline investment and employment figures, with both the resources minister, Martin Ferguson, and the treasurer, Wayne Swan, acutely focused on the decision. Ferguson had already raised eyebrows with a request that the attorney-general's department monitor the activity of green activists. Did that mean monitoring the environment minister?, a few colleagues wondered aloud. I suspected Swan, who'd always supported me, would also be happy to see me out of the environment portfolio, especially given the number of knockbacks I'd given to projects in Queensland over the past two and a half years.

While plenty of wind shear had come with the role, I felt I'd been an effective minister, with all decisions made soundly. I'd finally shaken off the wobbles, even though, with the wisdom of hindsight, I could see how some issues might have been better handled. I had good relationships with most of the senior leadership team by now and would call on them if necessary, but only if factional plays threatened to spiral out of control and take me with them. At the very least, I was sane and reasonable, which was more than could be said for quite a few people around the place. In the harem-like atmosphere of the Caucus, where gossip and game-playing were rife and where Rudd was sure to create mischief, there probably weren't that many people whom Gillard could trust not to be diverted by internal politics, who would simply concentrate on bringing the education reforms home. And so it turned out that Julia Gillard offered me the position of Minister for School Education, Early Childhood and Youth, a fresh start and a hefty agenda, working closely with the prime minister and her office—something I had no problem with at all.

The agenda was definitely ambitious—a good thing—but it needed to be signed off and delivered in quick time: a new needs-based school funding system, the national curriculum, an agreement on Indigenous education with the states to better support Aboriginal students, and the rollout of new national childcare standards were priorities that would normally take a couple of terms to bed down properly. That we managed this and more over the next thirty or so months was testament to the hard work of many people—advisers, staff, bureaucrats, sector leaders. It really was nothing short of a miracle, as swirling leadership tensions generated by Rudd's 'will he, won't he?' game guaranteed that the government appeared to be perpetually under siege.

At the top of the list of reforms, legislating a new school funding system was especially daunting. The career of one recent Labor leader—Mark Latham—had been seriously damaged when he promised to change the funding formula. Even though the policy was reasonable, an over-the-top scare campaign by the Catholic and independent schools sector, arguing that Labor had a 'hit list' of schools whose funding would be slashed, succeeded in belting Latham out of the park. The sector was well cashed up and had proved to be a formidable adversary, and some current ministers, like Jenny Macklin, the shadow education minister at the time, were still wearing the scars.

My old mate, the knockabout troubadour Billy Bragg, who'd thought a lot about politics and history, once remarked that music doesn't change the world, education does. There was certainly no arguing its importance, and a moment's reflection brought it home. After all, where would I have ended up had it not been for the education I'd received at school, and then at university, courtesy of the Whitlam government? I was ready for the second leg.

It's a mistake to think of human progress as one straight line of continual improvement. It is possible for countries to go backwards, and the history of school funding in Australia confirmed this unpleasant fact.

How was it that in a markedly secular society, the non-government school sector, much of which was operated by Anglican and Catholic churches and more recently Islamic and fundamentalist Christian organisations, had flourished while the government sector, especially secondary schools, floundered?

Part of the answer lay in the way schools were funded. A New South Wales parliamentary committee looking into education recommended as early as 1884 that 'one uniform system be established for the whole of the colony and that an adherence to that system be made an indispensable condition under which, and how, it [a uniform system] could be granted'.

Despite this, the churches had insisted on establishing their own schools, which, in time, were supported by both sides of politics, with a great deal of soul searching by Labor when Gough Whitlam first advocated state aid for non-government schools in the late 1960s. While the states had primary responsibility for providing school education, the private-school sector, particularly the many Catholic parish schools, was a powerful force and came to find a friendly ear in Canberra—none more so than that of the previous Howard government, which skewed the budget to ensure a privileged funding position was maintained. This, among other things, kept perpetuating privilege.

In the Whitlam era, government schools received 70 per cent of Commonwealth funding and private schools received just less than 30 per cent, an amount roughly equivalent to enrolment proportions. Both the Hawke and Keating governments had ensured a greater proportion of funding went to government schools. By the end of John Howard's term, however, the ratio had been reversed. Now government schools were receiving about 31 per cent of Commonwealth funding, while private schools had 69 per cent, despite public schools having around two-thirds of the enrolments.

To my way of thinking, private schools are simply part of a plural education system, and shouldn't be discriminated against. Unlike John Howard, I'd been to a church-run school, and at different times my daughters had attended independent schools, but I never considered that these schools should be generously supported by the government.

Labor policy affirmed the right of parents to choose this kind of education for their children while aiming for a new funding system that would remedy the large equity gap which had opened up across the Australian education landscape. This gap, which saw kids from low socioeconomic backgrounds, including Aboriginal and Torres Strait Islander students, being as many as three years behind their peers from more affluent suburbs, was confirmed in an extensive report on school funding by an eminent panel drawn from both sides of the politics and education fence, and chaired by Sydney business-man David Gonski. Commissioned when Labor came to power in 2007, the report was released as we began our second term in 2010. The problem was clear: children from disadvantaged backgrounds were concentrated in an underfunded public system, while wealthy independent schools were bastions of privilege. As a result we were falling behind in education performance. The report recommended a new, needs-based school funding model so that extra funds could be applied to narrowing this gap. The Gonski report provided the impetus and the template for this long overdue change, and was ultimately endorsed by most dispassionate education observers. The notable exception was shadow education minister Christopher Pyne, who dismissed the clearly argued 200-page report only twenty minutes after it was released.

It is an understatement to say that changing the way the Common-wealth funded school education was a complex undertaking. It would take every available hour, and all the skills and resources at our disposal, to see it through to a successful conclusion, but there was no question it was a nation-changing task to get excited about. At the same time, the raft of other big changes—including a new national curriculum and early childhood education standards, which required agreement of the mainly Coalition states—had to be delivered as well.

Naturally, extra funding would be required to support a new model. To allay the fears of private schools and lessen the likelihood of a scare campaign being mounted against any changes, the govern-ment had determined that no school would lose money as a result of the changes. This made the development of a nationally consistent funding model painfully difficult, given thousands of schools would have to make the transition to the new system.

To get a new bill through the parliament would involve reaching agreement with the states and between the various parties in the education sector, balancing the interests of government and non-government schools, getting agreement from cabinet for the extra money, all the while working with advisers from the prime minister's office who had a strong interest in the policy but were often preoccupied with warding off the many gremlins surrounding them after a difficult election.

Once a final model was decided on, the perils of federation were again on full display. Surprisingly only New South Wales (with National Party education minister Adrian Piccoli), South Australia (with Labor's Jay Wetherill) and Tasmania (with the Greens' Nick McKim) showed a clear appreciation of the benefits of increased funding and a fairer system. These states didn't play games or try to obstruct the process.

Western Australia had already shown its stripes by blocking the national curriculum until the eleventh hour, forcing me to engineer a series of last-minute interventions until agreement was reached. But still they remained aloof from the new funding model, confident that overflowing coffers from the mining boom could secure enough resources for education and fixated on resisting imaginary Canberra control of Western Australian schools.

Victoria's Coalition government had a split personality, wanting to be part of the brave new world they, in part, had already embraced, but caught up in the politics of states versus Canberra and attacking the proposal for political effect.

Under Labor's Cameron Dick as education minister, Queensland had been positive. Once the Coalition regained power there, education minister John-Paul Langbroek remained supportive, but the gloves soon came off, with incoming premier Campbell Newman declaring the reform was a 'bucket of vomit', despite the fact that hundreds of Queensland schools would be better off under the new model. To reinforce his education priorities, in a laughable gesture Newman later banned me from heading across the border to talk about the changes—so much for freedom of speech in Queensland.

The Country Liberal Party in the Northern Territory had turned over three education ministers in less than a year, and, not surprisingly, they were at sea from day one. Queensland and the Northern Territory, as it happened, also had the poorest education records.

As ever, self-interest and greed were on full display, especially in relation to the independent private schools. They played hard and as negotiations became difficult would go around my office and straight to the prime minister's. I understood the strategy, as the final sign-off would happen there and I'd done the same thing more than a few times as a conservation activist.

In the background hovered the mitres and robes of a bevy of Catholic bishops who would marshal their troops if they believed the Catholic education system was going to be denied. George Pell, then the Archbishop of Sydney, climate change sceptic and apparently Tony Abbott's quasi-spiritual and political adviser, could hardly be expected to engage objectively, although we always approached him in good faith.

But it's harder for any one sector to secure too much advantage if both the prime minister and ministers' offices hold a consistent position. This wasn't always the case and in one instance they were inadvertently helped by the prime minister's adviser, Tom Bentley, who in one of many discussions with the private schools, concerned that local Catholic schools had been advantaged, agreed they would get commensurate increases the model did not provide for, which resulted in a $15 million bonus for them in the ACT.

Julia Gillard was always rock solid on the new funding model reform. It meant a great deal to her and to the government's legacy. She stuck by the model and by me, even when we were under siege from her department, trying to corral spending and mindful of the competing budget demand of other big-ticket items like the

National Disability Insurance Scheme (NDIS). Other ministers were lukewarm in support, including Jenny Macklin, who'd worked assiduously on the NDIS and was concerned that funds would be diverted away from disability towards schools. Finance minister Penny Wong didn't appear to care for the reform at all.

I cannot think of any other significant issue, with the exception of climate change, that received as much attention from cabinet as the school funding package. Numerous versions of the cabinet submission from the prime minister and me were pored over and picked apart, sometimes as part of a larger dynamic of interrogation of the prime minister; Wayne Swan, Craig Emerson and Brendan O'Connor—key Gillard allies—assisted in fending off these complaints. The arguments for a new model were strong, it was a landmark Labor reform and, by the time the final submission was due to be agreed, everyone fell into line. (Interestingly, the NDIS, which I supported, was never subject to the same level of scrutiny, nor was it required to provide the same level of detail as the National Plan for School Improvement, as the funding reform was formally titled.)

The biggest danger, other than a change of leader or the government imploding, was a breakout of old-style class warfare (such as had brought Latham's earlier efforts undone) between the private and public school sectors, with the Australian Education Union (AEU), made up of primary and secondary school teachers, leading the charge.

I was surprised to find that some of my colleagues were more inclined to support the non-government school sector than the AEU. Repairing relations with the union, one of the largest in the country, was an early task. It is to the credit of their senior leadership, especially federal president Angelo Gavrielatos, that the union ended up playing a constructive role, embarking on a nationwide 'I give a Gonski' campaign, despite serious opposition from key state branches. This meant eschewing old ideological battles which had put noses out of joint in the past, and facing up to the reality of a diverse school sector in which many parents opted to send their kids to a non-government school in the secondary years. The union could no longer resist sensible reforms, especially in the area of improving teacher quality; they needed to be part of the solution to addressing worsening student performance and not characterise the reform as us versus them.

Gavrielatos, a man who wears his passions on his sleeve, understood this better than most, and he and my chief of staff, Denise Spinks, were in constant contact as the legislation intensified. At the previous election, the teachers had deserted Labor, to the extent that some country polling booths struggled to find volunteers, a role many teachers had previously taken on. Now, along with the primary and secondary school principals' organisations, teachers became strong allies in the quest for a fairer funding system.

The business community was also in favour, aware of the connection between education and productivity, and mindful that as the mining boom started to taper off, the record high standard of living many Australians took for granted would be under threat unless we stemmed the education decline.

The travel schedule was relentless as I visited school after school, crisscrossing the country to spruik the benefits of better schools.

The contrast between the state of most government schools and high-end private schools was stark. Visiting Abbotsleigh—an all-girls school (which, coincidentally, my mum had attended) on Sydney's Upper North Shore—was mind-blowing. The neatly manicured gardens were on a par with those at Parliament House, and its new library, which boasted native wood panelling, generous skylights and row upon row of gleaming Macs, was superior to any I had visited.

I didn't begrudge the school this level of opulence—its fees are stratospheric for starters and much of the student body, encouraged by their parents, was highly motivated to succeed—but it beggared belief that the substantial endowment of many non-government schools should be continually supplemented by Commonwealth funds when teachers in some government schools were dipping into their own pockets to supply pens and stationery to their needy students.

The gap between the education haves and have-nots was now so great that it threatened to spawn a two-tier society. Only a proactive national government could get things in order and close the gap, with a well-thought-out policy backed by a substantial budget, to give all young Australians a decent start in life.

This was the mission we had embarked on, and it consumed us right through three chaotic years of government.

34

JOKER IN THE PACK

I WAS MIDWAY through the term, and entangled in the continuing wrestle with the independent school sector and the states over the fate of the 'Gonski' school funding reforms, when life-sized cardboard cut-outs of me started appearing at clubs and hotels—of which there was no shortage—across my electorate. Banners and signs exhorted the public to 'Tell Peter Garrett!' what they thought of the government's 'un-Australian' policy of trying to reduce the scale of problem gambling by restricting the use of poker machines. On the basis that just about any publicity is good publicity, I was touched by the efforts of the gambling lobby to remind everyone what their local federal member looked like.

Tim Freedman, of Sydney band the Whitlams, had spotlighted this issue with his song, 'Blow Up the Pokies'. We were part of a generation of Sydney musicians who'd seen firsthand the impact poker machines had on those who used them and on the hotels that hosted them. The once-vibrant pub scene that nourished so many artists had collapsed, and local watering holes had become soulless, sad gambling dens. The fact is Australians lose more money per person on gambling than any other nation. Problem gamblers were responsible for nearly half of the total amounts lost on poker machines, and the personal fallout, in terms of social, emotional and financial cost to those individuals and their families, was huge.

The campaign against poker-machine reform mounted by the clubs and hotels turned out to have a nasty edge right from the start, when they shot out of the blocks with specially generated polling, always framed to put a positive spin on policies while highlighting the alleged negative consequences of any reforms, which they 'leaked' to sympathetic media.

I soon found myself carrying the flag for a battle that most Labor MPs from New South Wales didn't have the stomach for, and which had come about only because a small number of independent MPs, in particular Andrew Wilkie from Tasmania—whose vote was needed by the minority government if we were to get legislation through parliament—were strongly committed to poker-machine reform.

The measures under consideration were modest enough, including limiting the amount that could be spent on each wager, and introducing what was called pre-commitment technology so players could voluntarily set their spending limit.

Still, ClubsNSW and the Australian Hotel Association, whose members stacked as many machines in their premises as they were allowed, were trenchant in their opposition, as was, albeit in a quieter vein, the NSW Labor government.

Pro-poker-machine letters flooded the local paper, my office was bombarded with emails and indignant phone calls, and talkback radio raged hot. Across Sydney, especially in the western suburbs, the clubs were carpet-bombing electorates. A deputation of club leaders, including Ken Murray, a senior ALP member who was the current president of the Randwick Labor Club, paid me a visit.

My position was simple. I recognised the clubs were an important part of the community, and acknowledged the (modest) support they gave to local community groups and sporting bodies. At the same time, I believed genuine steps to reduce the harm that gambling addictions cause were long overdue. As it happened, the preponderance of clubs and hotels in Kingsford Smith meant the electorate had one of the highest concentrations of poker machines in the state. They were literally everywhere and the social cost was borne by a number of my constituents.

The deputation didn't see it that way. Murray was a fixer from way back, so it was a case of the old fallback, agreeing to disagree. I would note their objections and relay them to the government but continue to support the reforms. Discussion over, it was time for me to get back to work on education.

But the clubs campaign showed no signs of slowing. They had a big war chest, and had visited the National Rifle Association in the US to learn new campaign techniques from masters of the dark arts. They targeted MPs in marginal seats and had a pervasive media presence. Sydney was so awash with pro-gambling propaganda that I decided to write to every household in the electorate, explaining the proposed changes and pointing out the harm—broken homes, bank-ruptcies, suicides—caused by addiction to poker machines.

The reaction was immediate. 'The gloves are off,' declared Murray, threatening to cut the support the Randwick Labor Club automatically provided to the local member without even convening a board meeting to discuss this unprecedented action. The cardboard cut-outs proliferated and a public rally to denounce the government's plans was scheduled to take place at Souths Juniors, the Taj Mahal of gambling meccas in the local area.

The umbilical cord between the clubs and the party was now clearly visible. Most of the leaders of the pro-pokies push were current or former Labor office-bearers. The clubs were generous donors to candidates. In fact, a ClubsNSW representative had given me an envelope containing a cheque made out to my electorate council at an early meet-the-candidates event for NSW MPs. When I realised what it was I gave it back.

A number of local Labor colleagues joined the rally and when the time came for me to take the stage at Souths, facing a sea of angry faces bussed in and holding ready-made signs saying 'Hands off our club' and the like, my isolation was complete.

Support for the proposals in the Caucus had moved from lukewarm to freezing: a rational position given that most members in NSW seats were battling to hold their vote in an already-hostile political environment. Rudd was reported to have sent a signal to the clubs that, if returned to the leadership, he'd take a softer line, despite having earlier confessed to hating poker machines. The Australian Hotels Association, meanwhile, sent letters to school principals listing the projects they funded, but double counted some to make their contribution seem more generous.

Labor was too reliant on the clubs—some of which were their own—for patronage and support. The political will to see such a difficult issue through simply wasn't strong enough to withstand the weight of opposition, including from within. The reform sputtered out, with weak legislation introduced that would achieve nothing. It could not have ended any other way.

A subsequent straw poll of Kingsford Smith voters found a majority in favour of the reforms and against poker machines. There is still plenty of support for sensible anti-gambling measures in the suburbs.

Later on, the Randwick Labor Club—the spiritual home and headquarters of Labor in the area since former member Lionel Bowen's mother had founded the club in 1963—removed 'Labor' from its title to become the Randwick Club.

Later still, I informed Ken Murray I wouldn't accept any donations from the club for the upcoming election. It wasn't pride or payback; I just felt ill at the thought that a once-great political institution had fallen so far. I didn't want to be part of its further decline.

. . .

There were still plenty of good people around willing to stand their ground and act on their values, but would they continue to choose Labor? As our second term ground on, it was becoming harder to tell.

Some branch meetings of party members suggested it was all over. Monday nights were set aside for these gatherings, even though it was the one night of the week people preferred to stay in, and despite my suggestion that branches might stagger their meetings so they didn't all take place on the same evening. And so my routine when home in Sydney was simple: drive across the electorate at breakneck speed and try to visit as many meetings as I could before they packed up and turned in for the night.

I'd start at the southern end and work north, beginning at an ugly 1960s-style community centre in Matraville that had seen better days. A tired-looking punching bag hung in the front room, and leaves and litter blown in from the street lay in piles along the corridors.

In the meeting room, a handful of middle-aged, down-at-heel members, part of Botany mayor Ron Hoenig's machine, would sit glumly, waiting for the local member to arrive. Through the prism of the past week's talkback wisdom, spiced with their ingrained prejudices, they'd listen to my report, including the latest twists and turns concerning refugees, the fate of budget measures and whatever else was making news: arms crossed, brows furrowed, heads occasionally nodding. Arguments would sporadically break out across the table. Some nights people were so desperate to get home there would be no questions for me at all. The smell of a decaying political corpse hung heavy in the air, all the more so as the branch secretary worked at the morgue.

Then I'd set off to a Catholic school hall in Maroubra, home to the biggest branch in the electorate, run by two party godfathers, Ken Murray and Johno Johnson. Bob Carr was also a member. Between serving as NSW premier and as a senator in the federal parliament, he showed up one night to argue the toss on nuclear power (Bob was in favour) when I was giving the member's report.

After we volleyed points back and forth for ten minutes to no discernible end, the branch president called us to order with a reminder to the faithful who'd come out on a cold Monday night that, in any other circumstances, 'You'd have to pay big dollars to hear a debate like this anywhere else, so please thank Bob and Peter for their contribution.' Faint applause.

Typical issues of the week would again be traversed: Afghanistan, biosecurity, disability policy, the intricacies of the proposed school funding model, the Obama visit and an assortment of other topics. Some members of this branch had taken exception to my stance on gay marriage; one had even sent a letter via the media detailing the reasons why gay marriage was a threat to our way of life and demanding a rethink on my part or else. 'Garrett faces a mutiny' the local rag screamed before it hit the recycling box—the member in question was in thrall to a church that had lost sight of its mission.

The questions were usually perfunctory, occasionally pointed if a nerve like gay marriage had been touched. But debate was contained, the meeting was always well run, the membership books were closely guarded and the machine rolled on.

Then I'd dash out and tear up to the School of Arts hall at Coogee, to a branch populated by party activists, long-time union members and a smattering of professionals.

Here the branch meeting was alive and cooking, with members active in local issues and closely following the national debate. The spirit of genuine inquiry I encountered here was an elixir as I addressed thoughtful questions concerning the education reforms and the progress of election promises. Passions ran high and the question-and-answer session would usually veer off into a free-ranging discussion on how to achieve a fairer nation and what progress Labor was making in that task.

The heart of the party was still beating. I could feel its pulse in this room, and in a handful of others across the electorate. It helped keep me blazing away day in and day out, waging crazy peace, attending to the things I had some control over and not fixating too long over those I didn't.

...

This energising pulse was difficult to find at the biennial ALP National Conference held in December 2011 at the Sydney Convention Centre.

In theory, the conference was Labor's pre-eminent decision-making body, a place where the whole party got together to decide its future direction and sign off on policy. In practice it had become a ritual event with decisions determined in advance by the factions and powerful voting blocs controlled by the union movement.

On the agenda for this meeting was a motion moved by Julia Gillard to relax party policy and allow sales of uranium to India, notwithstanding its continuing refusal to sign the Treaty on the Non-Proliferation of Nuclear Weapons, known as the Non-Proliferation Treaty (NPT), or give any real guarantee that Australian uranium wouldn't end up as part of India's nuclear weapons program.

The conference wouldn't roll the leader and the numbers had been locked in, although the vote was closer than expected. Three cabinet ministers opposed to the change—myself, Stephen Conroy and Anthony Albanese—took to the stage to argue the no case. David Bradbury and a couple of other activists had snuck into the hall and were heckling from the wings.

The rejoinder from those pushing to change the policy was that adequate safeguards would be part of any agreement. These were hollow words given the history of uranium exports, but all the more so as the final agreement—concluded in 2014 by the Abbott government—didn't include any substantial controls, and India skipped away laughing.

This was yet another example of how negligent senior Australian politicians can be on such an important issue, and how urgent it now is to push for a nuclear weapons treaty to eradicate the threat of these monstrous armaments once and for all.

...

After defeats like this, it was important to focus on the positive changes we were making. For the majority of our second term of government, we were fixed on the school funding changes. Whether parliament was sitting or not, wherever I happened to be, there would be daily meetings or phone hook-ups to track the progress of the Gonski/early childhood education reforms campaign.

A departmental task force, led by secretary Lisa Paul, was responsible for refining the model and conducting the bulk of negotiations—no mean task. In time a second task force involving the Department of Prime Minister and Cabinet would become involved as well. Working from information laid out on a huge matrix running over multiple pages, various components of the project would be discussed and analysed with senior officials, and actions determined. This included media strategy, timelines for the outreach campaign, progress of legislation and negotiations, public appearances and so on, and was revised and updated daily. This was the only way to keep abreast of the many-headed beast we needed to tame.

In the midst of this activity an urgent issue arose seemingly from nowhere, in a brief sent up from the department without any prior warning—an occupational hazard faced by ministers since time immemorial. It concerned a case that had been taken to the Human Rights Commission by Tobias Nganbe, an elder and teacher from the Wadeye community, one of the largest towns in the Northern Territory, and a place where Midnight Oil had played aeons ago. Nganbe had argued that the Commonwealth government, the Northern Territory administration and the Northern Territory Catholic Education Office were guilty of historical neglect of the community, resulting in chronic underfunding of their schools. And he had a point. The Wadeye claim was now outstanding, and was being pursued by Melbourne law firm Arnold Bloch Leibler, which had provided its services pro bono and could now sniff victory.

I met with a delegation Nganbe led down to Canberra, which included a familiar face—William Parmbuk, the skinny gig-crasher and anti-alcohol activist, now in his early forties and still active in community affairs at Wadeye. These leaders weren't belligerent, although they had every right to feel aggrieved, but their patience had worn thin and they wanted resolution. So did I, and after numerous discussions to see how we could rejig available resources and source some extra funds, I visited Wadeye determined to work something out.

Flying in, I could see below us a patchwork of tracks leading to a huddle of roofs, with a single road winding eastwards across the vast expanse that surrounds the town. Remote it might be, but Wadeye deserved to have its voice heard, and we would need to use the short time we had well.

As was often the case, the only way to push things through was to ask departmental officials to leave the meeting, and with the air cleared of complex language and caution, I promised Tobias that the government would make amends, that a genuine commitment to the community and the programs that worked on the ground would now be forthcoming. With that undertaking in place I was sure we had a good chance of settling the case.

Eighteen months later we signed the agreement at a special ceremony in Melbourne, characterised by senior *Age* journalist Michael Gordon as 'the shaking leg of happiness'.

Tobias Nganbe, exhausted by the struggle, smiled at me and said, 'Now we can move ahead.'

My last visit to Wadeye was to commemorate the signing and inspect a new boarding school that had just been completed with Commonwealth support. We stayed overnight, sleeping in shipping containers that had been turned into modest accommodation. A concert had been scheduled to coincide with our visit but I only lasted an hour. Lying on a camp stretcher I could just hear the opening chords of 'Beds Are Burning' echoing off the walls of the new community hall, and then William took the mike and started singing with great gusto. I fell asleep before the second verse.

The next morning we posed together for photos on the site of the stage where we'd danced together twenty-eight years earlier, before I rushed back to Canberra. There we were doing a different kind of dance, a daily corroboree with our sleeves rolled up that would take us through to the end.

35

ARE WE THERE YET?

T HE DIARY I carried around with me was for the most part filled with meeting reminders, interspersed sporadically with random notes. I tried to at least make brief entries recording the weather, as the tundra kept evaporating and glaciers were melting before our eyes. Dangerous climate change hadn't gone away. Every couple of days there was another article or a further piece of research: climate chaos, arguably the biggest and most confronting issue of our times, upon us.

So it was a red-letter day when finally, in Labor's second term, the first faltering steps to reduce carbon pollution were taken. At early cabinet meetings I'd warned my colleagues that the very modest targets being proposed wouldn't keep global warming in check. Still, we had to start somewhere. The beauty of the scheme was that it penalised big polluters, and used the revenue to support low-emissions businesses and technologies. That in turn would stimulate a climate-friendly economy and generate employment.

The climate bills were finally put to the vote by the prime minister on 13 September 2011: forty-three years after ACF's *Habitat* magazine had featured the greenhouse effect on its front page, seventeen years after climate change was first addressed in policy by Labor, and seven years after I stood up for the first time in Caucus and urged the party to develop a strong climate change policy.

The week before the bill became law, scientists had pointed out that with greenhouse pollution continuing to increase, coral reefs—those wondrous, multicoloured reservoirs of ocean life—would be the first entire ecosystem to be destroyed by climate change, and it could happen in our lifetime.

A few scribbled lines in the diary read: 'I'm hurting. I know what good things humans are capable of, and at the same time how incapable of acting in the planet's and our interests we still are.'

Throughout the second term a redneck wonderland, urged on by the News Limited tabloids and given constant succour by the Coalition, had been in full flight. Tony Abbott welcomed first the 'no carbon tax rally' and later the 'convoy of no confidence' to Canberra. This was the so-called 'people's revolt', spawned by the shock jocks and parasites who spewed dumb hate and saw the climate change debate as a cover for extremists, gays and greenies to take over the world.

Standing in front of signs calling Gillard a witch, Abbott was at home with the crowd. While he wouldn't endorse everything they said, he could 'understand' their frustration and so the tone was set for the remainder of the government's term.

Kevin Rudd, who'd been appointed foreign minister by Gillard, later announced from New York that he was resigning and coming home 'in the interests of the country'. It would only be a matter of time before Rudd mounted several challenges for the leadership, and the eyes of the Canberra press pack were perpetually squinting in his direction.

At close quarters it was too frustrating to watch: a tragic drama on repeat, while the core business of government, and a positive narrative that went with our reforms, was swept under the carpet. In the midst of the sourness permeating the political debate and lack of confidence in Labor's project, it was important that we kept the flame burning on the home front. So in Kingsford Smith we organised a rally for a Clean Energy Future, and marched to Coogee Beach with a solid turnout and an absence of malice—a positive sign that there still was a wellspring of support for strong climate action.

More than ever, it seemed to me that getting the education agenda embedded was critical, for in the long run our polity—all of us—needed to grow up. A better-educated populace might see through the major delusions that were holding Australia back: that climate change was a chimera; that the good times would keep on rolling; that in a global economy we could become isolationists when it suited us; that our region—with the rise of China—was benign; that we could have continued economic growth without seriously damaging our way of life; and, finally, that governments were responsible for everything that went wrong and had to provide for everybody, not only the poor and infirm, at all times.

The talk of the end of history, and the funeral rites commentators increasingly performed on democracy, were so much tosh: just witness the growing presence of civil society in many countries, and the increase in the number of democracies as well. While the major parties clearly needed rejuvenation, government would continue to be the central force in the political system. But the entitlement addiction that government had facilitated and that Australians had fallen prey to needed to be cured, so systemic change—that might create short-term losers but benefit everybody in the long run—could begin.

Part of the learning that a better education encompassed would be for every student to know something of how the current political system works. I got behind the Constitution Education Fund, led by my old friend the novelist and republican Tom Keneally, and Kerry Jones, an avowed monarchist who'd worked with Tony Abbott to derail the last push for a republic. Together they had developed excellent education materials for the classroom to deepen young people's understanding of Australia's democratic system, focusing on the constitution, on the premise that if we don't understand it, we'll neglect it.

Currently, not everybody values the freedom to choose his or her representative. Lots of people don't know what democracy means and large numbers of young adults don't even bother to vote.

It's been reported that a quarter of young Australians say they would support a non-democracy in some circumstances. If true, this is an astonishing figure.

The young might contemplate this for a microsecond maybe, till reality bit them on the bum: after all, as writer Martin Flanagan has observed, the only alternative to elected leaders is non-elected ones, followed closely by secret police and torture cells. And then, to save their skins, they'd join the long queues outside the consulate of a country like Australia, where functional democracy was still intact.

...

Throughout these years I spent way more time with my staff, in both the ministerial and electorate offices, than with Doris and our daughters, whose warp-speed journey into womanhood I very much wanted to be around for. In effect, your staff becomes a second family: my chief of staff Denise Spinks, a tungsten-tough former union official, a great ally in a blue; deputy Kate Pasterfield, cheerful and smart, who had been with me from the beginning and was adept at managing our way through the thicket of tricky Labor politics while keeping an eye on the big picture; and senior press secretary Lisa Miller, who had a sharp eye for detail and, having worked at *The Daily Telegraph*, could knock out snappy one-liners when needed. These three women made up the senior squad.

From early on I wasn't confident about some of the advice the prime minister was receiving, particularly after she hired a former adviser to British prime minister Tony Blair, John McTernan, to run strategy. At the beginning of the term, the suggestion was that the government simply note, rather than endorse, the Gonski report when it was handed down and, according to McTernan, we should avoid mentioning 'fairness' when discussing the new funding model. We ended up marking time for months as a result, but by the time the campaign for a needs-based system was in full swing I simply ignored the second dopey instruction—the new scheme was specifically intended to be fairer, and wasn't fairness a core Labor value?—and the debate lifted.

The other plank of the strategy was to delay a commitment to the funding model so as to draw out the Coalition states and the federal Opposition, in order to go to an election fighting for the new school funding system.

The problem with this approach was that extending the negotiations almost indefinitely gave space to those who wanted to sabotage the reform. It also gave rise to the impression that the government wasn't fully committed and risked jeopardising the effort if Rudd should take the leadership again and abandon the model, as he had, in private conversations, suggested could happen. And what if we lost government before the new arrangements had been sufficiently bedded down?

At one stage, in an attempt to mollify the non-government school sector, the prime minister promised that every private school would get more money. After months of bridge-building with the AEU, the suggestion that non-government schools would do better than government schools had the capacity to set off the public school lobby and escalate a debate that could easily spin out of control.

Fortunately, Tony Abbott came to the rescue by responding that existing funding to government schools was an 'injustice', a sobering insight into his perspective, and in the furore that followed Julia's comments were forgotten.

...

One of the interesting duties for ministers is to represent the prime minister at functions or ceremonies when the PM has other commitments.

On one occasion I was asked to greet the Dalai Lama, a regular visitor to Australia. We shared a cup of tea in a holding room at Sydney airport, and I asked him to reflect on the long campaign for recognition of Tibet and where it might end up.

He paused and then remarked with a doleful smile that, in his experience, when dealing with China there should be no appeasement, that China only respected strength.

I had some understanding of what he meant. Once, while still environment minister, I'd met with Madame Chen Zhili, vice chair of the standing committee of the 11th National People's Congress, a senior position in the most important nation in our region.

The meeting—ostensibly to discuss climate change policy—was arranged at short notice and as our group—my two advisers, with a couple of officials from the Department of Foreign Affairs—entered the room, we were faced with at least seventeen Chinese officials, with the undersecretary resolutely planted in the centre. It is commonplace for some countries to bring substantial delegations to Parliament House, and granted there was a big difference in population— 1.3 billion to 23 million—but the disparity here was so marked it had all the hallmarks of a serious loss of face.

I whispered over my shoulder to no one in particular to get back-up, and courtesy of a couple of text messages three more staff members, looking a little perplexed, rushed in to join us. It was now seventeen to eight.

It was pure symbolism, of course, but this gelled with the feeling I had about China's growing confidence: the Central Kingdom was throwing its weight around in the region, and Australia was very much within reach. (Since then, China's actions in whitewashing the massacre in Tiananmen Square, frustrating the transition to democracy for Hong Kong, laying claim to areas outside its sovereign borders and placing infrastructure and personnel to secure those claims have escalated. These actions urgently require a careful but firm response.)

I started the meeting with a formal welcome and then went on to reprise the Australian government's position on climate change.

'We will decide how best to reduce greenhouse gas emissions, Mr Minister,' Chen Zhili said evenly, and after a few more pleasantries, the discussion ended.

The negotiations to agree on the school funding model lasted a good deal longer. It was a painfully long process, as all sides took advantage of the government's declining popularity to try to improve their position or, in the case of some Coalition state governments, press for political advantage. The media coverage was extensive, with *The Australian* focusing closely and seriously on the reforms. Journalists, including Justine Ferrari from *The Oz* and Anna Patty from *The Sydney Morning Herald*, were so thoroughly backgrounded, they knew the intimate details of who'd said what to whom and when, and so could highlight the pressure points in what were meant to be confidential negotiations.

The marathon process saw burn-out start to take its toll on the department's modelling team and the taskforce, and in my office, where ridiculously long working hours were already taken for granted, people were stretched to breaking point.

Notwithstanding this, in the eye of the public, education remained one of the few pluses for the Gillard government. Once Gonski's report had been made public at the beginning of 2011, I was convinced there was no turning back; the train had left the station and from then on we just persevered.

During the internal battles over costings with the departments of Prime Minister and Cabinet, Treasury and Finance, David Gonski had remarked to me, and I happened to agree, that ultimately it wasn't about the dollars; it was about implementing the model. Still, we would aim to draw as much out of the budget as possible, partly to manage the difficult transition under which no school, no matter how well provisioned, couldn't be left worse off, but also because education was a justifiable investment as long as the extra money was well targeted. The reform architecture that Julia Gillard and her team had initiated when she was education minister contained a raft of initiatives that, if well resourced, would improve results. But a fairer funding system, which distributed funds to schools that needed the most support, was the Holy Grail. Opportunities like this didn't come along often and we couldn't afford to fail. And time was running out . . .

. . .

By the beginning of 2012, the rumblings from the Rudd forces had become a crescendo. Gillard flushed him out and a tentative challenge foundered. Despite the media talking him up at every opportunity, Rudd didn't have the numbers; it was a cruel joke really. But if the government's position worsened, then backbenchers sitting on narrow margins would clutch at any straw, and he'd be back trying again.

It was only May, but with leadership speculation dominating it felt like we'd been going for a year, and there was another year of nothing but leadership talk to go: Rudd back on *Sunrise*, the morning TV program, saying the government wasn't selling the education reforms; Rudd's family weighing in with a social media blitz; Rudd visiting marginal seats to talk about foreign aid; Rudd refusing to use the prime minister's name in interviews; Rudd appearing on ABC's *7.30 Report* to trail his coat three days after Julia Gillard's father died . . . on and on it went.

By the time the third anniversary of the Gillard government came around on 24 June, the polls were stuck so low the government was like a death star, burning energy but invisible to the naked eye. A sullen torpor had enveloped the Labor side in Parliament House.

The next day—Tuesday—Caucus was flatter than a dead cat's bounce. Those who dreaded a return to Rudd were morose, and those agitating for another leadership challenge concentrated on keeping a lid on their emotions in case it imploded as before.

I'd long since resigned myself to the possibility that there could be another change of leader and, if that should eventuate, I'd go. In the outbreak of commentary by ministers following Rudd's removal in 2010, when asked I'd said I wouldn't work with him again. This was simply an acknowledgement of how difficult and precarious the business of government had become under Rudd. But that wasn't my only reason. The fact was I couldn't trust him as a leader. In the aftermath of Rudd's removal, Wayne Swan had claimed Rudd didn't 'hold Labor values' and was a dysfunctional decision-maker. I agreed with Swan's assessment, but my judgement was that Rudd was also a threat to national security. So unstable was the experience of government when he was leader, and so utterly ruthless his pursuit of Gillard at the expense of the party he once led, it was difficult to know which way someone with such a malevolent and punitive personality would jump when the pressure was really on. He'd cocked his trigger finger at George Bush in public and characterised the Chinese as 'rat fuckers' while masquerading as an international statesman who had all the answers. This kind of megalomaniac could get the country into trouble without a moment's reflection. He wouldn't be getting my vote or my service under any circumstances.

Meanwhile, the anxiety levels in my office were rising inexorably.

It had been an excruciatingly difficult exercise to get the new school funding proposal this far; tears had been shed, careers had gone off the rails. Throughout, we'd been fixed on getting the job done without any stuff-ups, derailments or diversions. I'd introduced the Australian Education Bill a fortnight earlier and now, only two days before the parliament broke, with the government at rock bottom and Rudd's forces gathering for one last tilt, it was due to be voted on. But the bill was still stuck in the Senate. One of the senators with the responsibility for its carriage was a likely Rudd supporter, and she had suddenly gone quiet in the past twenty-four hours.

The parliament was now flooding with lobbyists and out-of-town media types, all smelling blood. The press gallery, openly salivating, was in overdrive, reporting every trickle of information, poring over every nuance.

Kevin Michael Rudd, who'd vowed never to try to remove an elected leader of the Labor Party, was on the move again.

The following morning—Wednesday—we shouted, screamed, cajoled and finally got movement in the Senate. The Australian

Education Bill went through at ten minutes past one in the afternoon as I sat in the public gallery looking down on the Senate chamber. There were a few wet eyes and thumbs up all round.

Fifty minutes later, question time in the House of Representatives was due to begin when Mark Butler, a leading convenor of the left, entered the chamber, his expression sombre. Bill Shorten from the right followed, ashen-faced.

The faction bosses and the South Australians from Gillard's home state had switched sides, convinced the government would be obliterated at the next election. It would be Julia Gillard's last appearance in the parliament as prime minister.

Later that afternoon, Labor MPs trooped in to a special meeting of the Caucus to finally pull the scab from the festering sore that had dogged us since day one.

The great underminer prevailed by a margin of twelve votes.

Rudd approached me immediately following the ballot and asked me to stay on as education minister, followed by Anthony Albanese, who'd supported my entry into parliament, who said, 'We need you.'

But I'd had enough. Everyone has a limit and I'd reached mine—end of story. I called Doris to let her know it was over. She wasn't surprised; like most people, she was impatient with the constant game playing that had infected the government. I wrote out my resignation letter the following day.

...

In the run up to the 2013 election, Tony Abbott promised he was 'on a unity ticket' with Kevin Rudd on the new school funding model. He needed to make this promise he was never going to keep, as an election eve poll had judged him more trustworthy than Rudd but Labor was considered the best party on education by a large margin.

Rudd's campaign was a dud, full of last-minute changes and poorly conceived policies, such as announcing the navy would be relocated to Brisbane; the longer it went on, the more voters became dissatisfied. Once the Coalition was elected, new education minister Christopher Pyne tried to change the funding model and was howled down. Since then, he's snipped away at it off line in various ways, including reducing the indexation rate, cutting funding and decoupling the agreement with the states.

My hope and expectation is that the changes will stick, and as things stand a needs-based funding model is still in place. It is a once-in-a-generation improvement in a fundamental area of the nation's affairs. Getting a good start in life is a fundamental birth right—it's the Australian dream of fairness, in which every single citizen has the best chance of happiness and a successful life. What better promise can a government deliver? It was a privilege to see it through.

...

I didn't jump I wasn't pushed
I went of my own accord to do what I could
My eyes were open I had a go
To try to even up the score I had to leave the show

Now there may be a perfect paradise where black and white
    don't meet
Where the clicking mouse is a substitute for the sound of
    marching feet
You might think we can have it all that no one has to fall
But if I ever go around
I would do it again

I saw the best of men I saw the worst
I saw the best of women too, from governor to nurse
I straightened up and turned my cheek, I was lonely in
    the night
You only get one chance at things to try and do what's right

Whilst all the glory hunters were basking in false smiles
Twisted egos and ambition mile after mile
I went to find a quiet place away from the madding mob
To try and make a difference to get on with the job and do
    it again

Then I was simply waiting for a moment to be free
When they pull the curtain back you know it's time to leave
So I set my face towards the sun to let those seasons run
    and run
But on any day in any way if I was asked to join the fray
I would do it again

EPILOGUE

I'T'S 26 JANUARY 2013, and the Randwick council staff have been at it from first light, erecting tents and stalls in the park next to Coogee Beach, cheerfully bustling about, offering the occasional 'Happy Australia Day' to passers-by.

Of the many tasks a local member of parliament is called on to perform, representing the government at citizenship ceremonies was my favourite. And today's ceremony, taking place on Australia Day, is extra special.

As well as the induction of new Aussies by the mayor, there will be community service awards, and a speech by an Australia Day ambassador: someone with a distinguished career or track record of helping the community—they seldom miss the mark.

My role is to read the letter from the immigration minister welcoming the new citizens, outlining their rights and responsibilities. And then the member says 'a few words'.

I always felt the official communication didn't go far enough so I also offer a welcome of my own and tell the expectant crowd that indeed they are lucky to be joining the Australian nation.

I acknowledge the huge step they are taking, and express great confidence (on the basis of all I've seen of previous migrants' progress) that it's going to work out well.

I say that wherever they look, they can see extraordinary beauty in their new country and that Aboriginal people—the First

Peoples—actually still live here, just fifteen minutes down the road. I remind them that not long ago this beautiful place we now occupy belonged to the Aboriginal people and that we are working our way through this aspect of our past.

I point out, although many hardly need to be reminded, the precious state of peace we enjoy. For those who've survived unspeakable experiences in countries racked by ancient grudges, I urge them to take a deep breath: importing religious or ethnic rivalries is heavy baggage that shouldn't count in this modern country on the far side of the world.

I explain the sacrifice of young soldiers and why we commemorate Anzac Day, adding that we should always take very seriously the act of committing a nation to war.

I emphasise that they aren't expected to leave their culture behind when they join us, that in fact we are greatly enriched by it. We are one and we are many, as the alternative national anthem goes.

I tell them that within a stone's throw of where they are sitting there are good schools and hospitals, well-tended sports grounds and well-stocked libraries—all freely accessible, because this is a fair nation where everyone gets a go.

Our democracy is a rare jewel, I say. Yes, we should aim to make it better, but it is like this for a reason. Our forefathers and -mothers got a lot of things right. We have separation between church and state, and between the courts and elected representatives. Elections are free and fair, and citizens not only have the right to vote, they can stand for public office too. These important institutions are there to serve everyone, and no one party or person should be able to buy their way into power.

I acknowledge that getting work and putting food on the table for their families, and the education of their children, will be their most important tasks.

Yet I urge them to consider, once they've got a foothold, how they might give something back—as those who received recognition for community service today have done.

We seesaw through the national anthem, for the second time this morning. A portion of the crowd is dressed for the occasion, a few in the national costume of their country of origin, among whom a number beam and sing proudly. There's another cohort that has already drifted away, indifferent to the lyric, taking a clue from Aussie casual, in thongs, jeans, T-shirts.

The sun, now higher in the sky, is as bright as the faces of the excited new arrivals. Blazing yellow light splashes on the flash mansions hugging the cliffs nearby, and on the red-brick public housing flats further south, where quite a few of these recent arrivals will spend their early years.

Surging up against the cliffs that bookend the beach, the ocean is a well-cooked broth, warm and getting warmer: after millions of years of natural selection, and thousands of years of humans accumulating survival skills and taking over the planet, these new Australians are part of the generation that has outrun evolution, and, in their case, escaped their past as well—for them anything is possible.

As ever, the panorama takes my breath away. I look up to Dolphin Point on the Coogee headland. It hosts a memorial to the victims of a terrorist bombing in Bali that killed and wounded members of a local footy club and families from the area who'd gone there on holidays. It's a symbol of the frailties of our region and a reminder, like this morning's event, that we are an Asian nation.

The ceremony over, I wander past family groups and gatherings of young people who've come to the park to celebrate; many are covered in tattoos, fake and real, their summer gear prominently featuring the Australian flag. The Union Jack in the corner is still an eyesore to me, a reminder that we've got some way to go.

A CD is punched into a ghetto blaster and out chimes *Essential Oils*. 'Give us a song, Pete!' comes the shout. I can but smile and wave.

'Happy Australia Day!' someone else yells, as kids play chasings and cricket and the holiday mood radiates across the beach. If all these young people can get the best start possible, with a true love for their neighbours and this country, then nothing should hold them, and us, back. So much lies in wait, and there's so much to experience, so much to do, living in what to me is the best place on earth.

...

Finally I get back to my car and aim for Mittagong to catch up with my sweetheart. It will be a very late lunch and I don't even notice the drive out of town, lost in thought after a big day of mixed emotions.

Oh, our beloved Rowe. I can't wait to get back home.

Rowe had been our sanctuary and a labour of love, a never-ending project of repair and improvements undertaken in whatever spare hours we could snatch. A home shaped by laughter and occasional tears, and the routine of getting on with life, creating new memories.

The outside markers were school holidays and the two sets of important celebrations: Christmas and Easter from the old world, and Australia Day and Anzac Day from the new. Then came the rites of passage: birthdays celebrated with joy each time, as the family grew before our eyes.

Sometimes friends would gather and we'd eat and drink and play games—adults and kids—and listen to the music we grew up with, laughing about the silly, brave things we did, amazed at how quickly the years fly past.

In the Southern Highlands the seasons are distinct, more turbulent, less predictable. They arrive with changes you can sense—flora and fauna stirring—as if someone left the back door open and night air flowed in and filled the rooms.

Leaving autumn's letting-go and dropping into winter, cooling nights and the still days give way to frigid. Winds sweep long distance over the ranges from the west and occasional frosts crackle the gardens and fields.

As it warms there come a few brief weeks when perfumes and aromas fill the paddocks and linger in the air, as the glorious colours

of spring erupt. There are stems and branches and flowers budding
and blossoming into the softer, dreamy days.

Then soft gives way to harsh—and to hot, of course. But here
in the Highlands it could still double back, as clammy fog pushes
over the escarpment from the east, holding the heat of summer at
bay, while mists drift, otherworldly, in the valleys.

Once summer really took hold, if we were stuck fast, we'd just
have to suck it up and bake for a week or so, and hope the bush
wouldn't erupt in flames.

The small block next to the house was my special project. Here
weeds ruled, but bit by bit they'd been punished, pulled, poisoned
and then holes were dug and scribbly gums, snow gums, waratahs—
anything that 'used to grow round here'—planted in to bring some
lustre.

If the naysayers were out in force, and torrents of whinge from
talkback tyrants, media mavens and professional pessimists were
pouring down like a summer storm, I'd get out for a couple of hours
and meander in the glade. With the solar radio delivering cricket
live and Jim Maxwell and the ABC crew swapping yarns, I could
drink in the cool shade, catch up with my brothers and far-flung
mates by phone and refresh while planning some more landscape
changes. From little things . . .

I've been faithful in love and friendship, I can say that much. And
I've tried to be faithful to my inner voice, to my God, and to the
future. I've stumbled, fallen and then got up again, but I can still
hum a tune, and even wrote a few while finishing this account, so
I know that while there's life there's hope.

The wisdom of the elders is the cliché used to describe the learning
of a long innings, but we are so addicted to the shiny and the new,
our elders are mostly ignored altogether. But now even I'm starting to
feel like an elder, only too aware that life moves fast and in circles—
and here it comes again.

The moon tracks across the northern sky, its creamy shine

reflecting off the roof. The end of another day is announced by the frogs and birds, the sound drifting up from the dam as the evening cools and the passing traffic dies away.

The night sky showers its forever light, as I in turn look out—head filled with preoccupations, dreams and plans—into the cluster of constellations.

I call up moments of pure happiness: when each of my girls first called out 'Dada'; a blue-green day driving in the hills of France, just Doris and me, when the wind died away and the floating calm seemed to last forever; on my own at my favourite faraway break, catching a crest of water all the way to shore.

If I wait long enough I'll see a shooting star, try and catch it, and put it in my pocket. It carries the stuff we all came from, now falling from the heavens back to earth.

I can see new life taking root in the ground, new lives fuelled by love, bound one to the other, growing into tomorrow.

ACKNOWLEDGEMENTS

For the many friendships and collaborations that permeate *Big Blue Sky*, I am truly grateful. In music, conservation and politics, my life has been shared with many others and I greatly value these numerous, often unnamed partnerships.

Thanks to my band mates—Rob Hirst, Jim Moginie, Martin Rotsey, Bones Hillman, Peter Gifford and Andrew James—and our manager Gary Morris, who are such a big part of this memoir. Thanks also to friend and legal adviser Peter Thompson, Arlene Brookes in the Oils Office who assisted greatly, Paula Jones, Craig Allan and Sony Music Australia.

Part of this book concerns the Australian conservation movement. I commend those dedicated activists and many volunteers who have made such a difference to the health of our precious environment, and who I enjoyed working with over many years.

Thanks to my Aboriginal and Torres Strait Islander friends and colleagues who have allowed me a unique insight into Indigenous Australia, and whose struggle for proper recognition and a fair go remains unfinished business.

I would also like to thank the many staff, volunteers and advisers, including Wayne Smith, Bryce Wilson, Louise Moes, Rick Youssef, Sarah McCormack, Chrissie Mallon, Jill Morante, Cara Davis, Kate Sullivan, Phillipa Dimakis, Liam O'Dwyer and Paul Martin, who worked in my electorate and ministerial offices, and whose commitment to Labor values underpinned our joint efforts.

Additional thanks to the electors of Kingsford Smith, the Kingsford Smith Federal Electoral Council, including Tony Bowen, Dominic Sullivan, Matt Thistlethwaite and Chris Bastic; and to Labor Party members, including Tony Slevin, Geoff Gallop, Sandra Strong, Paul and Sue Tracy, Sue Myerhoffer, Christine Kibble, Patricia and Peter O'Brien, Peter Castaldi and Zoe Reynolds—among others— who never wavered in their support.

I am especially grateful for the assistance of Judy Middlebrook, Mark Dodshon, Kate Pasterfield, Denise Spinks, Ben Pratt, Simon Balderstone, Jenny Hunter, Phillip Toyne, Donna Petrachenko, Cameron Mellor, Peter Wright, Andy Palfreyman, Lisa Paul, Laurie Brereton, Craig Emerson, Warren Snowden, Alan James, Robyn Kruk, Penny Kerr, Paul Gilding, Charlie McMahon, John Connor, Don Henry, and Andrew and Matt Garrett, who all took time to provide additional information, review sections or make helpful suggestions.

To fill the gaps in my memory, I have drawn on Mark Dodshon's *Beds Are Burning*, Andrew McMillan's *Strict Rules*, Paul Kelly's *The End of Certainty*, Kerry-Anne Walsh's *The Stalking of Julia Gillard* and George Megalogenis's *The Australian Moment*. Of course any errors or factual distortions are my responsibility alone.

Many thanks are owed to Richard Walsh, who first encouraged me to consider a memoir; Jane Palfreyman, my publisher at Allen & Unwin, for her enthusiasm and advice; Ali Lavau and Sarah Baker, for their judicious editing and suggestions; and my agent, Deb Callaghan, for her constant support.

Finally, my heartfelt thanks to Doris for her sound counsel during the writing of this book, and to my daughters, Emily, May and Grace, for hanging in.

INDEX